Hayate the combat butler

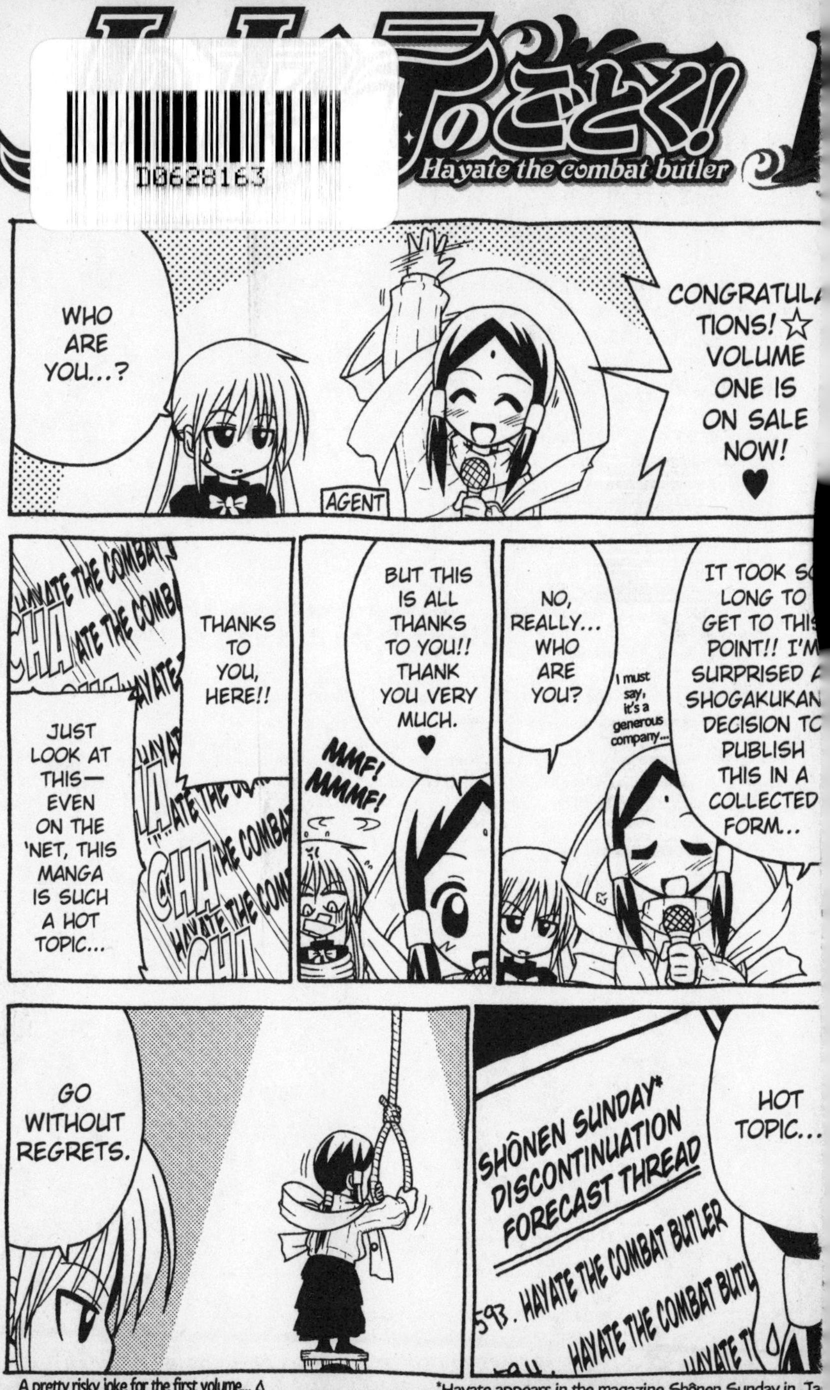
CONGRATULATIONS! ☆ VOLUME ONE IS ON SALE NOW! ♥
AGENT
WHO ARE YOU...?
IT TOOK SO LONG TO GET TO THIS POINT!! I'M SURPRISED AT SHOGAKUKAN'S DECISION TO PUBLISH THIS IN A COLLECTED FORM...
I must say, it's a generous company...
NO, REALLY... WHO ARE YOU?
BUT THIS IS ALL THANKS TO YOU!! THANK YOU VERY MUCH. ♥
MMF! MMMF!
THANKS TO YOU, HERE!!
JUST LOOK AT THIS— EVEN ON THE 'NET, THIS MANGA IS SUCH A HOT TOPIC...
HOT TOPIC...
SHÔNEN SUNDAY* DISCONTINUATION FORECAST THREAD
HAYATE THE COMBAT BUTLER
593. HAYATE THE COMBAT BUTL
GO WITHOUT REGRETS.

A pretty risky joke for the first volume... ∆

*Hayate appears in the magazine Shônen Sunday in Ja

HAYATE THE COMBAT BUTLER
VOL. 1

STORY AND ART BY
KENJIRO HATA

English Adaptation/Mark Giambruno
Translation/Yuki Yoshioka & Cindy H. Yamauchi
Touch-up Art & Lettering/Freeman Wong
Design/Yukiko Whitley
Editor/Kit Fox

Editor in Chief, Books/Alvin Lu
Editor in Chief, Magazines/Marc Weidenbaum
VP, Publishing Licensing/Rika Inouye
VP, Sales and Product Marketing/Gonzalo Ferreyra
VP, Creative/Linda Espinosa
Publisher/Hyoe Narita

The rights of the author(s) of the work(s) in this publication to be so identified have been asserted in accordance with the Copyright, Designs and Patents Act 1988. A CIP catalogue record for this book is available from the British Library.

Printed in Canada

Published by VIZ Media, LLC
P.O. Box 77010
San Francisco, CA 94107

10 9 8 7 6 5 4 3
First printing, November 2006
Third printing, June 2008

Hayate
the Combat Butler

KENJIRO HATA

CONTENTS

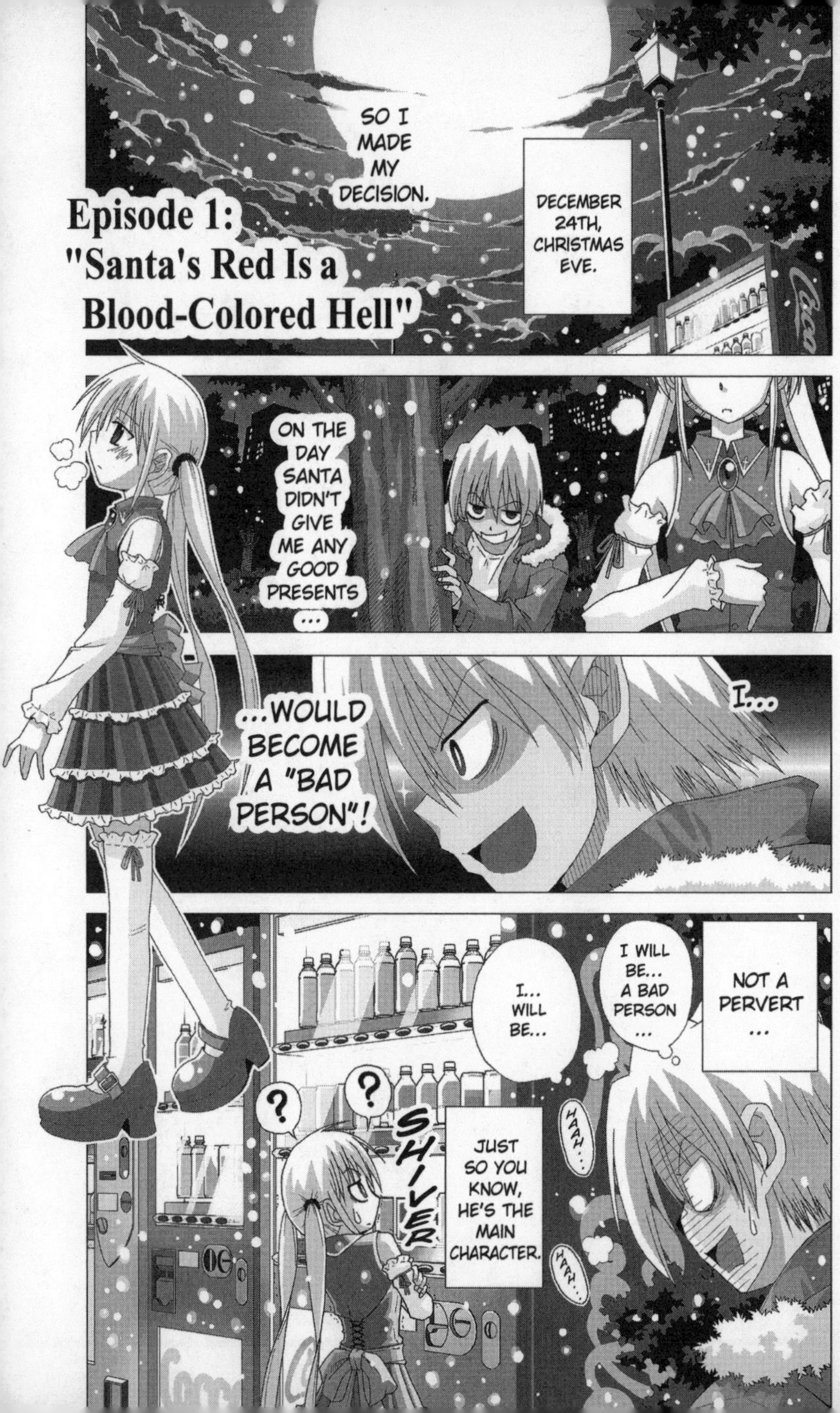

DECEMBER 24TH, CHRISTMAS EVE.
SO I MADE MY DECISION.
Episode 1: "Santa's Red Is a Blood-Colored Hell"
ON THE DAY SANTA DIDN'T GIVE ME ANY GOOD PRESENTS...
I...
...WOULD BECOME A "BAD PERSON"!
NOT A PERVERT...
I WILL BE... A BAD PERSON...
I... WILL BE...
HAAH...
HAAH...
JUST SO YOU KNOW, HE'S THE MAIN CHARACTER.
SHIVER
?
?

Episode 1: "Santa's Red Is a Blood-Colored Hell"

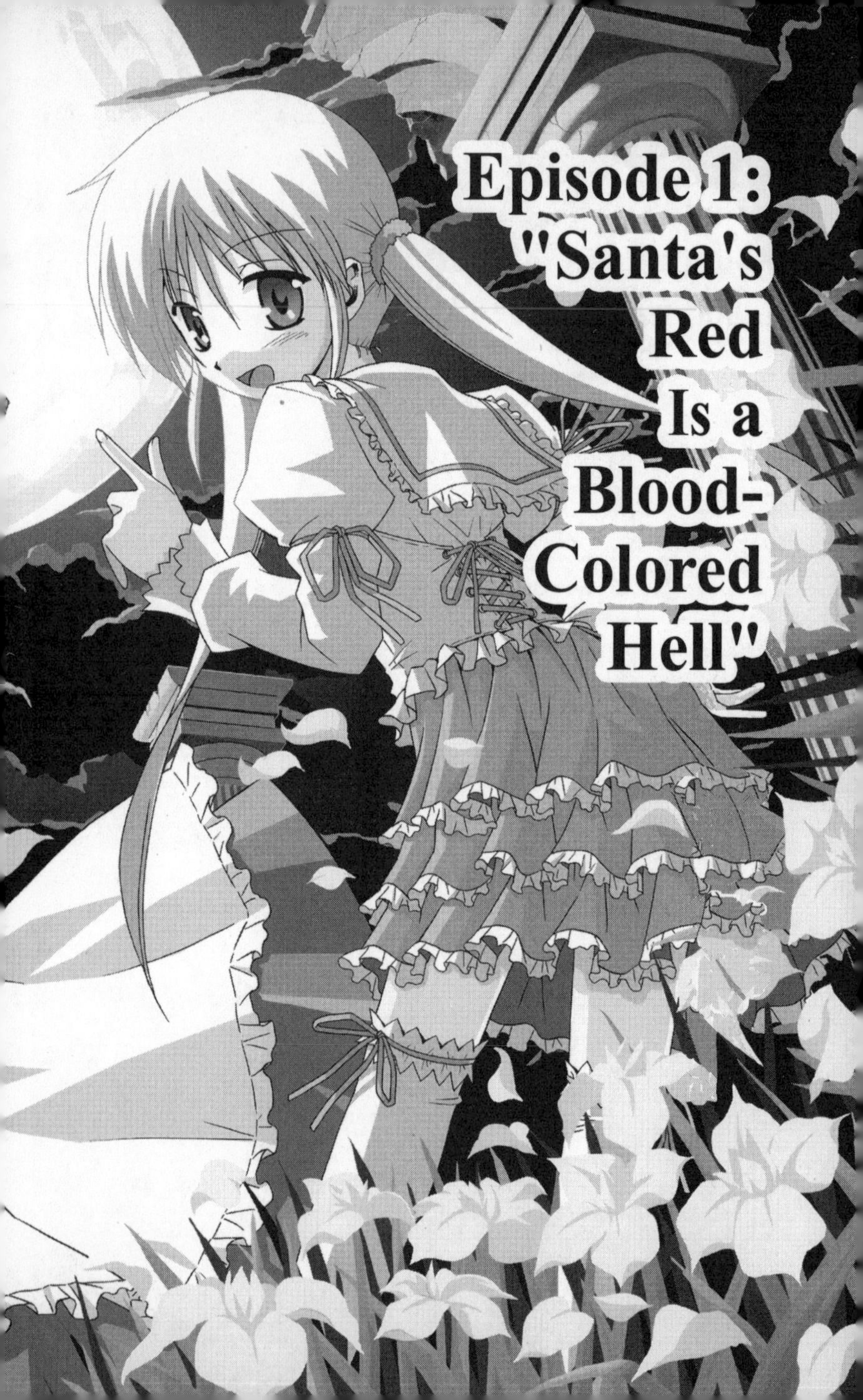

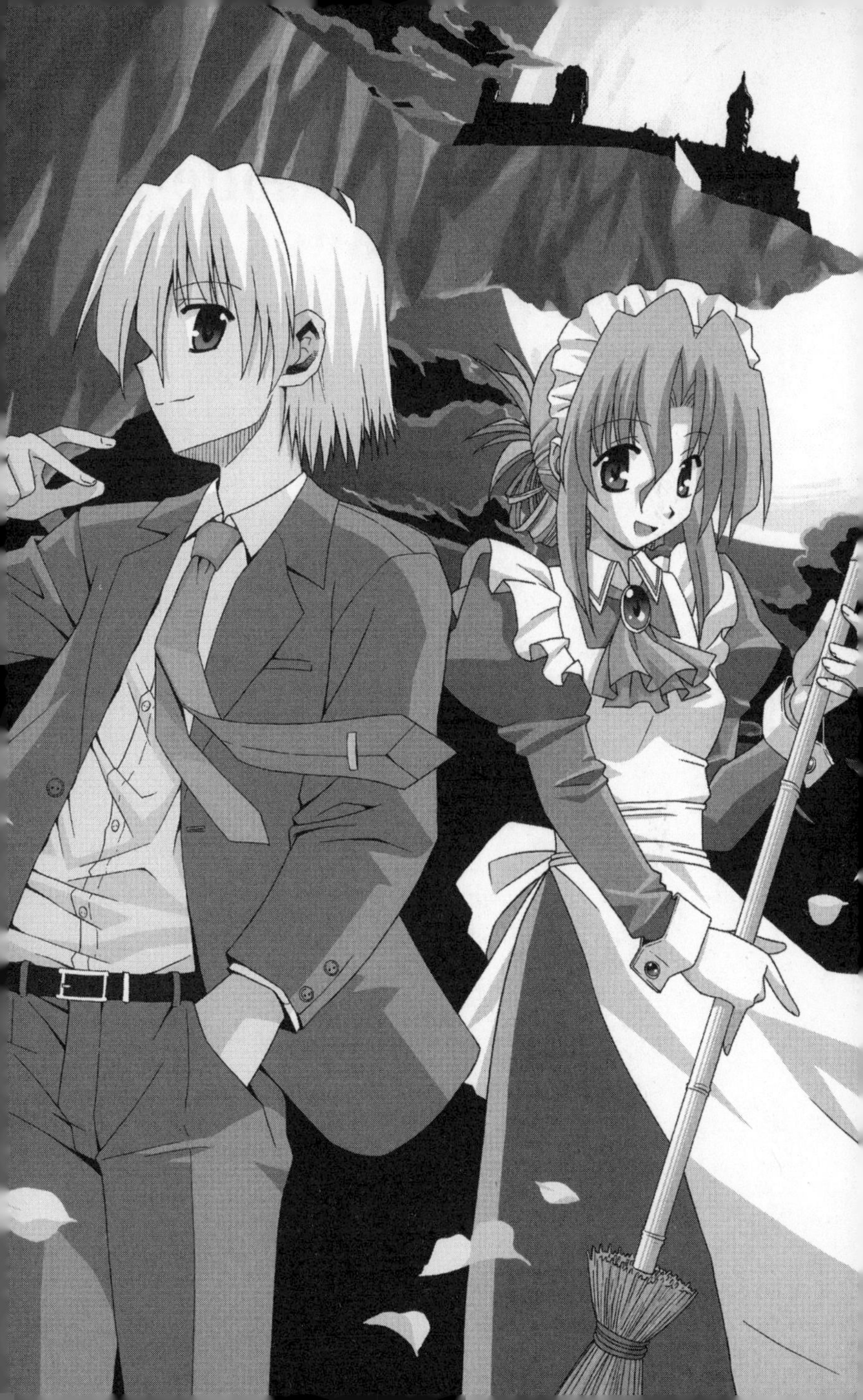

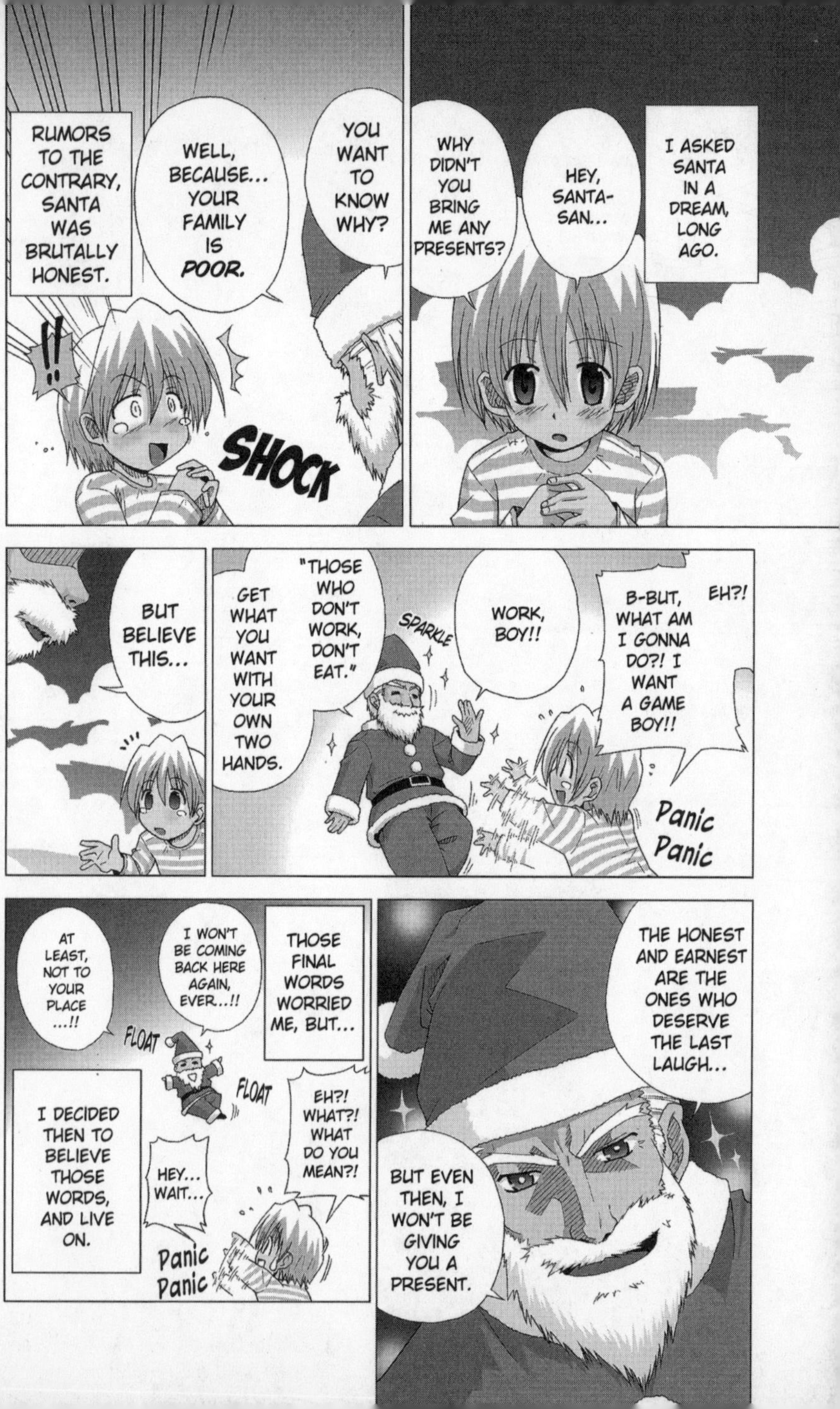
I ASKED SANTA IN A DREAM, LONG AGO.
HEY, SANTA-SAN...
WHY DIDN'T YOU BRING ME ANY PRESENTS?
YOU WANT TO KNOW WHY?
WELL, BECAUSE... YOUR FAMILY IS POOR.
RUMORS TO THE CONTRARY, SANTA WAS BRUTALLY HONEST.
!!
SHOCK
EH?!
B-BUT, WHAT AM I GONNA DO?! I WANT A GAME BOY!!
Panic Panic
WORK, BOY!!
SPARKLE
"THOSE WHO DON'T WORK, DON'T EAT."
GET WHAT YOU WANT WITH YOUR OWN TWO HANDS.
BUT BELIEVE THIS...
THE HONEST AND EARNEST ARE THE ONES WHO DESERVE THE LAST LAUGH...
BUT EVEN THEN, I WON'T BE GIVING YOU A PRESENT.
THOSE FINAL WORDS WORRIED ME, BUT...
I WON'T BE COMING BACK HERE AGAIN, EVER...!!
AT LEAST, NOT TO YOUR PLACE ...!!
FLOAT
FLOAT
EH?! WHAT?! WHAT DO YOU MEAN?!
HEY... WAIT...
Panic Panic
I DECIDED THEN TO BELIEVE THOSE WORDS, AND LIVE ON.

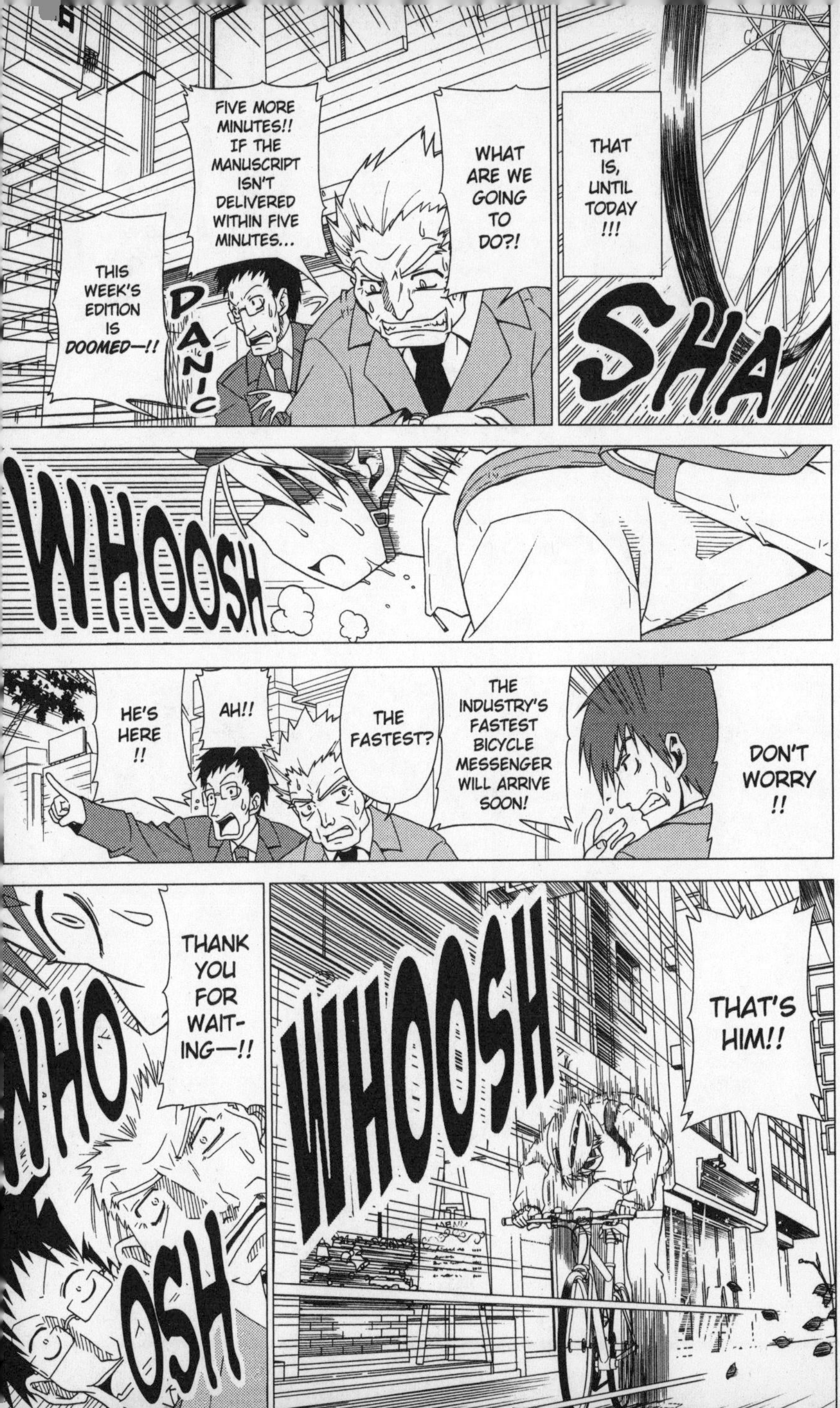
THAT IS, UNTIL TODAY!!!
SHA
WHAT ARE WE GOING TO DO?!
FIVE MORE MINUTES!! IF THE MANUSCRIPT ISN'T DELIVERED WITHIN FIVE MINUTES...
THIS WEEK'S EDITION IS DOOMED—!!
PANIC
WHOOSH
DON'T WORRY!!
THE INDUSTRY'S FASTEST BICYCLE MESSENGER WILL ARRIVE SOON!
THE FASTEST?
AH!!
HE'S HERE!!
THAT'S HIM!!
WHOOSH
THANK YOU FOR WAITING—!!
WHOOSH

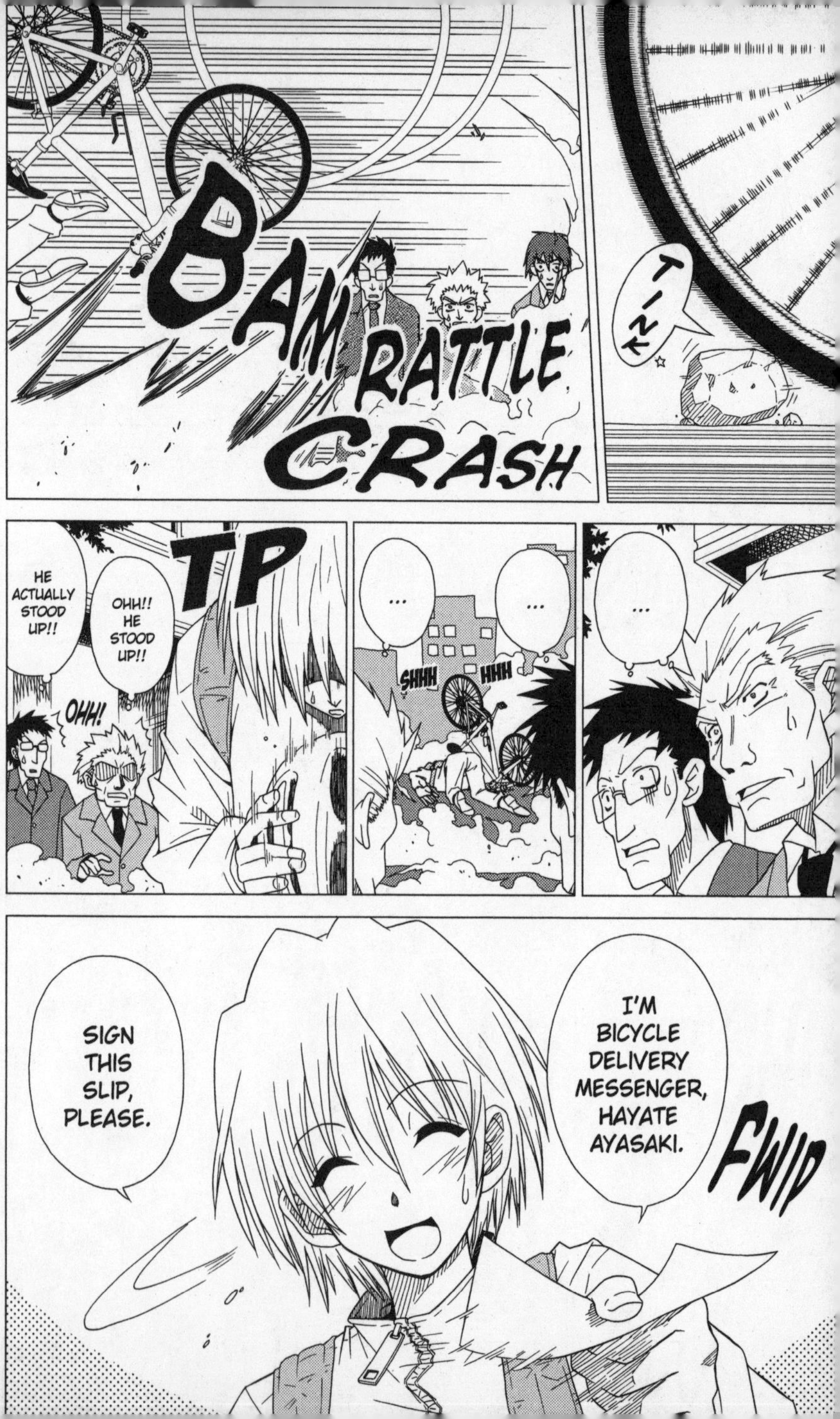
TINK
BAM
RATTLE
CRASH
...
...
...
SHHH
HHH
TP
OHH!! HE STOOD UP!!
HE ACTUALLY STOOD UP!!
OHH!
I'M BICYCLE DELIVERY MESSENGER, HAYATE AYASAKI.
SIGN THIS SLIP, PLEASE.
FWIP

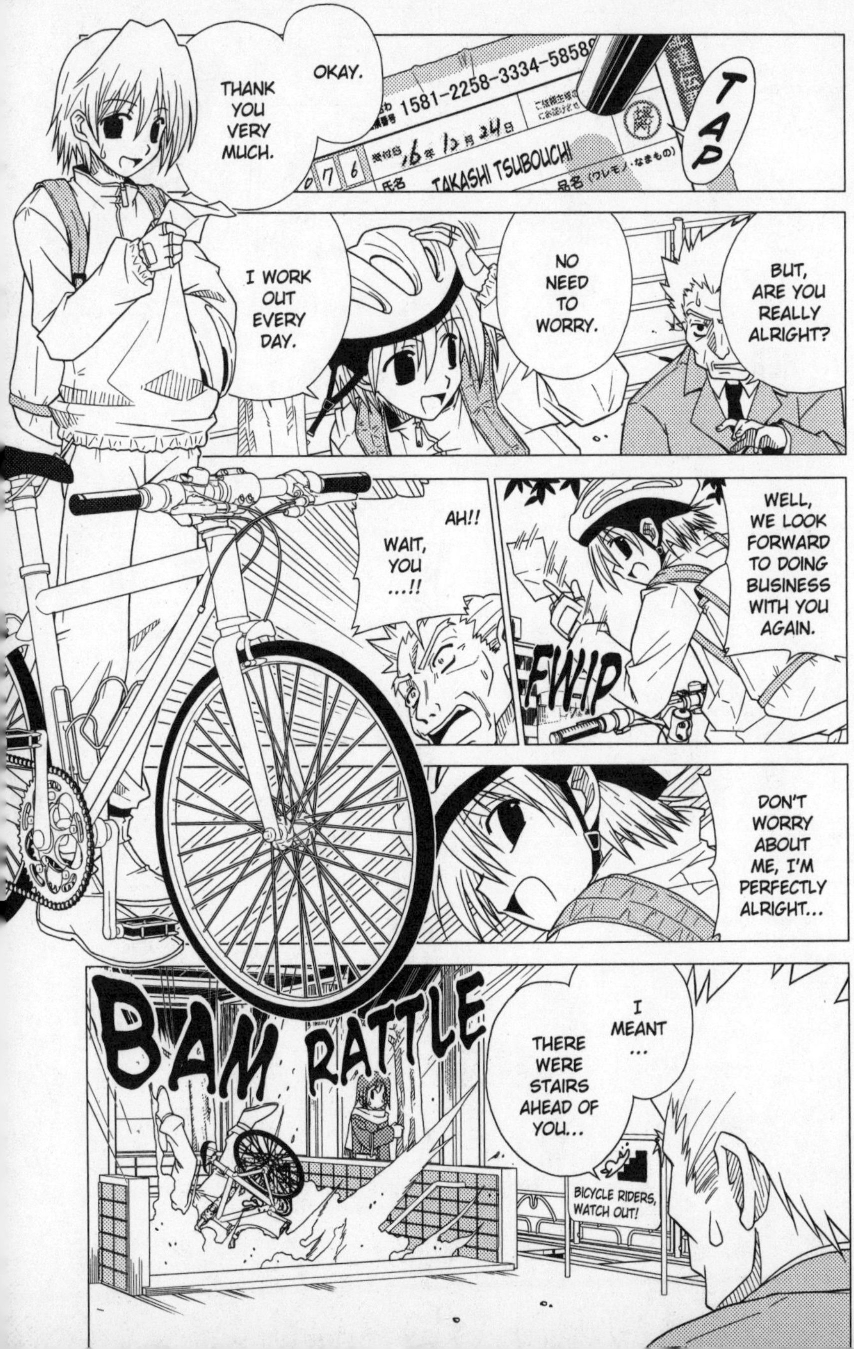
TAP
1581-2258-3334-5858
TAKASHI TSUBOUCHI
OKAY.
THANK YOU VERY MUCH.
BUT, ARE YOU REALLY ALRIGHT?
NO NEED TO WORRY.
I WORK OUT EVERY DAY.
WELL, WE LOOK FORWARD TO DOING BUSINESS WITH YOU AGAIN.
FWIP
AH!!
WAIT, YOU ...!!
DON'T WORRY ABOUT ME, I'M PERFECTLY ALRIGHT...
I MEANT ...
THERE WERE STAIRS AHEAD OF YOU...
BICYCLE RIDERS, WATCH OUT!
BAM RATTLE

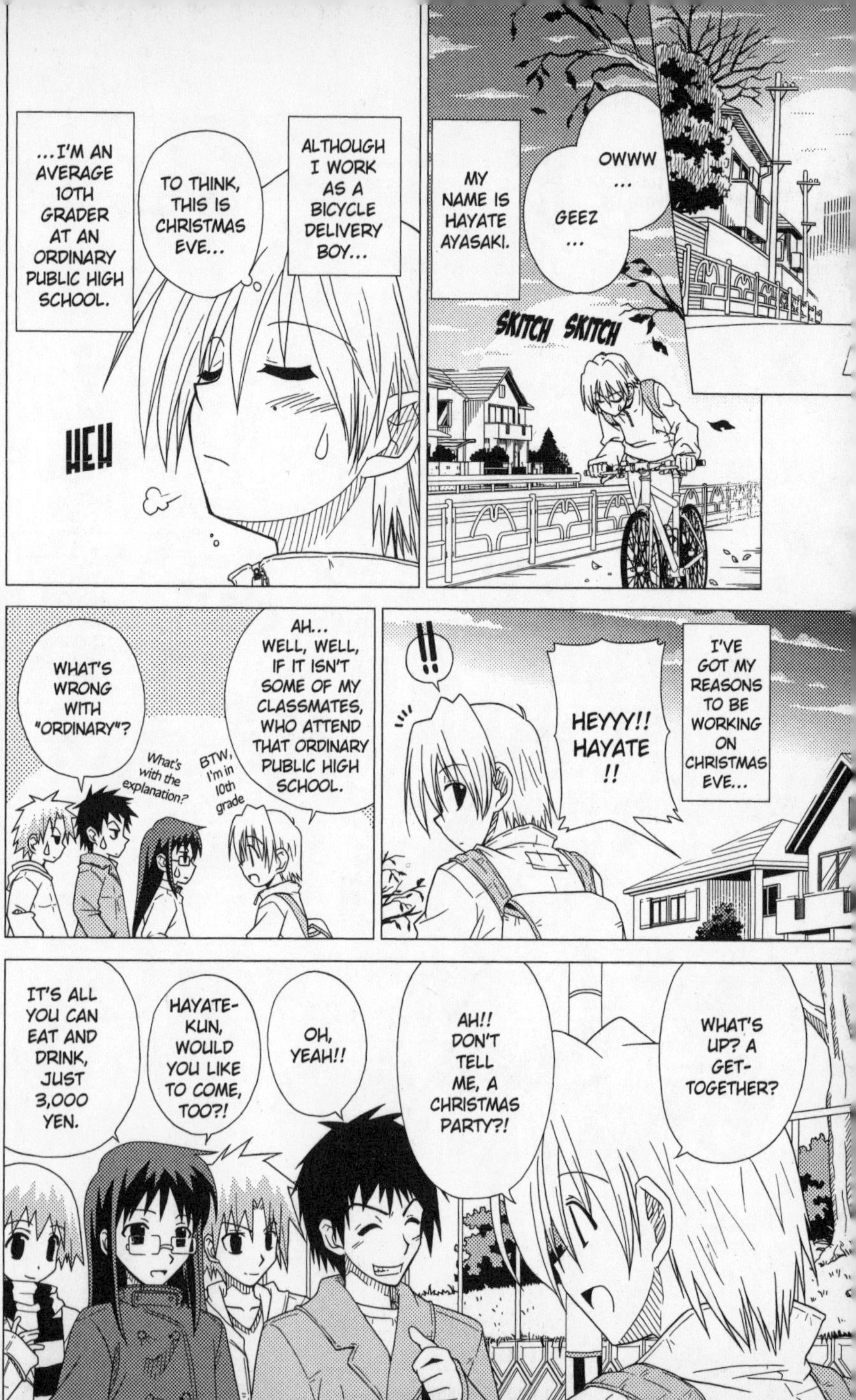
MY NAME IS HAYATE AYASAKI.
OWWW... GEEZ...
SKITCH SKITCH
ALTHOUGH I WORK AS A BICYCLE DELIVERY BOY...
TO THINK, THIS IS CHRISTMAS EVE...
...I'M AN AVERAGE 10TH GRADER AT AN ORDINARY PUBLIC HIGH SCHOOL.
HEH
I'VE GOT MY REASONS TO BE WORKING ON CHRISTMAS EVE...
HEYYY!! HAYATE!!
!!
AH... WELL, WELL, IF IT ISN'T SOME OF MY CLASSMATES, WHO ATTEND THAT ORDINARY PUBLIC HIGH SCHOOL.
BTW, I'm in 10th grade
What's with the explanation?
WHAT'S WRONG WITH "ORDINARY"?
WHAT'S UP? A GET-TOGETHER?
AH!! DON'T TELL ME, A CHRISTMAS PARTY?!
OH, YEAH!!
HAYATE-KUN, WOULD YOU LIKE TO COME, TOO?!
IT'S ALL YOU CAN EAT AND DRINK, JUST 3,000 YEN.

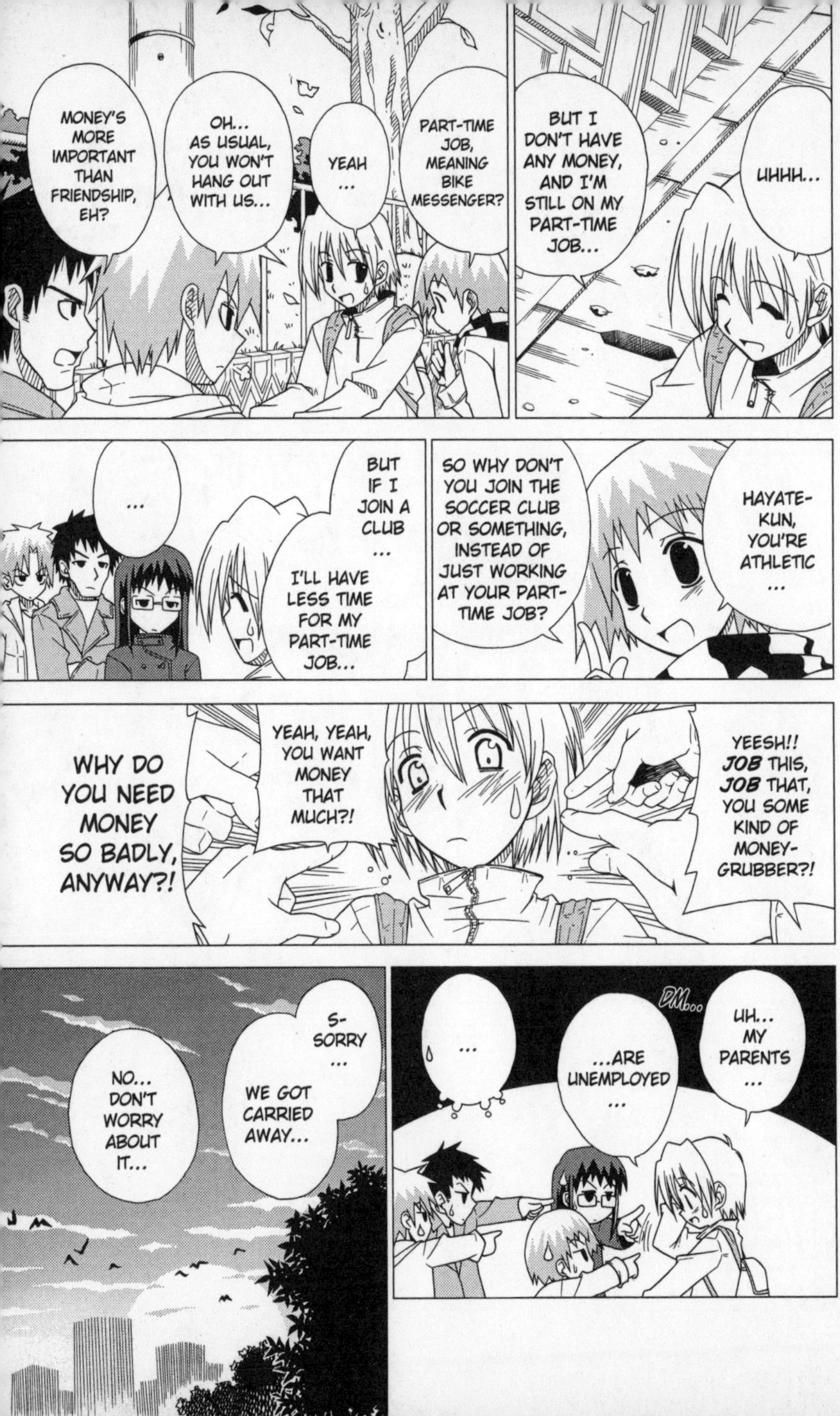
UHHH...
BUT I DON'T HAVE ANY MONEY, AND I'M STILL ON MY PART-TIME JOB...
PART-TIME JOB, MEANING BIKE MESSENGER?
YEAH...
OH... AS USUAL, YOU WON'T HANG OUT WITH US...
MONEY'S MORE IMPORTANT THAN FRIENDSHIP, EH?
HAYATE-KUN, YOU'RE ATHLETIC...
SO WHY DON'T YOU JOIN THE SOCCER CLUB OR SOMETHING, INSTEAD OF JUST WORKING AT YOUR PART-TIME JOB?
BUT IF I JOIN A CLUB...
I'LL HAVE LESS TIME FOR MY PART-TIME JOB...
...
YEESH!! JOB THIS, JOB THAT, YOU SOME KIND OF MONEY-GRUBBER?!
YEAH, YEAH, YOU WANT MONEY THAT MUCH?!
WHY DO YOU NEED MONEY SO BADLY, ANYWAY?!
UH... MY PARENTS...
...ARE UNEMPLOYED...
...
S-SORRY...
WE GOT CARRIED AWAY...
NO... DON'T WORRY ABOUT IT...

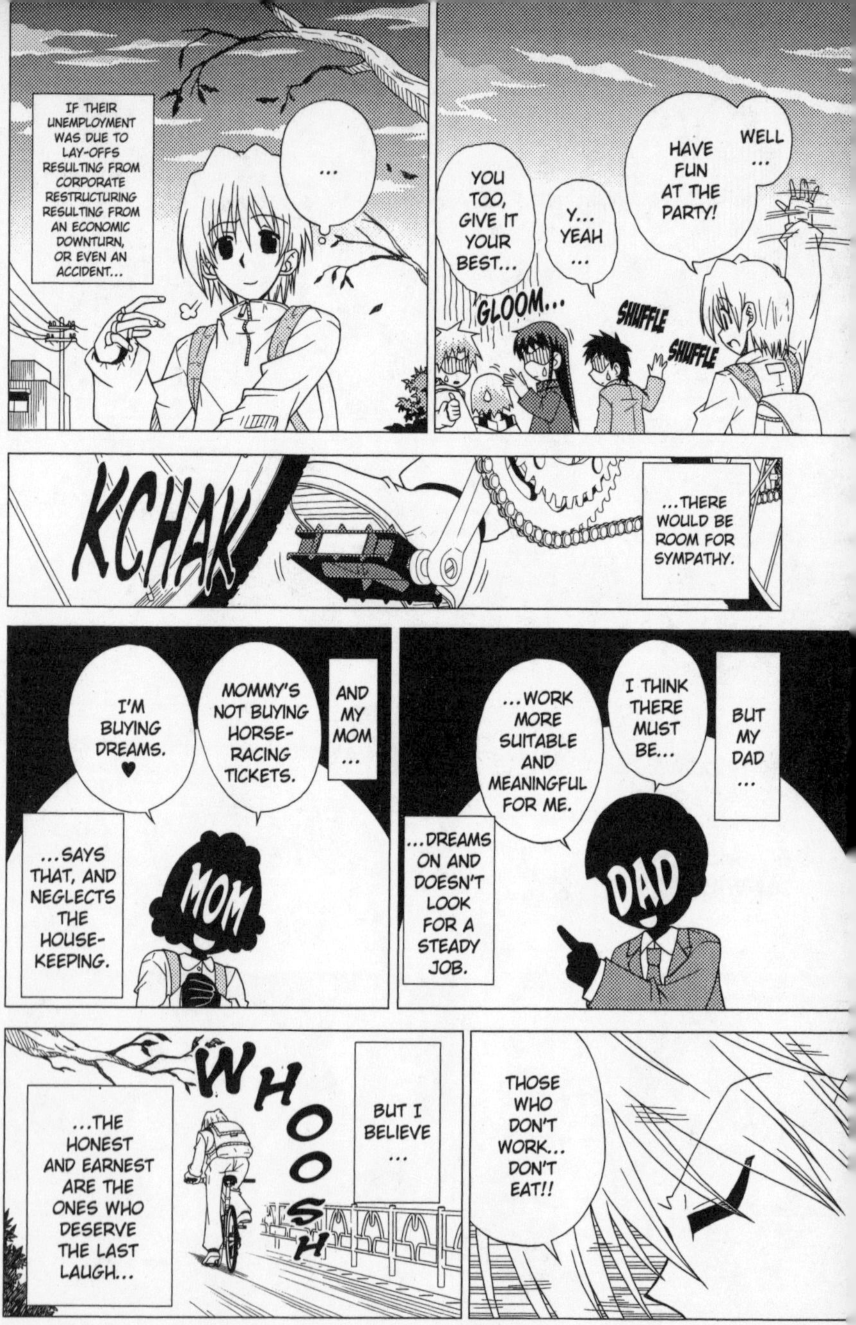
WELL...
HAVE FUN AT THE PARTY!
Y... YEAH...
YOU TOO, GIVE IT YOUR BEST...
GLOOM...
SHUFFLE
SHUFFLE
IF THEIR UNEMPLOYMENT WAS DUE TO LAY-OFFS RESULTING FROM CORPORATE RESTRUCTURING RESULTING FROM AN ECONOMIC DOWNTURN, OR EVEN AN ACCIDENT...
...
...THERE WOULD BE ROOM FOR SYMPATHY.
KCHAK
BUT MY DAD...
I THINK THERE MUST BE...
...WORK MORE SUITABLE AND MEANINGFUL FOR ME.
...DREAMS ON AND DOESN'T LOOK FOR A STEADY JOB.
DAD
AND MY MOM...
MOMMY'S NOT BUYING HORSE-RACING TICKETS.
I'M BUYING DREAMS. ♥
...SAYS THAT, AND NEGLECTS THE HOUSE-KEEPING.
MOM
THOSE WHO DON'T WORK... DON'T EAT!!
BUT I BELIEVE...
...THE HONEST AND EARNEST ARE THE ONES WHO DESERVE THE LAST LAUGH...
WHOOSH

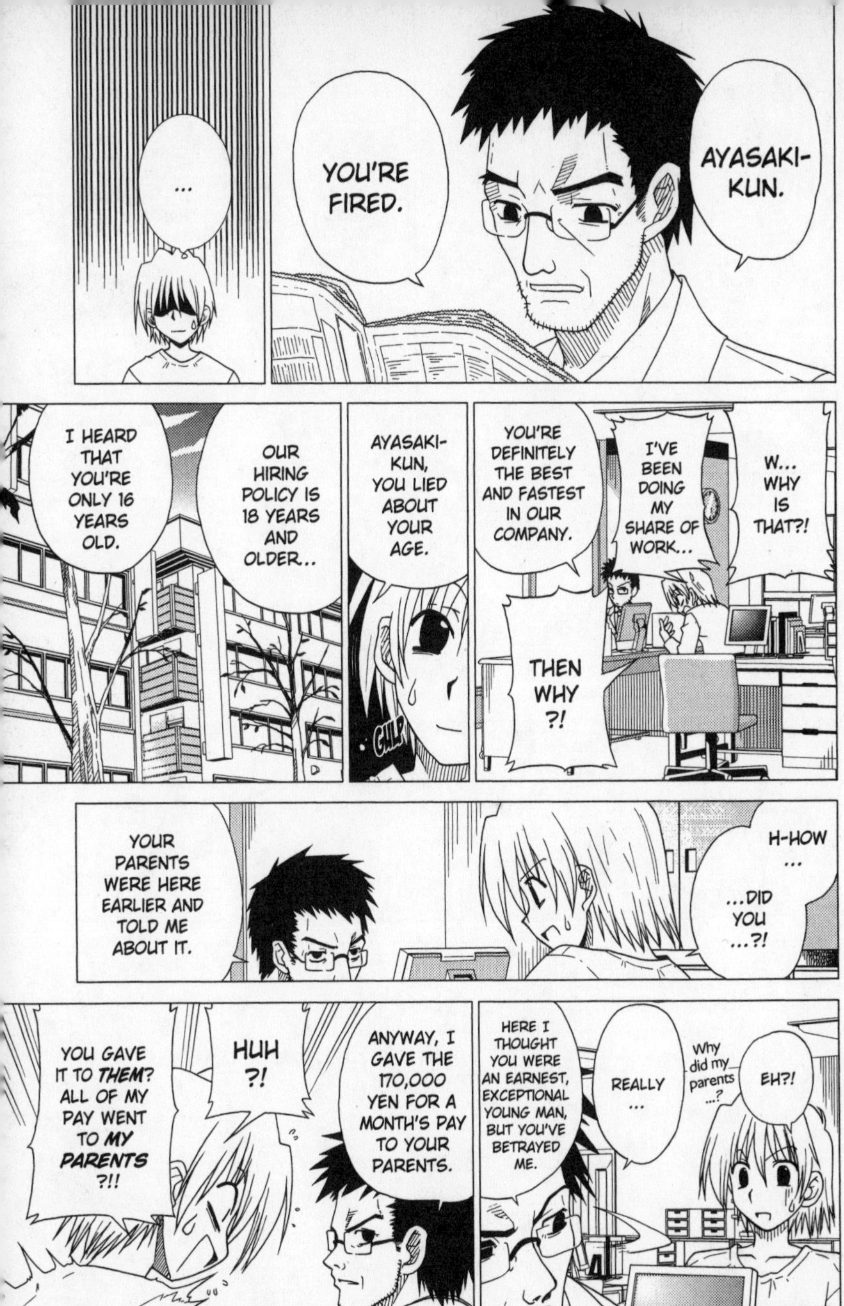
AYASAKI-KUN.
YOU'RE FIRED.
...
W... WHY IS THAT?!
I'VE BEEN DOING MY SHARE OF WORK...
YOU'RE DEFINITELY THE BEST AND FASTEST IN OUR COMPANY.
THEN WHY?!
AYASAKI-KUN, YOU LIED ABOUT YOUR AGE.
GULP
OUR HIRING POLICY IS 18 YEARS AND OLDER...
I HEARD THAT YOU'RE ONLY 16 YEARS OLD.
H-HOW... ...DID YOU...?!
YOUR PARENTS WERE HERE EARLIER AND TOLD ME ABOUT IT.
EH?!
Why did my parents...?
REALLY...
HERE I THOUGHT YOU WERE AN EARNEST, EXCEPTIONAL YOUNG MAN, BUT YOU'VE BETRAYED ME.
ANYWAY, I GAVE THE 170,000 YEN FOR A MONTH'S PAY TO YOUR PARENTS.
HUH?!
YOU GAVE IT TO *THEM*? ALL OF MY PAY WENT TO *MY PARENTS*?!!

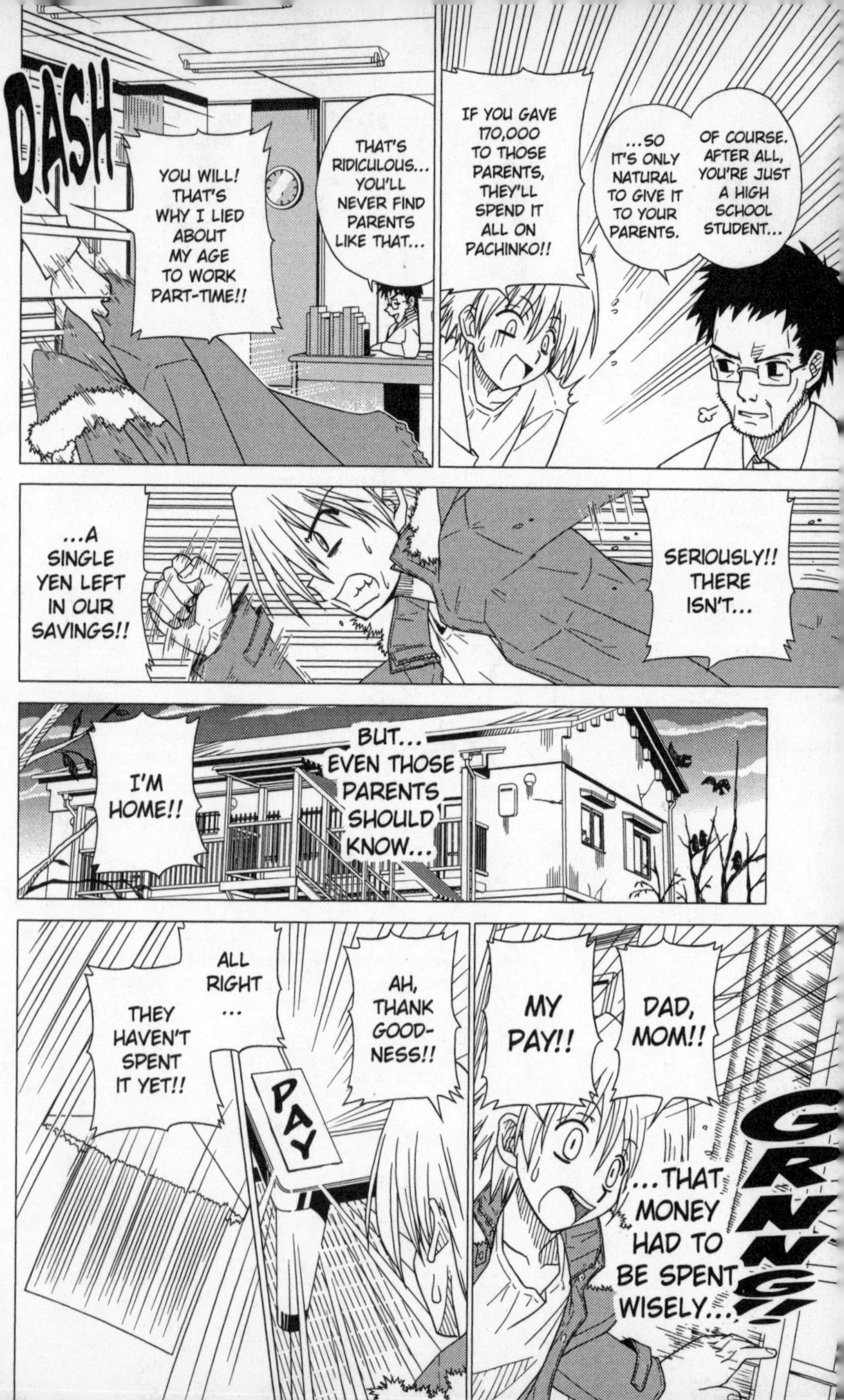
OF COURSE. AFTER ALL, YOU'RE JUST A HIGH SCHOOL STUDENT...
...SO IT'S ONLY NATURAL TO GIVE IT TO YOUR PARENTS.
IF YOU GAVE 170,000 TO THOSE PARENTS, THEY'LL SPEND IT ALL ON PACHINKO!!
THAT'S RIDICULOUS... YOU'LL NEVER FIND PARENTS LIKE THAT...
YOU WILL! THAT'S WHY I LIED ABOUT MY AGE TO WORK PART-TIME!!
DASH
SERIOUSLY!! THERE ISN'T...
...A SINGLE YEN LEFT IN OUR SAVINGS!!
BUT... EVEN THOSE PARENTS SHOULD KNOW...
I'M HOME!!
...THAT MONEY HAD TO BE SPENT WISELY...
GRNNG!!
DAD, MOM!!
MY PAY!!
AH, THANK GOODNESS!!
ALL RIGHT...
THEY HAVEN'T SPENT IT YET!!
PAY

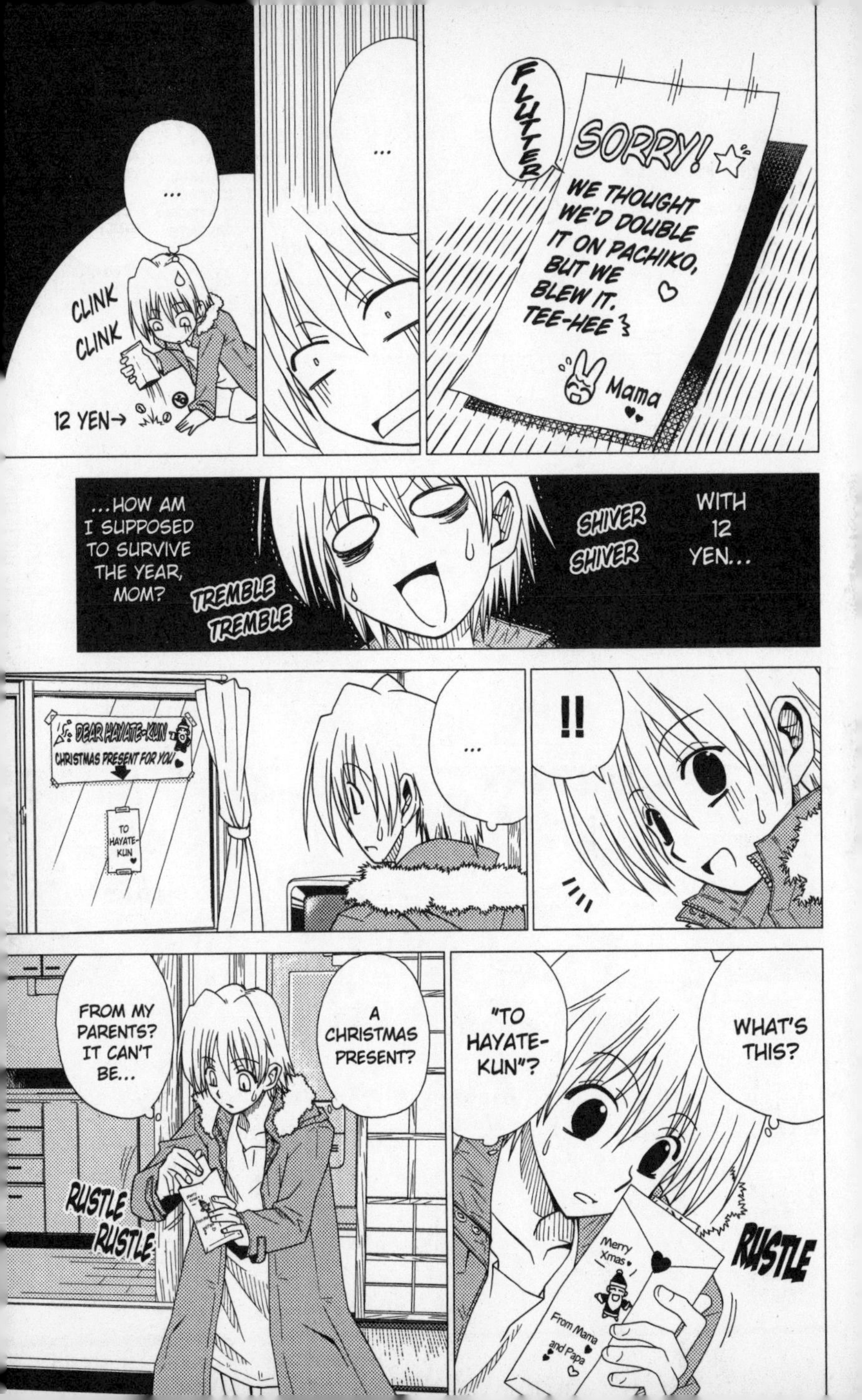
FLUTTER
SORRY!
WE THOUGHT WE'D DOUBLE IT ON PACHIKO, BUT WE BLEW IT. TEE-HEE
Mama
...
...
CLINK CLINK
12 YEN→
WITH 12 YEN...
SHIVER SHIVER
...HOW AM I SUPPOSED TO SURVIVE THE YEAR, MOM?
TREMBLE TREMBLE
!!
...
DEAR HAYATE-KUN
CHRISTMAS PRESENT FOR YOU
TO HAYATE-KUN
WHAT'S THIS?
"TO HAYATE-KUN"?
RUSTLE
Merry Xmas
From Mama and Papa
A CHRISTMAS PRESENT?
FROM MY PARENTS? IT CAN'T BE...
RUSTLE RUSTLE

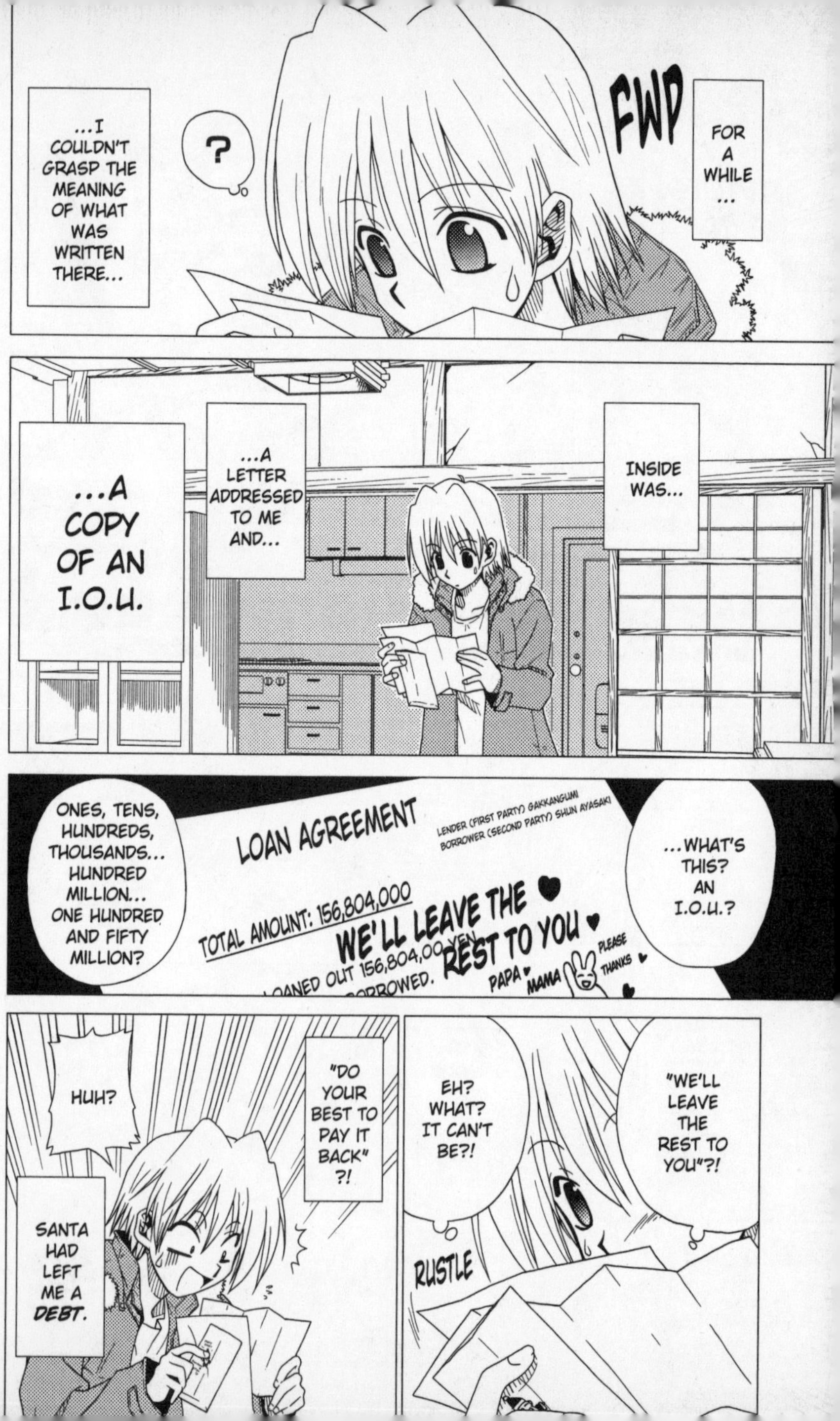
FOR A WHILE...
FWP
?
...I COULDN'T GRASP THE MEANING OF WHAT WAS WRITTEN THERE...
INSIDE WAS...
...A LETTER ADDRESSED TO ME AND...
...A COPY OF AN I.O.U.
...WHAT'S THIS? AN I.O.U.?
LOAN AGREEMENT
LENDER (FIRST PARTY) GAKKANGUMI
BORROWER (SECOND PARTY) SHUN AYASAKI
TOTAL AMOUNT: 156,804,000
WE'LL LEAVE THE REST TO YOU
BORROWED.
PAPA
MAMA
PLEASE
THANKS
ONES, TENS, HUNDREDS, THOUSANDS... HUNDRED MILLION... ONE HUNDRED AND FIFTY MILLION?
"WE'LL LEAVE THE REST TO YOU"?!
EH? WHAT? IT CAN'T BE?!
RUSTLE
"DO YOUR BEST TO PAY IT BACK"?!
HUH?
SANTA HAD LEFT ME A DEBT.

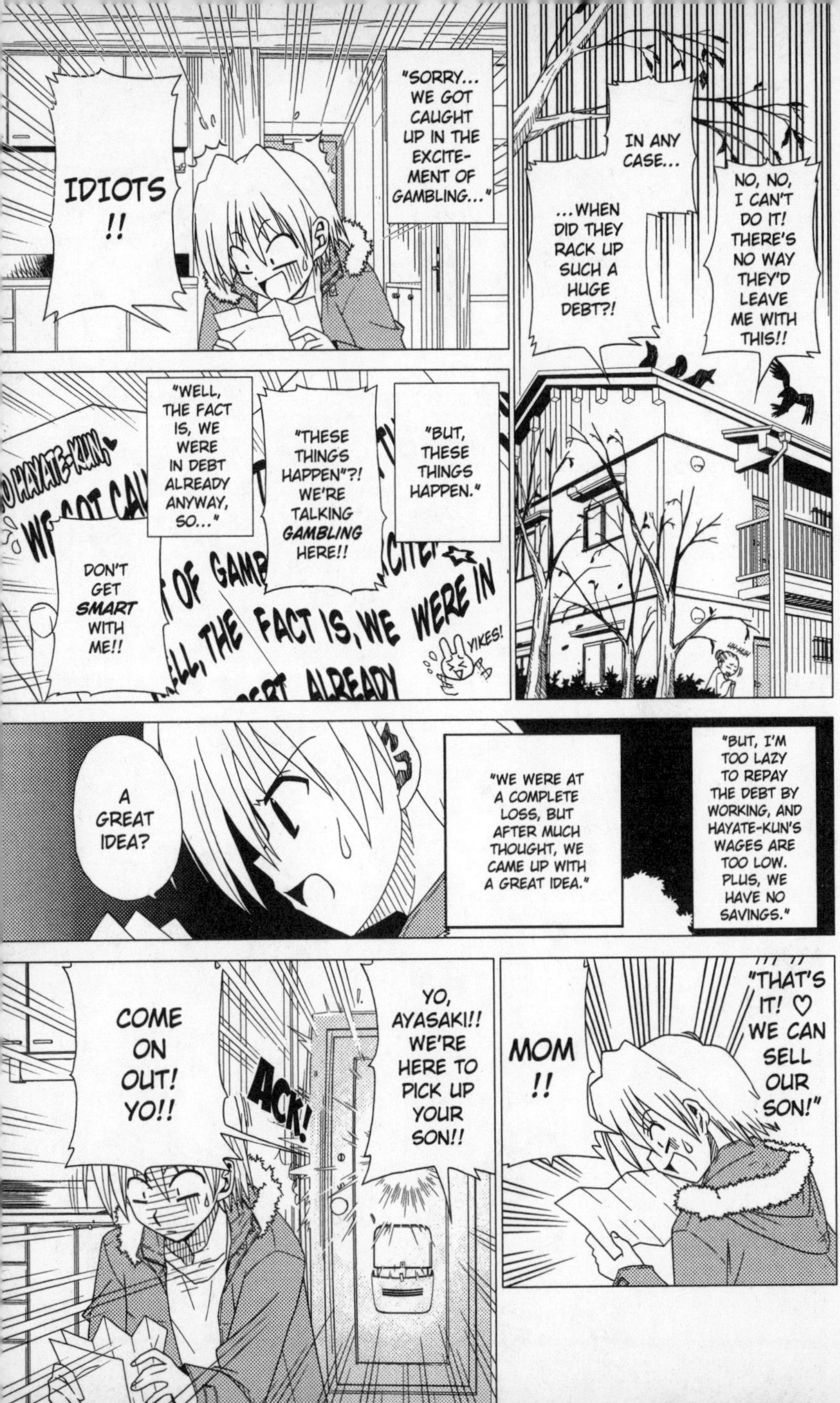
IN ANY CASE...
...WHEN DID THEY RACK UP SUCH A HUGE DEBT?!
NO, NO, I CAN'T DO IT! THERE'S NO WAY THEY'D LEAVE ME WITH THIS!!
"SORRY... WE GOT CAUGHT UP IN THE EXCITEMENT OF GAMBLING..."
IDIOTS!!
"BUT, THESE THINGS HAPPEN."
"THESE THINGS HAPPEN"?! WE'RE TALKING GAMBLING HERE!!
"WELL, THE FACT IS, WE WERE IN DEBT ALREADY ANYWAY, SO..."
DON'T GET SMART WITH ME!!
YIKES!
"BUT, I'M TOO LAZY TO REPAY THE DEBT BY WORKING, AND HAYATE-KUN'S WAGES ARE TOO LOW. PLUS, WE HAVE NO SAVINGS."
"WE WERE AT A COMPLETE LOSS, BUT AFTER MUCH THOUGHT, WE CAME UP WITH A GREAT IDEA."
A GREAT IDEA?
"THAT'S IT! ♡ WE CAN SELL OUR SON!"
MOM!!
YO, AYASAKI!! WE'RE HERE TO PICK UP YOUR SON!!
ACK!
COME ON OUT! YO!!

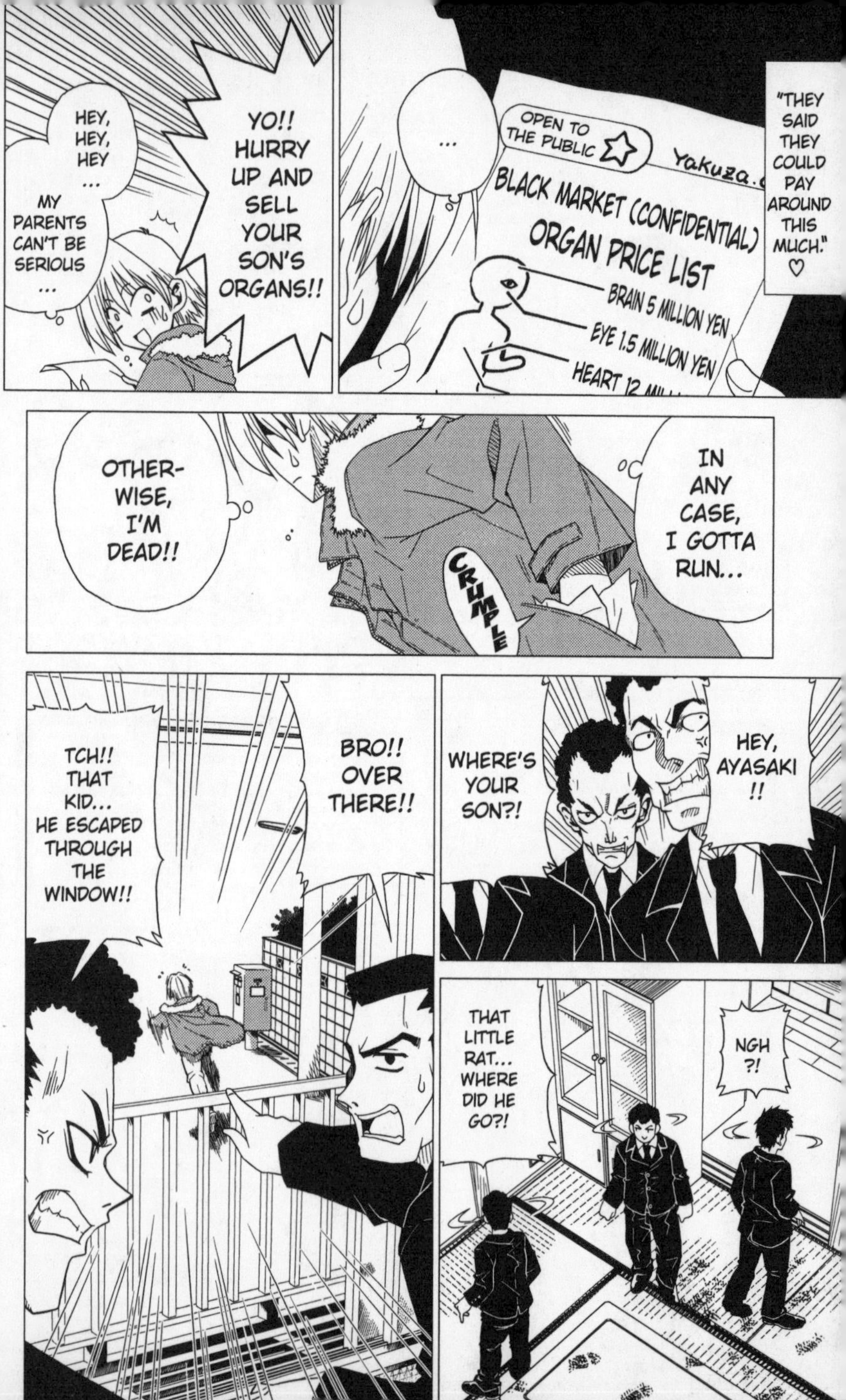
"THEY SAID THEY COULD PAY AROUND THIS MUCH." ♡
...
OPEN TO THE PUBLIC ☆
Yakuza.
BLACK MARKET (CONFIDENTIAL) ORGAN PRICE LIST
BRAIN 5 MILLION YEN
EYE 1.5 MILLION YEN
HEART 12
YO!! HURRY UP AND SELL YOUR SON'S ORGANS!!
HEY, HEY, HEY ... MY PARENTS CAN'T BE SERIOUS ...
IN ANY CASE, I GOTTA RUN...
OTHER-WISE, I'M DEAD!!
CRUMPLE
HEY, AYASAKI !!
WHERE'S YOUR SON?!
NGH ?!
THAT LITTLE RAT... WHERE DID HE GO?!
BRO!! OVER THERE!!
TCH!! THAT KID... HE ESCAPED THROUGH THE WINDOW!!

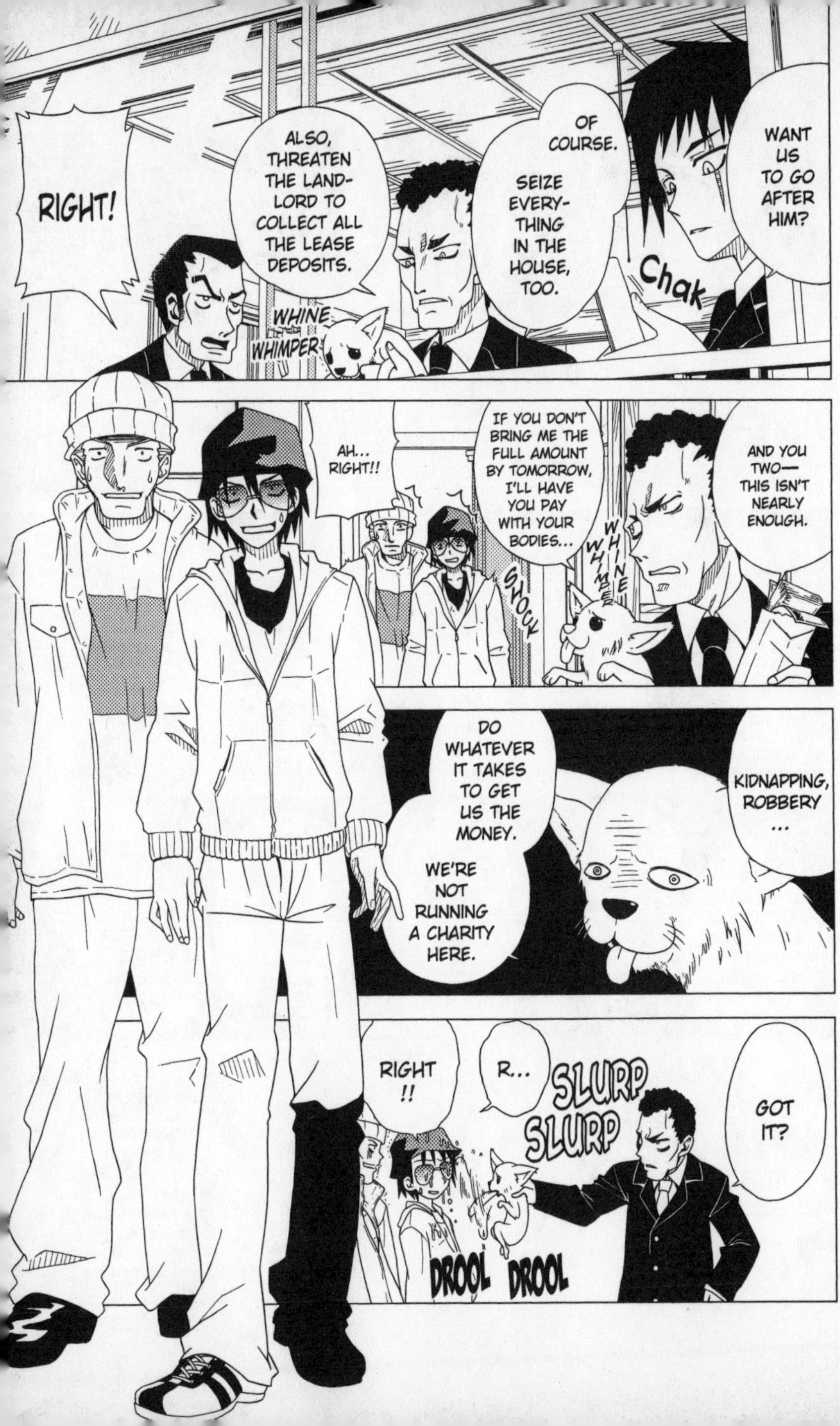

WANT US TO GO AFTER HIM?
Chak
OF COURSE.
SEIZE EVERY-THING IN THE HOUSE, TOO.
ALSO, THREATEN THE LAND-LORD TO COLLECT ALL THE LEASE DEPOSITS.
WHINE
WHIMPER
RIGHT!
AND YOU TWO— THIS ISN'T NEARLY ENOUGH.
WHINE
WHIMPER
IF YOU DON'T BRING ME THE FULL AMOUNT BY TOMORROW, I'LL HAVE YOU PAY WITH YOUR BODIES...
SHOCK
AH... RIGHT!!
KIDNAPPING, ROBBERY ...
DO WHATEVER IT TAKES TO GET US THE MONEY.
WE'RE NOT RUNNING A CHARITY HERE.
GOT IT?
SLURP
SLURP
R...
RIGHT !!
DROOL DROOL

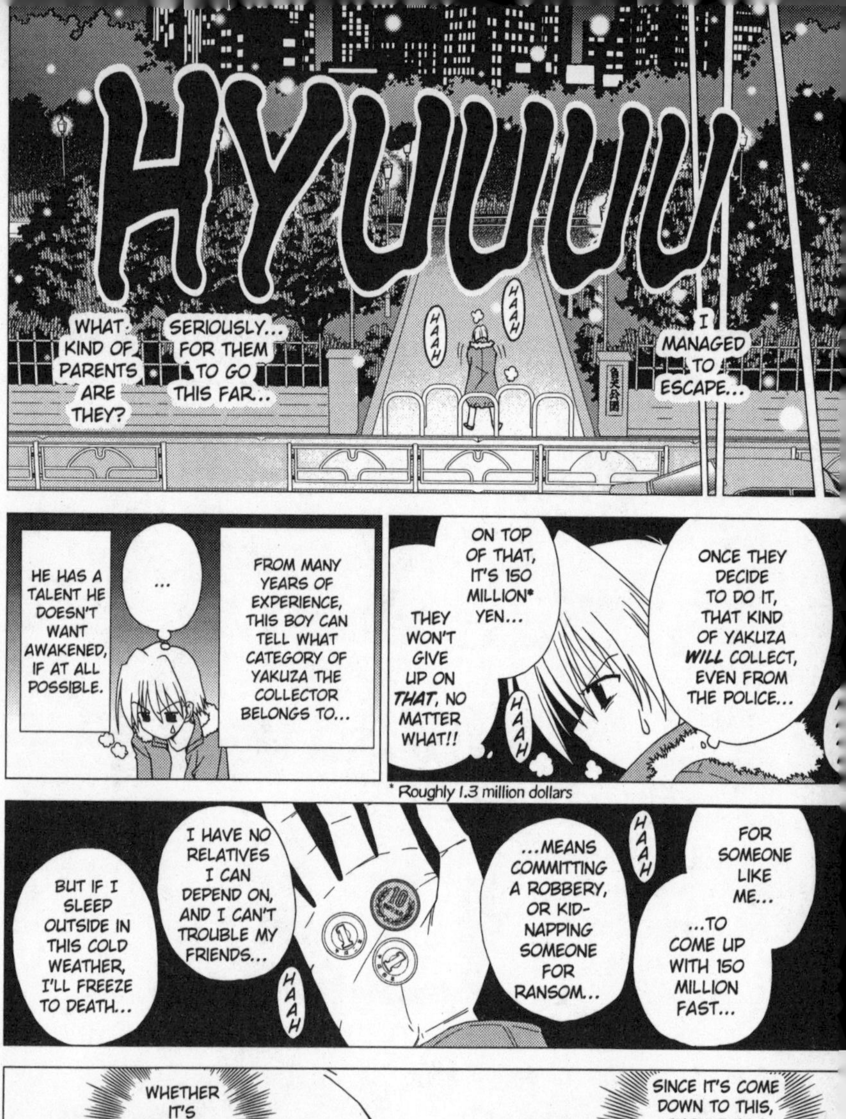
HYUUUU
I MANAGED TO ESCAPE...
HAAH
HAAH
SERIOUSLY... FOR THEM TO GO THIS FAR...
WHAT KIND OF PARENTS ARE THEY?
ONCE THEY DECIDE TO DO IT, THAT KIND OF YAKUZA *WILL* COLLECT, EVEN FROM THE POLICE...
ON TOP OF THAT, IT'S 150 MILLION* YEN...
THEY WON'T GIVE UP ON *THAT*, NO MATTER WHAT!!
HAAH
FROM MANY YEARS OF EXPERIENCE, THIS BOY CAN TELL WHAT CATEGORY OF YAKUZA THE COLLECTOR BELONGS TO...
...
HE HAS A TALENT HE DOESN'T WANT AWAKENED, IF AT ALL POSSIBLE.
FOR SOMEONE LIKE ME...
...TO COME UP WITH 150 MILLION FAST...
HAAH
...MEANS COMMITTING A ROBBERY, OR KID-NAPPING SOMEONE FOR RANSOM...
I HAVE NO RELATIVES I CAN DEPEND ON, AND I CAN'T TROUBLE MY FRIENDS...
BUT IF I SLEEP OUTSIDE IN THIS COLD WEATHER, I'LL FREEZE TO DEATH...
HAAH
SINCE IT'S COME DOWN TO THIS, SHOULDN'T I JUST BECOME A BAD GUY?! MY PARENTS, AS WELL AS THE YAKUZA, ARE TARGETING ME...
SOME WRONGDOING SHOULD BE FORGIVEN!! NO, IT *MUST* BE FORGIVEN!!
WHETHER IT'S ROBBERY, OR KID-NAPPING...
...IT'S TO SAVE MY OWN LIFE!!

* Roughly 1.3 million dollars

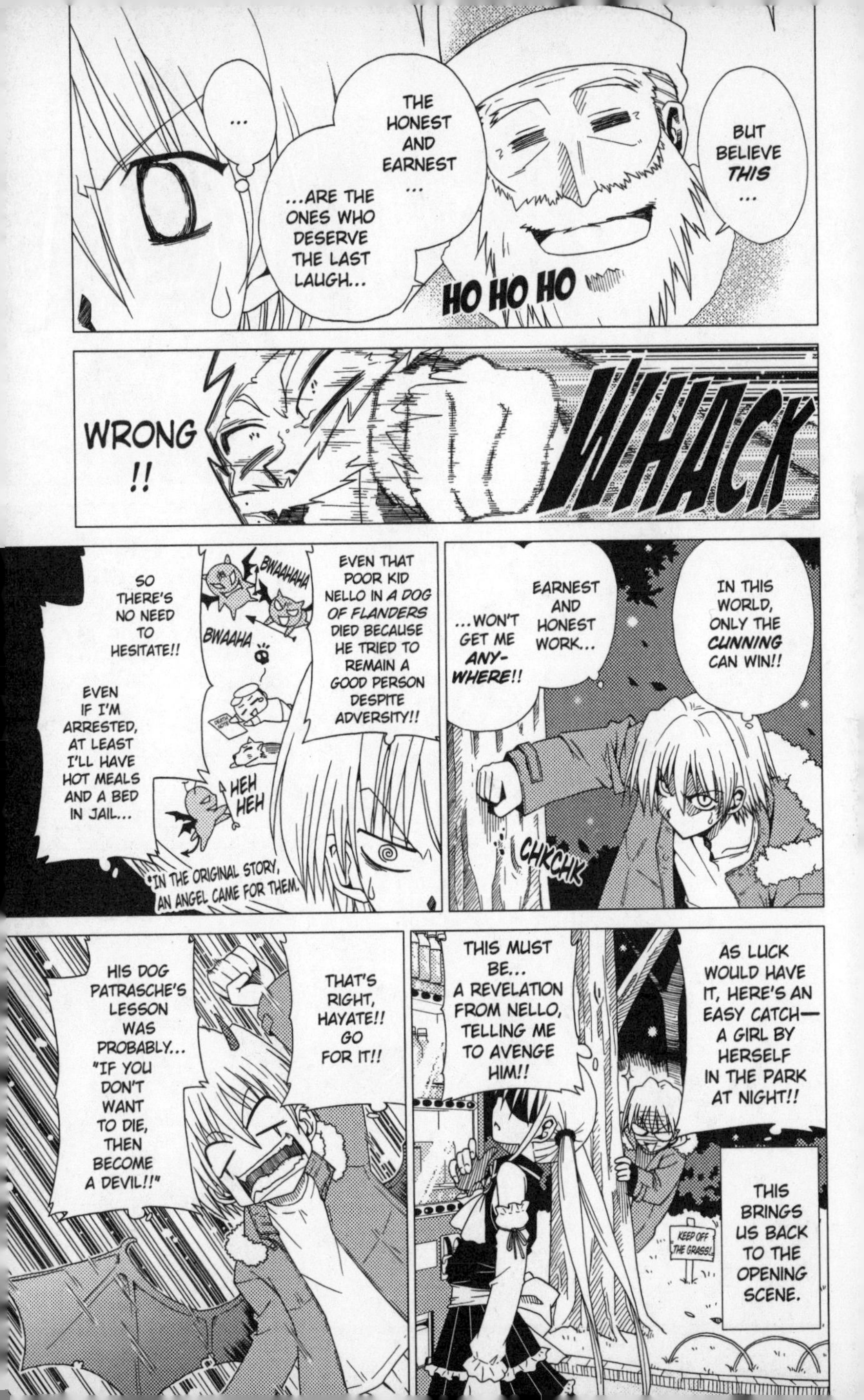
BUT BELIEVE THIS...
THE HONEST AND EARNEST...
...ARE THE ONES WHO DESERVE THE LAST LAUGH...
HO HO HO
...
WHACK
WRONG!!
IN THIS WORLD, ONLY THE CUNNING CAN WIN!!
EARNEST AND HONEST WORK...
...WON'T GET ME ANYWHERE!!
CHKCHK
EVEN THAT POOR KID NELLO IN A DOG OF FLANDERS DIED BECAUSE HE TRIED TO REMAIN A GOOD PERSON DESPITE ADVERSITY!!
BWAAHAHA
BWAAHA
SO THERE'S NO NEED TO HESITATE!!
EVEN IF I'M ARRESTED, AT LEAST I'LL HAVE HOT MEALS AND A BED IN JAIL...
HEH HEH
*IN THE ORIGINAL STORY, AN ANGEL CAME FOR THEM.
AS LUCK WOULD HAVE IT, HERE'S AN EASY CATCH— A GIRL BY HERSELF IN THE PARK AT NIGHT!!
THIS MUST BE... A REVELATION FROM NELLO, TELLING ME TO AVENGE HIM!!
KEEP OFF THE GRASS!
THIS BRINGS US BACK TO THE OPENING SCENE.
THAT'S RIGHT, HAYATE!! GO FOR IT!!
HIS DOG PATRASCHE'S LESSON WAS PROBABLY... "IF YOU DON'T WANT TO DIE, THEN BECOME A DEVIL!!"

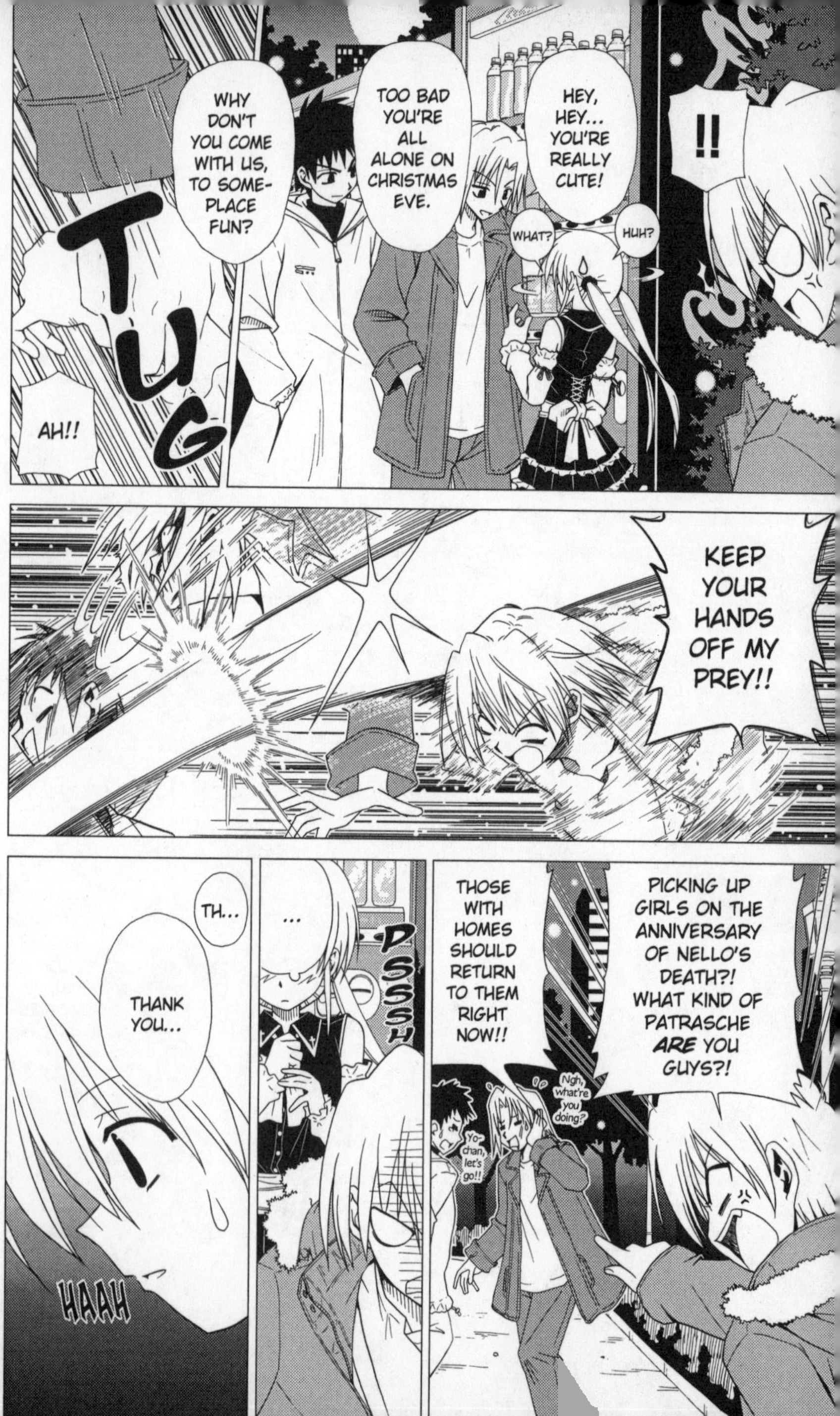
!!
HEY, HEY... YOU'RE REALLY CUTE!
HUH?
WHAT?
TOO BAD YOU'RE ALL ALONE ON CHRISTMAS EVE.
WHY DON'T YOU COME WITH US, TO SOME-PLACE FUN?
TUG
AH!!
KEEP YOUR HANDS OFF MY PREY!!
PICKING UP GIRLS ON THE ANNIVERSARY OF NELLO'S DEATH?! WHAT KIND OF PATRASCHE ARE YOU GUYS?!
THOSE WITH HOMES SHOULD RETURN TO THEM RIGHT NOW!!
Ngh, what're you doing?
Yo-chan, let's go!!
PSSSH
...
TH...
THANK YOU...
HAAH

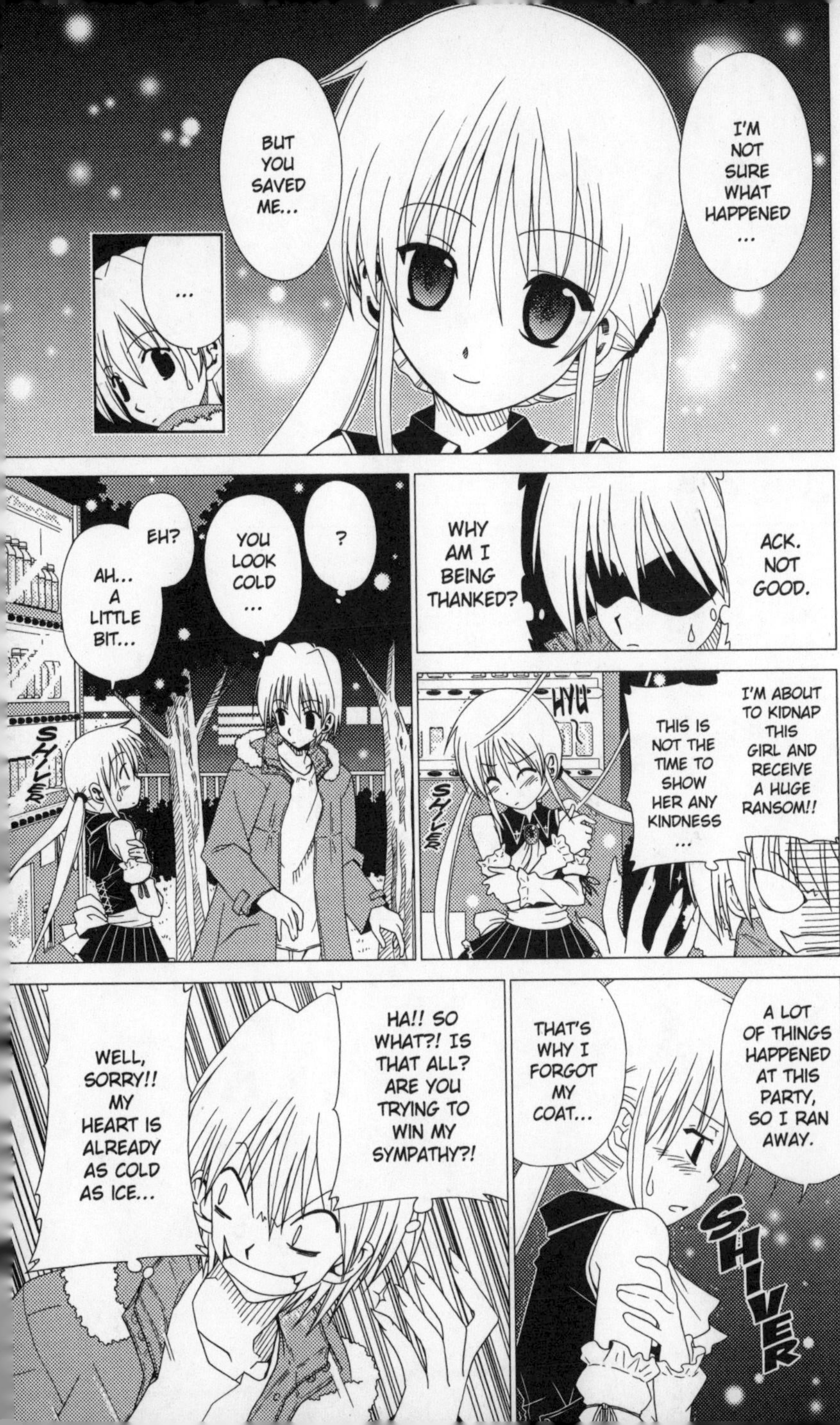
I'M NOT SURE WHAT HAPPENED ...
BUT YOU SAVED ME...
...
ACK. NOT GOOD.
WHY AM I BEING THANKED?
I'M ABOUT TO KIDNAP THIS GIRL AND RECEIVE A HUGE RANSOM!!
THIS IS NOT THE TIME TO SHOW HER ANY KINDNESS ...
HYU
SHIVER
?
YOU LOOK COLD ...
EH?
AH... A LITTLE BIT...
SHIVER
A LOT OF THINGS HAPPENED AT THIS PARTY, SO I RAN AWAY.
THAT'S WHY I FORGOT MY COAT...
SHIVER
HA!! SO WHAT?! IS THAT ALL? ARE YOU TRYING TO WIN MY SYMPATHY?!
WELL, SORRY!! MY HEART IS ALREADY AS COLD AS ICE...

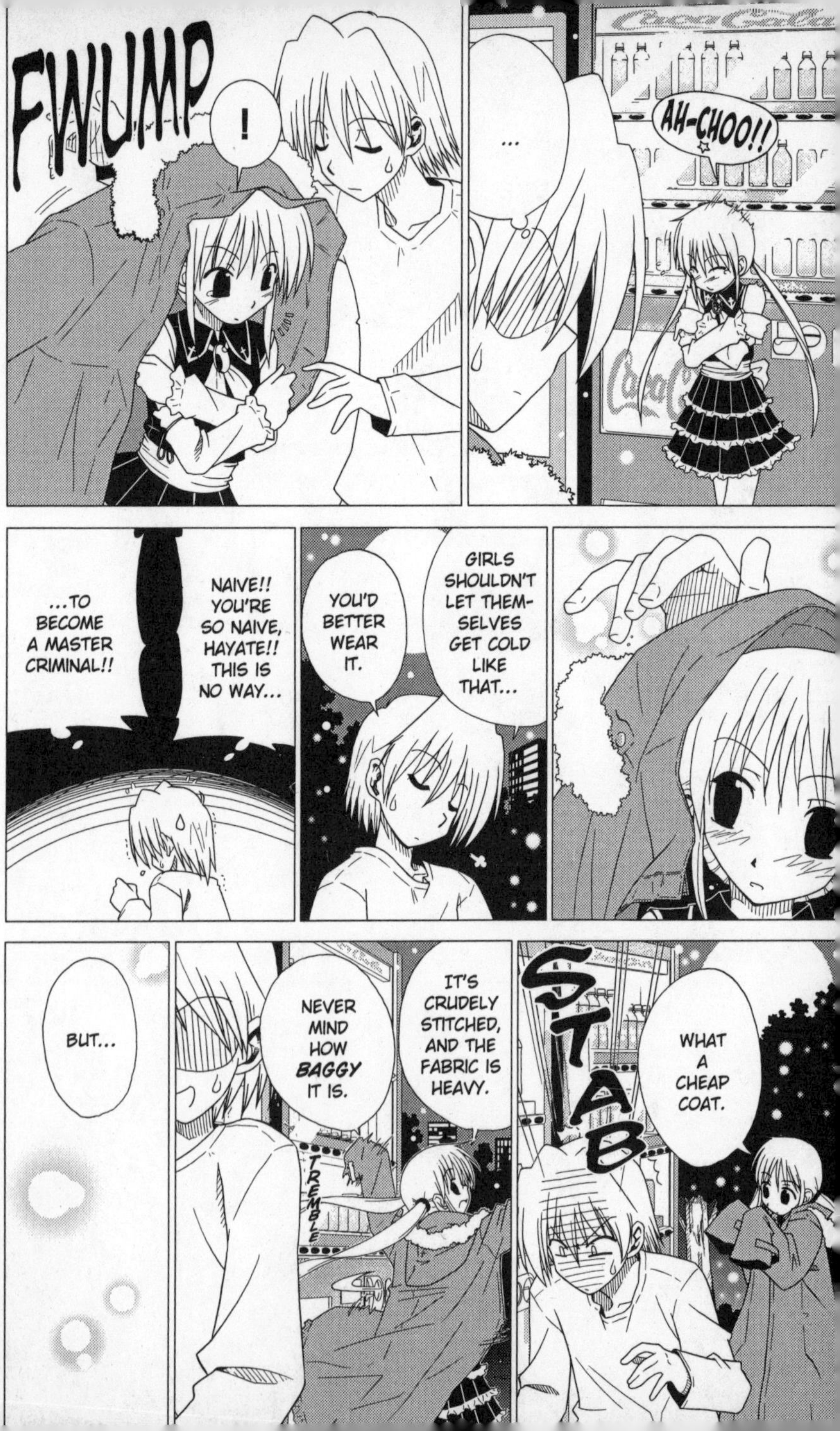
AH-CHOO!!
...
FWUMP
!
GIRLS SHOULDN'T LET THEM-SELVES GET COLD LIKE THAT...
YOU'D BETTER WEAR IT.
NAIVE!! YOU'RE SO NAIVE, HAYATE!! THIS IS NO WAY...
...TO BECOME A MASTER CRIMINAL!!
WHAT A CHEAP COAT.
STAB
IT'S CRUDELY STITCHED, AND THE FABRIC IS HEAVY.
NEVER MIND HOW *BAGGY* IT IS.
TREMBLE
BUT...

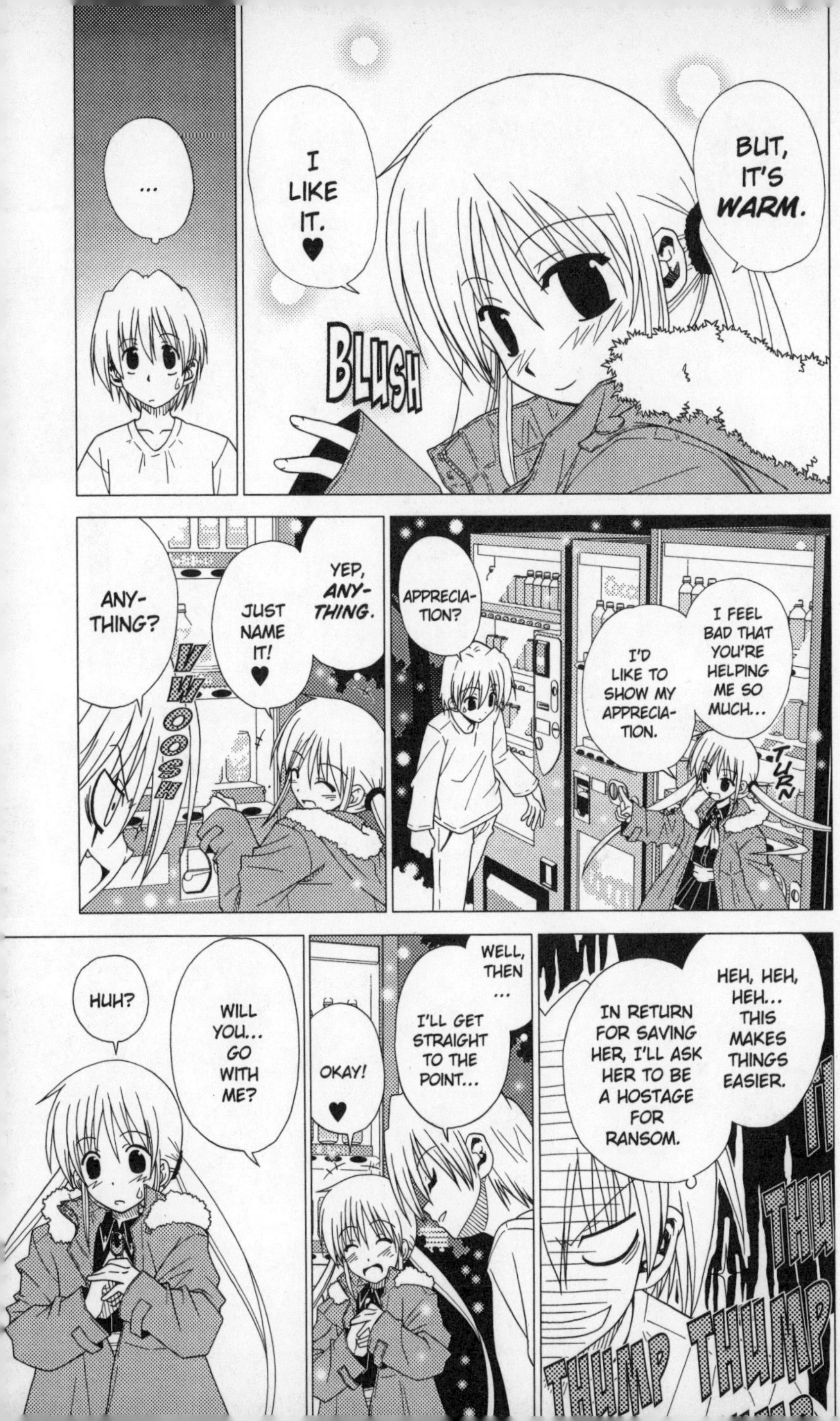
BUT, IT'S WARM.
I LIKE IT. ♥
BLUSH
...
I FEEL BAD THAT YOU'RE HELPING ME SO MUCH...
I'D LIKE TO SHOW MY APPRECIATION.
TURN
APPRECIATION?
YEP, ANYTHING.
JUST NAME IT! ♥
ANYTHING?
VWOOOSH
HEH, HEH, HEH... THIS MAKES THINGS EASIER.
IN RETURN FOR SAVING HER, I'LL ASK HER TO BE A HOSTAGE FOR RANSOM.
THUMP THUMP
WELL, THEN...
I'LL GET STRAIGHT TO THE POINT...
OKAY! ♥
WILL YOU... GO WITH ME?
HUH?

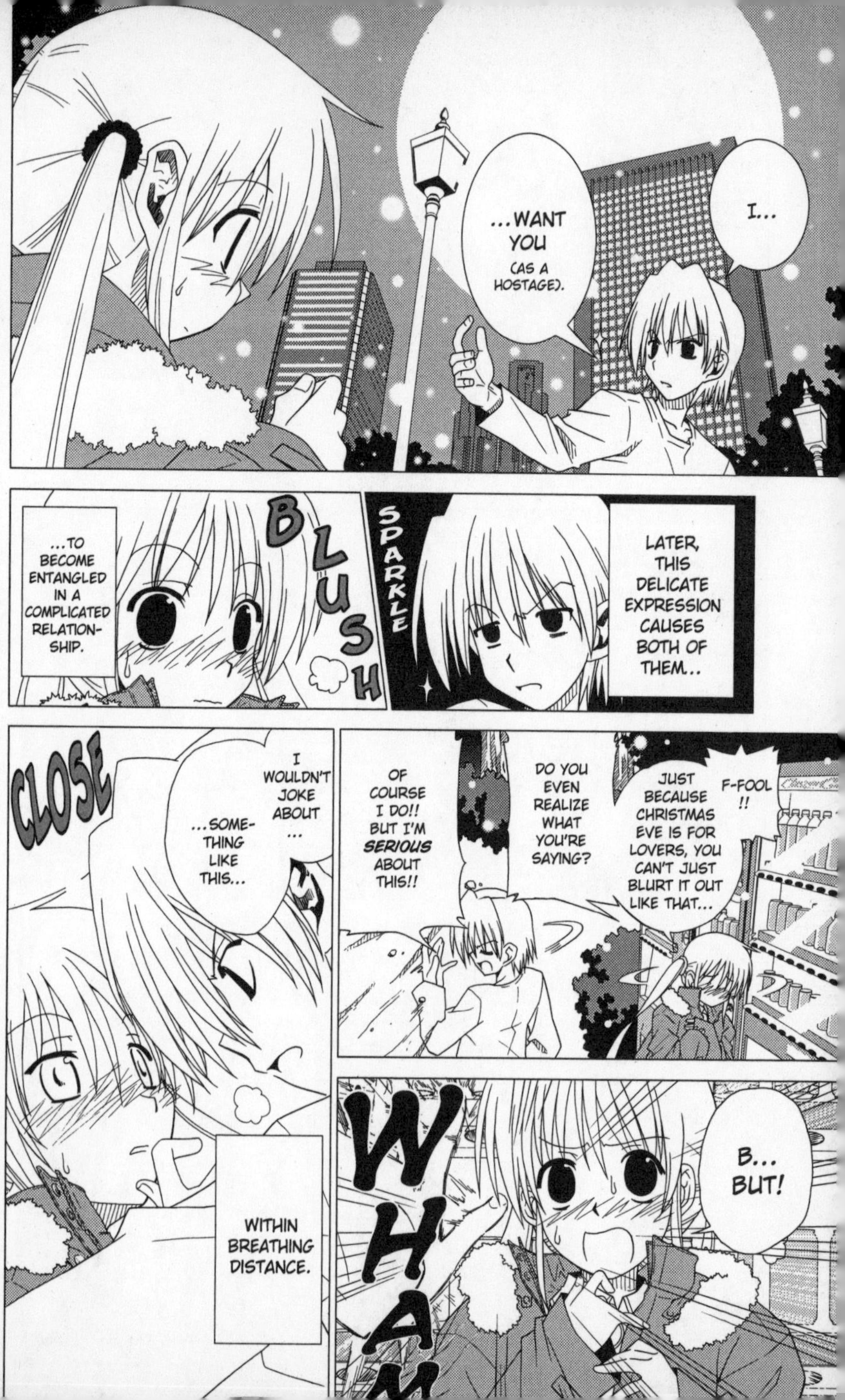
I...
...WANT YOU (AS A HOSTAGE).
LATER, THIS DELICATE EXPRESSION CAUSES BOTH OF THEM...
SPARKLE
BLUSH
...TO BECOME ENTANGLED IN A COMPLICATED RELATION-SHIP.
F-FOOL!!
JUST BECAUSE CHRISTMAS EVE IS FOR LOVERS, YOU CAN'T JUST BLURT IT OUT LIKE THAT...
DO YOU EVEN REALIZE WHAT YOU'RE SAYING?
OF COURSE I DO!! BUT I'M *SERIOUS* ABOUT THIS!!
B... BUT!
WHAM
CLOSE
I WOULDN'T JOKE ABOUT ...
...SOME-THING LIKE THIS...
WITHIN BREATHING DISTANCE.

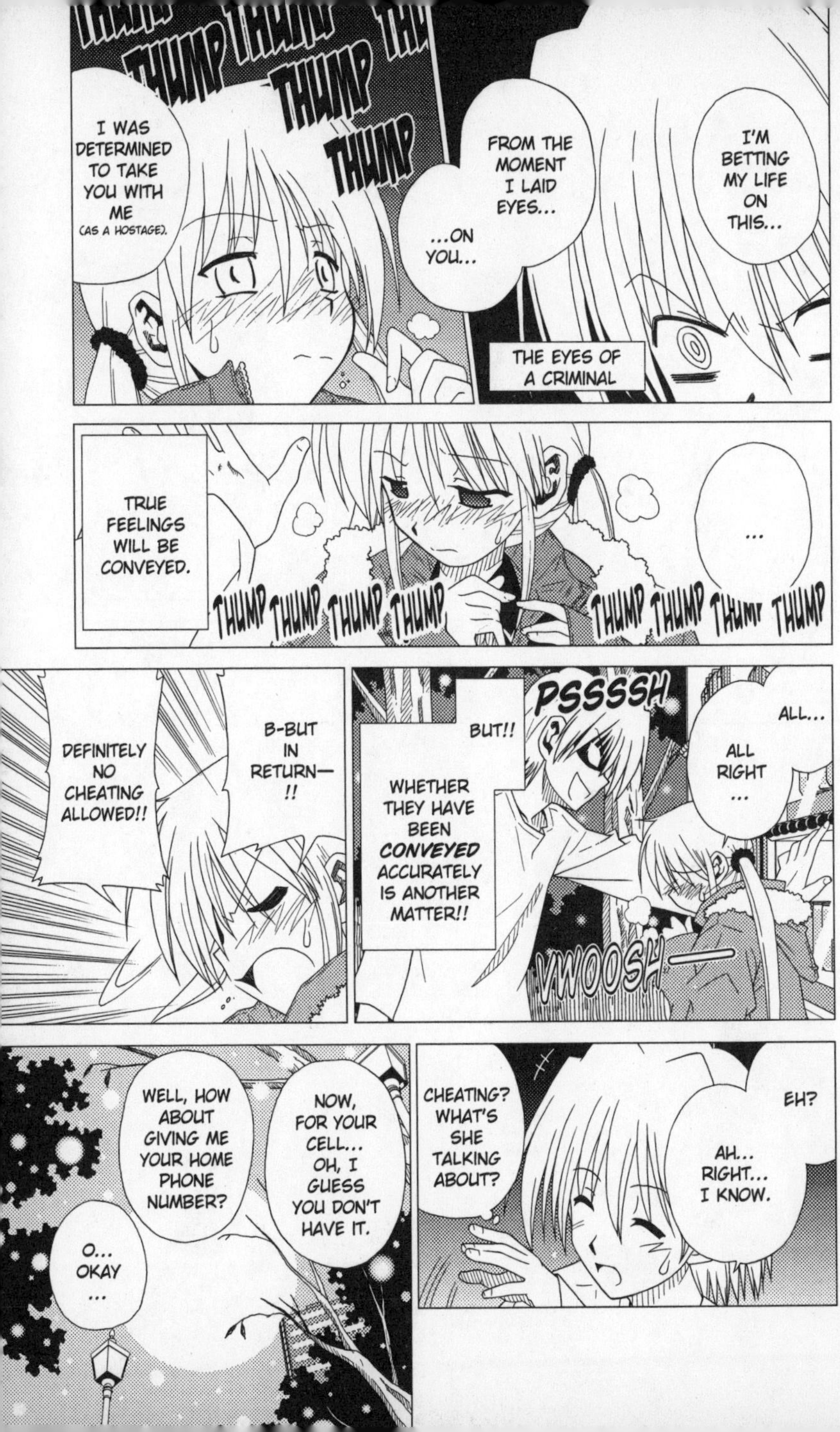
I'M BETTING MY LIFE ON THIS...
FROM THE MOMENT I LAID EYES...
...ON YOU...
THE EYES OF A CRIMINAL
THUMP THUMP THUMP THUMP
I WAS DETERMINED TO TAKE YOU WITH ME (AS A HOSTAGE).
...
THUMP THUMP THUMP THUMP THUMP THUMP THUMP THUMP
TRUE FEELINGS WILL BE CONVEYED.
ALL... ALL RIGHT ...
PSSSSH
BUT!!
WHETHER THEY HAVE BEEN **CONVEYED** ACCURATELY IS ANOTHER MATTER!!
VWOOSH—
B-BUT IN RETURN—!!
DEFINITELY NO CHEATING ALLOWED!!
EH?
AH... RIGHT... I KNOW.
CHEATING? WHAT'S SHE TALKING ABOUT?
NOW, FOR YOUR CELL... OH, I GUESS YOU DON'T HAVE IT.
WELL, HOW ABOUT GIVING ME YOUR HOME PHONE NUMBER?
O... OKAY ...

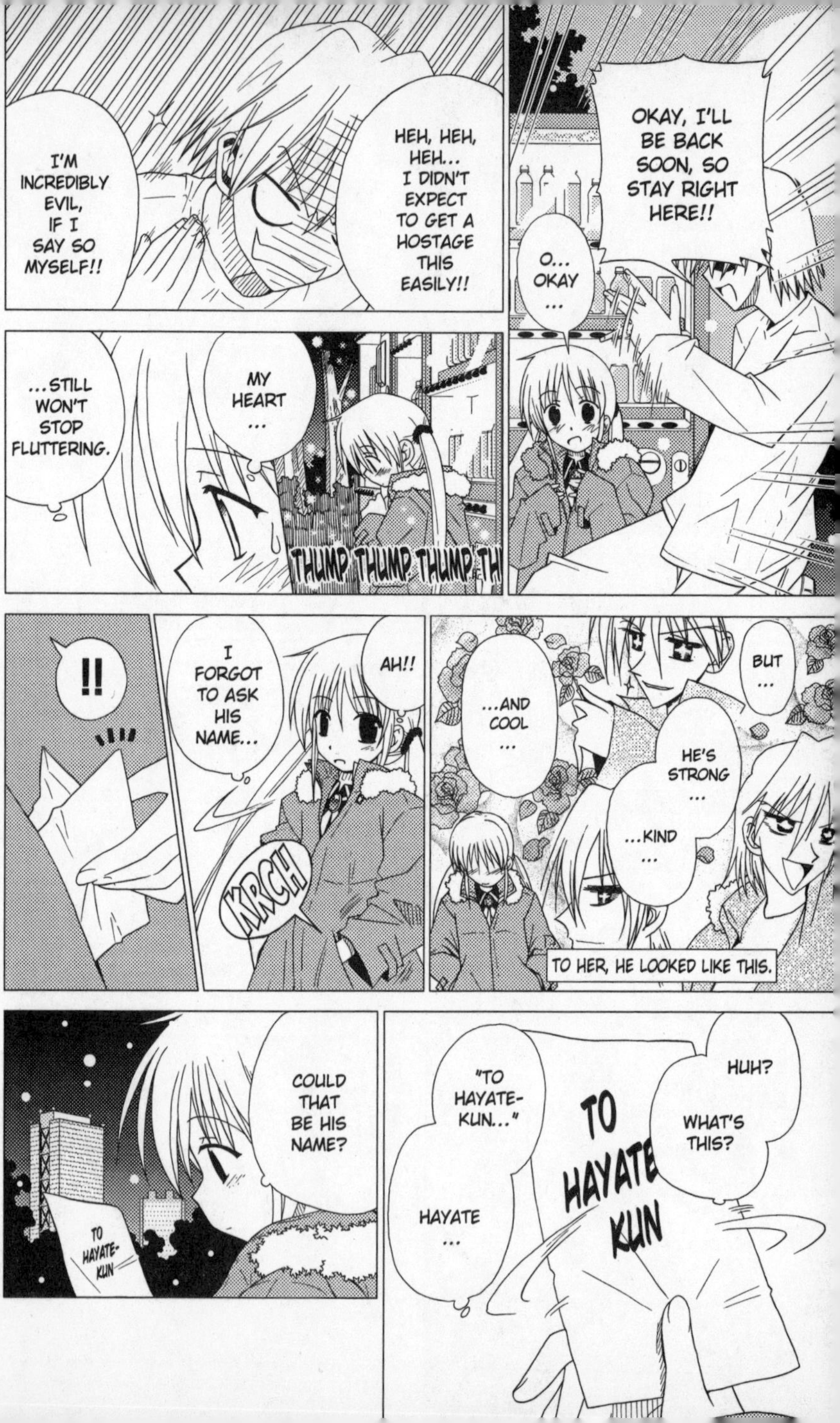
OKAY, I'LL BE BACK SOON, SO STAY RIGHT HERE!!
O... OKAY ...
HEH, HEH, HEH... I DIDN'T EXPECT TO GET A HOSTAGE THIS EASILY!!
I'M INCREDIBLY EVIL, IF I SAY SO MYSELF!!
MY HEART ...
...STILL WON'T STOP FLUTTERING.
THUMP THUMP THUMP TH
BUT ...
HE'S STRONG ...
...KIND ...
...AND COOL ...
TO HER, HE LOOKED LIKE THIS.
AH!!
I FORGOT TO ASK HIS NAME...
KRCH
!!
HUH?
WHAT'S THIS?
TO HAYATE KUN
"TO HAYATE-KUN..."
HAYATE ...
COULD THAT BE HIS NAME?
TO HAYATE-KUN

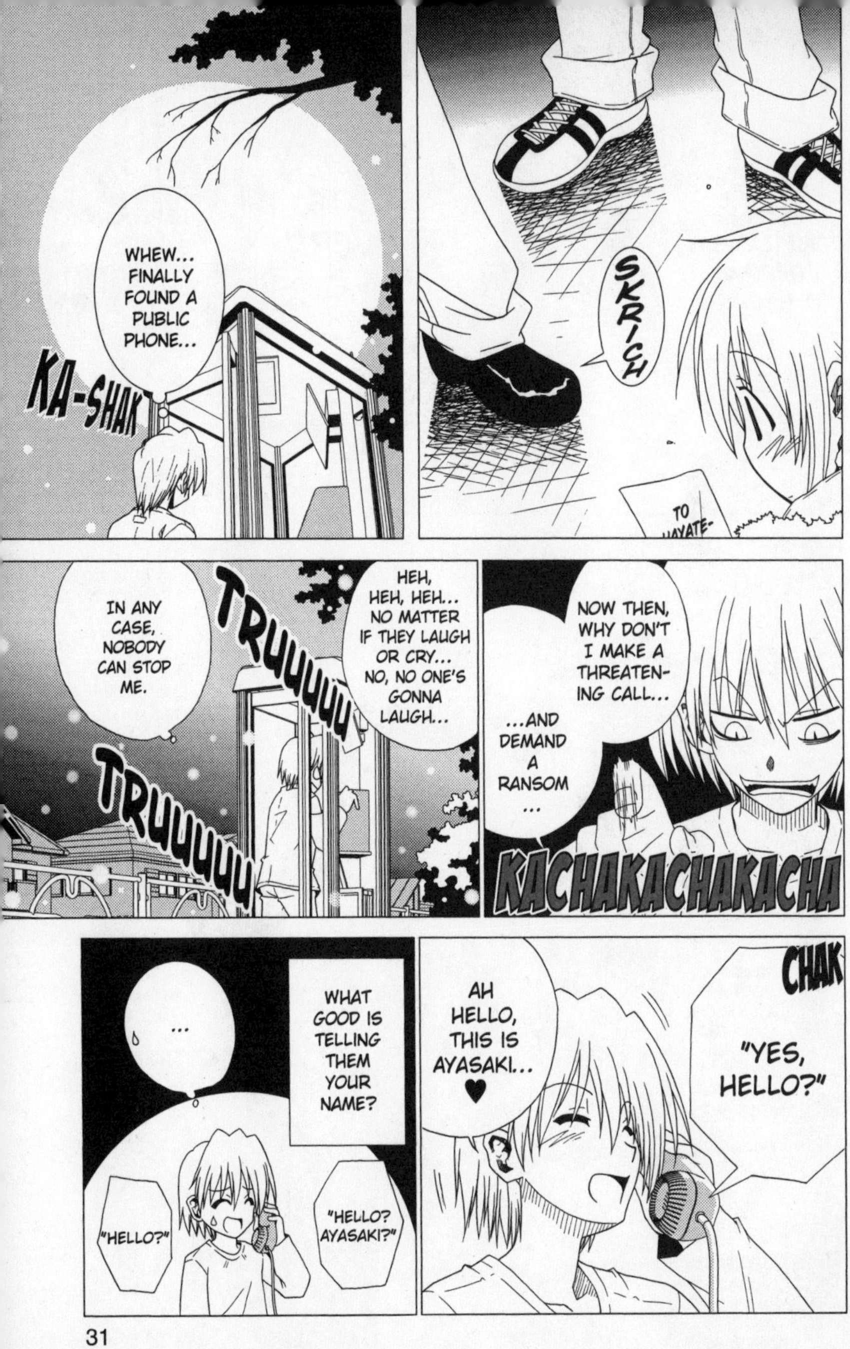
SKRICH
TO
KA-SHAK
WHEW... FINALLY FOUND A PUBLIC PHONE...
NOW THEN, WHY DON'T I MAKE A THREATENING CALL...
...AND DEMAND A RANSOM...
KACHAKACHAKACHA
HEH, HEH, HEH... NO MATTER IF THEY LAUGH OR CRY... NO, NO ONE'S GONNA LAUGH...
IN ANY CASE, NOBODY CAN STOP ME.
TRUUUUUU
TRUUUUUU
CHAK
"YES, HELLO?"
AH HELLO, THIS IS AYASAKI... ♥
WHAT GOOD IS TELLING THEM YOUR NAME?
"HELLO? AYASAKI?"
"HELLO?"
...

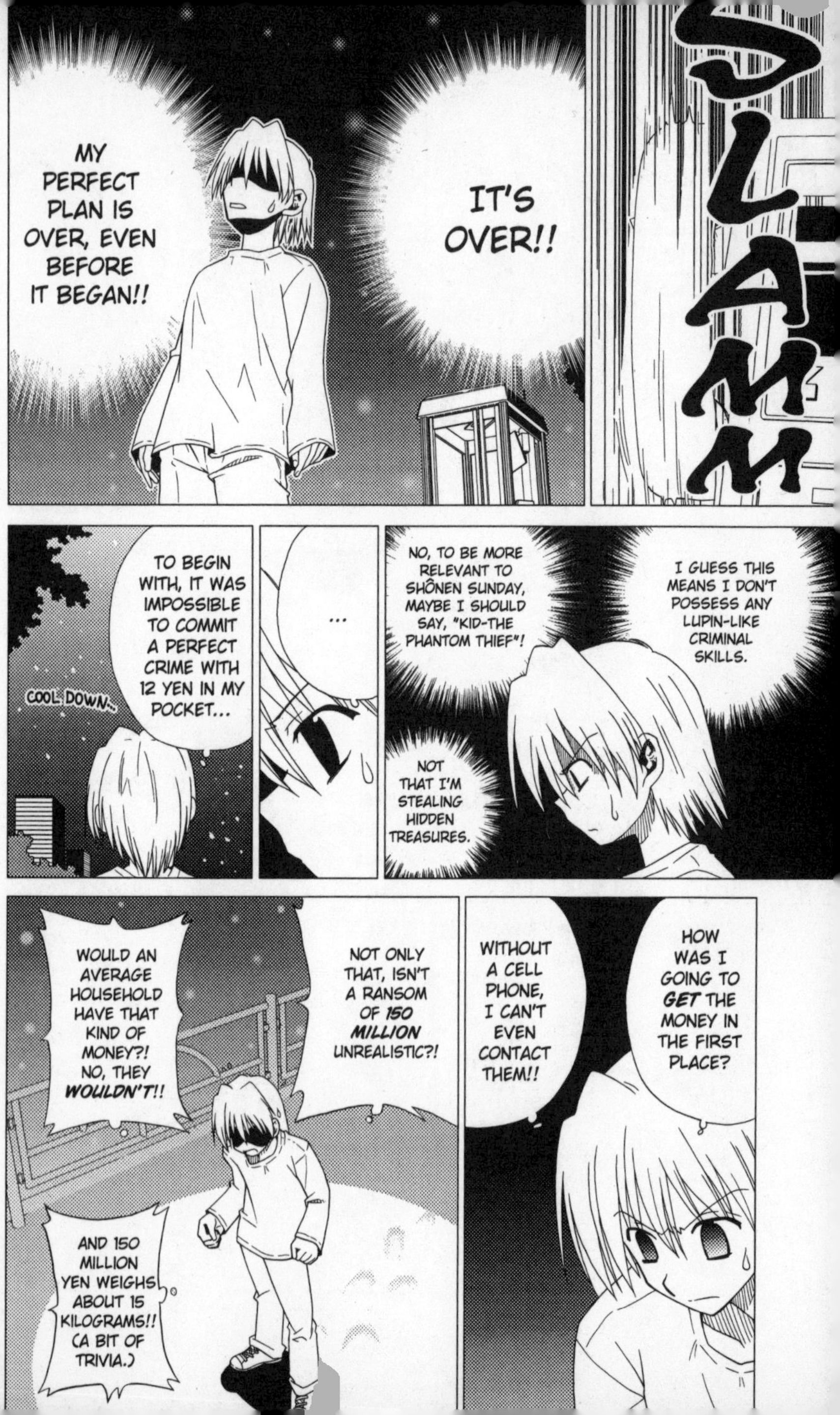
SLAMM
IT'S OVER!!
MY PERFECT PLAN IS OVER, EVEN BEFORE IT BEGAN!!
I GUESS THIS MEANS I DON'T POSSESS ANY LUPIN-LIKE CRIMINAL SKILLS.
NO, TO BE MORE RELEVANT TO SHÔNEN SUNDAY, MAYBE I SHOULD SAY, "KID-THE PHANTOM THIEF"!
NOT THAT I'M STEALING HIDDEN TREASURES.
...
TO BEGIN WITH, IT WAS IMPOSSIBLE TO COMMIT A PERFECT CRIME WITH 12 YEN IN MY POCKET...
COOL DOWN..
HOW WAS I GOING TO GET THE MONEY IN THE FIRST PLACE?
WITHOUT A CELL PHONE, I CAN'T EVEN CONTACT THEM!!
NOT ONLY THAT, ISN'T A RANSOM OF 150 MILLION UNREALISTIC?!
WOULD AN AVERAGE HOUSEHOLD HAVE THAT KIND OF MONEY?! NO, THEY WOULDN'T!!
AND 150 MILLION YEN WEIGHS ABOUT 15 KILOGRAMS!! (A BIT OF TRIVIA.)

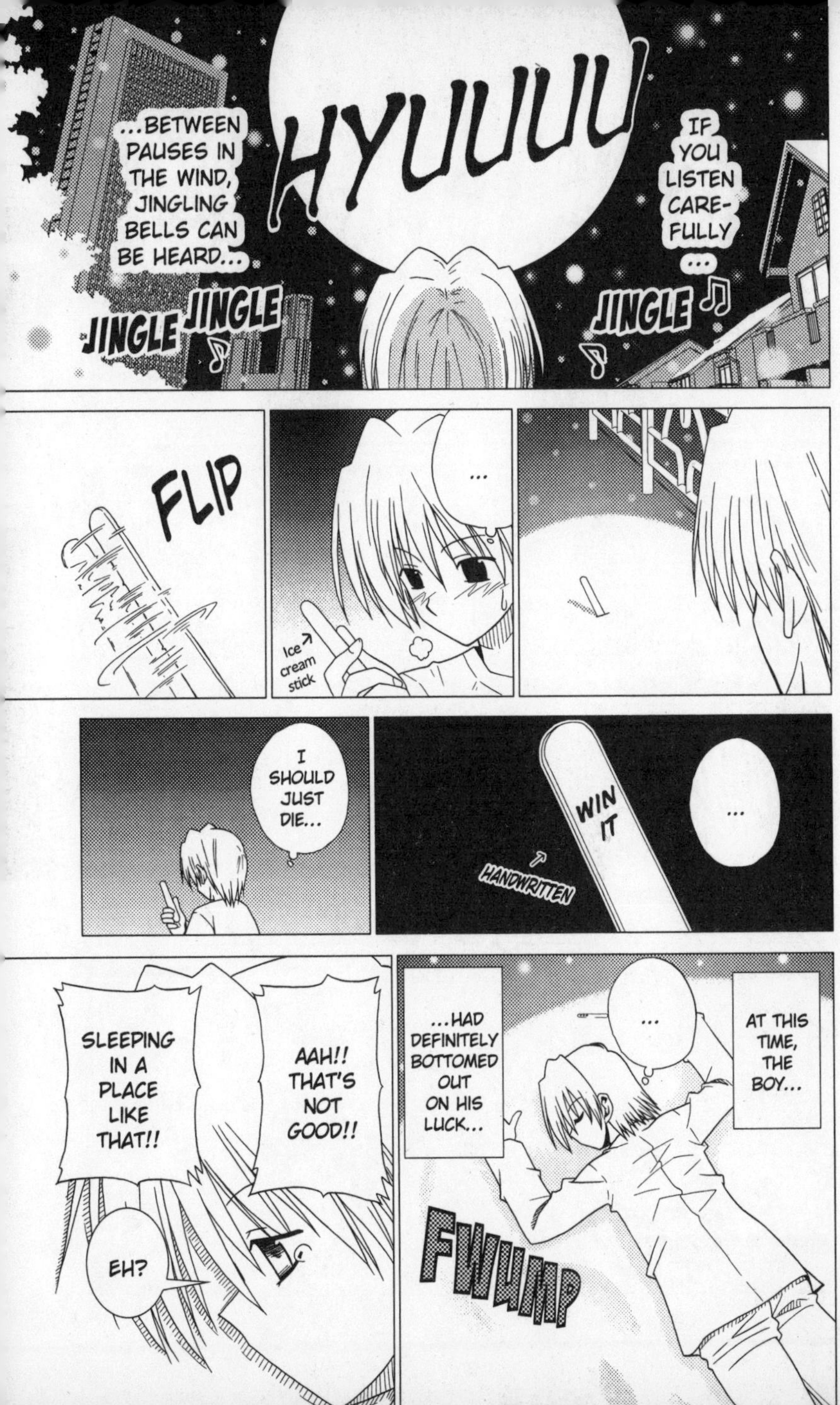
IF YOU LISTEN CARE-FULLY...
HYUUUU
...BETWEEN PAUSES IN THE WIND, JINGLING BELLS CAN BE HEARD...
JINGLE
JINGLE JINGLE
...
Ice cream stick
FLIP
...
WIN IT
HANDWRITTEN
I SHOULD JUST DIE...
AT THIS TIME, THE BOY...
...
...HAD DEFINITELY BOTTOMED OUT ON HIS LUCK...
FWUMP
AAH!! THAT'S NOT GOOD!!
SLEEPING IN A PLACE LIKE THAT!!
EH?

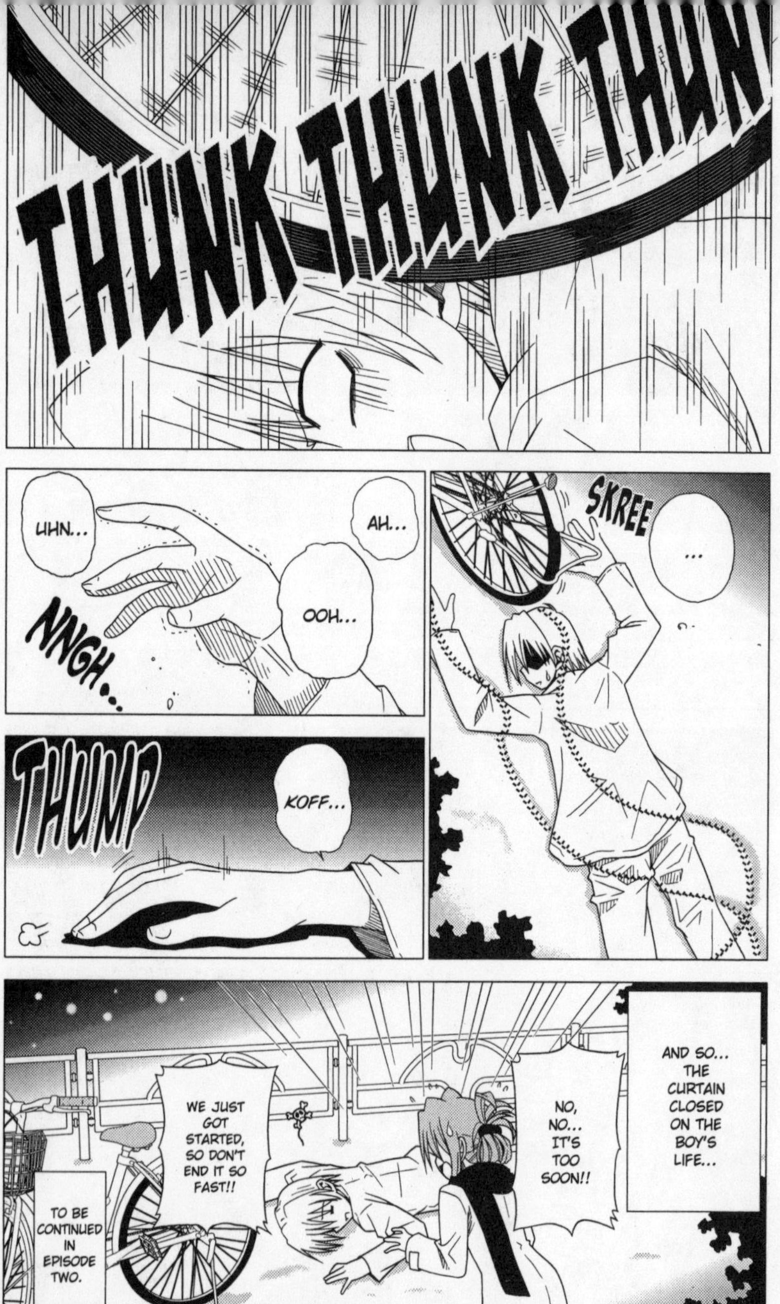
THUNK-THUNK-THUN
SKREE
...
AH...
UHN...
OOH...
NNGH...
KOFF...
THUMP
AND SO... THE CURTAIN CLOSED ON THE BOY'S LIFE...
NO, NO... IT'S TOO SOON!!
WE JUST GOT STARTED, SO DON'T END IT SO FAST!!
TO BE CONTINUED IN EPISODE TWO.

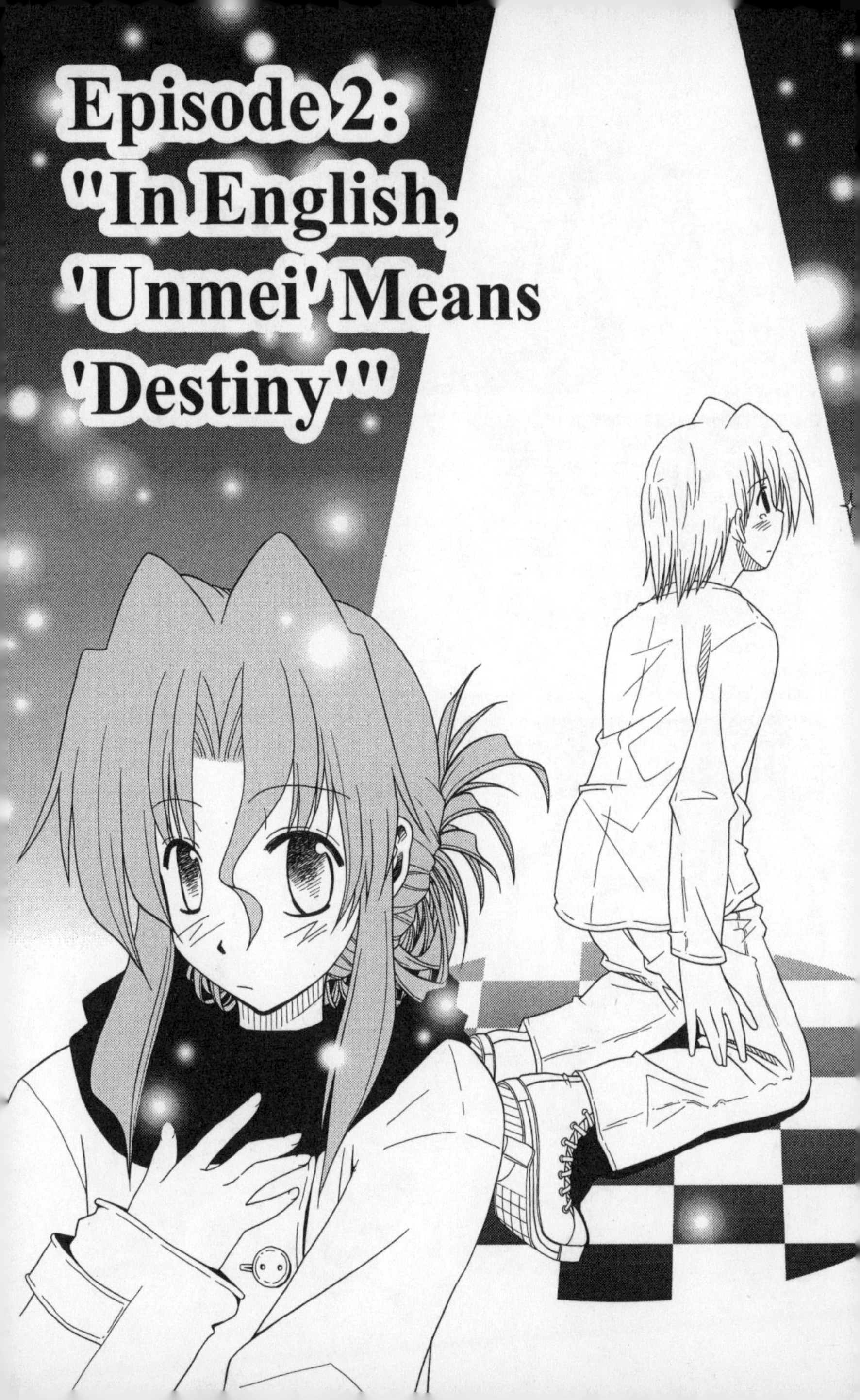
Episode 2:
"In English,
'Unmei' Means
'Destiny'"

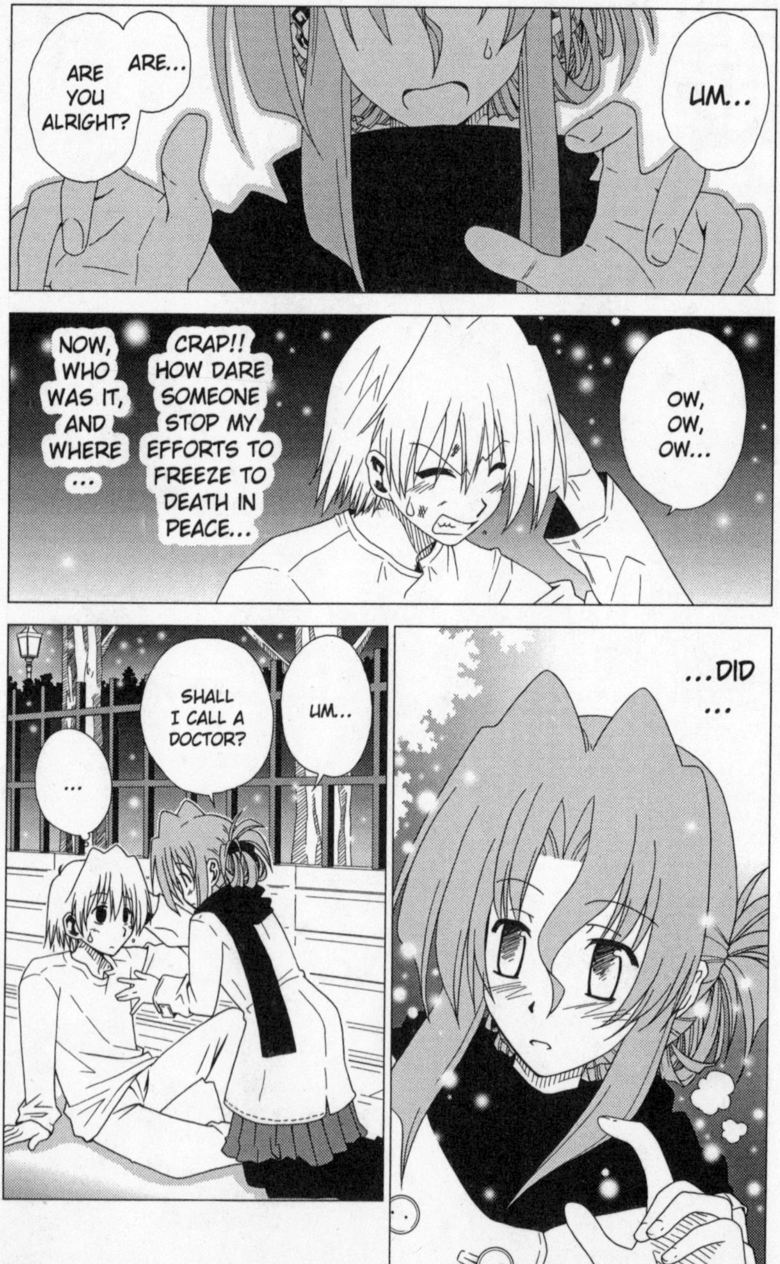
UM...
ARE...
ARE YOU ALRIGHT?
OW, OW, OW...
CRAP!! HOW DARE SOMEONE STOP MY EFFORTS TO FREEZE TO DEATH IN PEACE...
NOW, WHO WAS IT, AND WHERE ...
...DID ...
UM...
SHALL I CALL A DOCTOR?
...

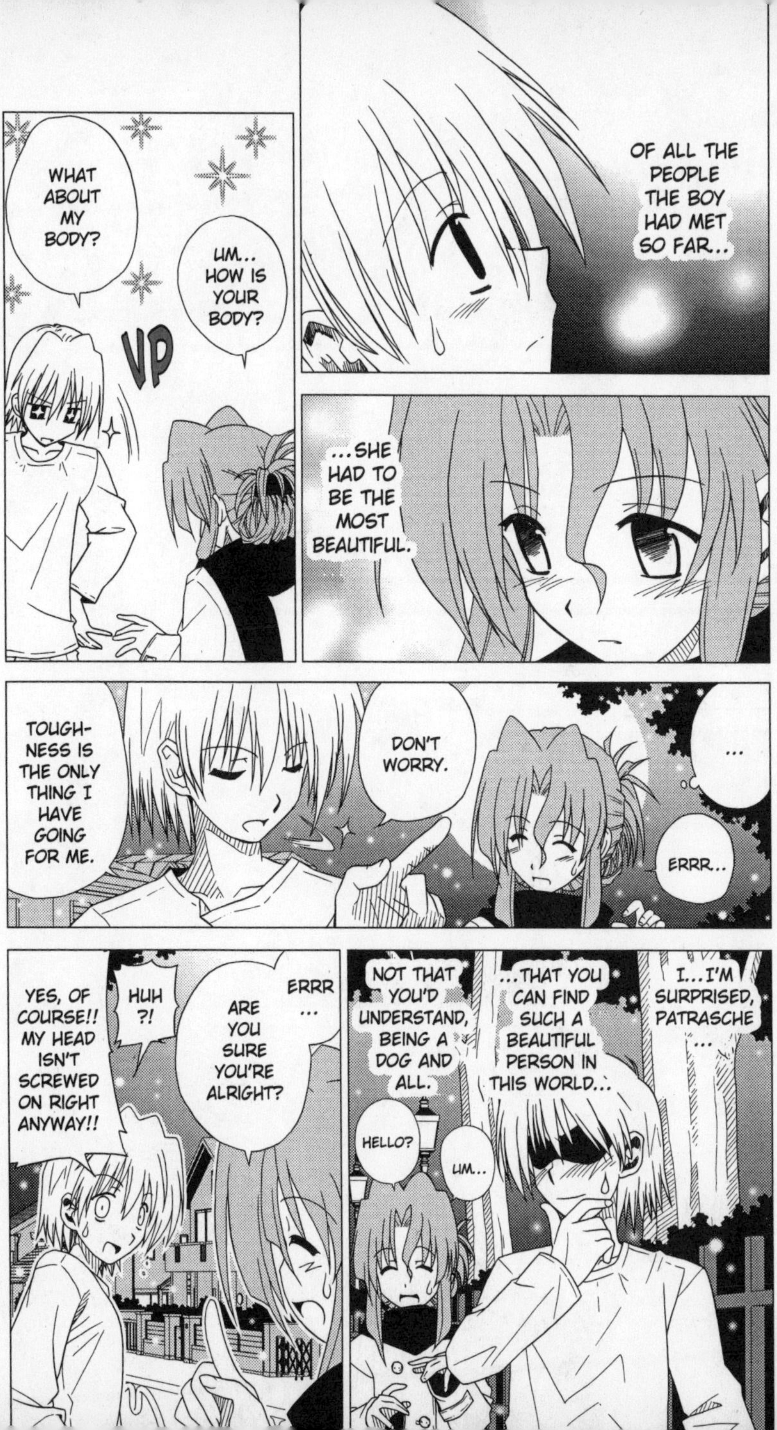
OF ALL THE PEOPLE THE BOY HAD MET SO FAR...
...SHE HAD TO BE THE MOST BEAUTIFUL.
WHAT ABOUT MY BODY?
UM... HOW IS YOUR BODY?
VP
...
ERRR...
DON'T WORRY.
TOUGHNESS IS THE ONLY THING I HAVE GOING FOR ME.
I...I'M SURPRISED, PATRASCHE...
...THAT YOU CAN FIND SUCH A BEAUTIFUL PERSON IN THIS WORLD...
NOT THAT YOU'D UNDERSTAND, BEING A DOG AND ALL.
UM...
HELLO?
ERRR...
ARE YOU SURE YOU'RE ALRIGHT?
HUH ?!
YES, OF COURSE!! MY HEAD ISN'T SCREWED ON RIGHT ANYWAY!!

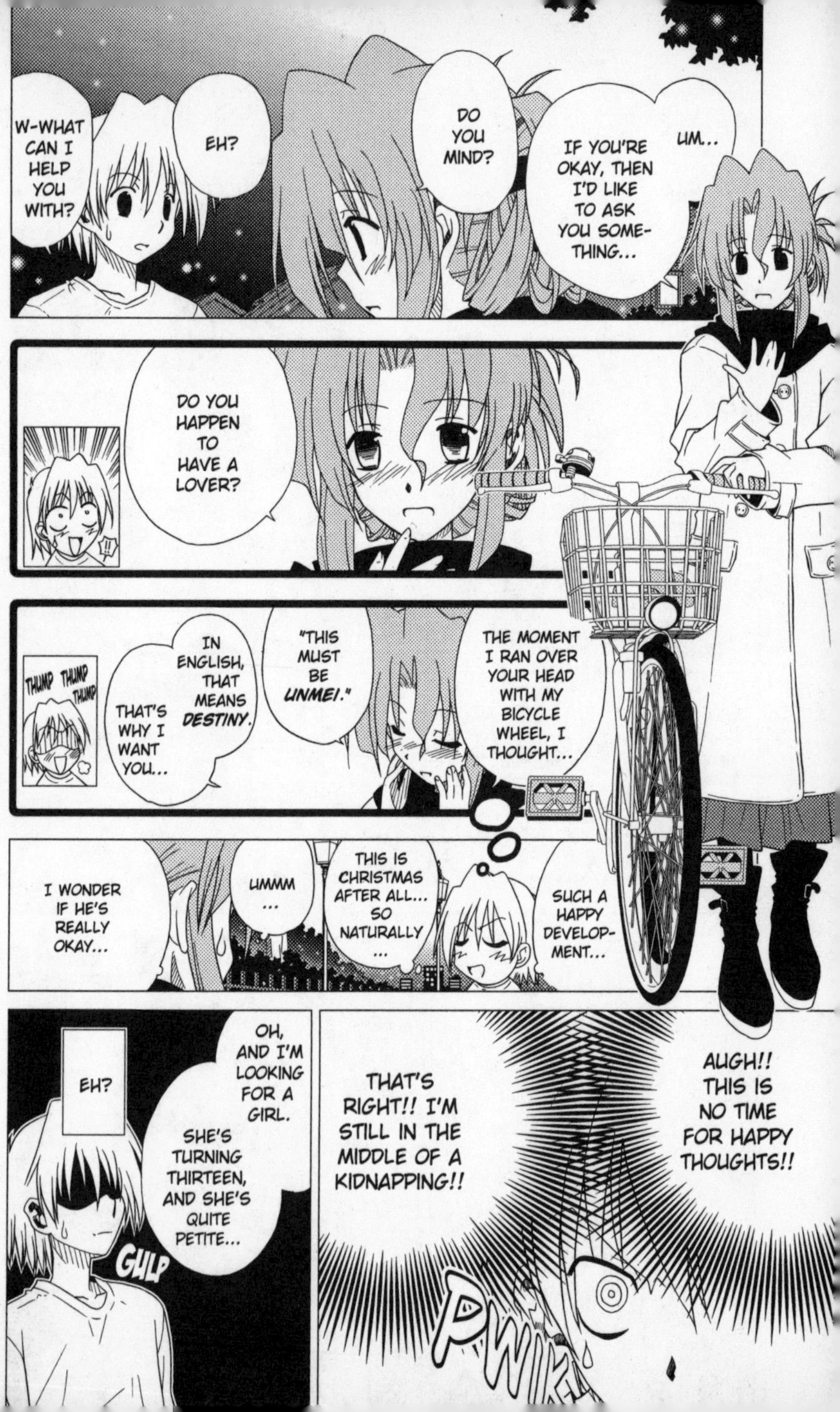
UM...
IF YOU'RE OKAY, THEN I'D LIKE TO ASK YOU SOME-THING...
DO YOU MIND?
EH?
W-WHAT CAN I HELP YOU WITH?
DO YOU HAPPEN TO HAVE A LOVER?
!!
THE MOMENT I RAN OVER YOUR HEAD WITH MY BICYCLE WHEEL, I THOUGHT...
"THIS MUST BE UNMEI."
IN ENGLISH, THAT MEANS DESTINY.
THAT'S WHY I WANT YOU...
THUMP THUMP THUMP
SUCH A HAPPY DEVELOP-MENT...
THIS IS CHRISTMAS AFTER ALL... SO NATURALLY...
UMMM...
I WONDER IF HE'S REALLY OKAY...
AUGH!! THIS IS NO TIME FOR HAPPY THOUGHTS!!
THAT'S RIGHT!! I'M STILL IN THE MIDDLE OF A KIDNAPPING!!
OH, AND I'M LOOKING FOR A GIRL.
SHE'S TURNING THIRTEEN, AND SHE'S QUITE PETITE...
EH?
GULP

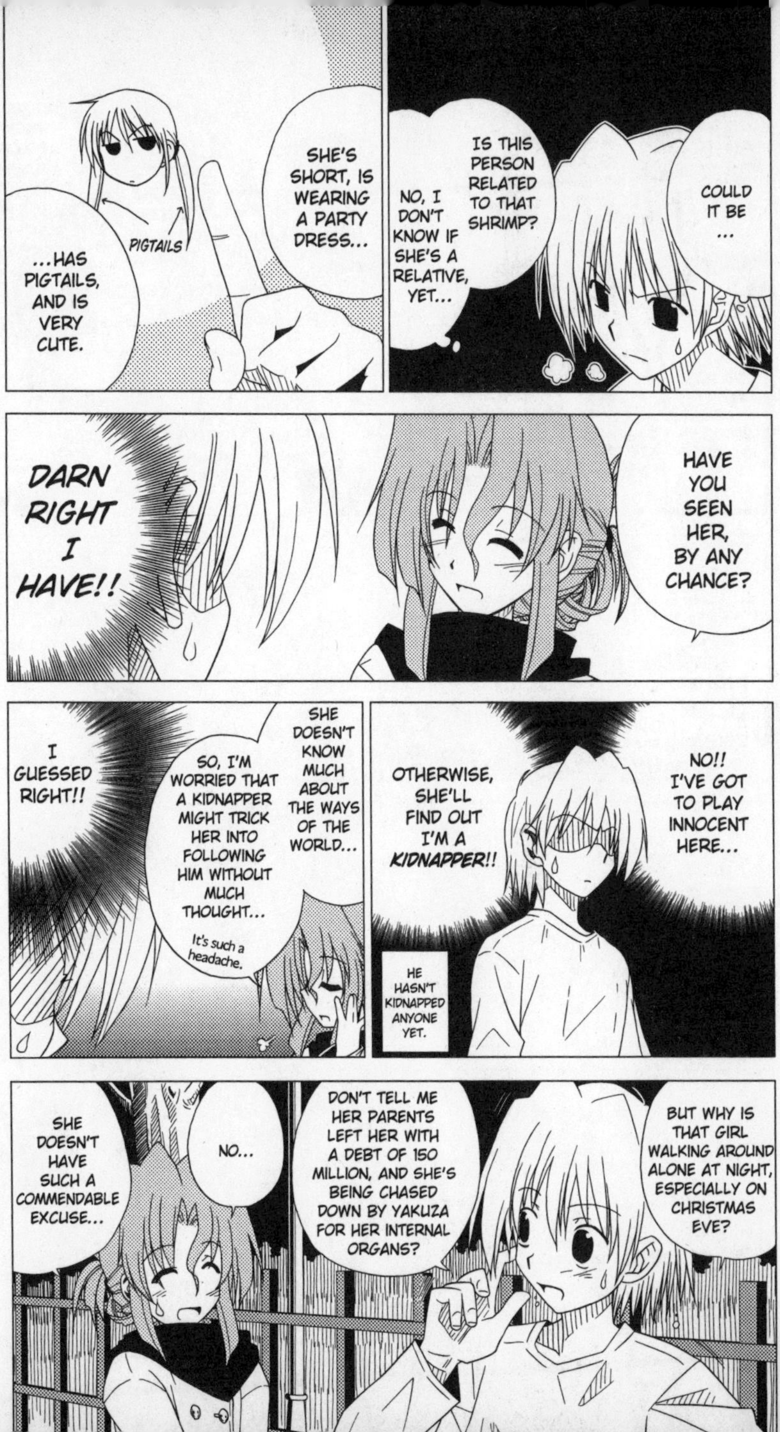
COULD IT BE ...
IS THIS PERSON RELATED TO THAT SHRIMP?
NO, I DON'T KNOW IF SHE'S A RELATIVE, YET...
SHE'S SHORT, IS WEARING A PARTY DRESS...
PIGTAILS
...HAS PIGTAILS, AND IS VERY CUTE.
HAVE YOU SEEN HER, BY ANY CHANCE?
DARN RIGHT I HAVE!!
NO!! I'VE GOT TO PLAY INNOCENT HERE...
OTHERWISE, SHE'LL FIND OUT I'M A KIDNAPPER!!
HE HASN'T KIDNAPPED ANYONE YET.
SHE DOESN'T KNOW MUCH ABOUT THE WAYS OF THE WORLD...
SO, I'M WORRIED THAT A KIDNAPPER MIGHT TRICK HER INTO FOLLOWING HIM WITHOUT MUCH THOUGHT...
It's such a headache.
I GUESSED RIGHT!!
BUT WHY IS THAT GIRL WALKING AROUND ALONE AT NIGHT, ESPECIALLY ON CHRISTMAS EVE?
DON'T TELL ME HER PARENTS LEFT HER WITH A DEBT OF 150 MILLION, AND SHE'S BEING CHASED DOWN BY YAKUZA FOR HER INTERNAL ORGANS?
NO...
SHE DOESN'T HAVE SUCH A COMMENDABLE EXCUSE...

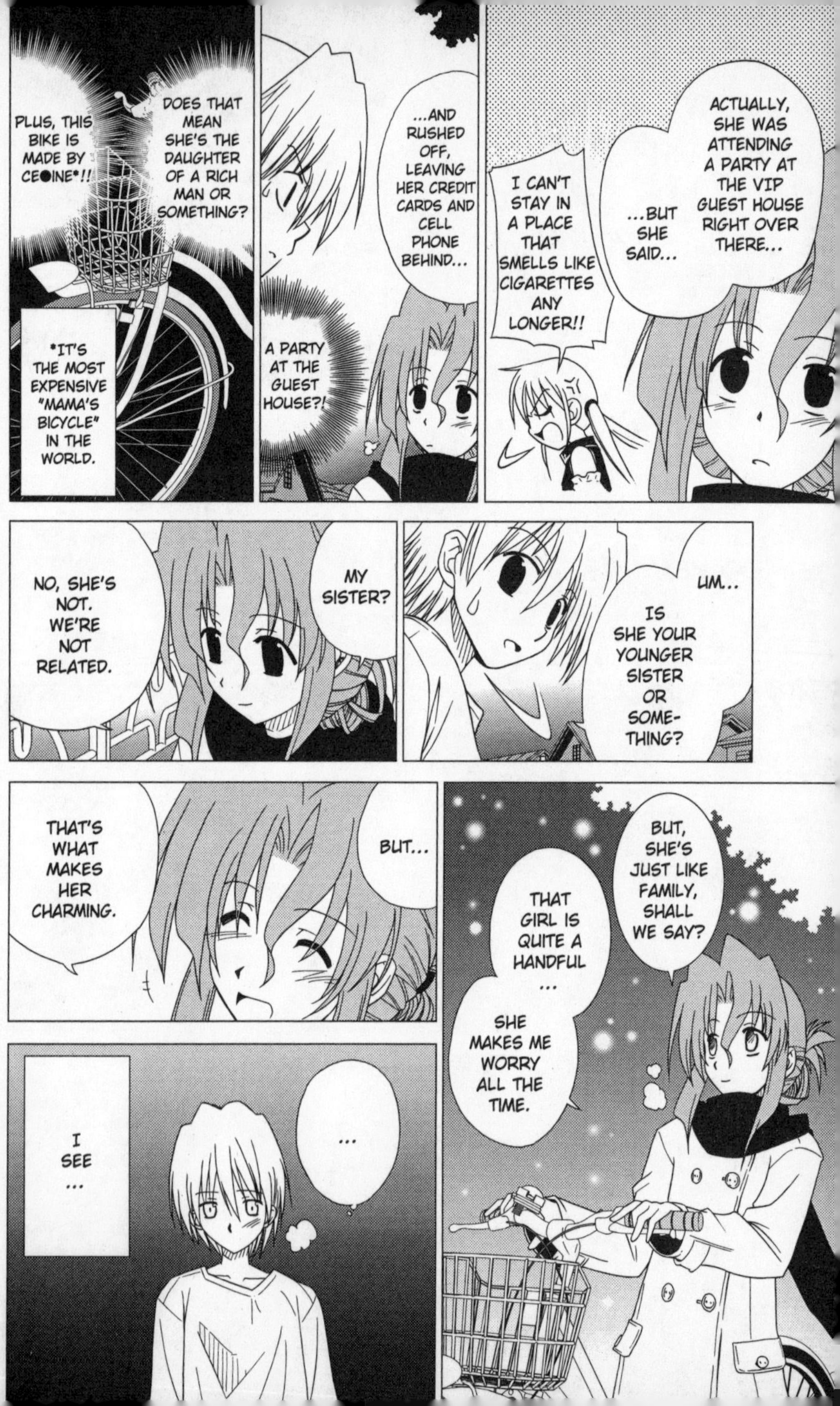
ACTUALLY, SHE WAS ATTENDING A PARTY AT THE VIP GUEST HOUSE RIGHT OVER THERE...
...BUT SHE SAID...
I CAN'T STAY IN A PLACE THAT SMELLS LIKE CIGARETTES ANY LONGER!!
...AND RUSHED OFF, LEAVING HER CREDIT CARDS AND CELL PHONE BEHIND...
A PARTY AT THE GUEST HOUSE?!
DOES THAT MEAN SHE'S THE DAUGHTER OF A RICH MAN OR SOMETHING?
PLUS, THIS BIKE IS MADE BY CE●INE*!!
*IT'S THE MOST EXPENSIVE "MAMA'S BICYCLE" IN THE WORLD.
UM...
IS SHE YOUR YOUNGER SISTER OR SOME-THING?
MY SISTER?
NO, SHE'S NOT. WE'RE NOT RELATED.
BUT, SHE'S JUST LIKE FAMILY, SHALL WE SAY?
THAT GIRL IS QUITE A HANDFUL ...
SHE MAKES ME WORRY ALL THE TIME.
BUT...
THAT'S WHAT MAKES HER CHARMING.
...
I SEE ...

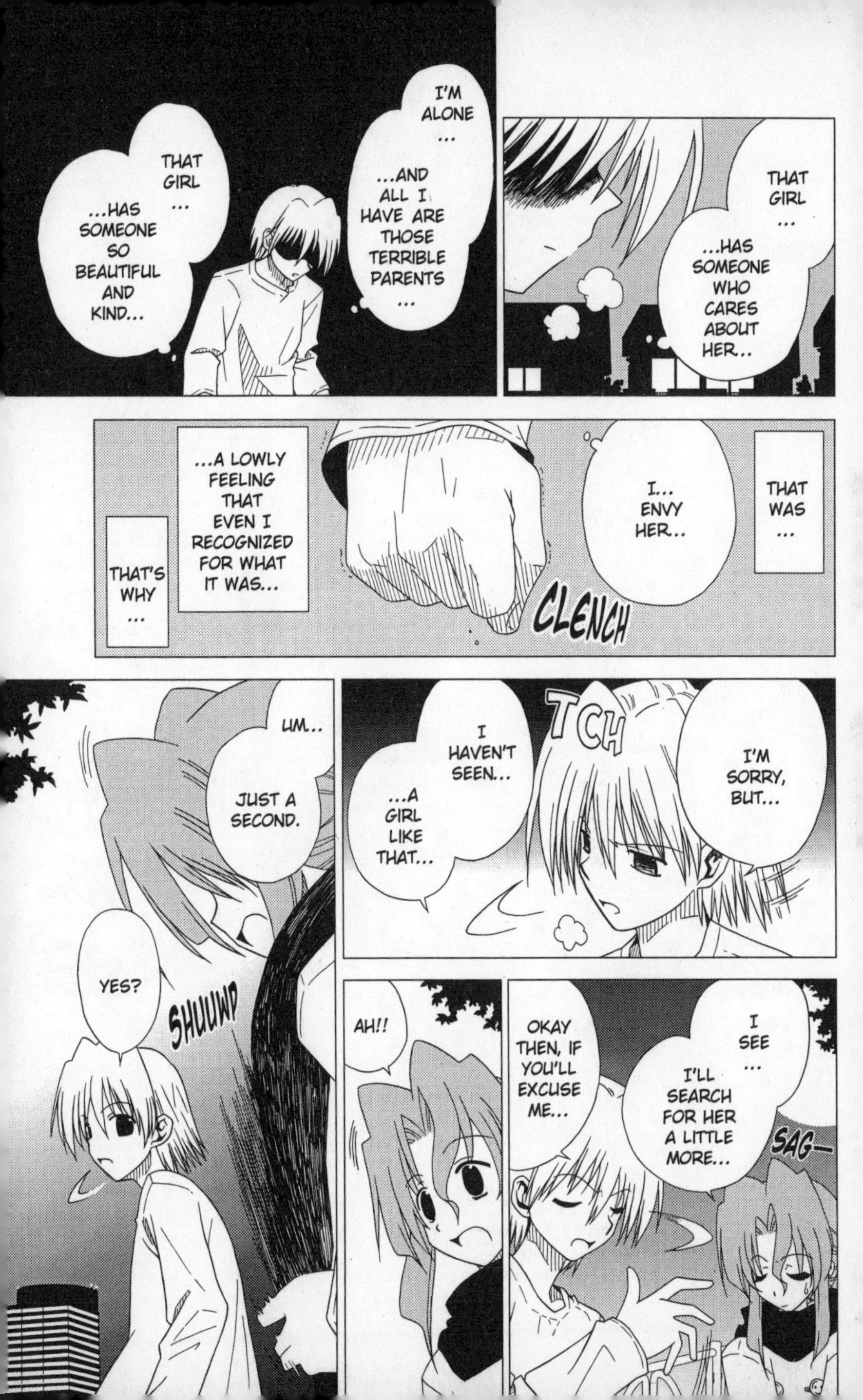
THAT GIRL ...
...HAS SOMEONE WHO CARES ABOUT HER...
I'M ALONE ...
...AND ALL I HAVE ARE THOSE TERRIBLE PARENTS ...
THAT GIRL ...
...HAS SOMEONE SO BEAUTIFUL AND KIND...
THAT WAS ...
I... ENVY HER...
CLENCH
...A LOWLY FEELING THAT EVEN I RECOGNIZED FOR WHAT IT WAS...
THAT'S WHY ...
I'M SORRY, BUT...
TCH
I HAVEN'T SEEN...
...A GIRL LIKE THAT...
I SEE ...
I'LL SEARCH FOR HER A LITTLE MORE...
SAG—
OKAY THEN, IF YOU'LL EXCUSE ME...
AH!!
UM...
JUST A SECOND.
SHUUWP
YES?

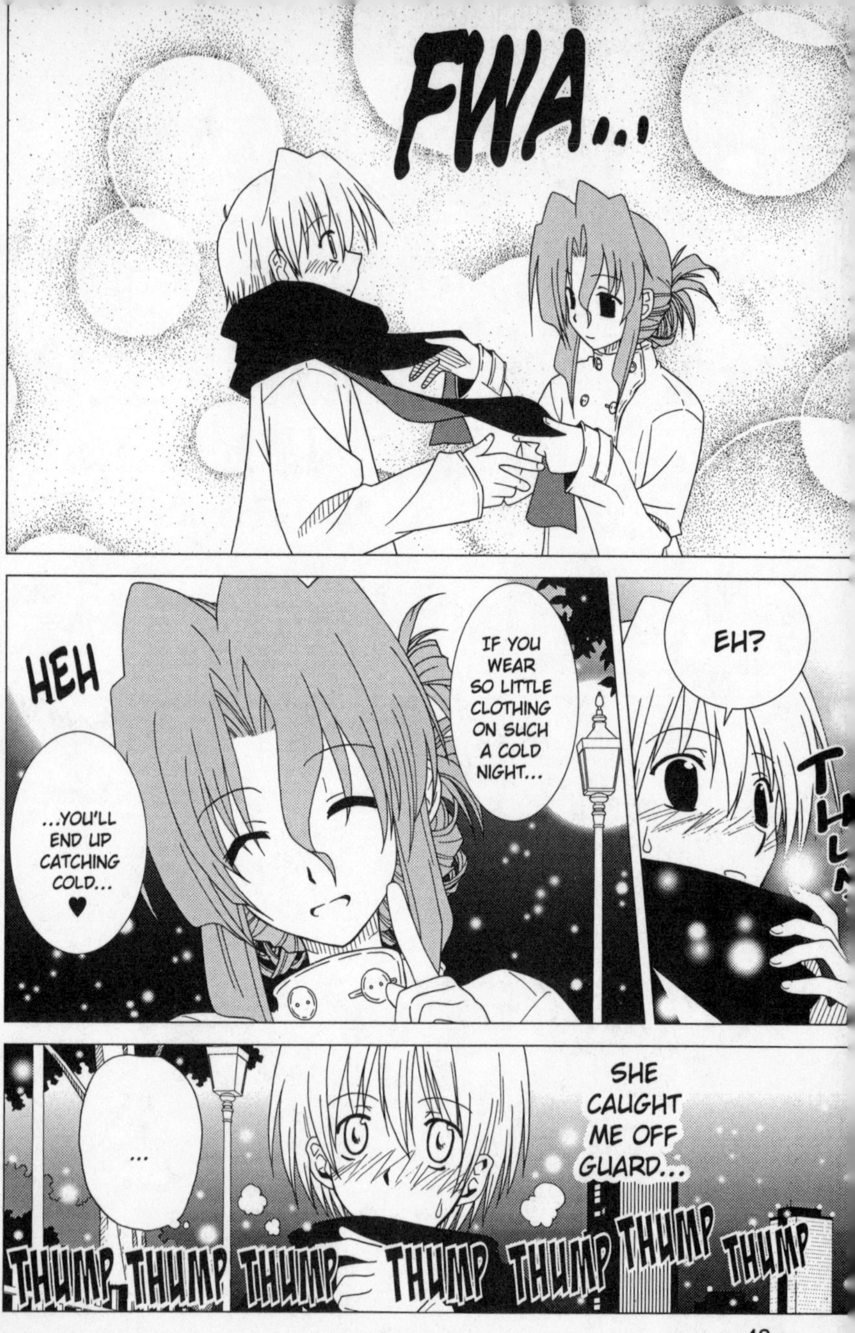
FWA...
EH?
IF YOU WEAR SO LITTLE CLOTHING ON SUCH A COLD NIGHT...
HEH
...YOU'LL END UP CATCHING COLD... ♥
SHE CAUGHT ME OFF GUARD...
...
THUMP THUMP THUMP THUMP THUMP THUMP THUMP

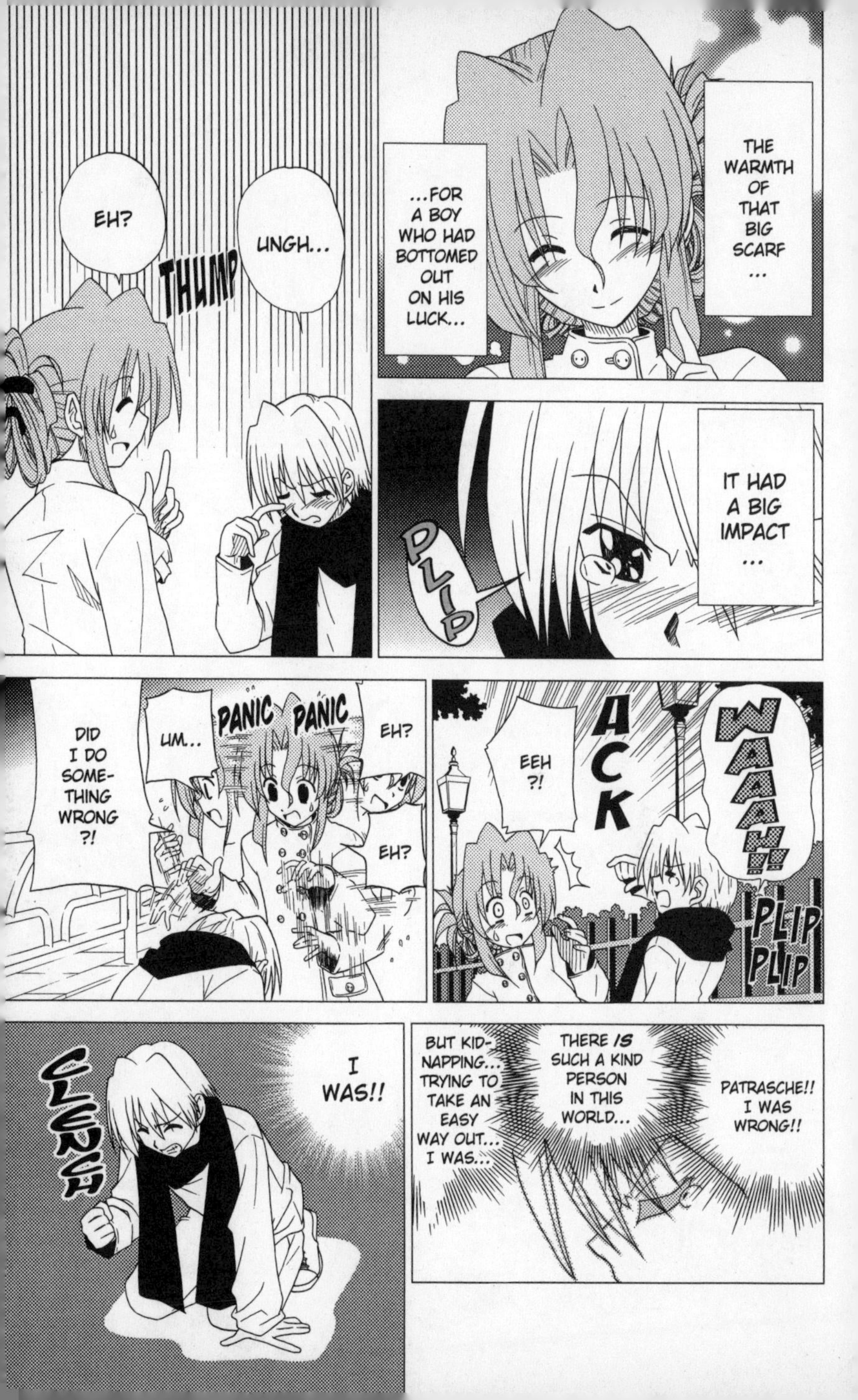
THE WARMTH OF THAT BIG SCARF...
...FOR A BOY WHO HAD BOTTOMED OUT ON HIS LUCK...
UNGH...
EH?
THUMP
IT HAD A BIG IMPACT...
PLIP
WAAAAH!!
PLIP PLIP
ACK
EEH?!
EH?
EH?
PANIC PANIC
UM...
DID I DO SOME-THING WRONG?!
PATRASCHE!! I WAS WRONG!!
THERE IS SUCH A KIND PERSON IN THIS WORLD...
BUT KID-NAPPING... TRYING TO TAKE AN EASY WAY OUT... I WAS...
I WAS!!
CLENCH

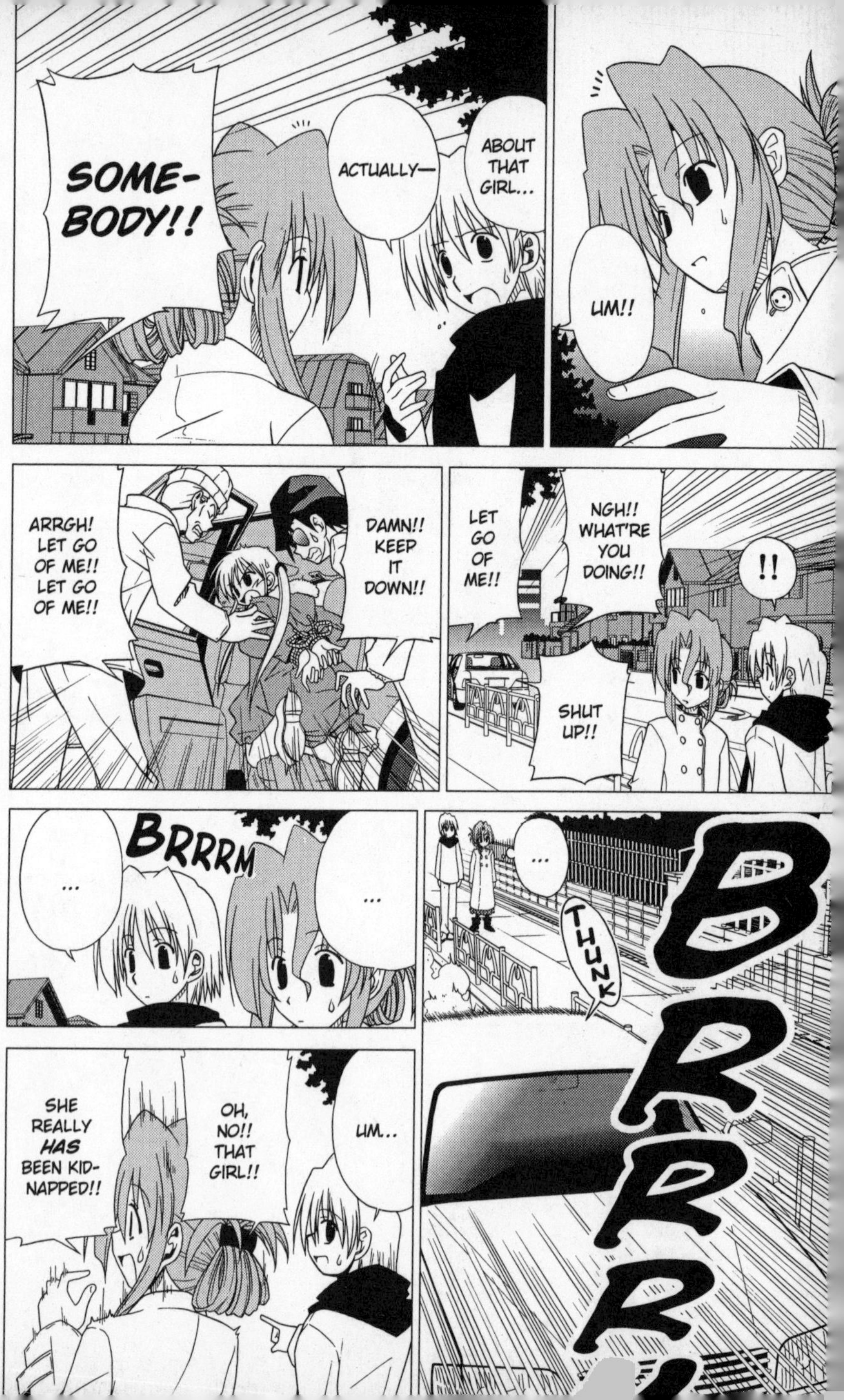
UM!!
ABOUT THAT GIRL...
ACTUALLY—
SOME-BODY!!
!!
NGH!! WHAT'RE YOU DOING!!
LET GO OF ME!!
SHUT UP!!
DAMN!! KEEP IT DOWN!!
ARRGH! LET GO OF ME!! LET GO OF ME!!
BRRR
THUNK
...
...
...
BRRRRM
UM...
OH, NO!! THAT GIRL!!
SHE REALLY *HAS* BEEN KID-NAPPED!!

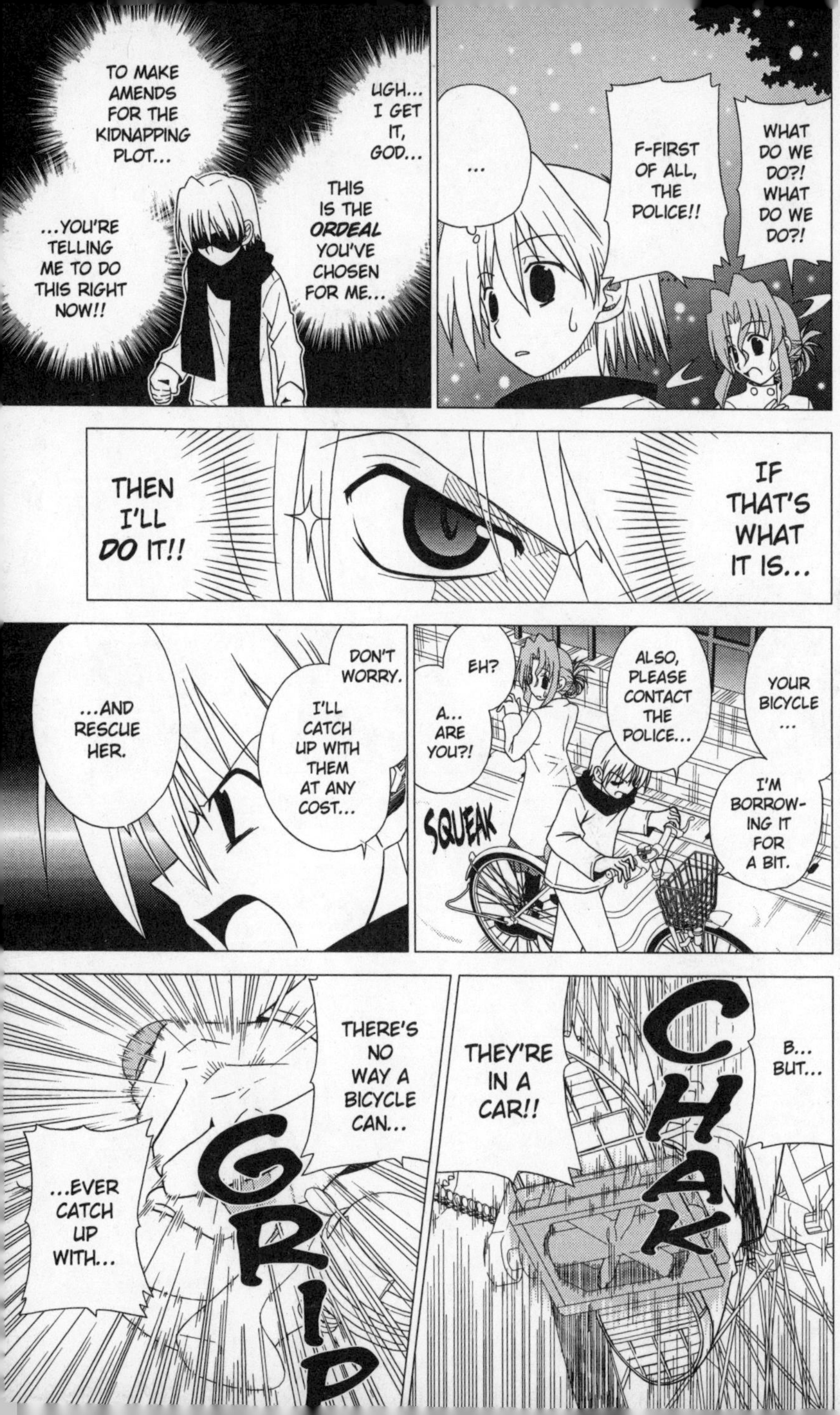
WHAT DO WE DO?! WHAT DO WE DO?!
F-FIRST OF ALL, THE POLICE!!
...
UGH... I GET IT, GOD...
THIS IS THE *ORDEAL* YOU'VE CHOSEN FOR ME...
TO MAKE AMENDS FOR THE KIDNAPPING PLOT...
...YOU'RE TELLING ME TO DO THIS RIGHT NOW!!
IF THAT'S WHAT IT IS...
THEN I'LL *DO* IT!!
YOUR BICYCLE...
I'M BORROWING IT FOR A BIT.
ALSO, PLEASE CONTACT THE POLICE...
EH?
A... ARE YOU?!
SQUEAK
DON'T WORRY.
I'LL CATCH UP WITH THEM AT ANY COST...
...AND RESCUE HER.
B... BUT...
CHAK
THEY'RE IN A CAR!!
THERE'S NO WAY A BICYCLE CAN...
...EVER CATCH UP WITH...
GRIP

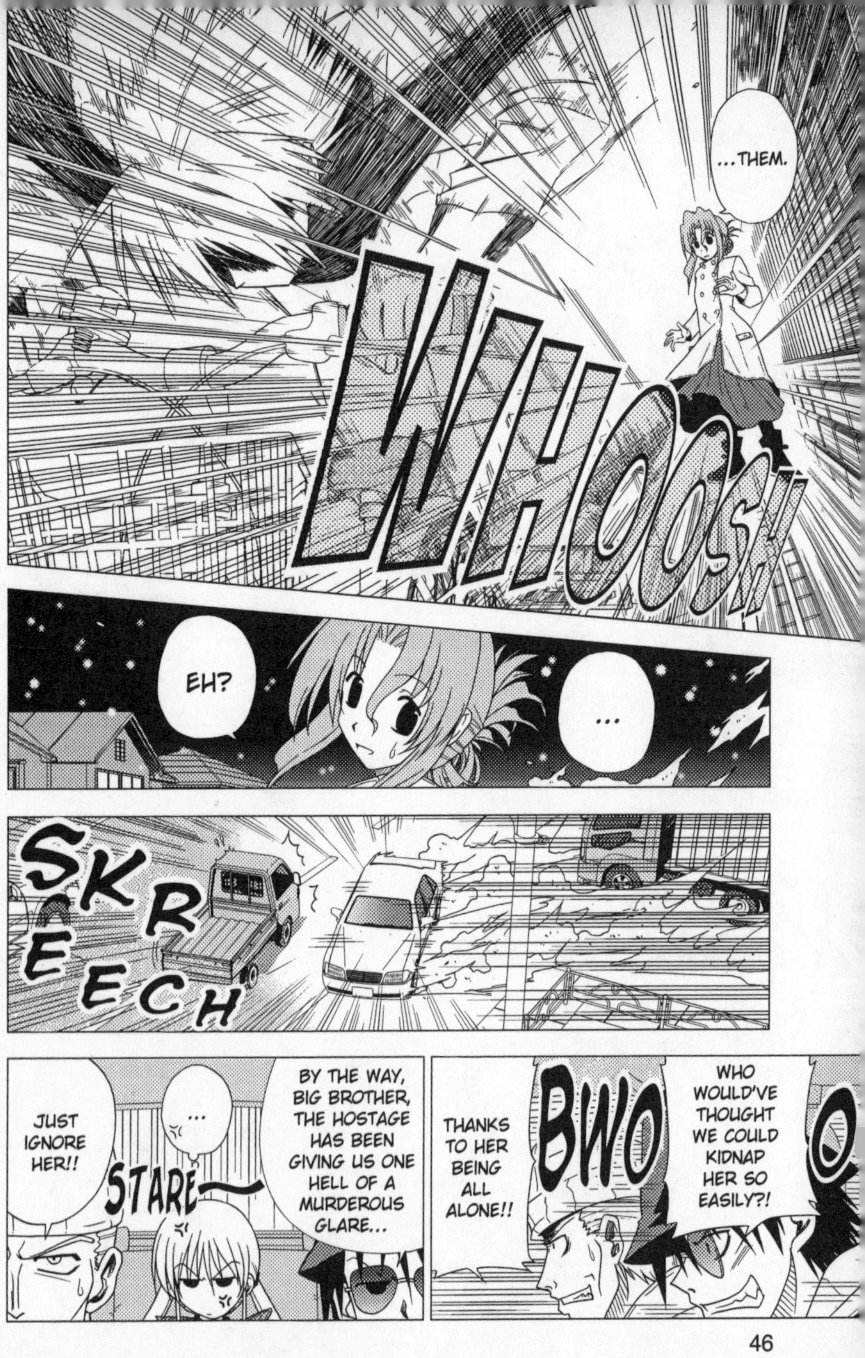
...THEM.
WHOOSH
...
EH?
SKREEECH
WHO WOULD'VE THOUGHT WE COULD KIDNAP HER SO EASILY?!
BWOO
THANKS TO HER BEING ALL ALONE!!
BY THE WAY, BIG BROTHER, THE HOSTAGE HAS BEEN GIVING US ONE HELL OF A MURDEROUS GLARE...
...
STARE—
JUST IGNORE HER!!

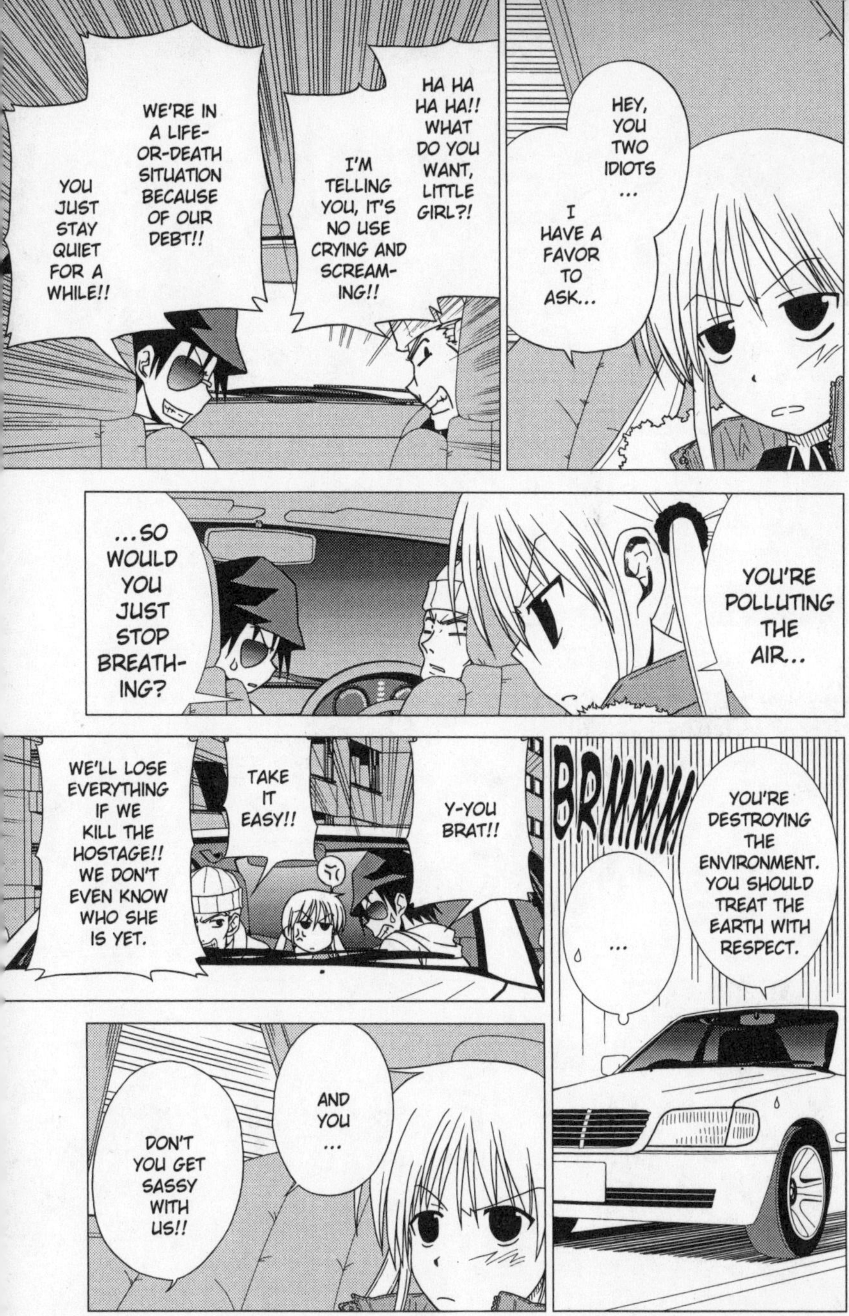
HEY, YOU TWO IDIOTS...
I HAVE A FAVOR TO ASK...
HA HA HA HA!! WHAT DO YOU WANT, LITTLE GIRL?!
I'M TELLING YOU, IT'S NO USE CRYING AND SCREAMING!!
WE'RE IN A LIFE-OR-DEATH SITUATION BECAUSE OF OUR DEBT!!
YOU JUST STAY QUIET FOR A WHILE!!
YOU'RE POLLUTING THE AIR...
...SO WOULD YOU JUST STOP BREATHING?
BRMMM
YOU'RE DESTROYING THE ENVIRONMENT. YOU SHOULD TREAT THE EARTH WITH RESPECT.
...
Y-YOU BRAT!!
TAKE IT EASY!!
WE'LL LOSE EVERYTHING IF WE KILL THE HOSTAGE!! WE DON'T EVEN KNOW WHO SHE IS YET.
AND YOU...
DON'T YOU GET SASSY WITH US!!

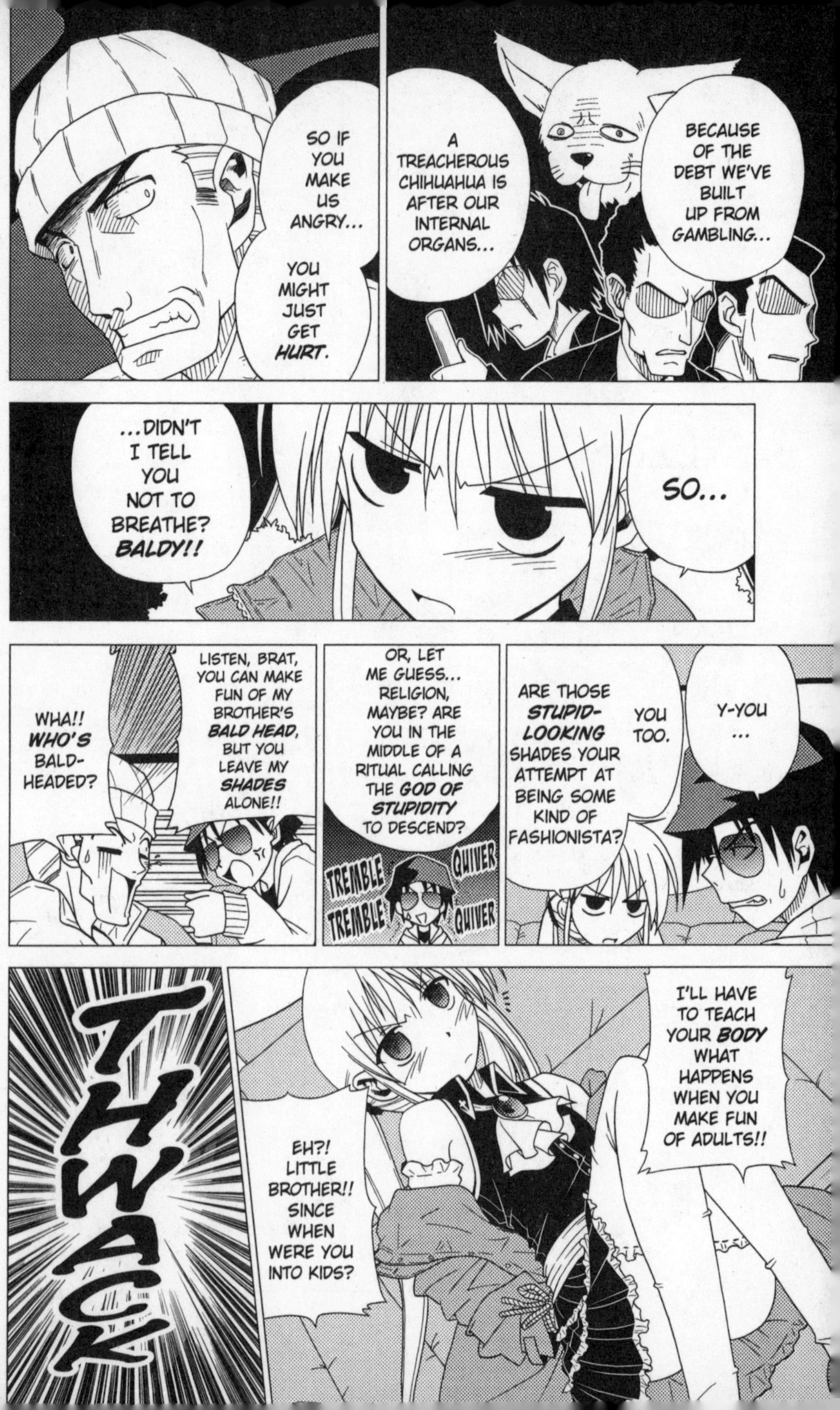
BECAUSE OF THE DEBT WE'VE BUILT UP FROM GAMBLING...
A TREACHEROUS CHIHUAHUA IS AFTER OUR INTERNAL ORGANS...
SO IF YOU MAKE US ANGRY...
YOU MIGHT JUST GET HURT.
SO...
...DIDN'T I TELL YOU NOT TO BREATHE? BALDY!!
Y-YOU ...
YOU TOO.
ARE THOSE STUPID-LOOKING SHADES YOUR ATTEMPT AT BEING SOME KIND OF FASHIONISTA?
OR, LET ME GUESS... RELIGION, MAYBE? ARE YOU IN THE MIDDLE OF A RITUAL CALLING THE GOD OF STUPIDITY TO DESCEND?
QUIVER QUIVER
TREMBLE TREMBLE
LISTEN, BRAT, YOU CAN MAKE FUN OF MY BROTHER'S BALD HEAD, BUT YOU LEAVE MY SHADES ALONE!!
WHA!! WHO'S BALD-HEADED?
I'LL HAVE TO TEACH YOUR BODY WHAT HAPPENS WHEN YOU MAKE FUN OF ADULTS!!
EH?! LITTLE BROTHER!! SINCE WHEN WERE YOU INTO KIDS?
THWACK

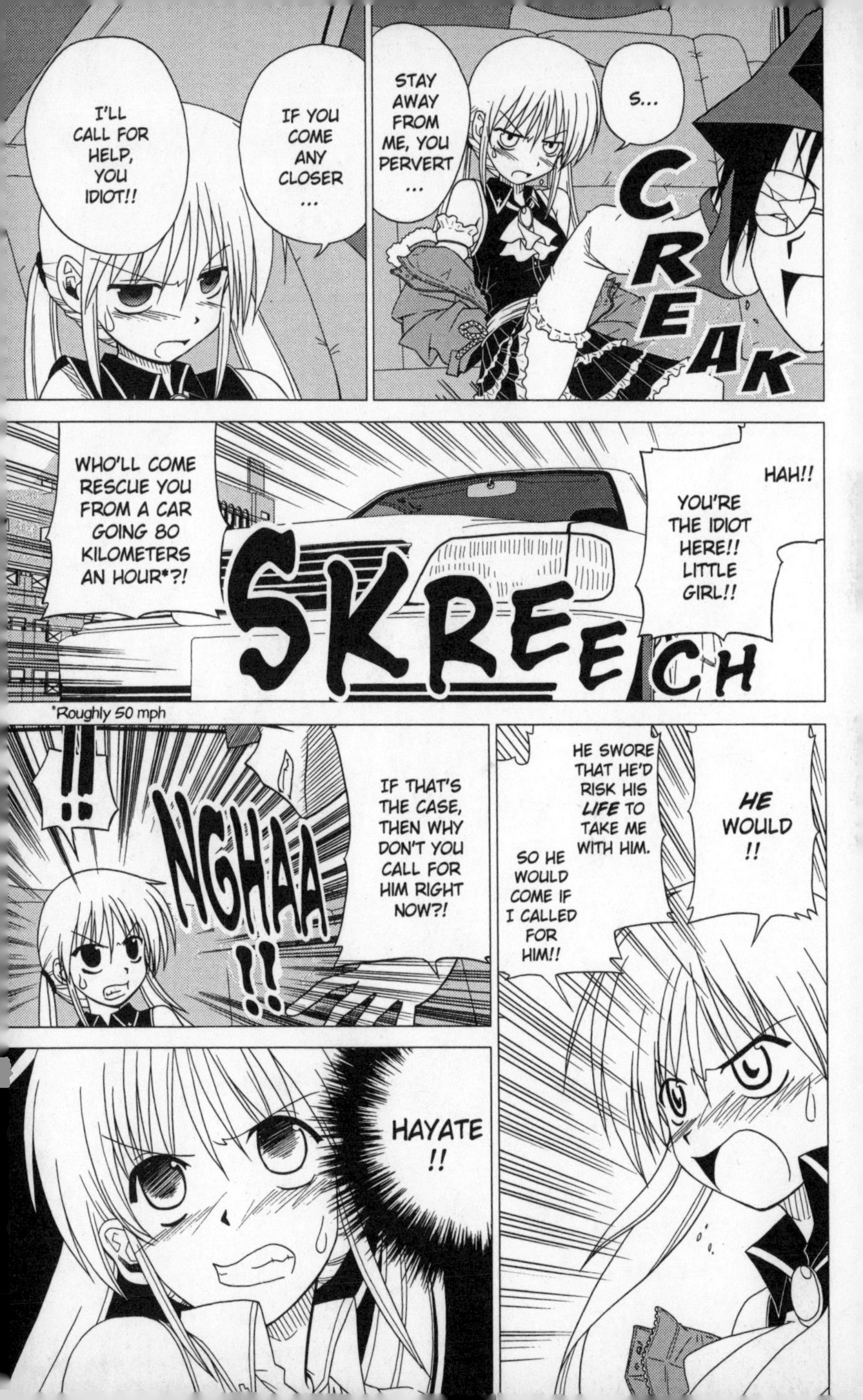
S...
CREAK
STAY AWAY FROM ME, YOU PERVERT...
IF YOU COME ANY CLOSER...
I'LL CALL FOR HELP, YOU IDIOT!!
HAH!!
YOU'RE THE IDIOT HERE!! LITTLE GIRL!!
SKREEECH
WHO'LL COME RESCUE YOU FROM A CAR GOING 80 KILOMETERS AN HOUR*?!
HE WOULD!!
HE SWORE THAT HE'D RISK HIS LIFE TO TAKE ME WITH HIM.
SO HE WOULD COME IF I CALLED FOR HIM!!
IF THAT'S THE CASE, THEN WHY DON'T YOU CALL FOR HIM RIGHT NOW?!
NGHAA!!
!!
HAYATE!!

*Roughly 50 mph

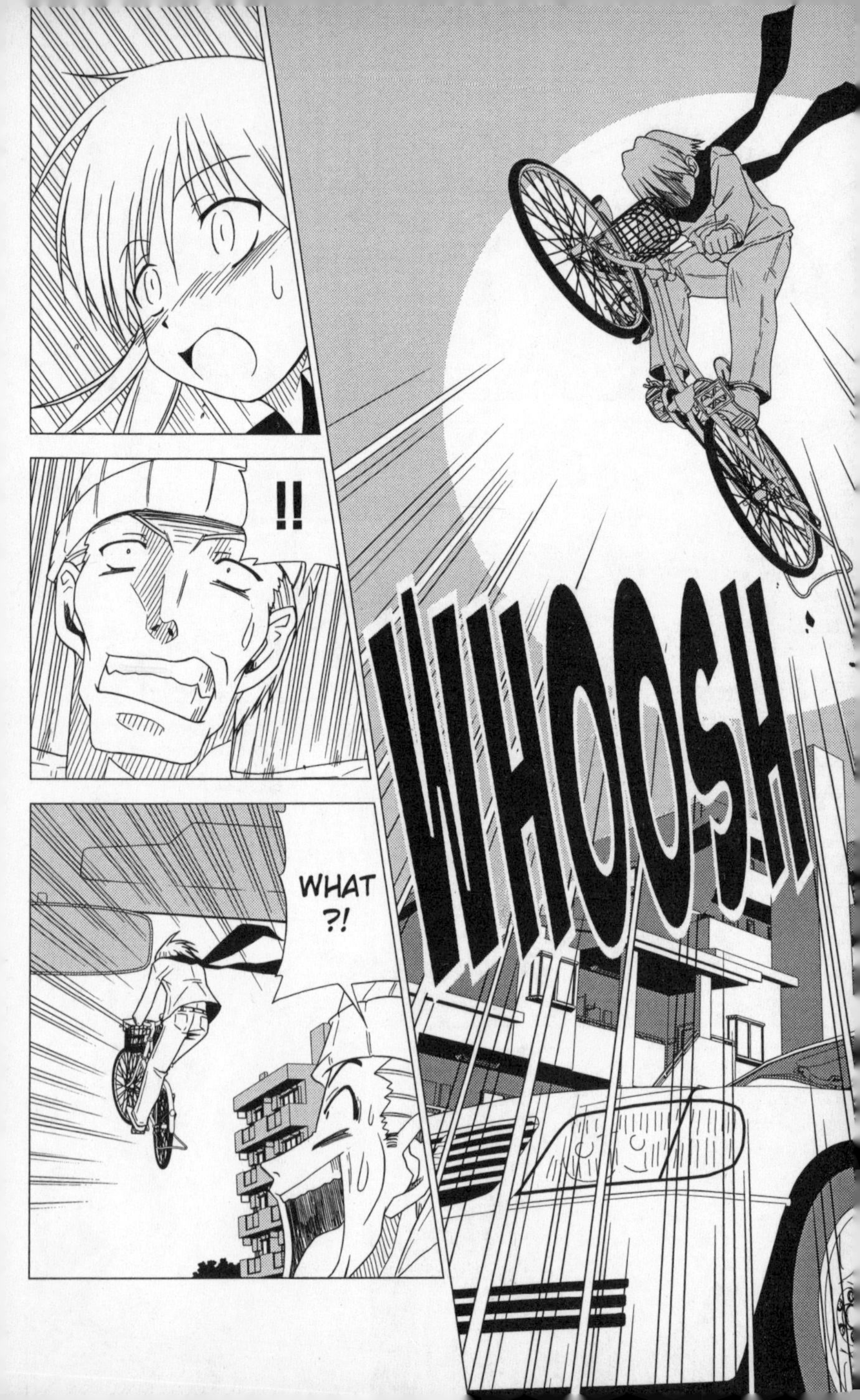
WHOOSH
!!
WHAT ?!

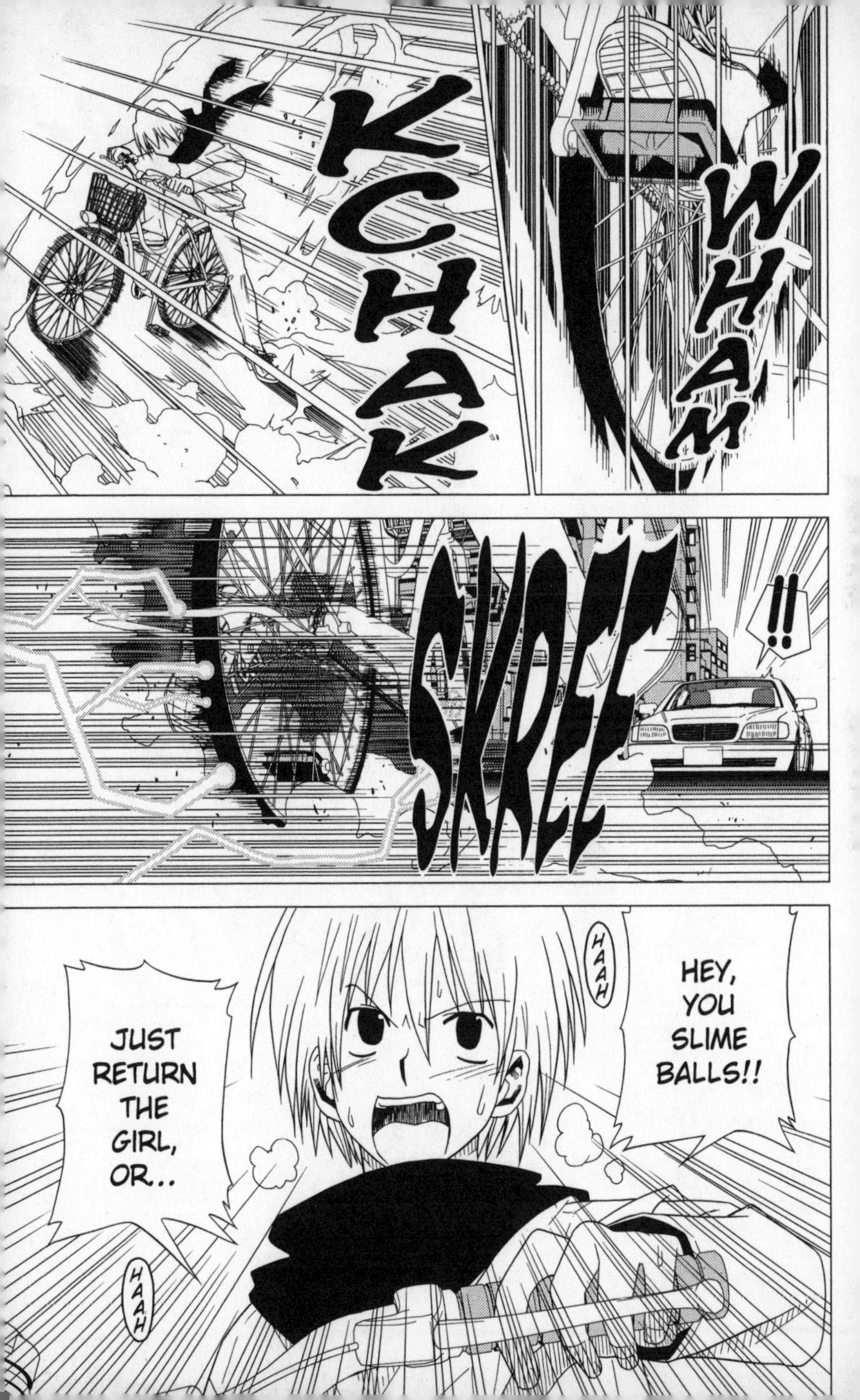
WHAM
KCHAK
SKREE
!!
HAAH
HEY, YOU SLIME BALLS!!
JUST RETURN THE GIRL, OR...
HAAH

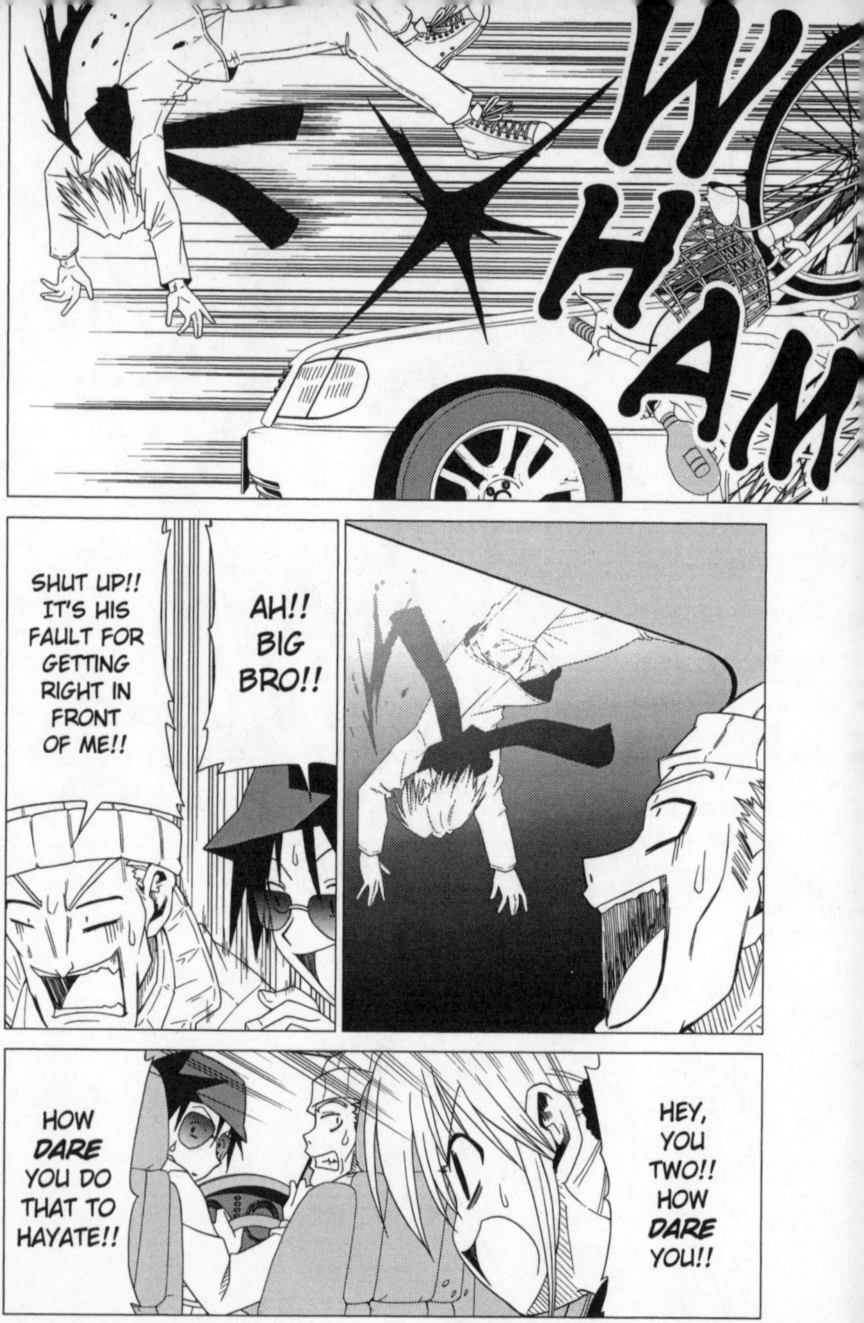
WHAM
AH!! BIG BRO!!
SHUT UP!! IT'S HIS FAULT FOR GETTING RIGHT IN FRONT OF ME!!
HEY, YOU TWO!! HOW DARE YOU!!
HOW DARE YOU DO THAT TO HAYATE!!

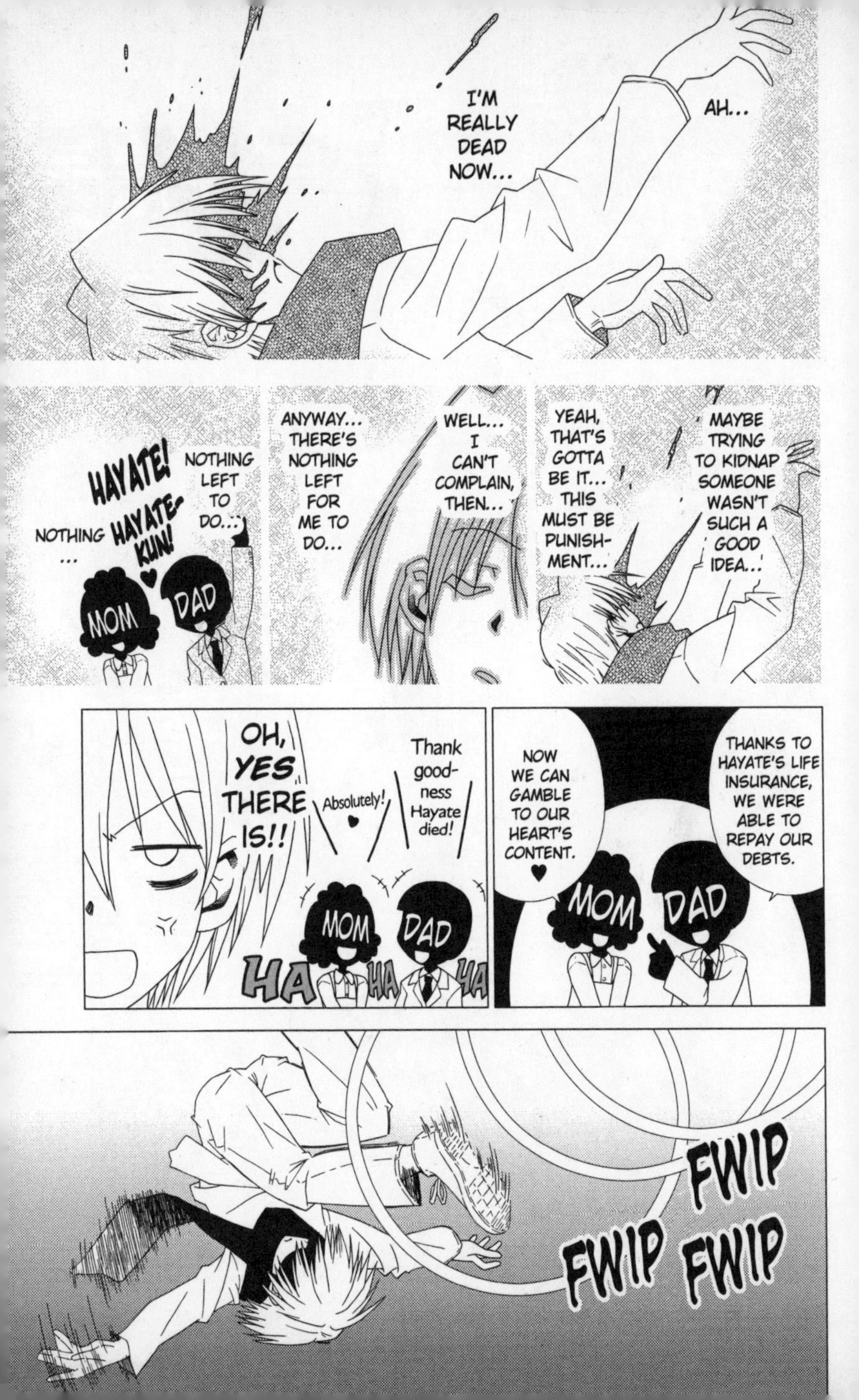
AH...
I'M REALLY DEAD NOW...
MAYBE TRYING TO KIDNAP SOMEONE WASN'T SUCH A GOOD IDEA...
YEAH, THAT'S GOTTA BE IT... THIS MUST BE PUNISHMENT...
WELL... I CAN'T COMPLAIN, THEN...
ANYWAY... THERE'S NOTHING LEFT FOR ME TO DO...
NOTHING LEFT TO DO...
NOTHING...
HAYATE!
HAYATE-KUN!
DAD
MOM
THANKS TO HAYATE'S LIFE INSURANCE, WE WERE ABLE TO REPAY OUR DEBTS.
NOW WE CAN GAMBLE TO OUR HEART'S CONTENT.
DAD
MOM
Thank goodness Hayate died!
Absolutely!
OH, YES THERE IS!!
DAD
MOM
HA HA HA
FWIP
FWIP FWIP

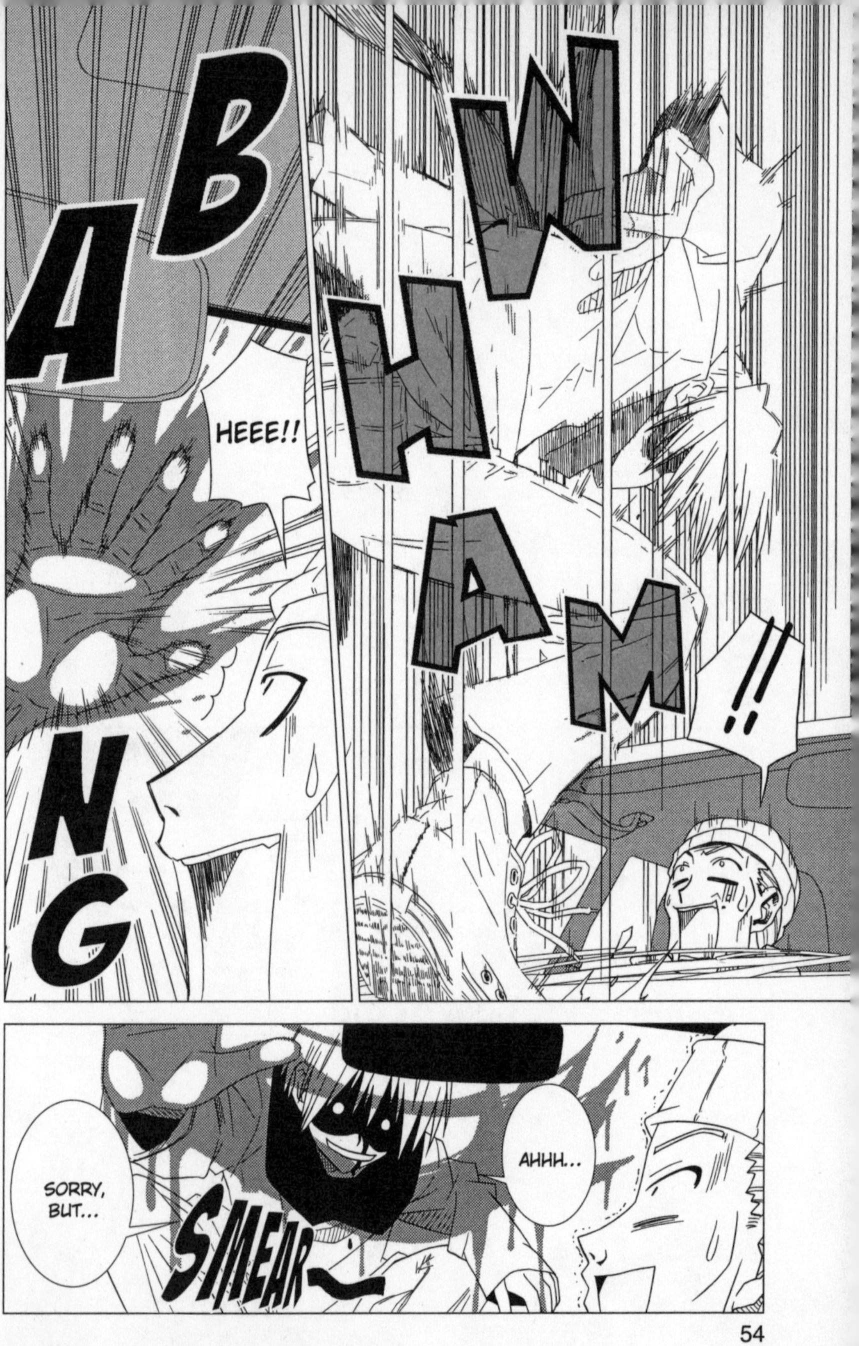
BWHAM!!
HEEE!!
BANG
AHHH...
SORRY, BUT...
SMEAR~

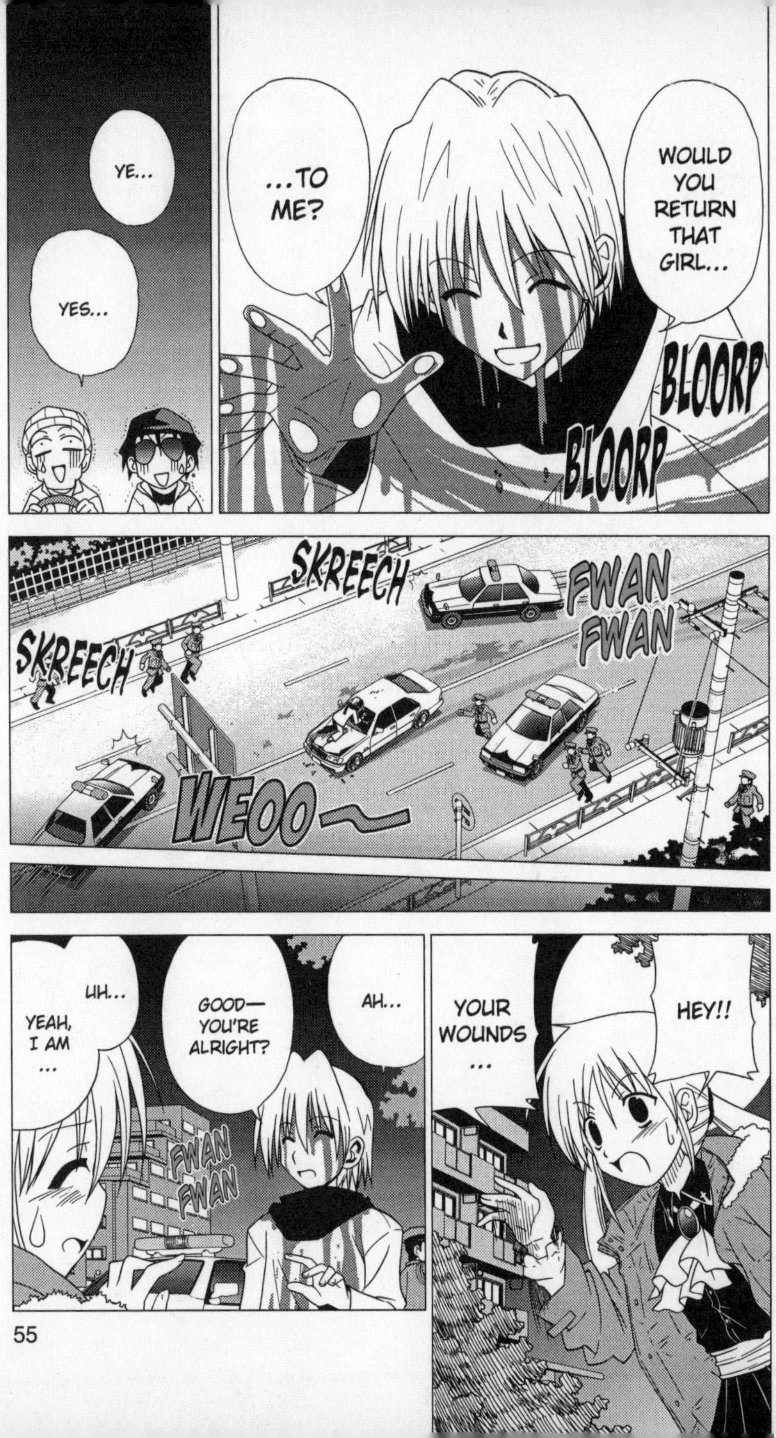
WOULD YOU RETURN THAT GIRL...
...TO ME?
BLOORP
BLOORP
YE...
YES...
SKREECH
FWAN FWAN
SKREECH
WEOO~
HEY!!
YOUR WOUNDS ...
AH...
GOOD— YOU'RE ALRIGHT?
UH...
YEAH, I AM ...
FWAN FWAN

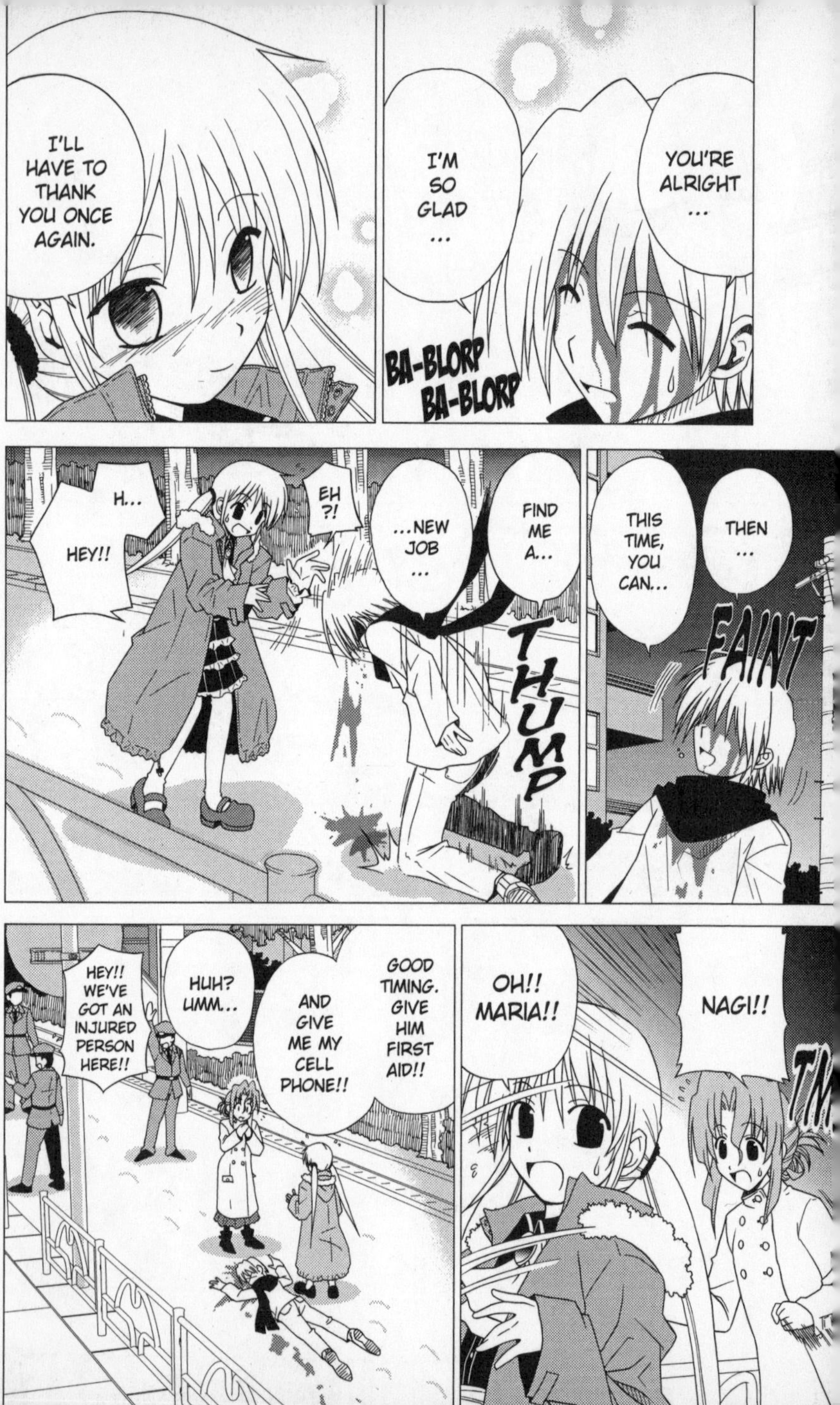
YOU'RE ALRIGHT ...
I'M SO GLAD ...
BA-BLORP BA-BLORP
I'LL HAVE TO THANK YOU ONCE AGAIN.
THEN ...
THIS TIME, YOU CAN...
FAINT
FIND ME A...
...NEW JOB ...
THUMP
EH ?!
H... HEY!!
NAGI!!
OH!! MARIA!!
GOOD TIMING. GIVE HIM FIRST AID!!
AND GIVE ME MY CELL PHONE!!
HUH? UMM...
HEY!! WE'VE GOT AN INJURED PERSON HERE!!

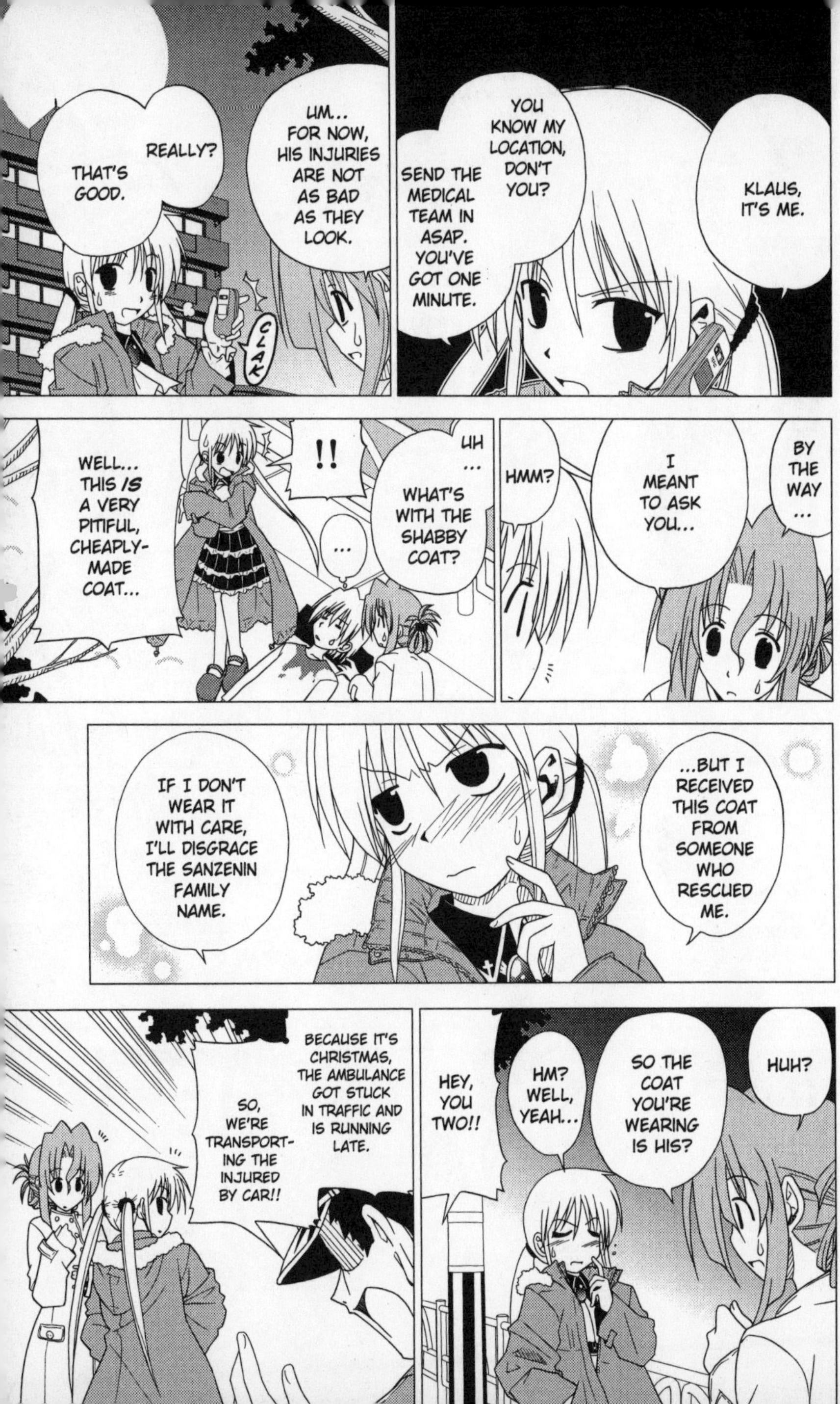
KLAUS, IT'S ME.
YOU KNOW MY LOCATION, DON'T YOU?
SEND THE MEDICAL TEAM IN ASAP. YOU'VE GOT ONE MINUTE.
UM... FOR NOW, HIS INJURIES ARE NOT AS BAD AS THEY LOOK.
CLAK
REALLY? THAT'S GOOD.
BY THE WAY...
I MEANT TO ASK YOU...
HMM?
UH... WHAT'S WITH THE SHABBY COAT?
!!
...
WELL... THIS *IS* A VERY PITIFUL, CHEAPLY-MADE COAT...
...BUT I RECEIVED THIS COAT FROM SOMEONE WHO RESCUED ME.
IF I DON'T WEAR IT WITH CARE, I'LL DISGRACE THE SANZENIN FAMILY NAME.
HUH?
SO THE COAT YOU'RE WEARING IS HIS?
HM? WELL, YEAH...
HEY, YOU TWO!!
BECAUSE IT'S CHRISTMAS, THE AMBULANCE GOT STUCK IN TRAFFIC AND IS RUNNING LATE.
SO, WE'RE TRANSPORTING THE INJURED BY CAR!!

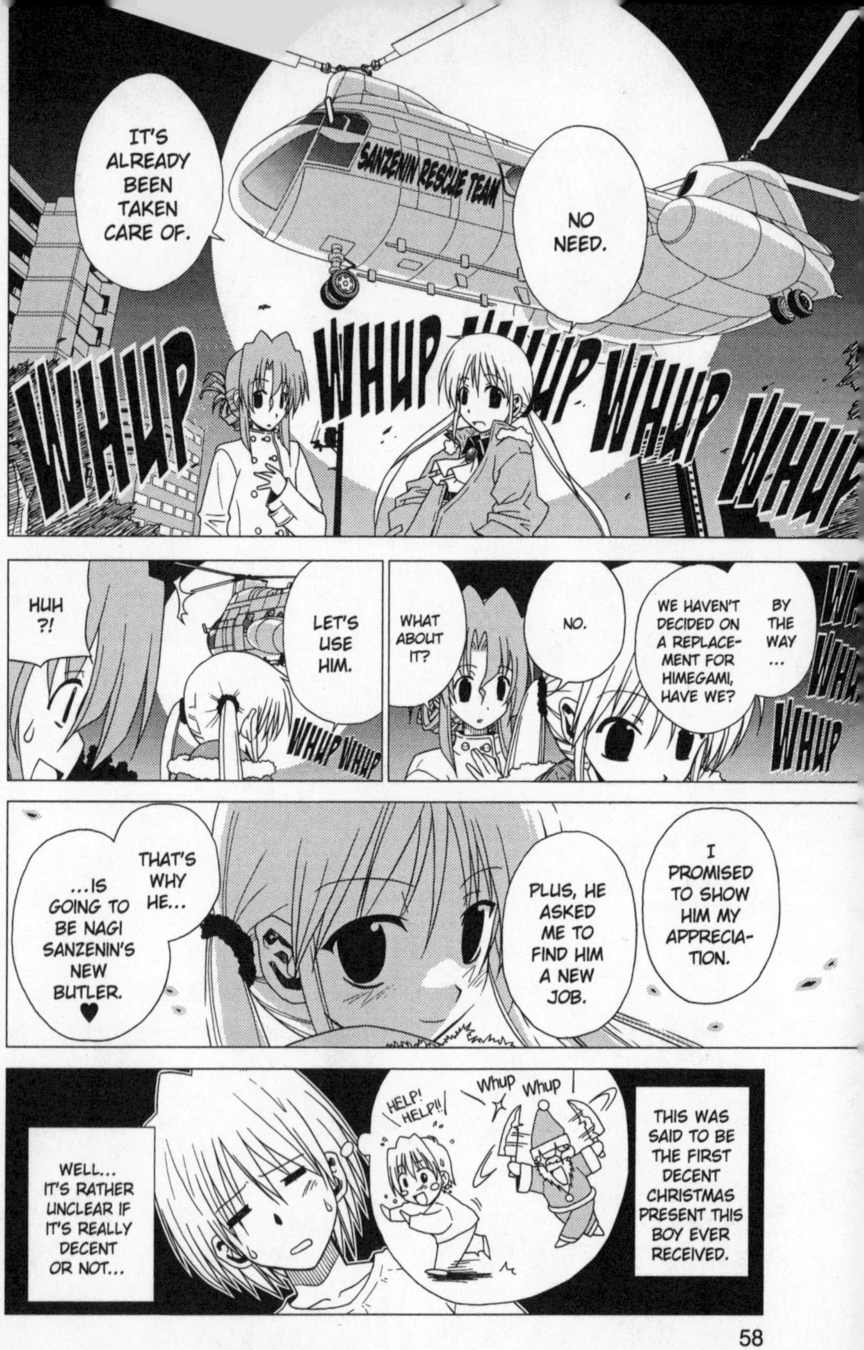
SANZENIN RESCUE TEAM
NO NEED.
IT'S ALREADY BEEN TAKEN CARE OF.
WHUP WHUP WHUP WHUP WHUP WHUP
BY THE WAY...
WE HAVEN'T DECIDED ON A REPLACEMENT FOR HIMEGAMI, HAVE WE?
NO.
WHAT ABOUT IT?
WHUP WHUP WHUP
LET'S USE HIM.
HUH?!
WHUP WHUP
I PROMISED TO SHOW HIM MY APPRECIATION.
PLUS, HE ASKED ME TO FIND HIM A NEW JOB.
THAT'S WHY HE...
...IS GOING TO BE NAGI SANZENIN'S NEW BUTLER. ♥
THIS WAS SAID TO BE THE FIRST DECENT CHRISTMAS PRESENT THIS BOY EVER RECEIVED.
Whup Whup
HELP! HELP!!
WELL... IT'S RATHER UNCLEAR IF IT'S REALLY DECENT OR NOT...

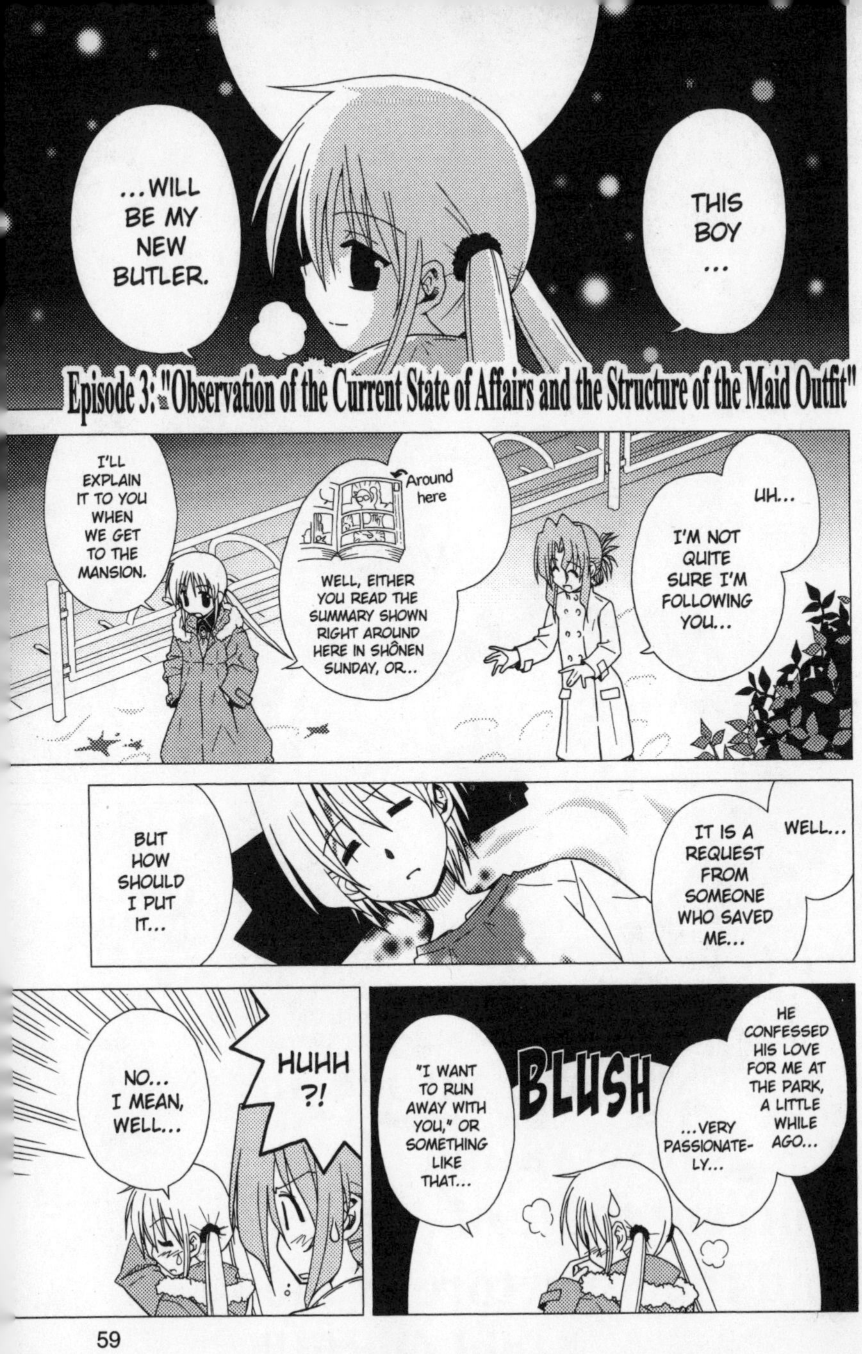
THIS BOY ...
...WILL BE MY NEW BUTLER.
Episode 3: "Observation of the Current State of Affairs and the Structure of the Maid Outfit"
UH...
I'M NOT QUITE SURE I'M FOLLOWING YOU...
Around here
WELL, EITHER YOU READ THE SUMMARY SHOWN RIGHT AROUND HERE IN SHÔNEN SUNDAY, OR..
I'LL EXPLAIN IT TO YOU WHEN WE GET TO THE MANSION.
WELL...
IT IS A REQUEST FROM SOMEONE WHO SAVED ME...
BUT HOW SHOULD I PUT IT...
HE CONFESSED HIS LOVE FOR ME AT THE PARK, A LITTLE WHILE AGO...
...VERY PASSIONATE-LY...
BLUSH
"I WANT TO RUN AWAY WITH YOU," OR SOMETHING LIKE THAT...
HUHH ?!
NO... I MEAN, WELL...

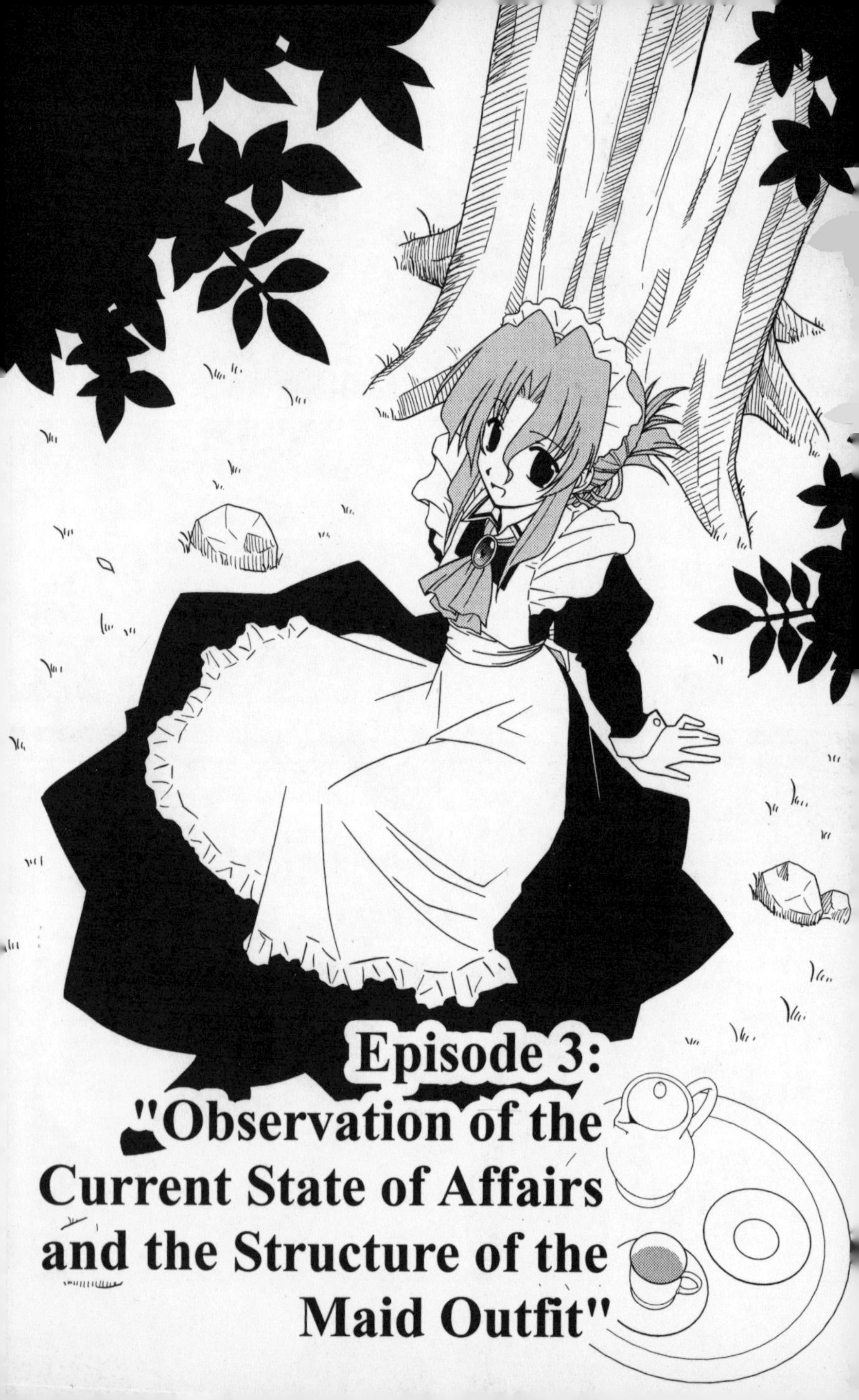

Episode 3: "Observation of the Current State of Affairs and the Structure of the Maid Outfit"

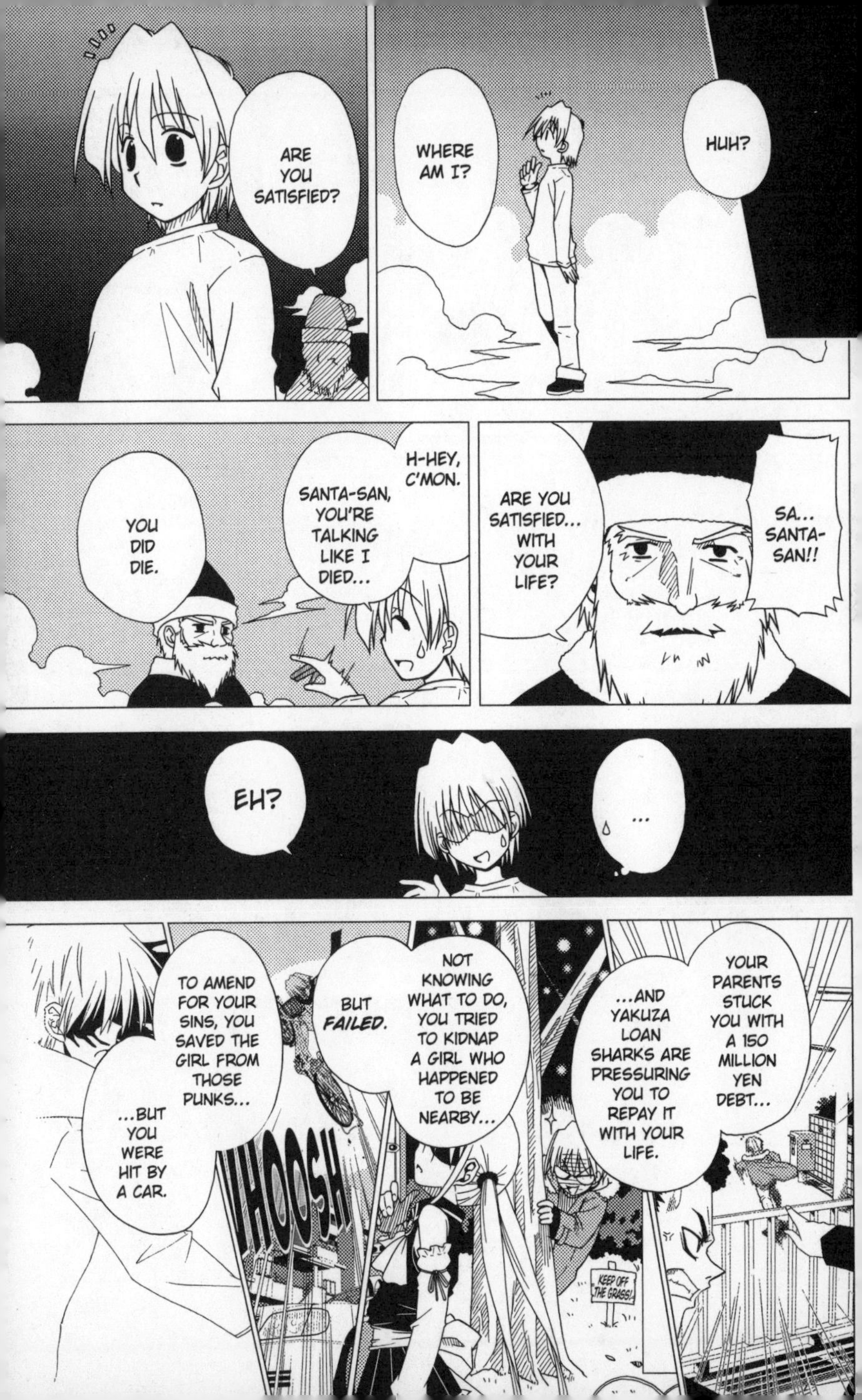
HUH?
WHERE AM I?
ARE YOU SATISFIED?
SA... SANTA-SAN!!
ARE YOU SATISFIED... WITH YOUR LIFE?
H-HEY, C'MON.
SANTA-SAN, YOU'RE TALKING LIKE I DIED...
YOU DID DIE.
...
EH?
YOUR PARENTS STUCK YOU WITH A 150 MILLION YEN DEBT...
...AND YAKUZA LOAN SHARKS ARE PRESSURING YOU TO REPAY IT WITH YOUR LIFE.
KEEP OFF THE GRASS!
NOT KNOWING WHAT TO DO, YOU TRIED TO KIDNAP A GIRL WHO HAPPENED TO BE NEARBY...
BUT *FAILED*.
TO AMEND FOR YOUR SINS, YOU SAVED THE GIRL FROM THOSE PUNKS...
WHOOSH
...BUT YOU WERE HIT BY A CAR.

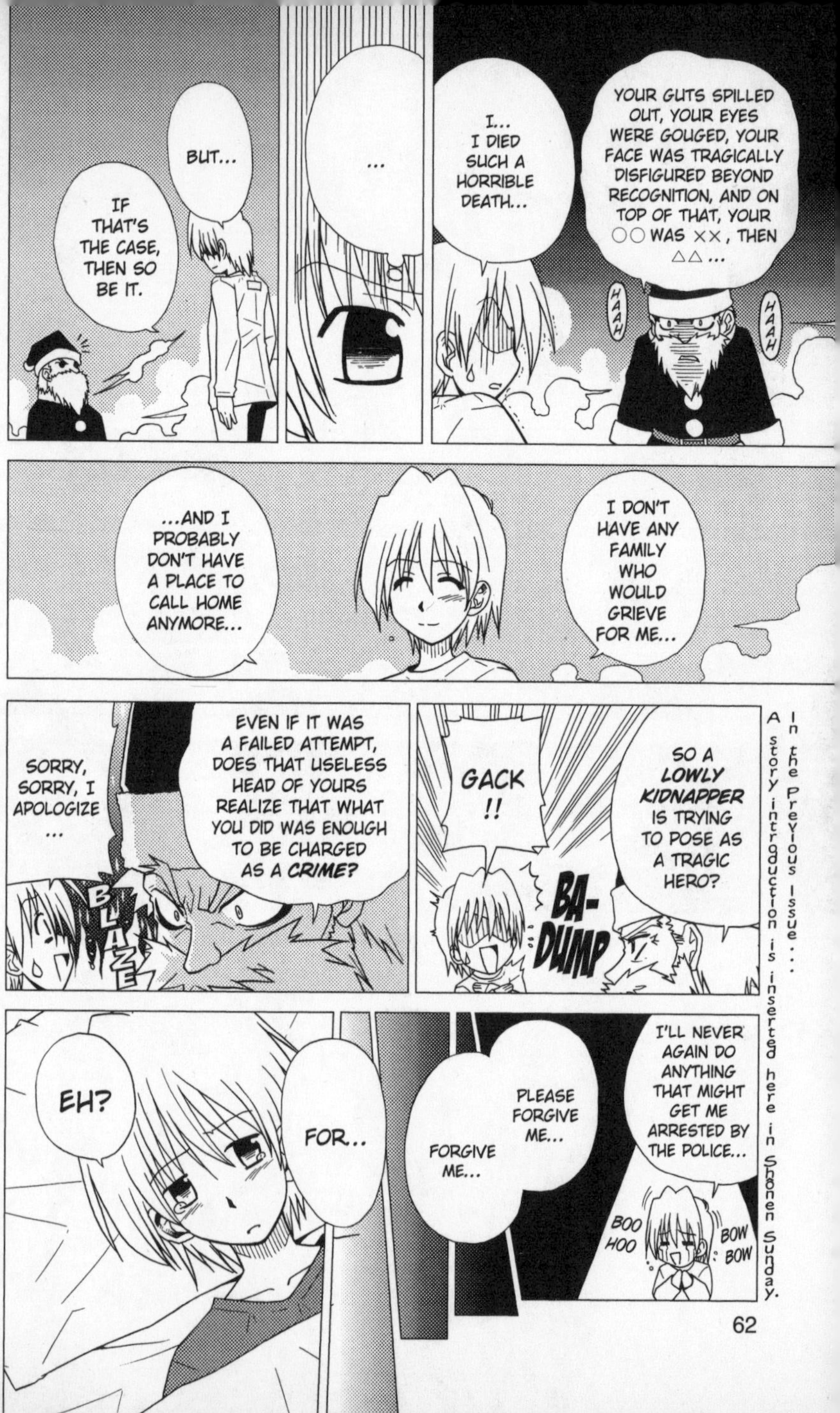
YOUR GUTS SPILLED OUT, YOUR EYES WERE GOUGED, YOUR FACE WAS TRAGICALLY DISFIGURED BEYOND RECOGNITION, AND ON TOP OF THAT, YOUR ○○ WAS ××, THEN △△...
HAAH
HAAH
I... I DIED SUCH A HORRIBLE DEATH...
...
BUT...
IF THAT'S THE CASE, THEN SO BE IT.
I DON'T HAVE ANY FAMILY WHO WOULD GRIEVE FOR ME...
...AND I PROBABLY DON'T HAVE A PLACE TO CALL HOME ANYMORE...
SO A LOWLY KIDNAPPER IS TRYING TO POSE AS A TRAGIC HERO?
GACK !!
BA-DUMP
EVEN IF IT WAS A FAILED ATTEMPT, DOES THAT USELESS HEAD OF YOURS REALIZE THAT WHAT YOU DID WAS ENOUGH TO BE CHARGED AS A CRIME?
BLAZE
SORRY, SORRY, I APOLOGIZE ...
I'LL NEVER AGAIN DO ANYTHING THAT MIGHT GET ME ARRESTED BY THE POLICE...
BOO HOO
BOW BOW
PLEASE FORGIVE ME...
FORGIVE ME...
FOR...
EH?

In the Previous Issue...
A story introduction is inserted here in Shonen Sunday.

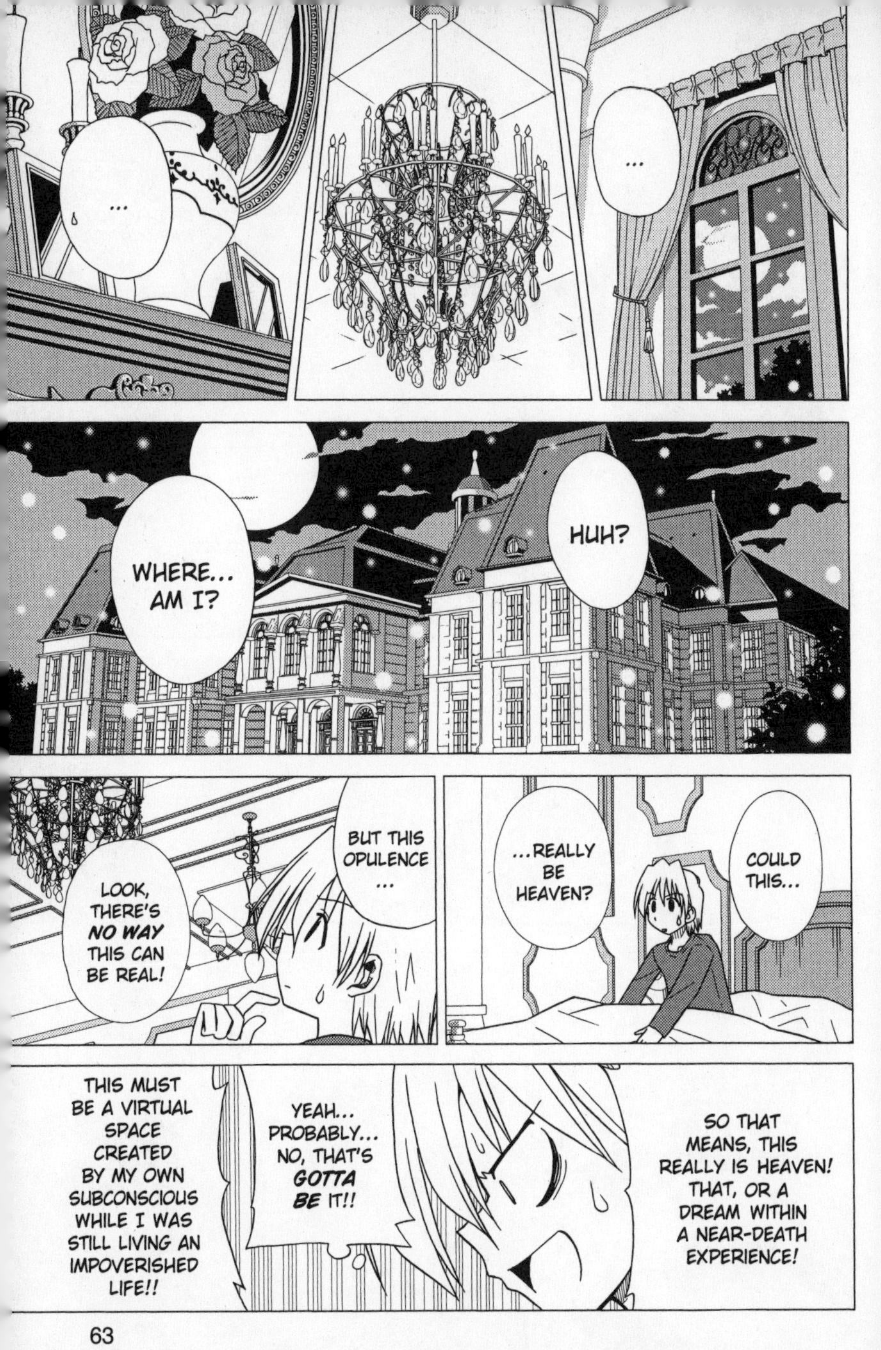
...
...
...
HUH?
WHERE... AM I?
COULD THIS...
...REALLY BE HEAVEN?
BUT THIS OPULENCE...
LOOK, THERE'S *NO WAY* THIS CAN BE REAL!
SO THAT MEANS, THIS REALLY IS HEAVEN! THAT, OR A DREAM WITHIN A NEAR-DEATH EXPERIENCE!
YEAH... PROBABLY... NO, THAT'S *GOTTA BE* IT!!
THIS MUST BE A VIRTUAL SPACE CREATED BY MY OWN SUBCONSCIOUS WHILE I WAS STILL LIVING AN IMPOVERISHED LIFE!!

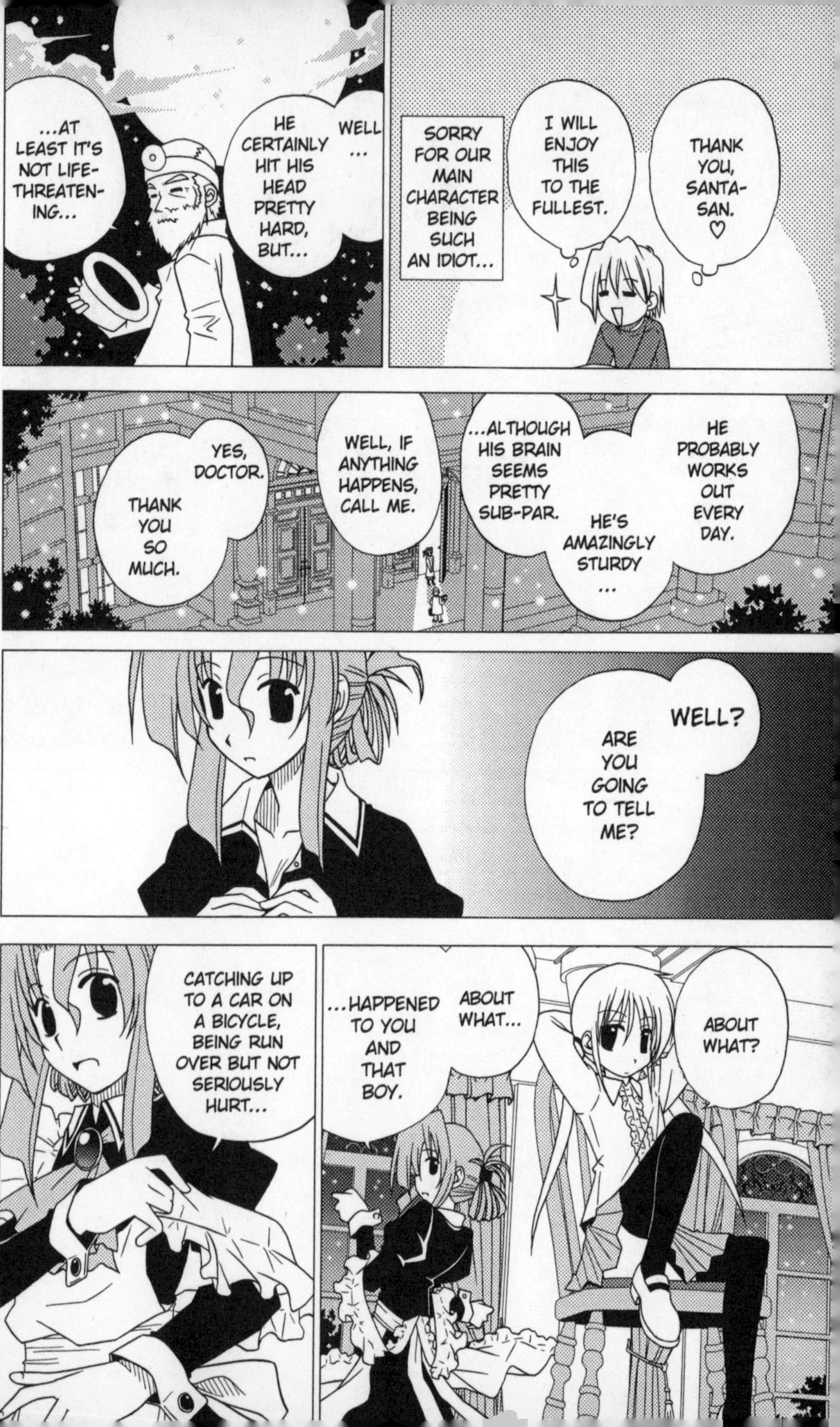
THANK YOU, SANTA-SAN. ♡
I WILL ENJOY THIS TO THE FULLEST.
SORRY FOR OUR MAIN CHARACTER BEING SUCH AN IDIOT...
WELL...
HE CERTAINLY HIT HIS HEAD PRETTY HARD, BUT...
...AT LEAST IT'S NOT LIFE-THREATENING...
HE PROBABLY WORKS OUT EVERY DAY.
HE'S AMAZINGLY STURDY...
...ALTHOUGH HIS BRAIN SEEMS PRETTY SUB-PAR.
WELL, IF ANYTHING HAPPENS, CALL ME.
YES, DOCTOR.
THANK YOU SO MUCH.
WELL?
ARE YOU GOING TO TELL ME?
ABOUT WHAT?
ABOUT WHAT...
...HAPPENED TO YOU AND THAT BOY.
CATCHING UP TO A CAR ON A BICYCLE, BEING RUN OVER BUT NOT SERIOUSLY HURT...

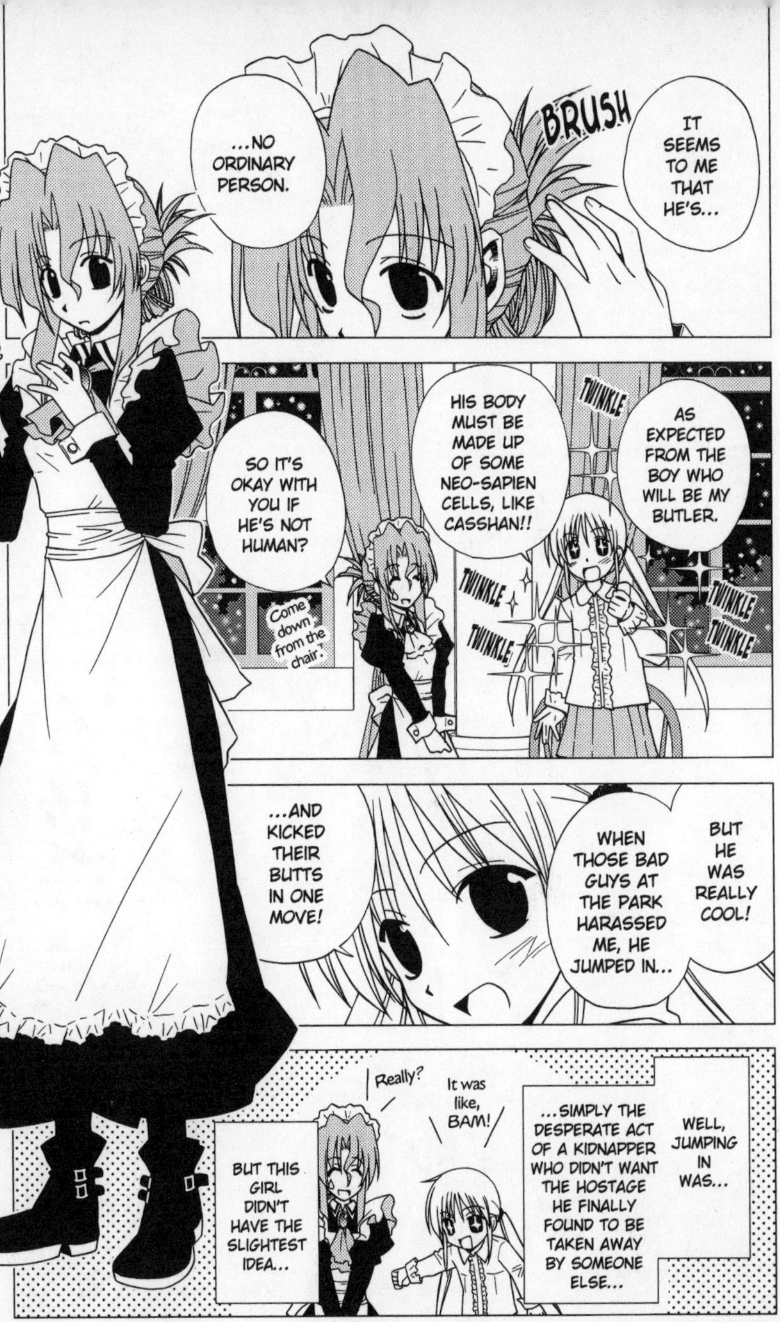
IT SEEMS TO ME THAT HE'S...
BRUSH
...NO ORDINARY PERSON.
AS EXPECTED FROM THE BOY WHO WILL BE MY BUTLER.
TWINKLE
TWINKLE
TWINKLE
HIS BODY MUST BE MADE UP OF SOME NEO-SAPIEN CELLS, LIKE CASSHAN!!
TWINKLE
TWINKLE
SO IT'S OKAY WITH YOU IF HE'S NOT HUMAN?
Come down from the chair.
BUT HE WAS REALLY COOL!
WHEN THOSE BAD GUYS AT THE PARK HARASSED ME, HE JUMPED IN...
...AND KICKED THEIR BUTTS IN ONE MOVE!
WELL, JUMPING IN WAS...
...SIMPLY THE DESPERATE ACT OF A KIDNAPPER WHO DIDN'T WANT THE HOSTAGE HE FINALLY FOUND TO BE TAKEN AWAY BY SOMEONE ELSE...
It was like, BAM!
Really?
BUT THIS GIRL DIDN'T HAVE THE SLIGHTEST IDEA...

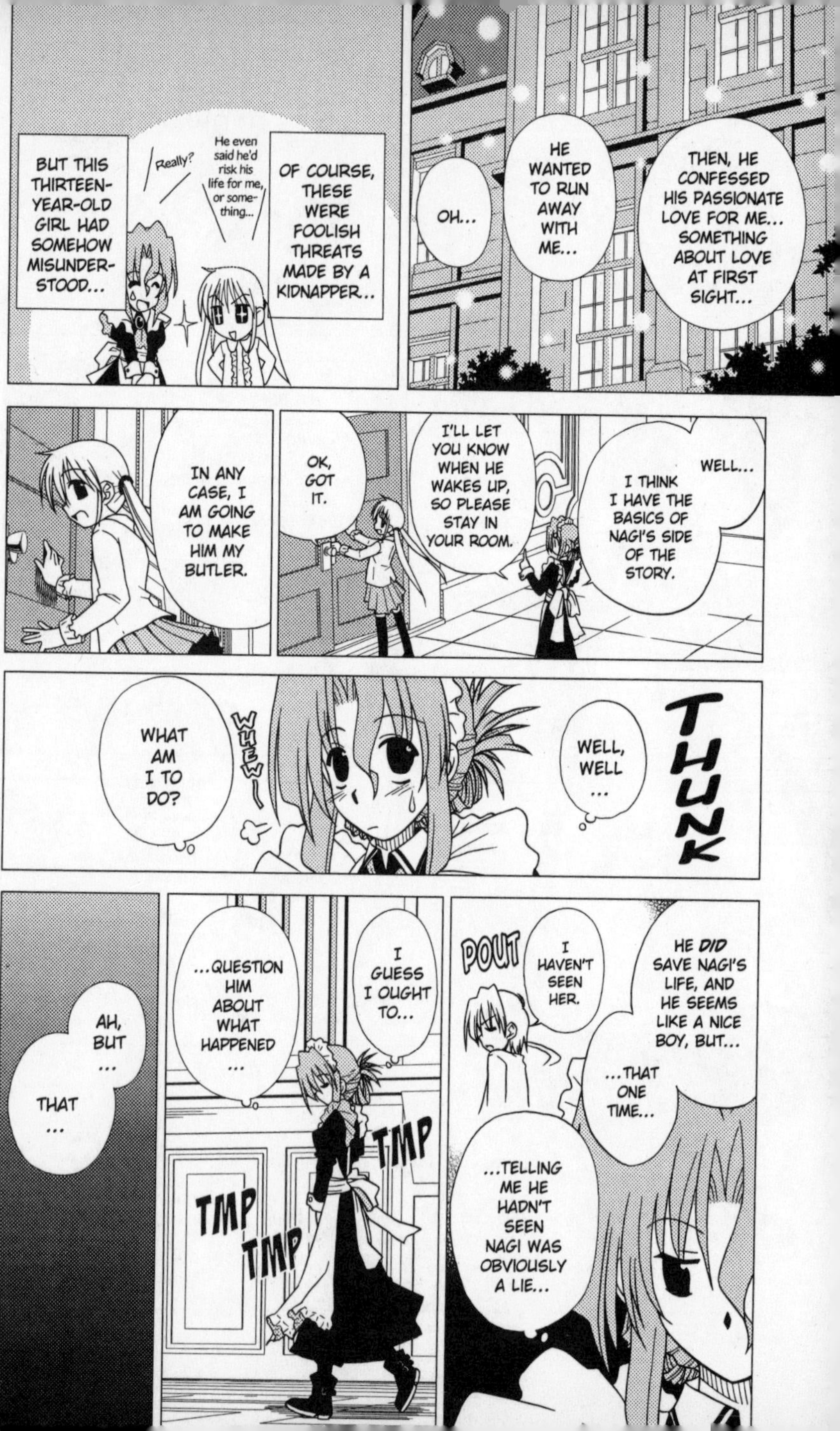
THEN, HE CONFESSED HIS PASSIONATE LOVE FOR ME... SOMETHING ABOUT LOVE AT FIRST SIGHT...
HE WANTED TO RUN AWAY WITH ME...
OH...
OF COURSE, THESE WERE FOOLISH THREATS MADE BY A KIDNAPPER...
He even said he'd risk his life for me, or some-thing...
Really?
BUT THIS THIRTEEN-YEAR-OLD GIRL HAD SOMEHOW MISUNDERSTOOD...
WELL...
I THINK I HAVE THE BASICS OF NAGI'S SIDE OF THE STORY.
I'LL LET YOU KNOW WHEN HE WAKES UP, SO PLEASE STAY IN YOUR ROOM.
OK, GOT IT.
IN ANY CASE, I AM GOING TO MAKE HIM MY BUTLER.
THUNK
WELL, WELL...
WHEW
WHAT AM I TO DO?
HE *DID* SAVE NAGI'S LIFE, AND HE SEEMS LIKE A NICE BOY, BUT...
I HAVEN'T SEEN HER.
POUT
...THAT ONE TIME...
...TELLING ME HE HADN'T SEEN NAGI WAS OBVIOUSLY A LIE...
I GUESS I OUGHT TO...
...QUESTION HIM ABOUT WHAT HAPPENED...
TMP
TMP
TMP
AH, BUT...
THAT...

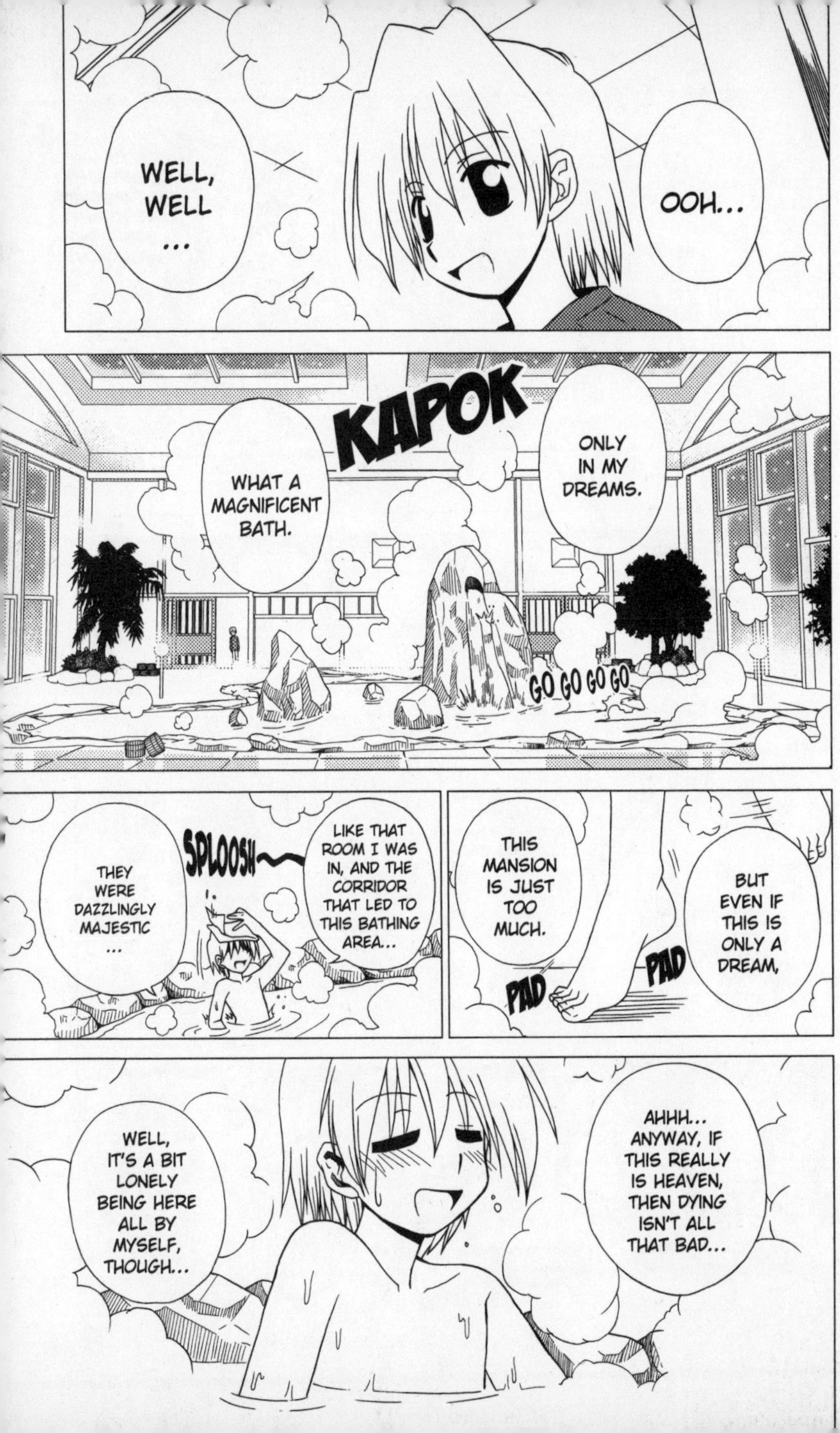
OOH...
WELL, WELL ...
ONLY IN MY DREAMS.
KAPOK
WHAT A MAGNIFICENT BATH.
GO GO GO GO
BUT EVEN IF THIS IS ONLY A DREAM,
PAD PAD
THIS MANSION IS JUST TOO MUCH.
LIKE THAT ROOM I WAS IN, AND THE CORRIDOR THAT LED TO THIS BATHING AREA...
SPLOOSH
THEY WERE DAZZLINGLY MAJESTIC ...
AHHH... ANYWAY, IF THIS REALLY IS HEAVEN, THEN DYING ISN'T ALL THAT BAD...
WELL, IT'S A BIT LONELY BEING HERE ALL BY MYSELF, THOUGH...

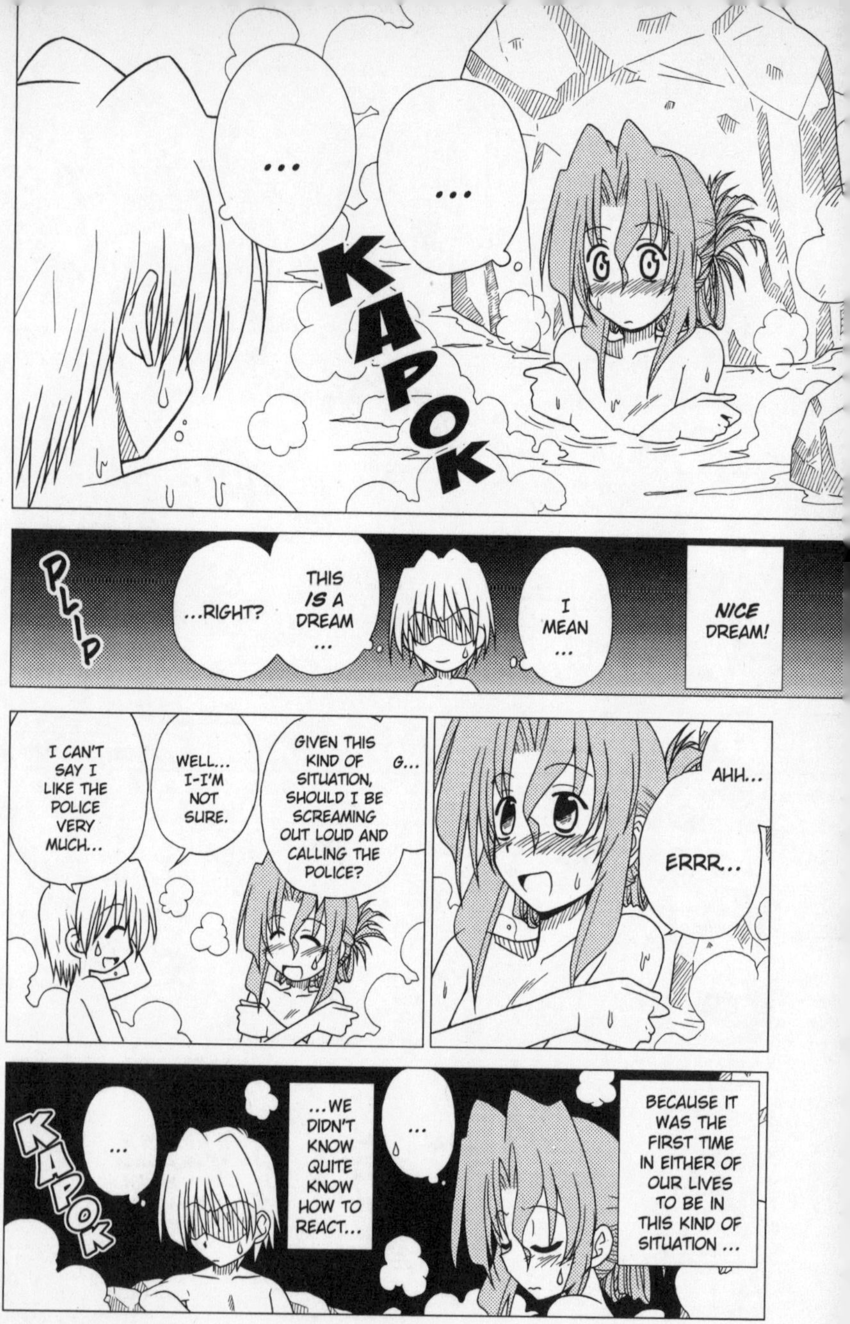
...
...
KAPOK
NICE DREAM!
I MEAN ...
THIS IS A DREAM ...
...RIGHT?
PLIP
AHH...
ERRR...
G...
GIVEN THIS KIND OF SITUATION, SHOULD I BE SCREAMING OUT LOUD AND CALLING THE POLICE?
WELL... I-I'M NOT SURE.
I CAN'T SAY I LIKE THE POLICE VERY MUCH...
BECAUSE IT WAS THE FIRST TIME IN EITHER OF OUR LIVES TO BE IN THIS KIND OF SITUATION ...
...
...WE DIDN'T KNOW QUITE KNOW HOW TO REACT...
...
KAPOK

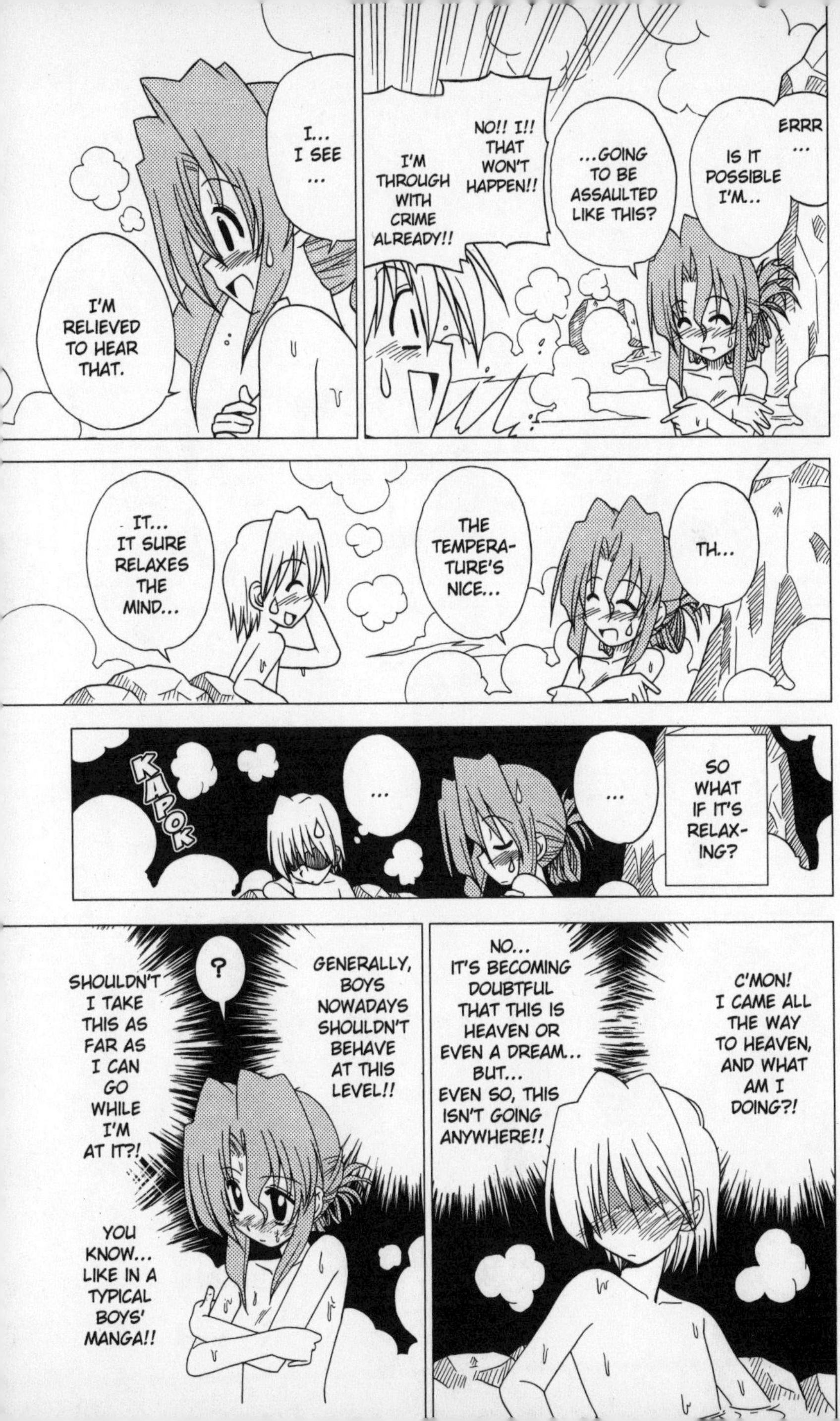
ERRR...
IS IT POSSIBLE I'M...
...GOING TO BE ASSAULTED LIKE THIS?
NO!! I!! THAT WON'T HAPPEN!!
I'M THROUGH WITH CRIME ALREADY!!
I... I SEE...
I'M RELIEVED TO HEAR THAT.
TH...
THE TEMPERA-TURE'S NICE...
IT... IT SURE RELAXES THE MIND...
SO WHAT IF IT'S RELAX-ING?
...
...
KAPOK
C'MON! I CAME ALL THE WAY TO HEAVEN, AND WHAT AM I DOING?!
NO... IT'S BECOMING DOUBTFUL THAT THIS IS HEAVEN OR EVEN A DREAM... BUT... EVEN SO, THIS ISN'T GOING ANYWHERE!!
GENERALLY, BOYS NOWADAYS SHOULDN'T BEHAVE AT THIS LEVEL!!
?
SHOULDN'T I TAKE THIS AS FAR AS I CAN GO WHILE I'M AT IT?!
YOU KNOW... LIKE IN A TYPICAL BOYS' MANGA!!

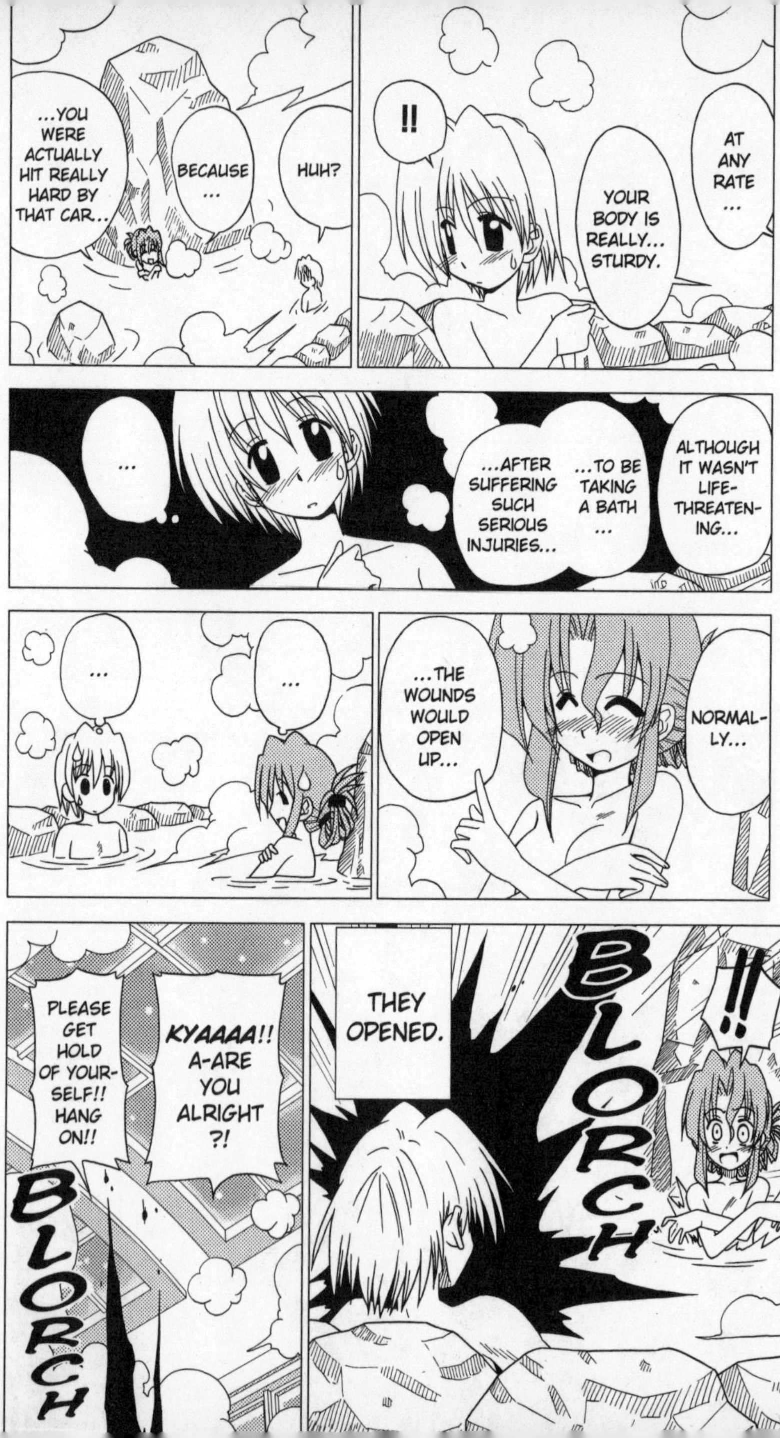
AT ANY RATE...
YOUR BODY IS REALLY... STURDY.
!!
HUH?
BECAUSE...
...YOU WERE ACTUALLY HIT REALLY HARD BY THAT CAR...
ALTHOUGH IT WASN'T LIFE-THREATENING...
...TO BE TAKING A BATH...
...AFTER SUFFERING SUCH SERIOUS INJURIES...
...
NORMALLY...
...THE WOUNDS WOULD OPEN UP...
...
...
!!
BLORCH
THEY OPENED.
KYAAAA!! A-ARE YOU ALRIGHT?!
PLEASE GET HOLD OF YOURSELF!! HANG ON!!
BLORCH

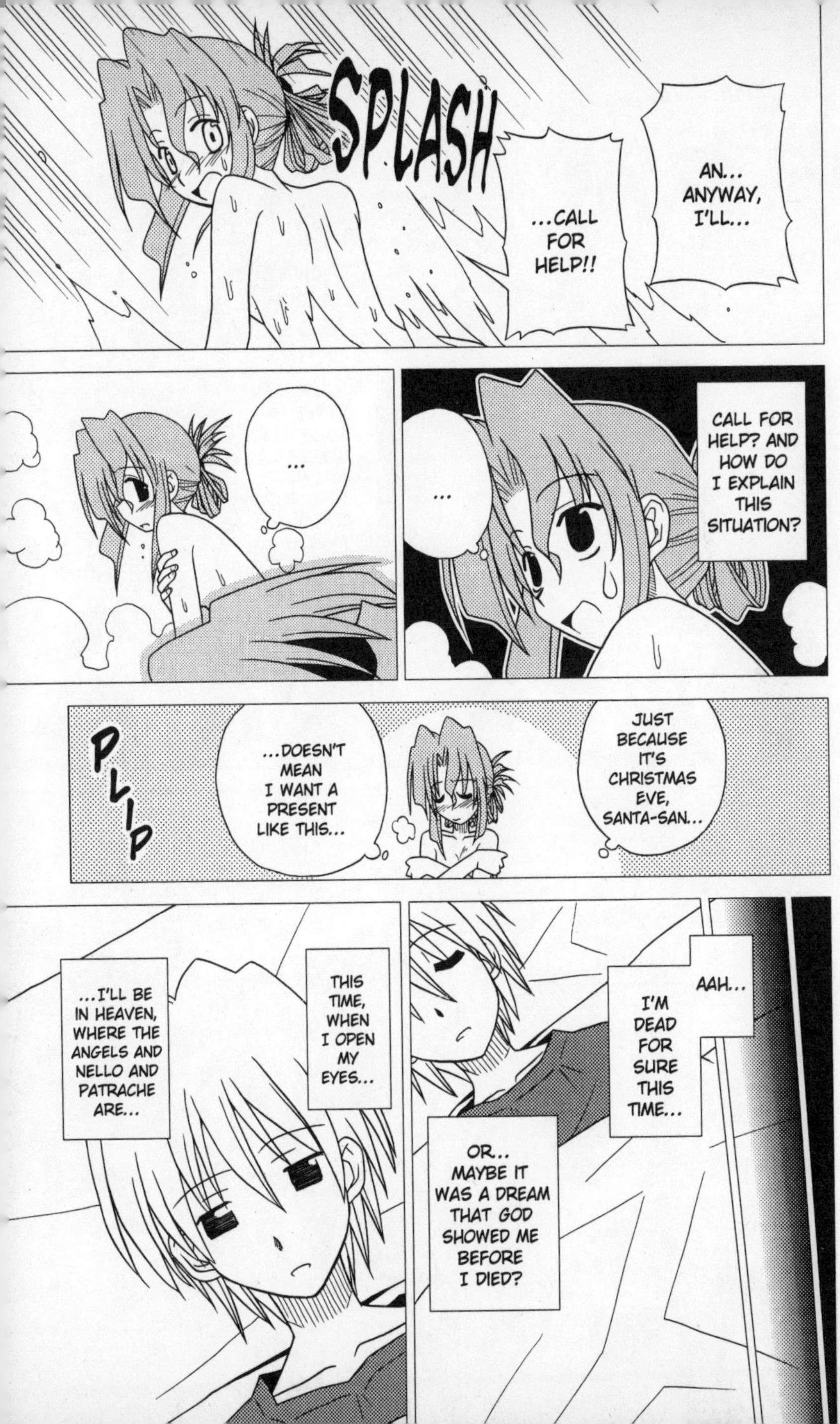
AN... ANYWAY, I'LL...
...CALL FOR HELP!!
SPLASH
CALL FOR HELP? AND HOW DO I EXPLAIN THIS SITUATION?
...
...
JUST BECAUSE IT'S CHRISTMAS EVE, SANTA-SAN...
...DOESN'T MEAN I WANT A PRESENT LIKE THIS...
PLIP
AAH...
I'M DEAD FOR SURE THIS TIME...
OR... MAYBE IT WAS A DREAM THAT GOD SHOWED ME BEFORE I DIED?
THIS TIME, WHEN I OPEN MY EYES...
...I'LL BE IN HEAVEN, WHERE THE ANGELS AND NELLO AND PATRACHE ARE...

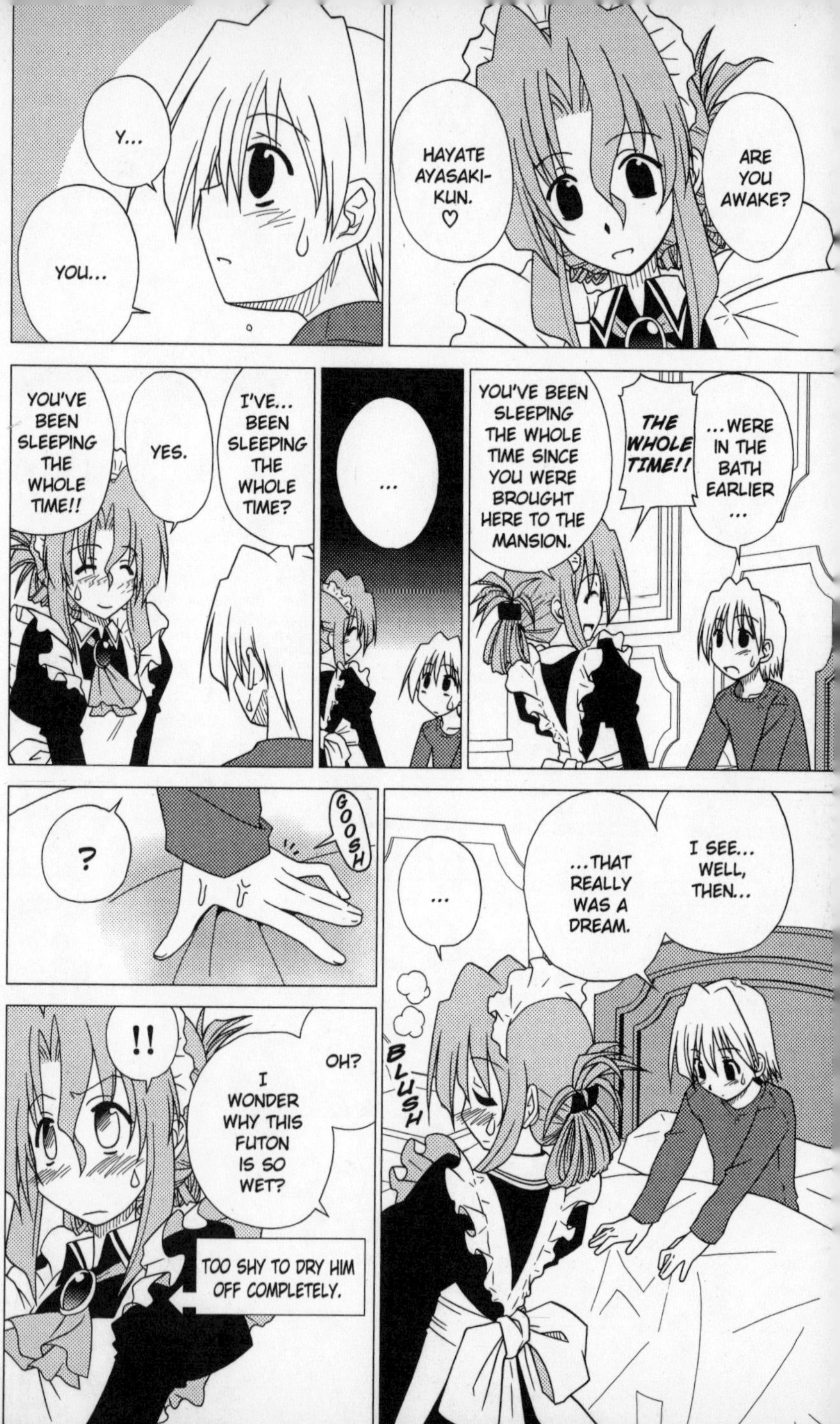
ARE YOU AWAKE?
HAYATE AYASAKI-KUN. ♡
Y...
YOU...
...WERE IN THE BATH EARLIER...
THE WHOLE TIME!!
YOU'VE BEEN SLEEPING THE WHOLE TIME SINCE YOU WERE BROUGHT HERE TO THE MANSION.
...
I'VE... BEEN SLEEPING THE WHOLE TIME?
YES.
YOU'VE BEEN SLEEPING THE WHOLE TIME!!
I SEE... WELL, THEN...
...THAT REALLY WAS A DREAM.
...
BLUSH
GOOSH
?
OH?
I WONDER WHY THIS FUTON IS SO WET?
!!
TOO SHY TO DRY HIM OFF COMPLETELY.

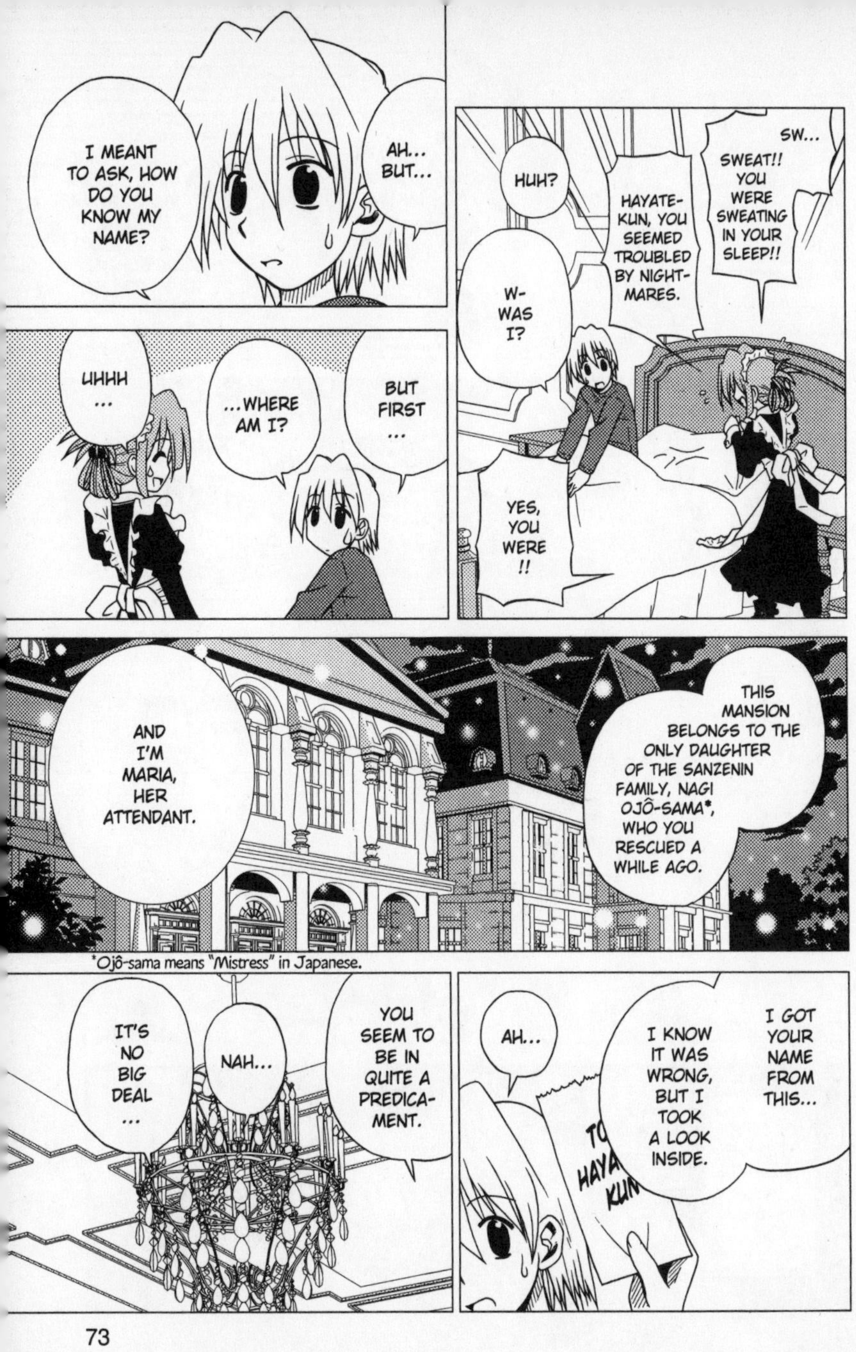
HAYATE-KUN, YOU SEEMED TROUBLED BY NIGHTMARES.
HUH?
SW...
SWEAT!! YOU WERE SWEATING IN YOUR SLEEP!!
W-WAS I?
YES, YOU WERE!!
AH... BUT...
I MEANT TO ASK, HOW DO YOU KNOW MY NAME?
BUT FIRST...
...WHERE AM I?
UHHH...
THIS MANSION BELONGS TO THE ONLY DAUGHTER OF THE SANZENIN FAMILY, NAGI OJÔ-SAMA*, WHO YOU RESCUED A WHILE AGO.
AND I'M MARIA, HER ATTENDANT.
I GOT YOUR NAME FROM THIS...
I KNOW IT WAS WRONG, BUT I TOOK A LOOK INSIDE.
AH...
YOU SEEM TO BE IN QUITE A PREDICAMENT.
NAH...
IT'S NO BIG DEAL...

*Ojô-sama means "Mistress" in Japanese.

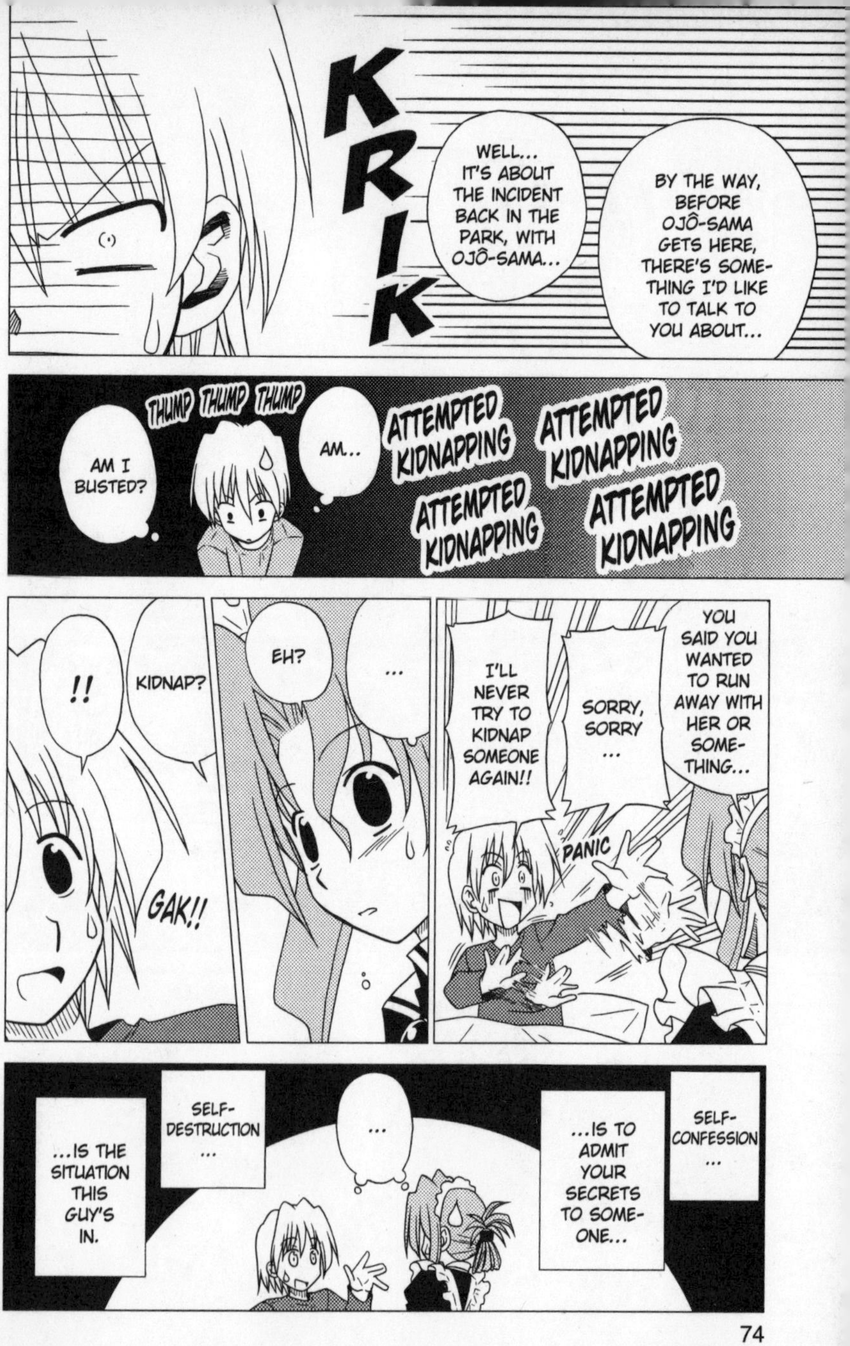
BY THE WAY, BEFORE OJÔ-SAMA GETS HERE, THERE'S SOMETHING I'D LIKE TO TALK TO YOU ABOUT...
WELL... IT'S ABOUT THE INCIDENT BACK IN THE PARK, WITH OJÔ-SAMA...
KRIK
ATTEMPTED KIDNAPPING
ATTEMPTED KIDNAPPING
ATTEMPTED KIDNAPPING
ATTEMPTED KIDNAPPING
AM...
THUMP THUMP THUMP
AM I BUSTED?
YOU SAID YOU WANTED TO RUN AWAY WITH HER OR SOMETHING...
SORRY, SORRY ...
I'LL NEVER TRY TO KIDNAP SOMEONE AGAIN!!
PANIC
...
EH?
KIDNAP?
!!
GAK!!
SELF-CONFESSION ...
...IS TO ADMIT YOUR SECRETS TO SOMEONE...
...
SELF-DESTRUCTION ...
...IS THE SITUATION THIS GUY'S IN.

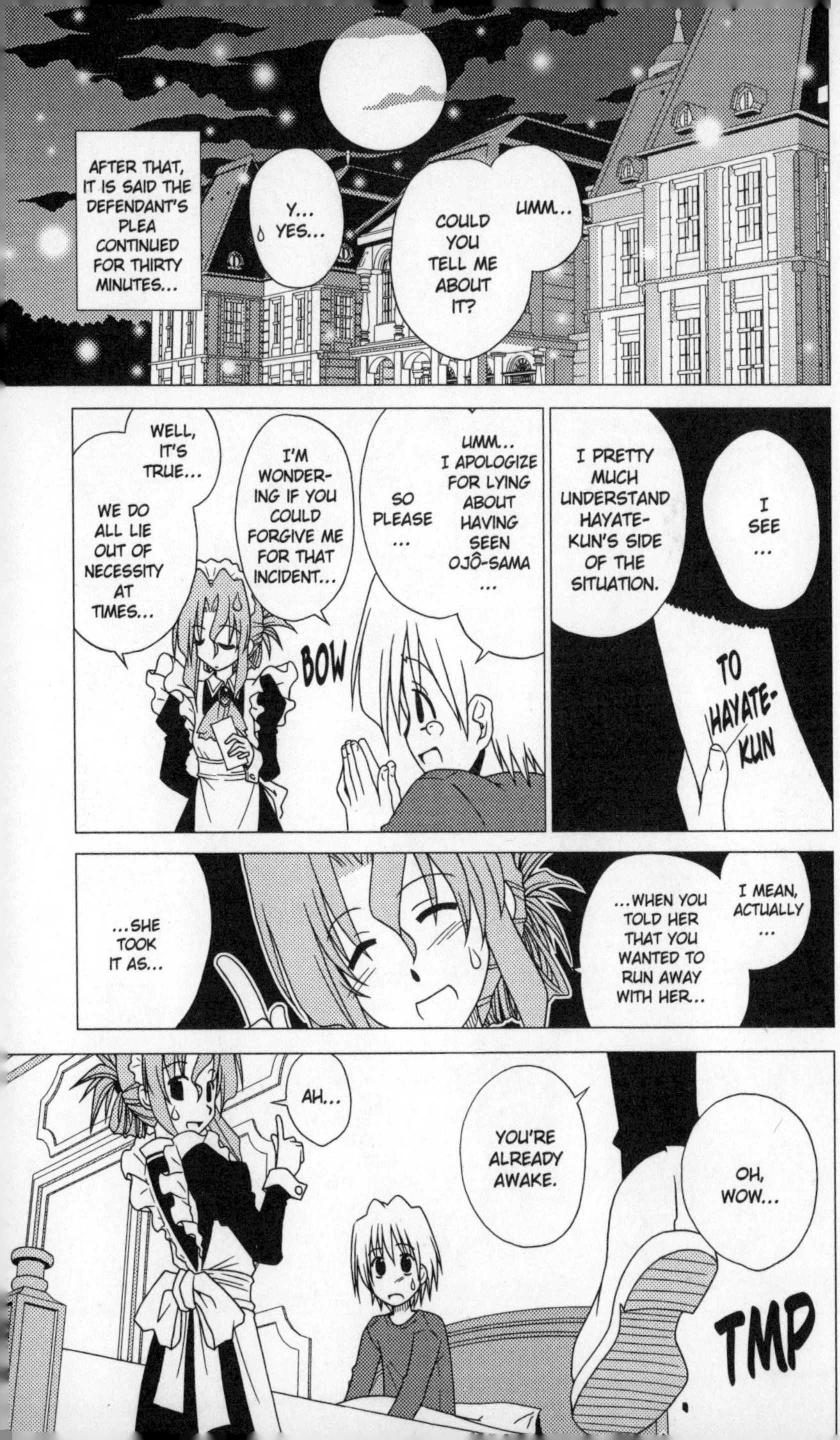
UMM...
COULD YOU TELL ME ABOUT IT?
Y... YES...
AFTER THAT, IT IS SAID THE DEFENDANT'S PLEA CONTINUED FOR THIRTY MINUTES...
I SEE...
I PRETTY MUCH UNDERSTAND HAYATE-KUN'S SIDE OF THE SITUATION.
TO HAYATE-KUN
UMM... I APOLOGIZE FOR LYING ABOUT HAVING SEEN OJÔ-SAMA...
SO PLEASE...
I'M WONDERING IF YOU COULD FORGIVE ME FOR THAT INCIDENT...
BOW
WELL, IT'S TRUE...
WE DO ALL LIE OUT OF NECESSITY AT TIMES...
I MEAN, ACTUALLY...
...WHEN YOU TOLD HER THAT YOU WANTED TO RUN AWAY WITH HER...
...SHE TOOK IT AS...
OH, WOW...
TMP
YOU'RE ALREADY AWAKE.
AH...

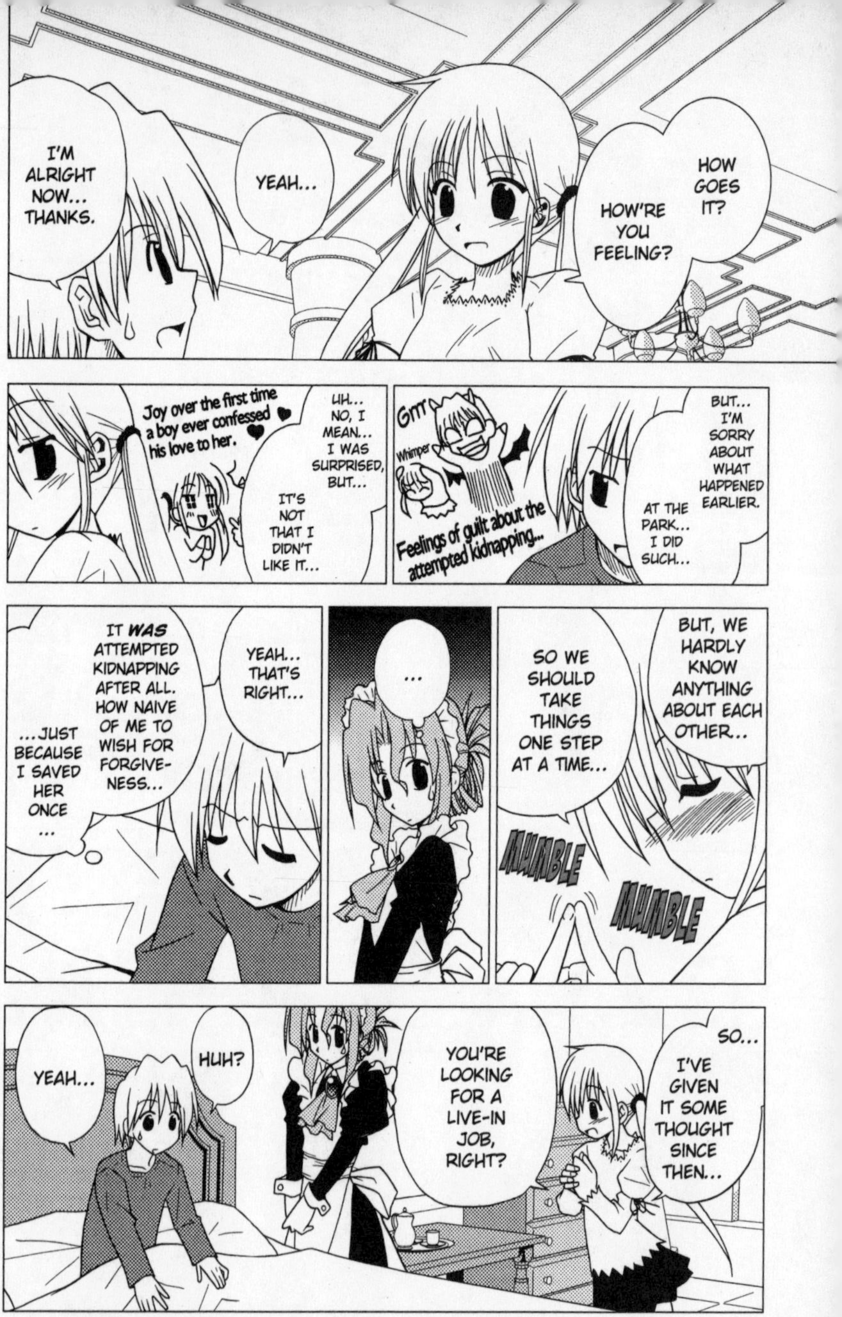
HOW GOES IT?
HOW'RE YOU FEELING?
YEAH...
I'M ALRIGHT NOW... THANKS.
BUT... I'M SORRY ABOUT WHAT HAPPENED EARLIER.
AT THE PARK... I DID SUCH...
Grrr
Whimper
Feelings of guilt about the attempted kidnapping...
UH... NO, I MEAN... I WAS SURPRISED, BUT...
IT'S NOT THAT I DIDN'T LIKE IT...
Joy over the first time a boy ever confessed his love to her.
BUT, WE HARDLY KNOW ANYTHING ABOUT EACH OTHER...
SO WE SHOULD TAKE THINGS ONE STEP AT A TIME...
MUMBLE
MUMBLE
...
YEAH... THAT'S RIGHT...
IT *WAS* ATTEMPTED KIDNAPPING AFTER ALL. HOW NAIVE OF ME TO WISH FOR FORGIVENESS...
...JUST BECAUSE I SAVED HER ONCE ...
SO... I'VE GIVEN IT SOME THOUGHT SINCE THEN...
YOU'RE LOOKING FOR A LIVE-IN JOB, RIGHT?
HUH?
YEAH...

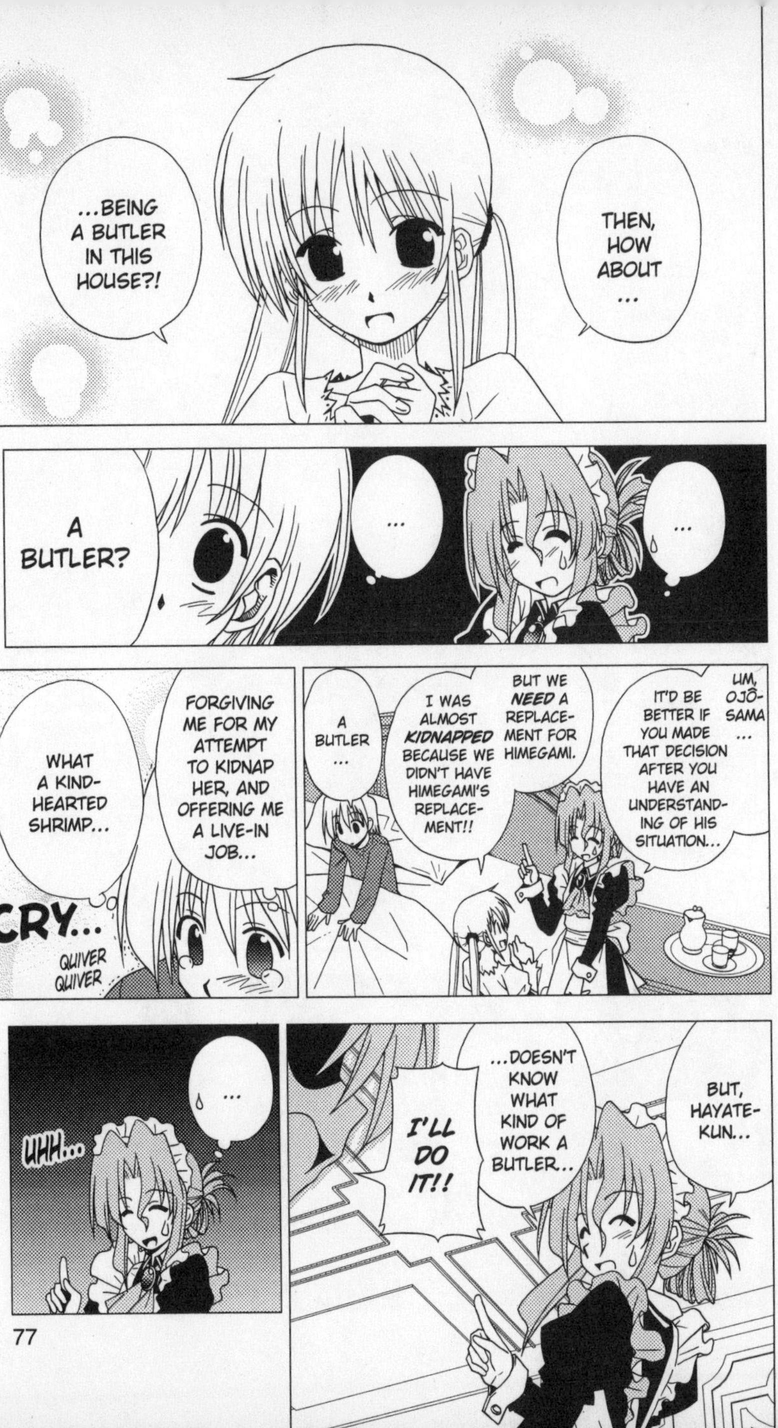
THEN, HOW ABOUT ...
...BEING A BUTLER IN THIS HOUSE?!
...
...
A BUTLER?
UM, OJÔ-SAMA ...
IT'D BE BETTER IF YOU MADE THAT DECISION AFTER YOU HAVE AN UNDERSTANDING OF HIS SITUATION...
BUT WE *NEED* A REPLACEMENT FOR HIMEGAMI.
I WAS ALMOST *KIDNAPPED* BECAUSE WE DIDN'T HAVE HIMEGAMI'S REPLACEMENT!!
A BUTLER ...
FORGIVING ME FOR MY ATTEMPT TO KIDNAP HER, AND OFFERING ME A LIVE-IN JOB...
WHAT A KIND-HEARTED SHRIMP...
CRY...
QUIVER QUIVER
BUT, HAYATE-KUN...
...DOESN'T KNOW WHAT KIND OF WORK A BUTLER...
I'LL DO IT!!
...
UHH...

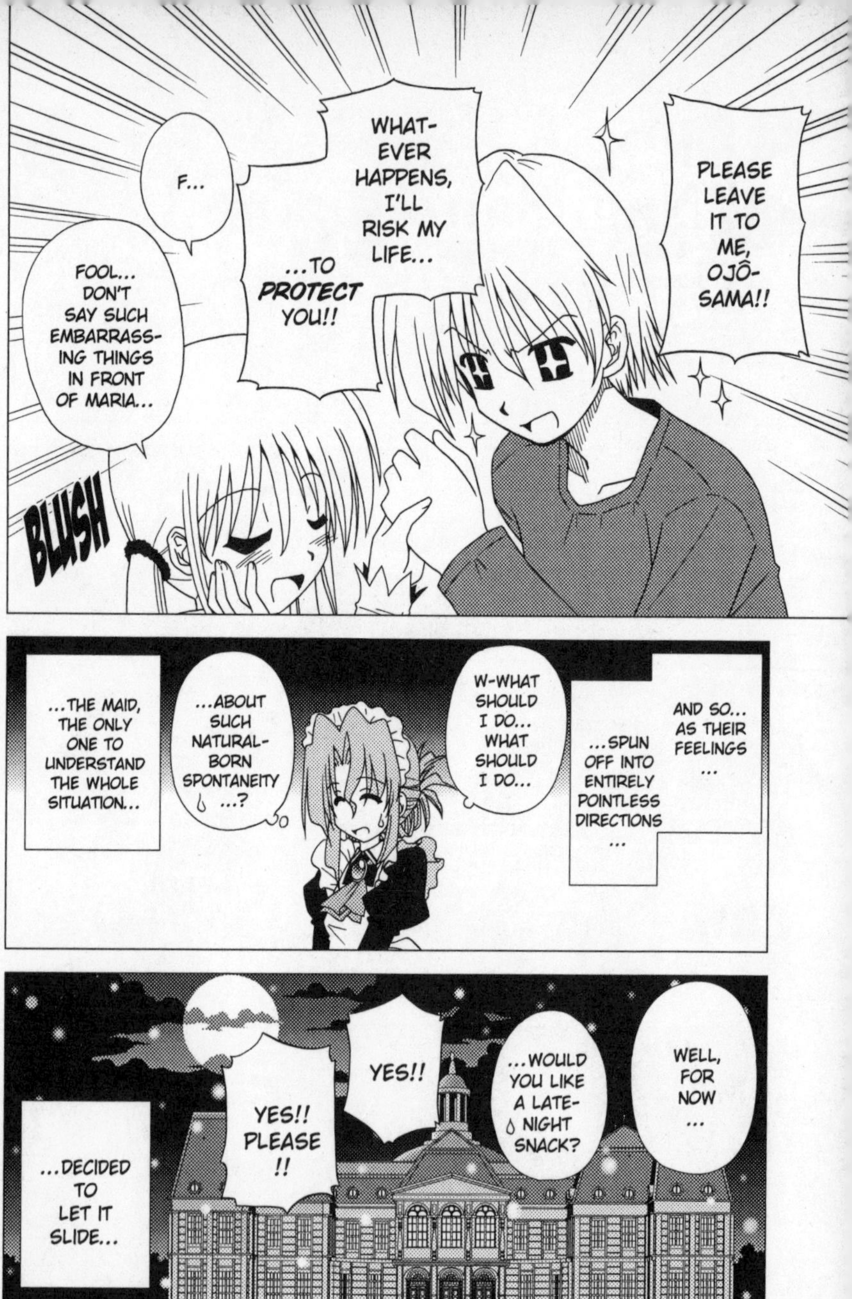
PLEASE LEAVE IT TO ME, OJÔ-SAMA!!
WHAT-EVER HAPPENS, I'LL RISK MY LIFE...
...TO PROTECT YOU!!
F...
FOOL... DON'T SAY SUCH EMBARRASS-ING THINGS IN FRONT OF MARIA...
BLUSH
AND SO... AS THEIR FEELINGS ...
...SPUN OFF INTO ENTIRELY POINTLESS DIRECTIONS ...
W-WHAT SHOULD I DO... WHAT SHOULD I DO...
...ABOUT SUCH NATURAL-BORN SPONTANEITY ...?
...THE MAID, THE ONLY ONE TO UNDERSTAND THE WHOLE SITUATION...
WELL, FOR NOW ...
...WOULD YOU LIKE A LATE-NIGHT SNACK?
YES!!
YES!! PLEASE !!
...DECIDED TO LET IT SLIDE...

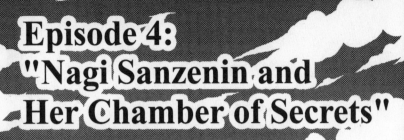

Episode 4:
"Nagi Sanzenin and
Her Chamber of Secrets"

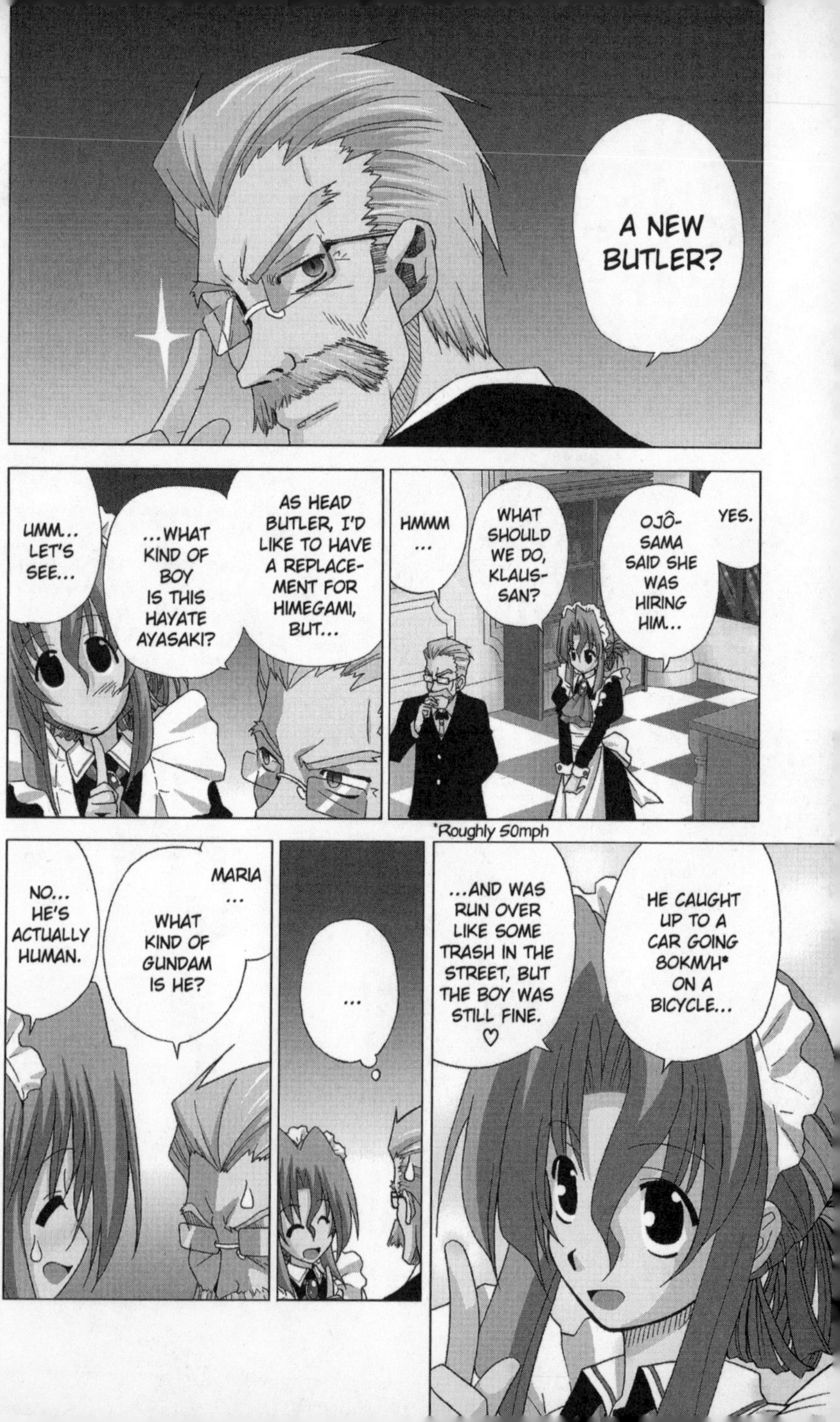
A NEW BUTLER?
YES.
OJÔ-SAMA SAID SHE WAS HIRING HIM...
WHAT SHOULD WE DO, KLAUS-SAN?
HMMM...
AS HEAD BUTLER, I'D LIKE TO HAVE A REPLACEMENT FOR HIMEGAMI, BUT...
...WHAT KIND OF BOY IS THIS HAYATE AYASAKI?
UMM... LET'S SEE...
HE CAUGHT UP TO A CAR GOING 80KM/H* ON A BICYCLE...
...AND WAS RUN OVER LIKE SOME TRASH IN THE STREET, BUT THE BOY WAS STILL FINE. ♡
...
MARIA...
WHAT KIND OF GUNDAM IS HE?
NO... HE'S ACTUALLY HUMAN.

*Roughly 50mph

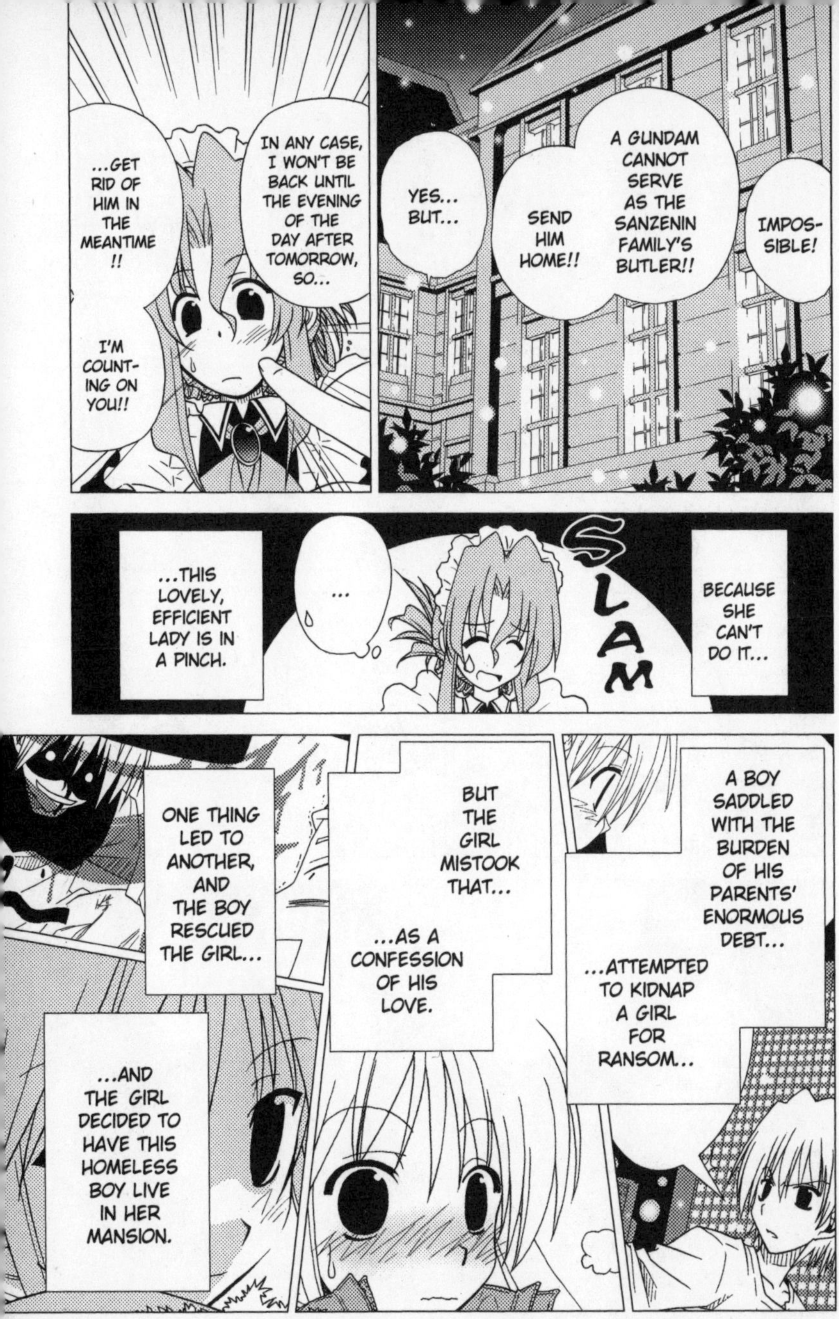
IMPOSSIBLE!
A GUNDAM CANNOT SERVE AS THE SANZENIN FAMILY'S BUTLER!!
SEND HIM HOME!!
YES... BUT...
IN ANY CASE, I WON'T BE BACK UNTIL THE EVENING OF THE DAY AFTER TOMORROW, SO...
...GET RID OF HIM IN THE MEANTIME!!
I'M COUNTING ON YOU!!
BECAUSE SHE CAN'T DO IT...
SLAM
...
...THIS LOVELY, EFFICIENT LADY IS IN A PINCH.
A BOY SADDLED WITH THE BURDEN OF HIS PARENTS' ENORMOUS DEBT...
...ATTEMPTED TO KIDNAP A GIRL FOR RANSOM...
ONE THING LED TO ANOTHER, AND THE BOY RESCUED THE GIRL...
BUT THE GIRL MISTOOK THAT...
...AS A CONFESSION OF HIS LOVE.
...AND THE GIRL DECIDED TO HAVE THIS HOMELESS BOY LIVE IN HER MANSION.

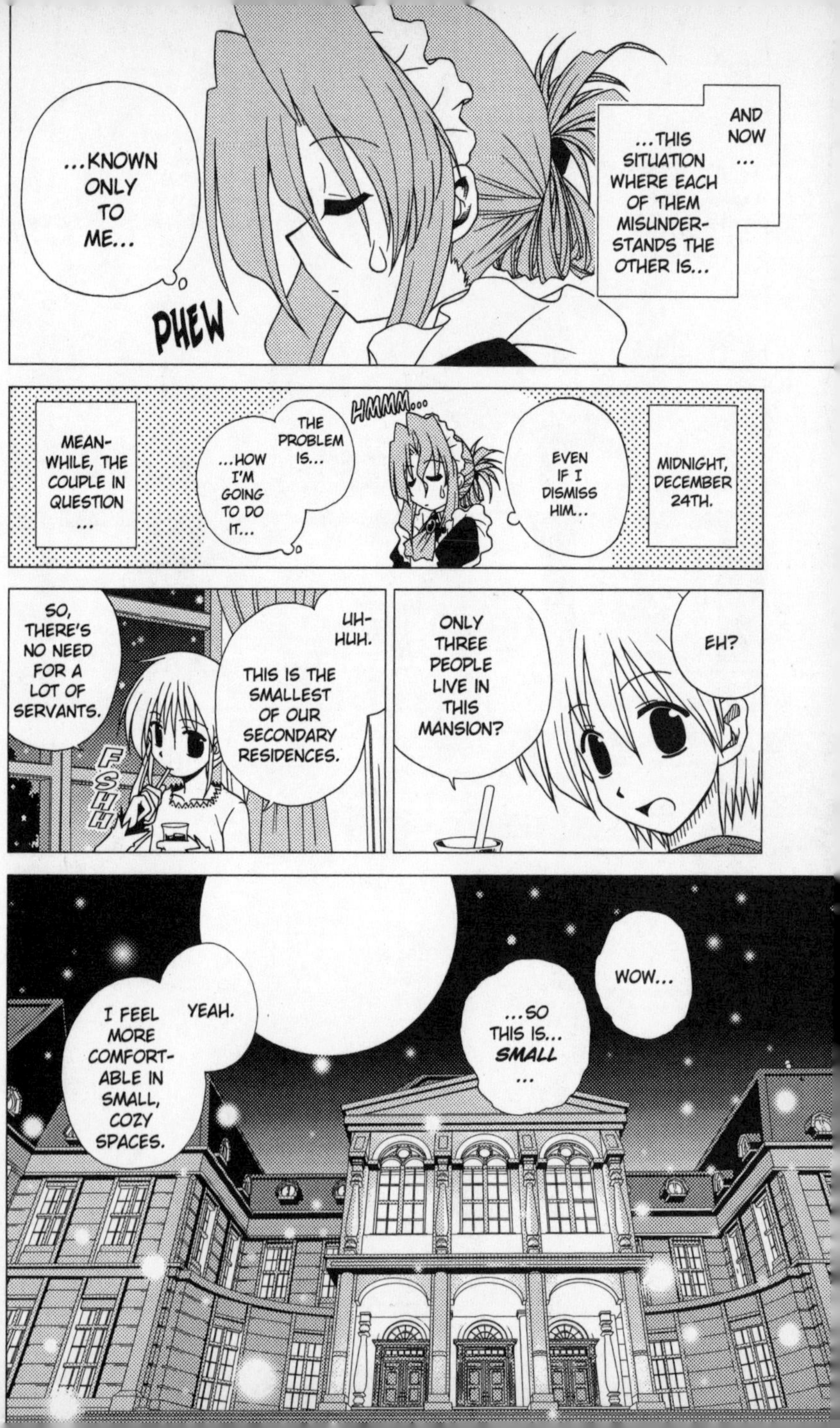
AND NOW ...
...THIS SITUATION WHERE EACH OF THEM MISUNDER-STANDS THE OTHER IS...
...KNOWN ONLY TO ME...
PHEW
MIDNIGHT, DECEMBER 24TH.
EVEN IF I DISMISS HIM...
HMMM...
THE PROBLEM IS...
...HOW I'M GOING TO DO IT...
MEAN-WHILE, THE COUPLE IN QUESTION ...
EH?
ONLY THREE PEOPLE LIVE IN THIS MANSION?
UH-HUH.
THIS IS THE SMALLEST OF OUR SECONDARY RESIDENCES.
SO, THERE'S NO NEED FOR A LOT OF SERVANTS.
FSHH
WOW...
...SO THIS IS... SMALL ...
YEAH.
I FEEL MORE COMFORT-ABLE IN SMALL, COZY SPACES.

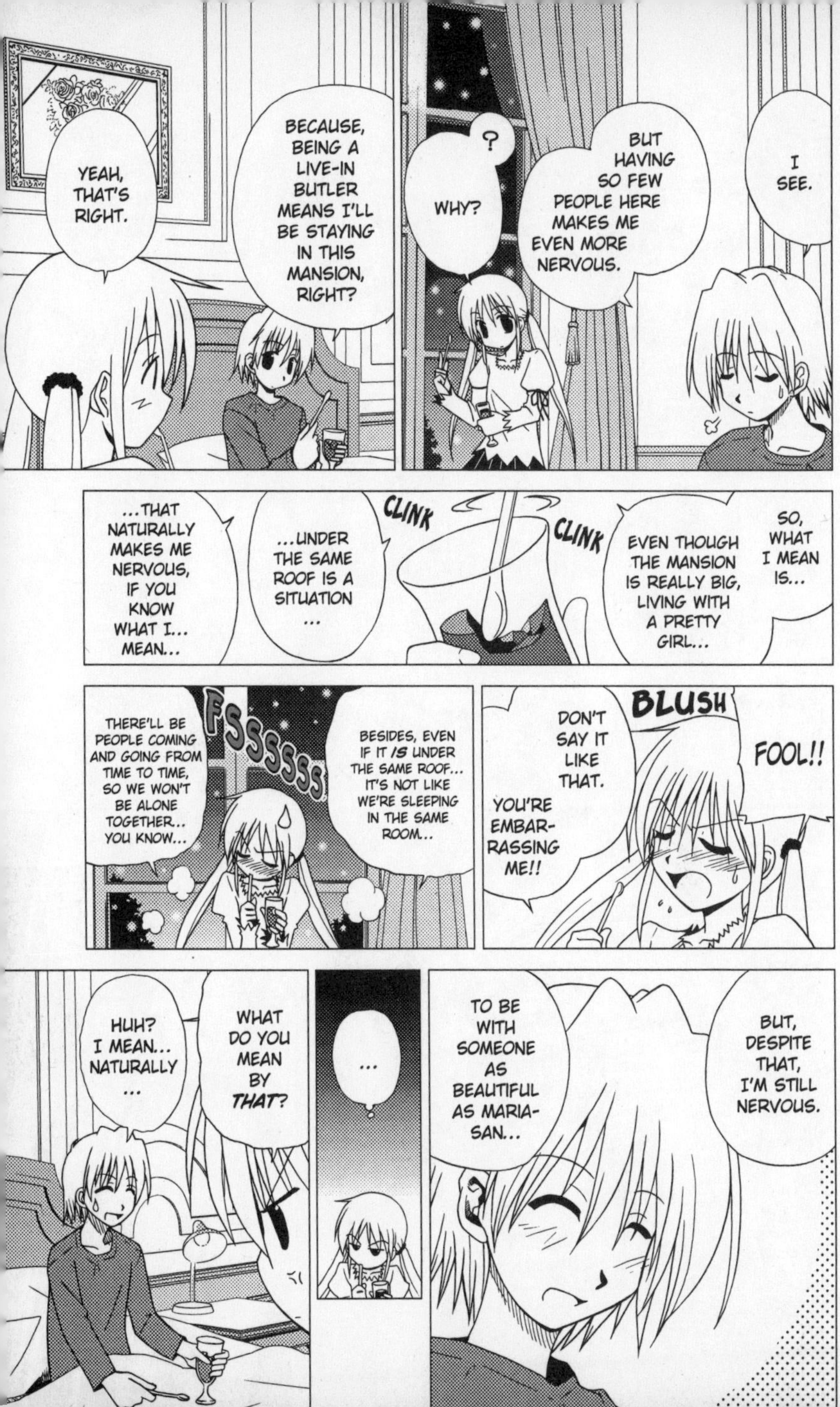
I SEE.
BUT HAVING SO FEW PEOPLE HERE MAKES ME EVEN MORE NERVOUS.
?
WHY?
BECAUSE, BEING A LIVE-IN BUTLER MEANS I'LL BE STAYING IN THIS MANSION, RIGHT?
YEAH, THAT'S RIGHT.
SO, WHAT I MEAN IS...
EVEN THOUGH THE MANSION IS REALLY BIG, LIVING WITH A PRETTY GIRL...
CLINK
CLINK
...UNDER THE SAME ROOF IS A SITUATION ...
...THAT NATURALLY MAKES ME NERVOUS, IF YOU KNOW WHAT I... MEAN...
BLUSH
FOOL!!
DON'T SAY IT LIKE THAT.
YOU'RE EMBARRASSING ME!!
BESIDES, EVEN IF IT *IS* UNDER THE SAME ROOF... IT'S NOT LIKE WE'RE SLEEPING IN THE SAME ROOM...
FSSSSSS
THERE'LL BE PEOPLE COMING AND GOING FROM TIME TO TIME, SO WE WON'T BE ALONE TOGETHER.. YOU KNOW...
BUT, DESPITE THAT, I'M STILL NERVOUS.
TO BE WITH SOMEONE AS BEAUTIFUL AS MARIA-SAN...
...
WHAT DO YOU MEAN BY *THAT*?
HUH? I MEAN... NATURALLY ...

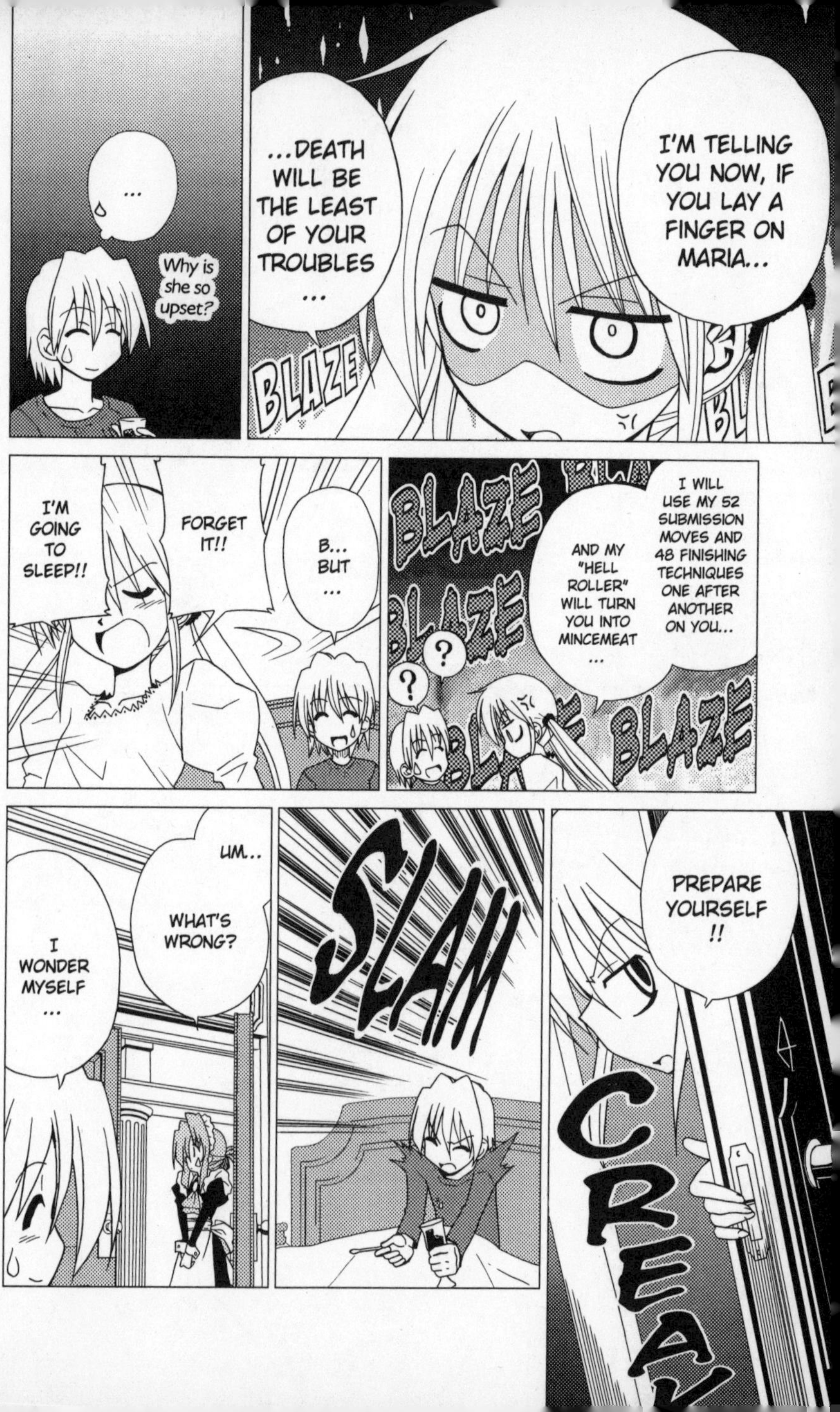
I'M TELLING YOU NOW, IF YOU LAY A FINGER ON MARIA...
...DEATH WILL BE THE LEAST OF YOUR TROUBLES ...
BLAZE
...
Why is she so upset?
I WILL USE MY 52 SUBMISSION MOVES AND 48 FINISHING TECHNIQUES ONE AFTER ANOTHER ON YOU...
AND MY "HELL ROLLER" WILL TURN YOU INTO MINCEMEAT ...
BLAZE
BLAZE
BLAZE
?
?
B... BUT ...
FORGET IT!!
I'M GOING TO SLEEP!!
PREPARE YOURSELF !!
CREA
SLAM
UM...
WHAT'S WRONG?
I WONDER MYSELF ...

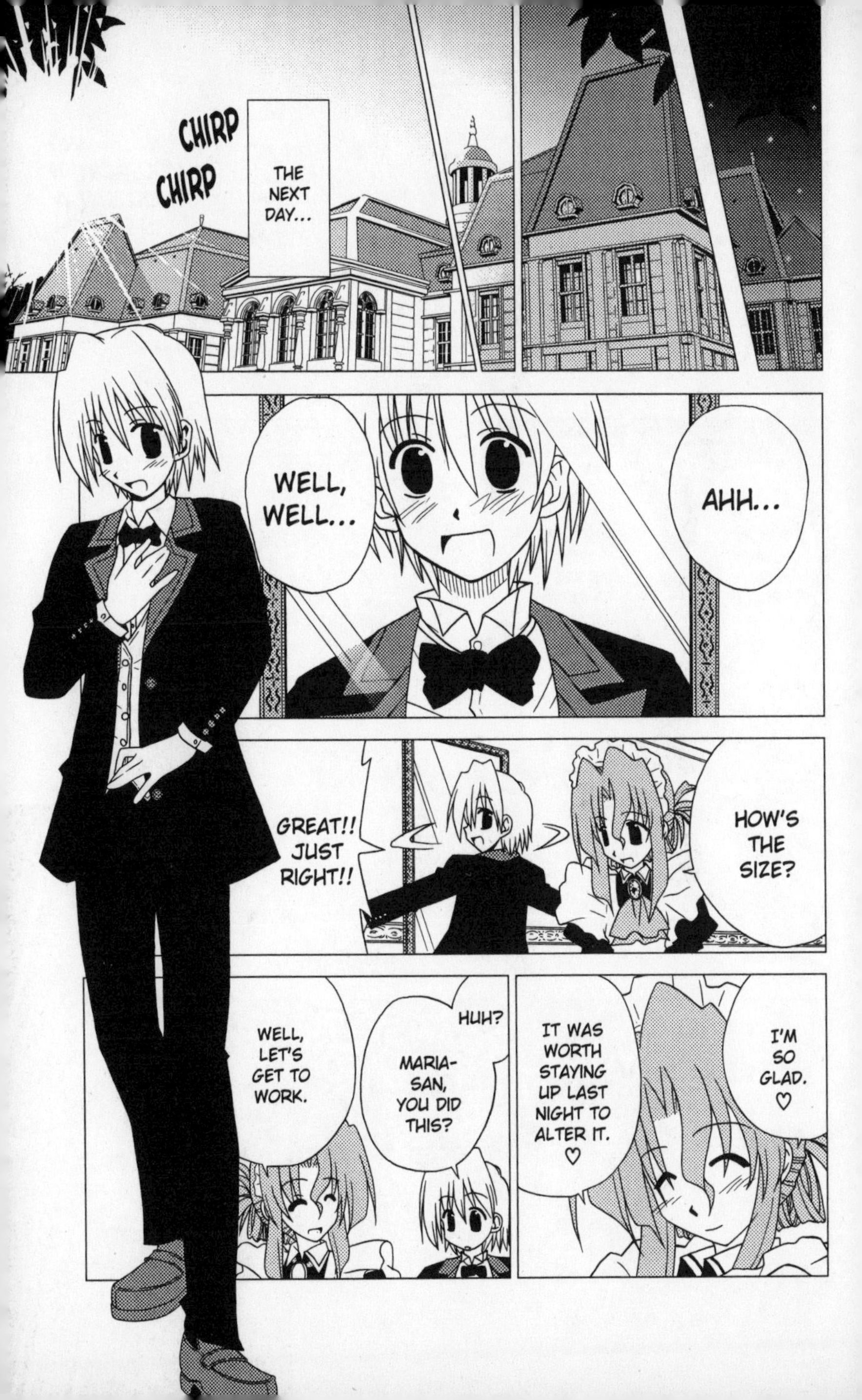
CHIRP
CHIRP
THE NEXT DAY...
AHH...
WELL, WELL...
HOW'S THE SIZE?
GREAT!! JUST RIGHT!!
I'M SO GLAD. ♡
IT WAS WORTH STAYING UP LAST NIGHT TO ALTER IT. ♡
HUH?
MARIA-SAN, YOU DID THIS?
WELL, LET'S GET TO WORK.

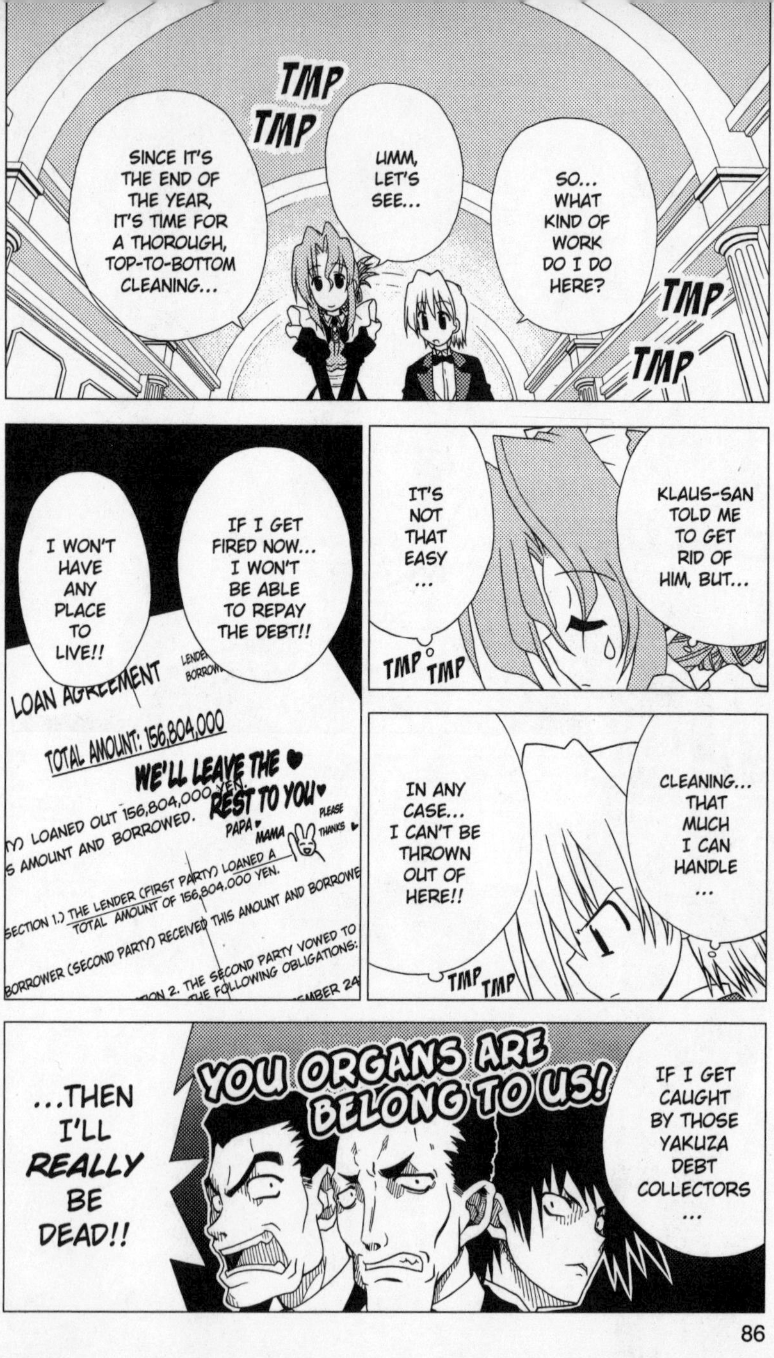
TMP TMP
SO... WHAT KIND OF WORK DO I DO HERE?
UMM, LET'S SEE...
SINCE IT'S THE END OF THE YEAR, IT'S TIME FOR A THOROUGH, TOP-TO-BOTTOM CLEANING...
TMP TMP
KLAUS-SAN TOLD ME TO GET RID OF HIM, BUT...
IT'S NOT THAT EASY ...
TMP TMP
CLEANING... THAT MUCH I CAN HANDLE ...
IN ANY CASE... I CAN'T BE THROWN OUT OF HERE!!
TMP TMP
IF I GET FIRED NOW... I WON'T BE ABLE TO REPAY THE DEBT!!
I WON'T HAVE ANY PLACE TO LIVE!!
LOAN AGREEMENT
TOTAL AMOUNT: 156,804,000
WE'LL LEAVE THE REST TO YOU
PAPA MAMA
PLEASE THANKS
SECTION 1.) THE LENDER (FIRST PARTY) LOANED A TOTAL AMOUNT OF 156,804.000 YEN.
IF I GET CAUGHT BY THOSE YAKUZA DEBT COLLECTORS ...
YOU ORGANS ARE BELONG TO US!
...THEN I'LL REALLY BE DEAD!!

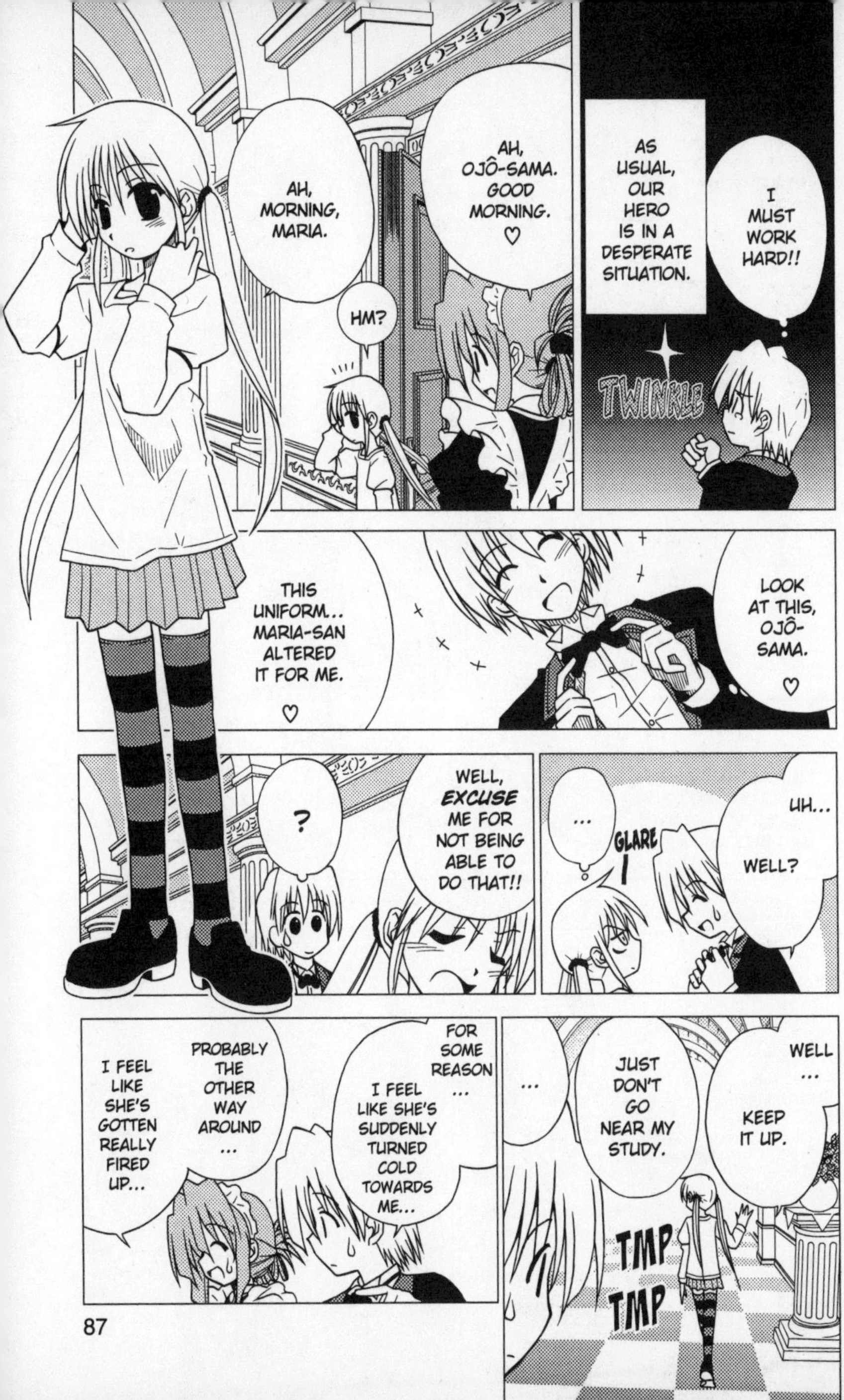
I MUST WORK HARD!!
AS USUAL, OUR HERO IS IN A DESPERATE SITUATION.
TWINKLE
AH, OJÔ-SAMA. GOOD MORNING. ♡
HM?
AH, MORNING, MARIA.
LOOK AT THIS, OJÔ-SAMA. ♡
THIS UNIFORM... MARIA-SAN ALTERED IT FOR ME. ♡
UH... WELL?
GLARE
...
WELL, *EXCUSE* ME FOR NOT BEING ABLE TO DO THAT!!
?
WELL ... KEEP IT UP.
JUST DON'T GO NEAR MY STUDY.
...
TMP TMP
FOR SOME REASON ... I FEEL LIKE SHE'S SUDDENLY TURNED COLD TOWARDS ME...
PROBABLY THE OTHER WAY AROUND ...
I FEEL LIKE SHE'S GOTTEN REALLY FIRED UP...

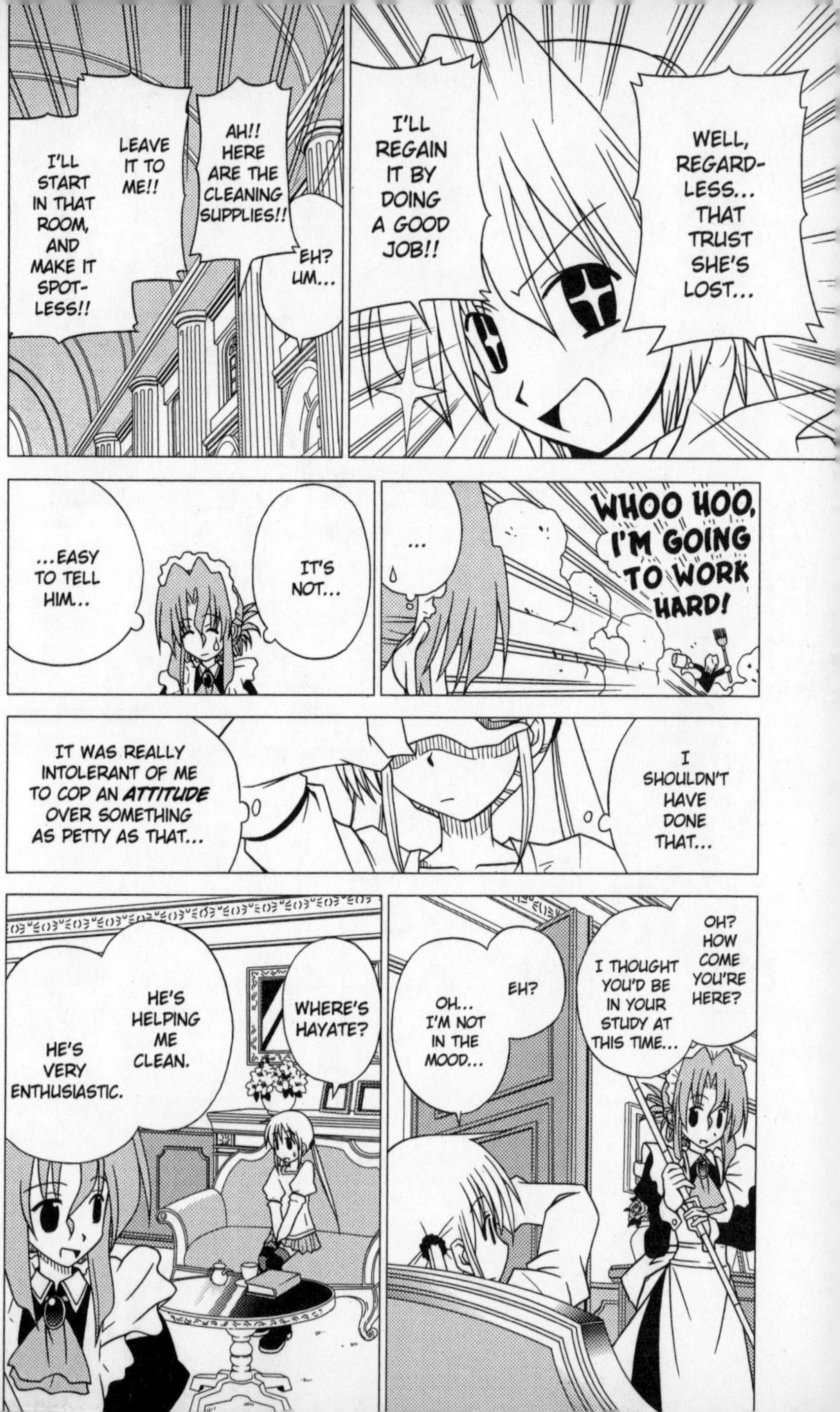
WELL, REGARDLESS... THAT TRUST SHE'S LOST...
I'LL REGAIN IT BY DOING A GOOD JOB!!
EH? UM...
AH!! HERE ARE THE CLEANING SUPPLIES!!
LEAVE IT TO ME!!
I'LL START IN THAT ROOM, AND MAKE IT SPOTLESS!!
WHOO HOO, I'M GOING TO WORK HARD!
...
IT'S NOT...
...EASY TO TELL HIM...
I SHOULDN'T HAVE DONE THAT...
IT WAS REALLY INTOLERANT OF ME TO COP AN ATTITUDE OVER SOMETHING AS PETTY AS THAT...
OH? HOW COME YOU'RE HERE?
I THOUGHT YOU'D BE IN YOUR STUDY AT THIS TIME...
EH?
OH... I'M NOT IN THE MOOD...
WHERE'S HAYATE?
HE'S HELPING ME CLEAN.
HE'S VERY ENTHUSIASTIC.

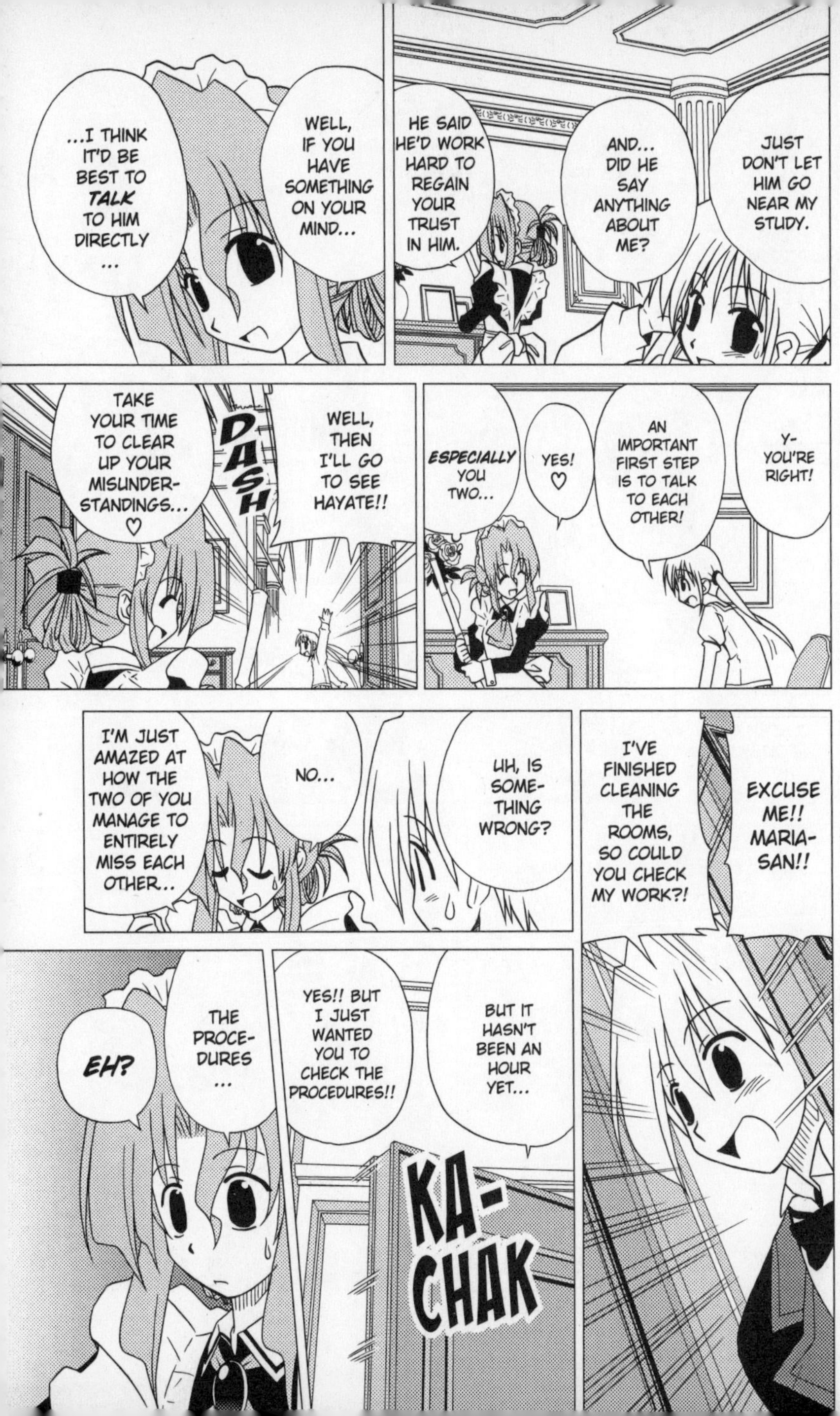
JUST DON'T LET HIM GO NEAR MY STUDY.
AND... DID HE SAY ANYTHING ABOUT ME?
HE SAID HE'D WORK HARD TO REGAIN YOUR TRUST IN HIM.
WELL, IF YOU HAVE SOMETHING ON YOUR MIND...
...I THINK IT'D BE BEST TO *TALK* TO HIM DIRECTLY...
Y-YOU'RE RIGHT!
AN IMPORTANT FIRST STEP IS TO TALK TO EACH OTHER!
YES! ♡
ESPECIALLY YOU TWO...
WELL, THEN I'LL GO TO SEE HAYATE!!
DASH
TAKE YOUR TIME TO CLEAR UP YOUR MISUNDERSTANDINGS... ♡
EXCUSE ME!! MARIA-SAN!!
I'VE FINISHED CLEANING THE ROOMS, SO COULD YOU CHECK MY WORK?!
UH, IS SOMETHING WRONG?
NO...
I'M JUST AMAZED AT HOW THE TWO OF YOU MANAGE TO ENTIRELY MISS EACH OTHER...
BUT IT HASN'T BEEN AN HOUR YET...
KA-CHAK
YES!! BUT I JUST WANTED YOU TO CHECK THE PROCEDURES!!
THE PROCEDURES...
EH?

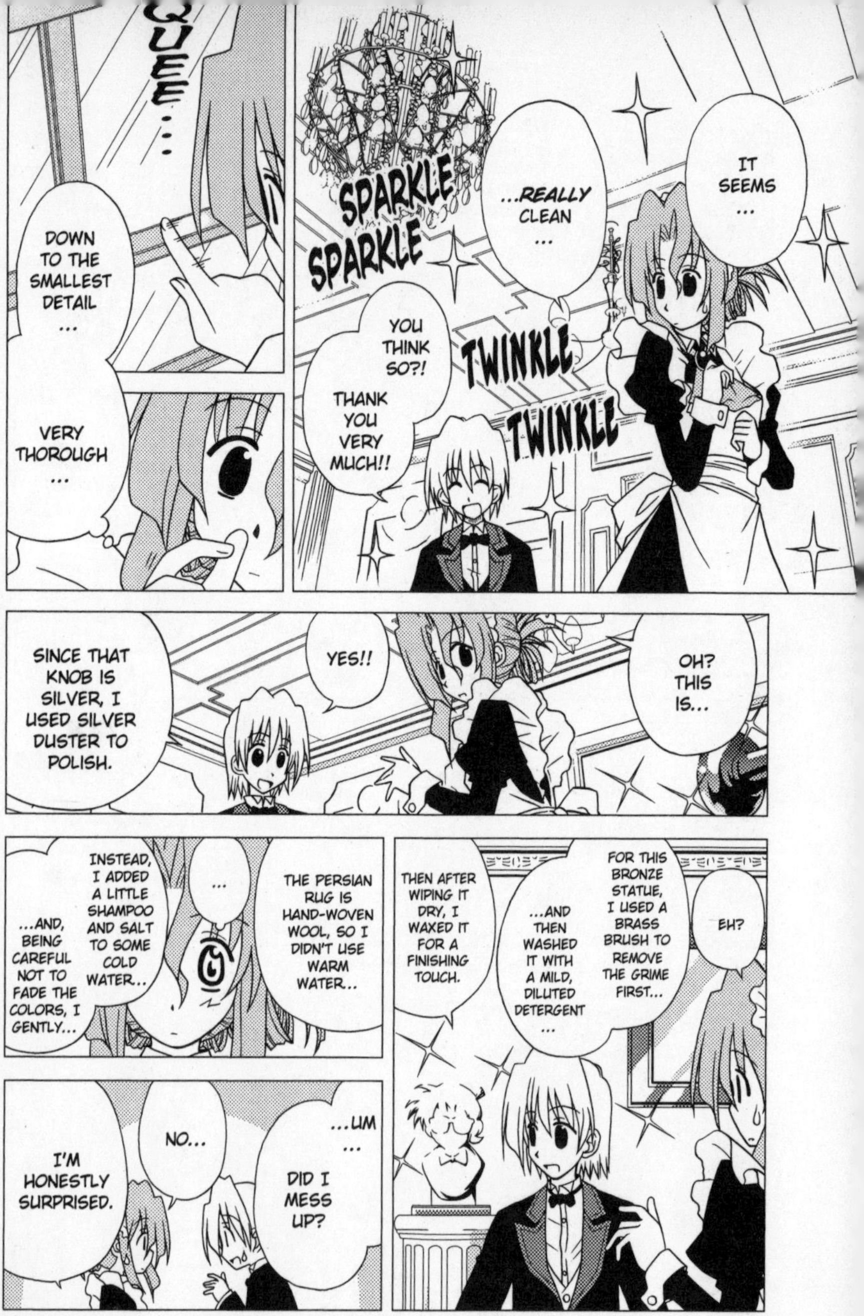
IT SEEMS...
...REALLY CLEAN...
SPARKLE SPARKLE
TWINKLE TWINKLE
YOU THINK SO?! THANK YOU VERY MUCH!!
QUEE...
DOWN TO THE SMALLEST DETAIL...
VERY THOROUGH...
OH? THIS IS...
YES!!
SINCE THAT KNOB IS SILVER, I USED SILVER DUSTER TO POLISH.
EH?
FOR THIS BRONZE STATUE, I USED A BRASS BRUSH TO REMOVE THE GRIME FIRST...
...AND THEN WASHED IT WITH A MILD, DILUTED DETERGENT...
THEN AFTER WIPING IT DRY, I WAXED IT FOR A FINISHING TOUCH.
THE PERSIAN RUG IS HAND-WOVEN WOOL, SO I DIDN'T USE WARM WATER...
...
INSTEAD, I ADDED A LITTLE SHAMPOO AND SALT TO SOME COLD WATER...
...AND, BEING CAREFUL NOT TO FADE THE COLORS, I GENTLY...
...UM... DID I MESS UP?
NO...
I'M HONESTLY SURPRISED.

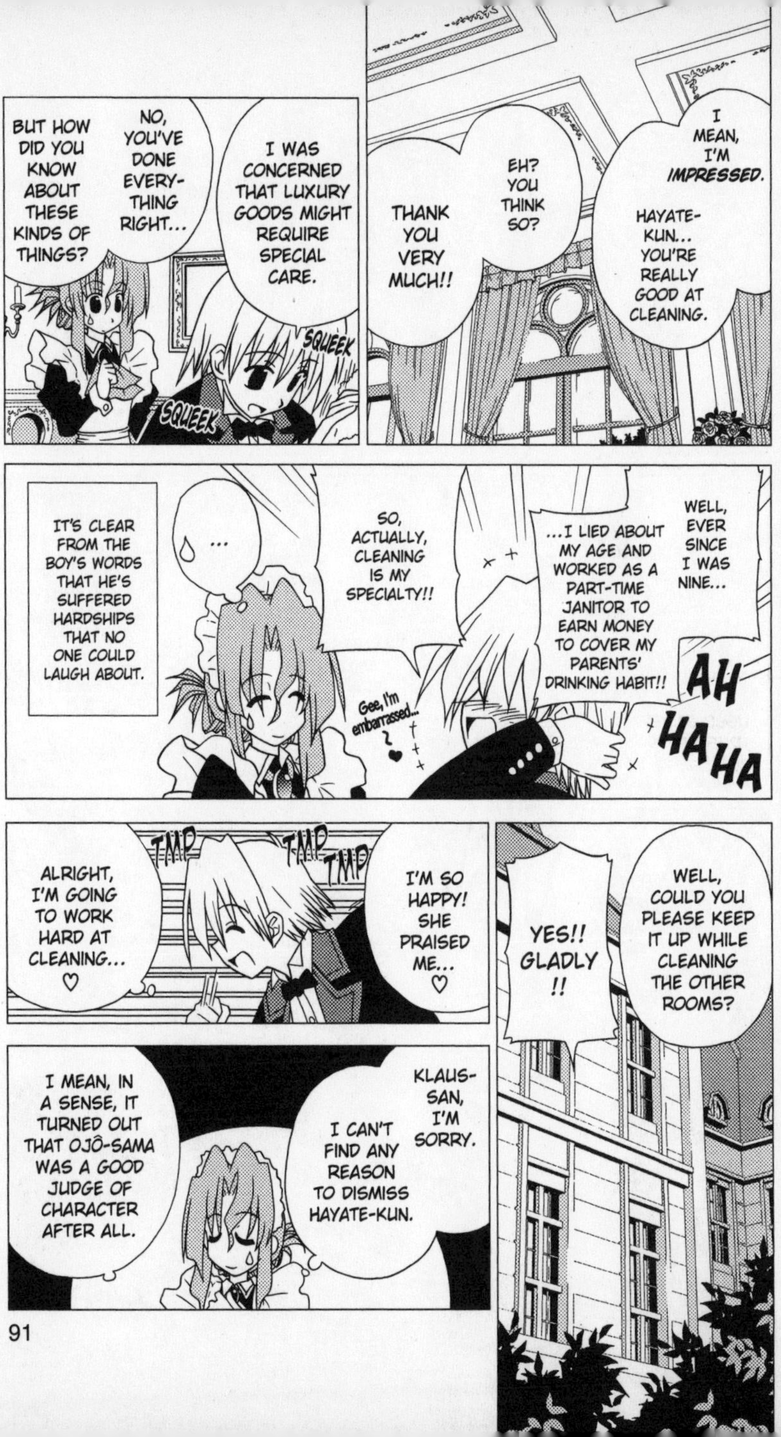
I MEAN, I'M *IMPRESSED*.
HAYATE-KUN... YOU'RE REALLY GOOD AT CLEANING.
EH? YOU THINK SO?
THANK YOU VERY MUCH!!
I WAS CONCERNED THAT LUXURY GOODS MIGHT REQUIRE SPECIAL CARE.
SQUEEK
SQUEEK
NO, YOU'VE DONE EVERY-THING RIGHT...
BUT HOW DID YOU KNOW ABOUT THESE KINDS OF THINGS?
WELL, EVER SINCE I WAS NINE...
...I LIED ABOUT MY AGE AND WORKED AS A PART-TIME JANITOR TO EARN MONEY TO COVER MY PARENTS' DRINKING HABIT!!
AH HAHAHA
SO, ACTUALLY, CLEANING IS MY SPECIALTY!!
Gee, I'm embarrassed...
...
IT'S CLEAR FROM THE BOY'S WORDS THAT HE'S SUFFERED HARDSHIPS THAT NO ONE COULD LAUGH ABOUT.
WELL, COULD YOU PLEASE KEEP IT UP WHILE CLEANING THE OTHER ROOMS?
YES!! GLADLY!!
I'M SO HAPPY! SHE PRAISED ME... ♡
TMP TMP TMP
ALRIGHT, I'M GOING TO WORK HARD AT CLEANING... ♡
KLAUS-SAN, I'M SORRY.
I CAN'T FIND ANY REASON TO DISMISS HAYATE-KUN.
I MEAN, IN A SENSE, IT TURNED OUT THAT OJÔ-SAMA WAS A GOOD JUDGE OF CHARACTER AFTER ALL.

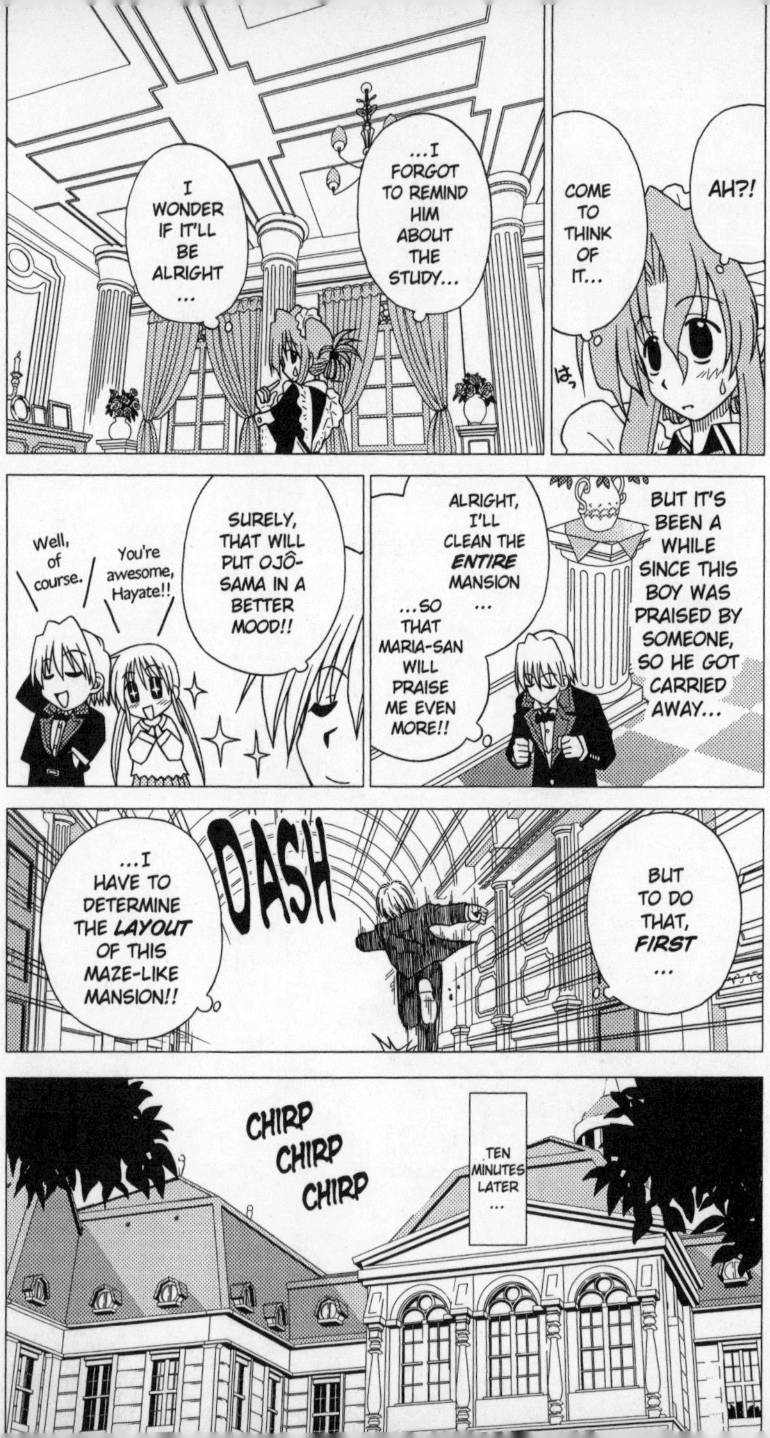
AH?!
COME TO THINK OF IT...
はっ
...I FORGOT TO REMIND HIM ABOUT THE STUDY...
I WONDER IF IT'LL BE ALRIGHT ...
BUT IT'S BEEN A WHILE SINCE THIS BOY WAS PRAISED BY SOMEONE, SO HE GOT CARRIED AWAY...
ALRIGHT, I'LL CLEAN THE *ENTIRE* MANSION ...
...SO THAT MARIA-SAN WILL PRAISE ME EVEN MORE!!
SURELY, THAT WILL PUT OJÔ-SAMA IN A BETTER MOOD!!
You're awesome, Hayate!!
Well, of course.
BUT TO DO THAT, *FIRST* ...
DASH
...I HAVE TO DETERMINE THE *LAYOUT* OF THIS MAZE-LIKE MANSION!!
TEN MINUTES LATER ...
CHIRP
CHIRP
CHIRP

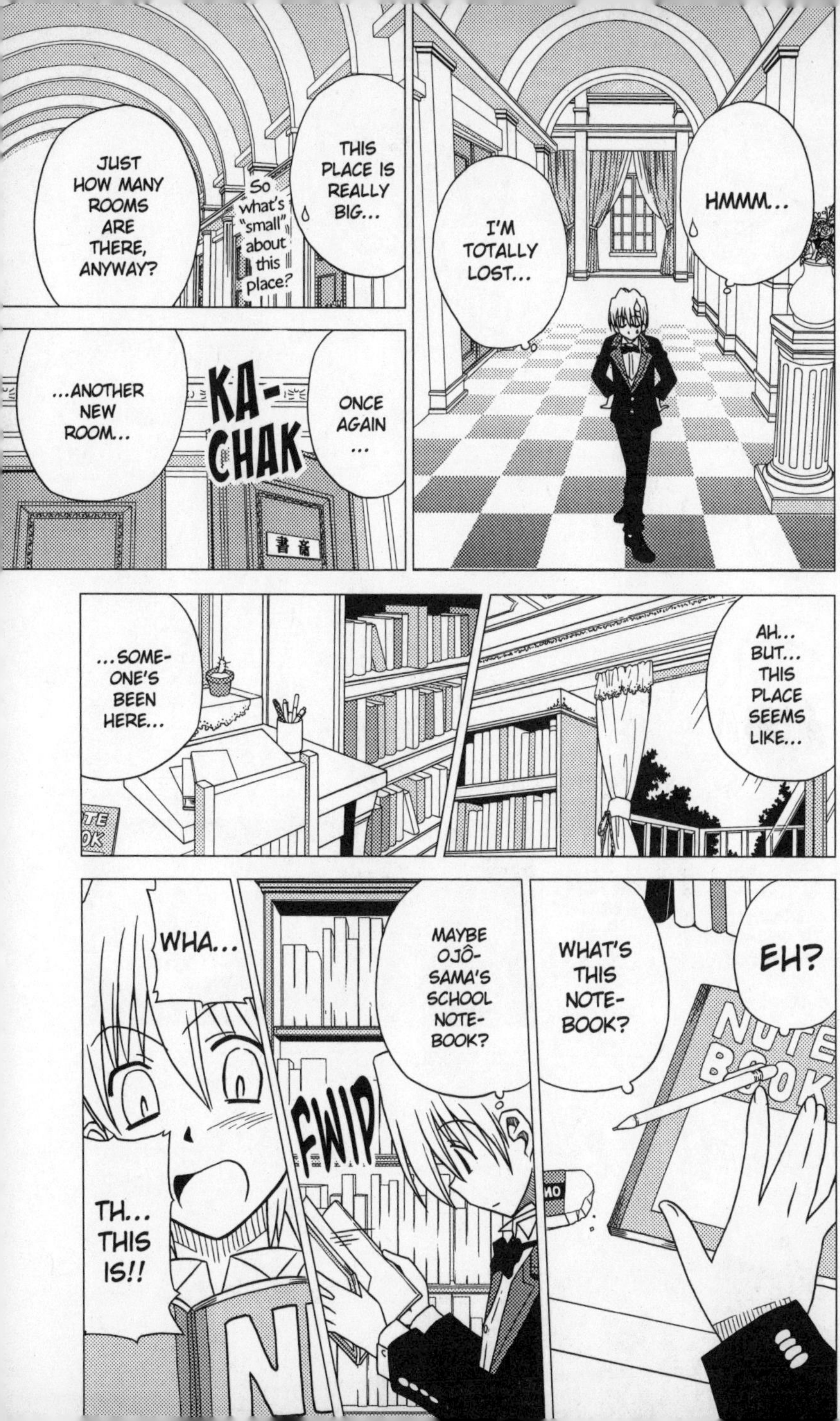
HMMM...
I'M TOTALLY LOST...
THIS PLACE IS REALLY BIG...
So what's "small" about this place?
JUST HOW MANY ROOMS ARE THERE, ANYWAY?
ONCE AGAIN...
KA-CHAK
...ANOTHER NEW ROOM...
書斎
AH... BUT... THIS PLACE SEEMS LIKE...
...SOME-ONE'S BEEN HERE...
EH?
NOTE BOOK
WHAT'S THIS NOTE-BOOK?
MAYBE OJÔ-SAMA'S SCHOOL NOTE-BOOK?
FWIP
WHA...
TH... THIS IS!!

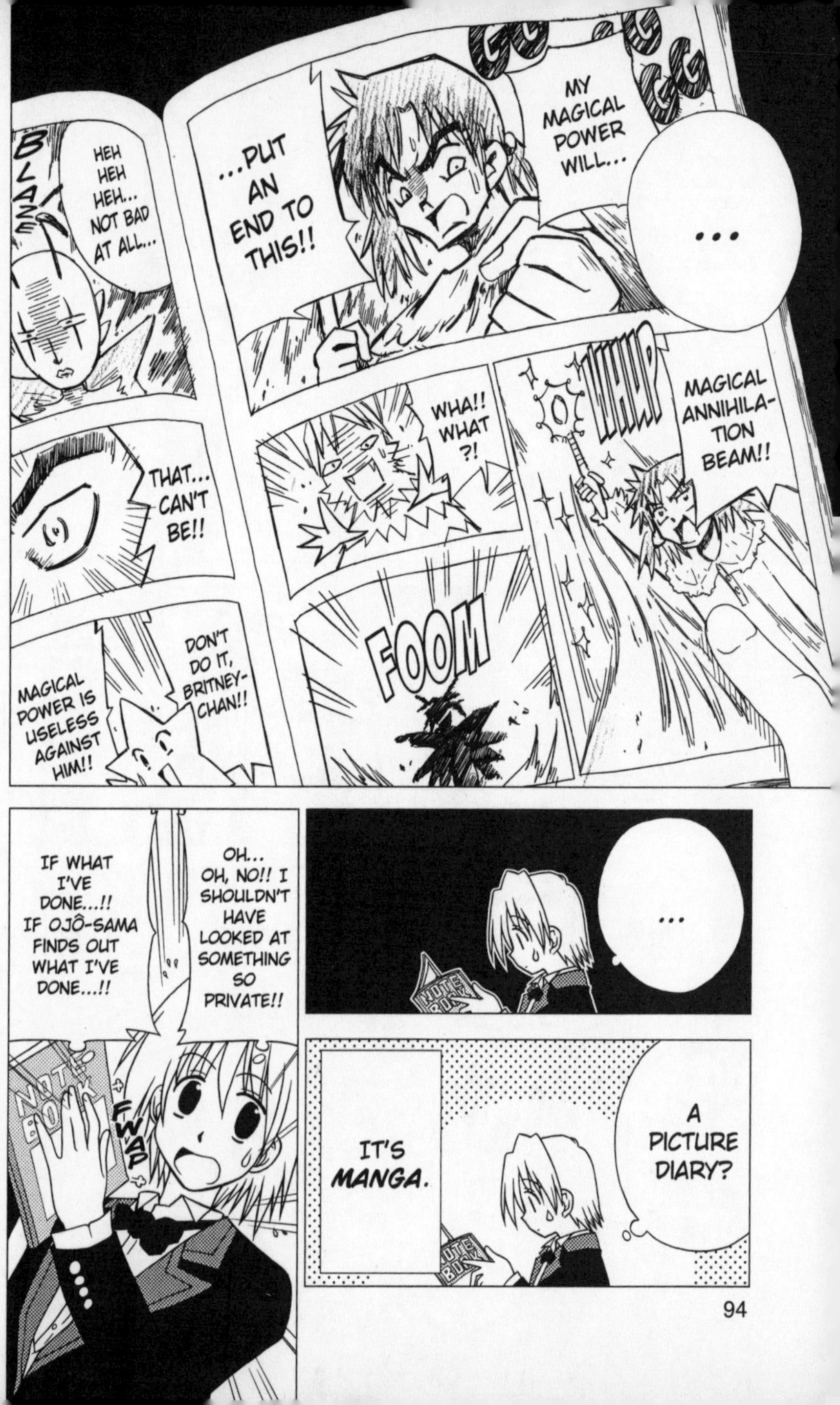
MY MAGICAL POWER WILL...
...
...PUT AN END TO THIS!!
MAGICAL ANNIHILATION BEAM!!
WHIP
WHA!! WHAT?!
FOOM
HEH HEH HEH... NOT BAD AT ALL...
BLAZE
THAT... CAN'T BE!!
DON'T DO IT, BRITNEY-CHAN!!
MAGICAL POWER IS USELESS AGAINST HIM!!
...
A PICTURE DIARY?
IT'S MANGA.
OH... OH, NO!! I SHOULDN'T HAVE LOOKED AT SOMETHING SO PRIVATE!!
IF WHAT I'VE DONE...!! IF OJÔ-SAMA FINDS OUT WHAT I'VE DONE...!!
FWAP

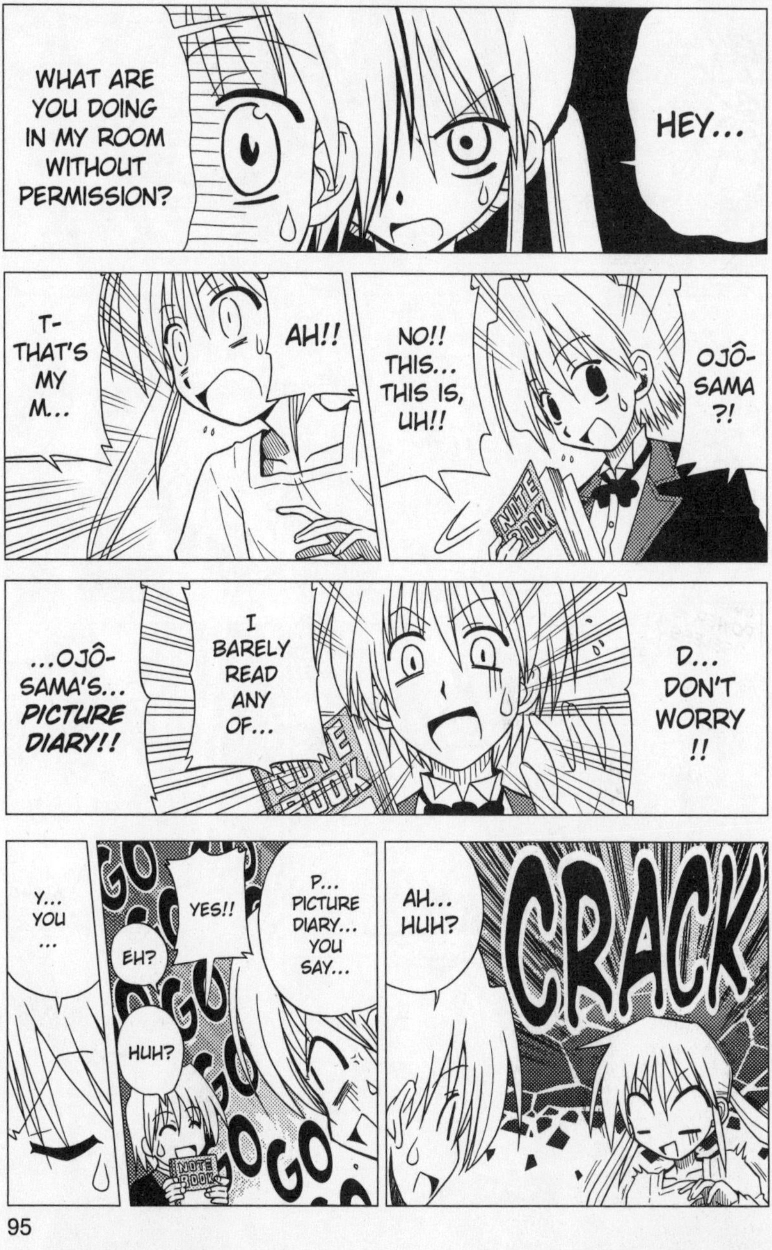
HEY...
WHAT ARE YOU DOING IN MY ROOM WITHOUT PERMISSION?
OJÔ-SAMA?!
NO!! THIS... THIS IS, UH!!
NOTE BOOK
AH!!
T-THAT'S MY M...
D... DON'T WORRY!!
I BARELY READ ANY OF...
...OJÔ-SAMA'S... PICTURE DIARY!!
NOTE BOOK
CRACK
AH... HUH?
P... PICTURE DIARY... YOU SAY...
YES!!
EH?
HUH?
GO GO GO GO
NOTE BOOK
Y... YOU...

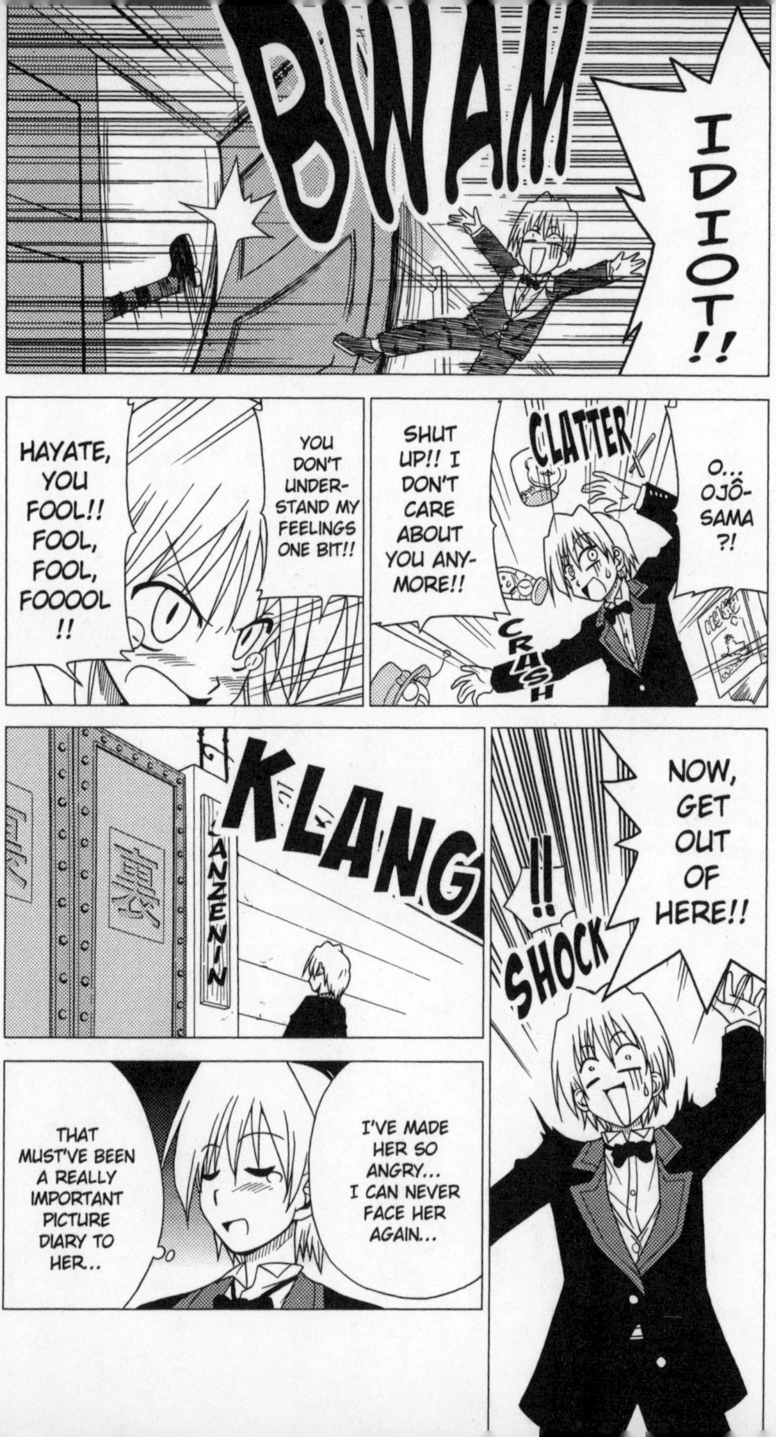
IDIOT!!
BWAM
O... OJÔ-SAMA?!
CLATTER
SHUT UP!! I DON'T CARE ABOUT YOU ANYMORE!!
CRASH
YOU DON'T UNDERSTAND MY FEELINGS ONE BIT!!
HAYATE, YOU FOOL!! FOOL, FOOL, FOOOOL!!
NOW, GET OUT OF HERE!!
!!
SHOCK
KLANG
ANZENIN
I'VE MADE HER SO ANGRY... I CAN NEVER FACE HER AGAIN...
THAT MUST'VE BEEN A REALLY IMPORTANT PICTURE DIARY TO HER...

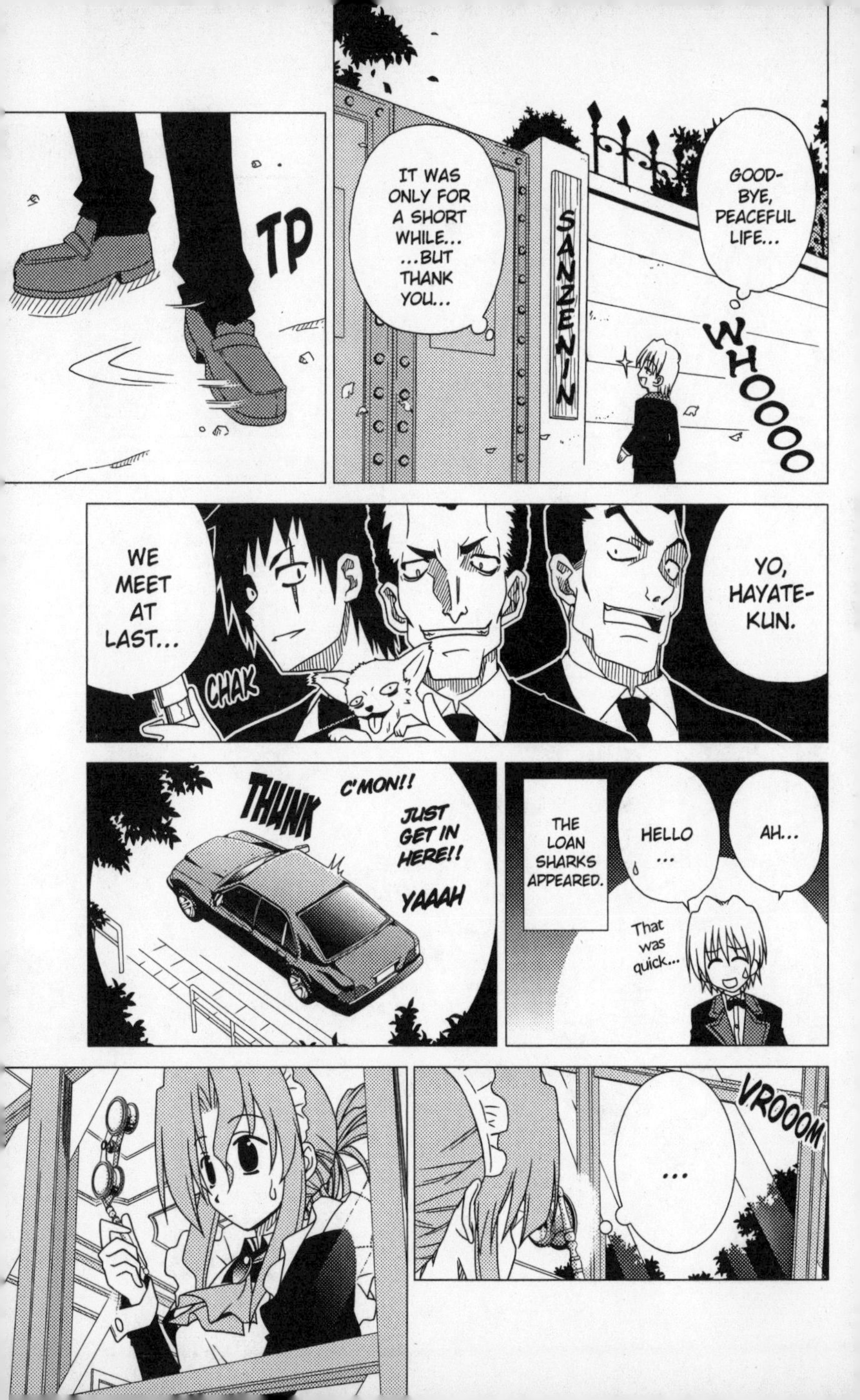
GOOD-BYE, PEACEFUL LIFE...
WHOOOOO
SANZENIN
IT WAS ONLY FOR A SHORT WHILE... ...BUT THANK YOU...
TP
YO, HAYATE-KUN.
WE MEET AT LAST...
CHAK
AH...
HELLO ...
THE LOAN SHARKS APPEARED.
That was quick...
C'MON!!
JUST GET IN HERE!!
YAAAH
THUNK
VROOOM
...

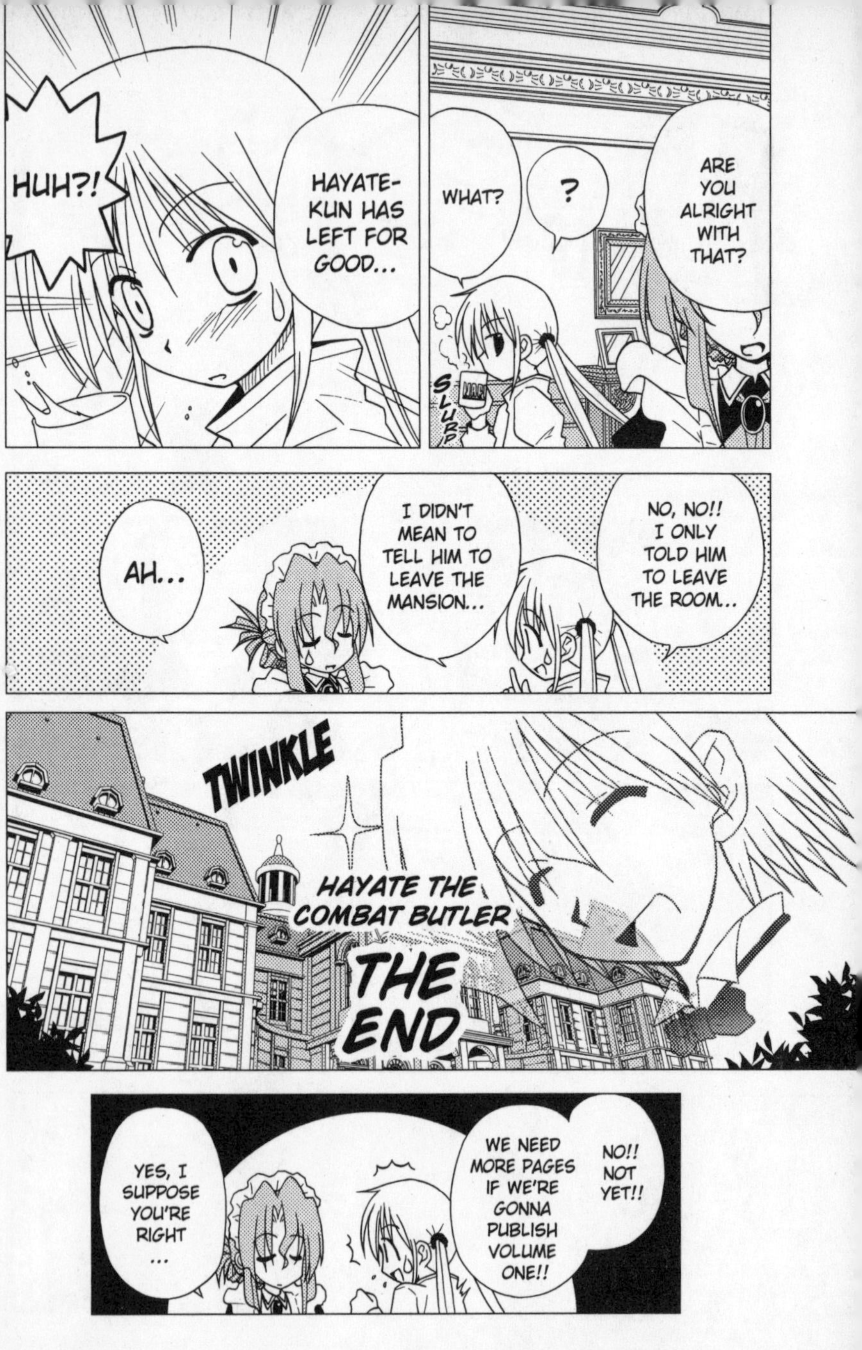
HAYATE-KUN HAS LEFT FOR GOOD...
HUH?!
ARE YOU ALRIGHT WITH THAT?
?
WHAT?
SLURP
NO, NO!! I ONLY TOLD HIM TO LEAVE THE ROOM...
I DIDN'T MEAN TO TELL HIM TO LEAVE THE MANSION...
AH...
TWINKLE
HAYATE THE COMBAT BUTLER
THE END
NO!! NOT YET!!
WE NEED MORE PAGES IF WE'RE GONNA PUBLISH VOLUME ONE!!
YES, I SUPPOSE YOU'RE RIGHT ...

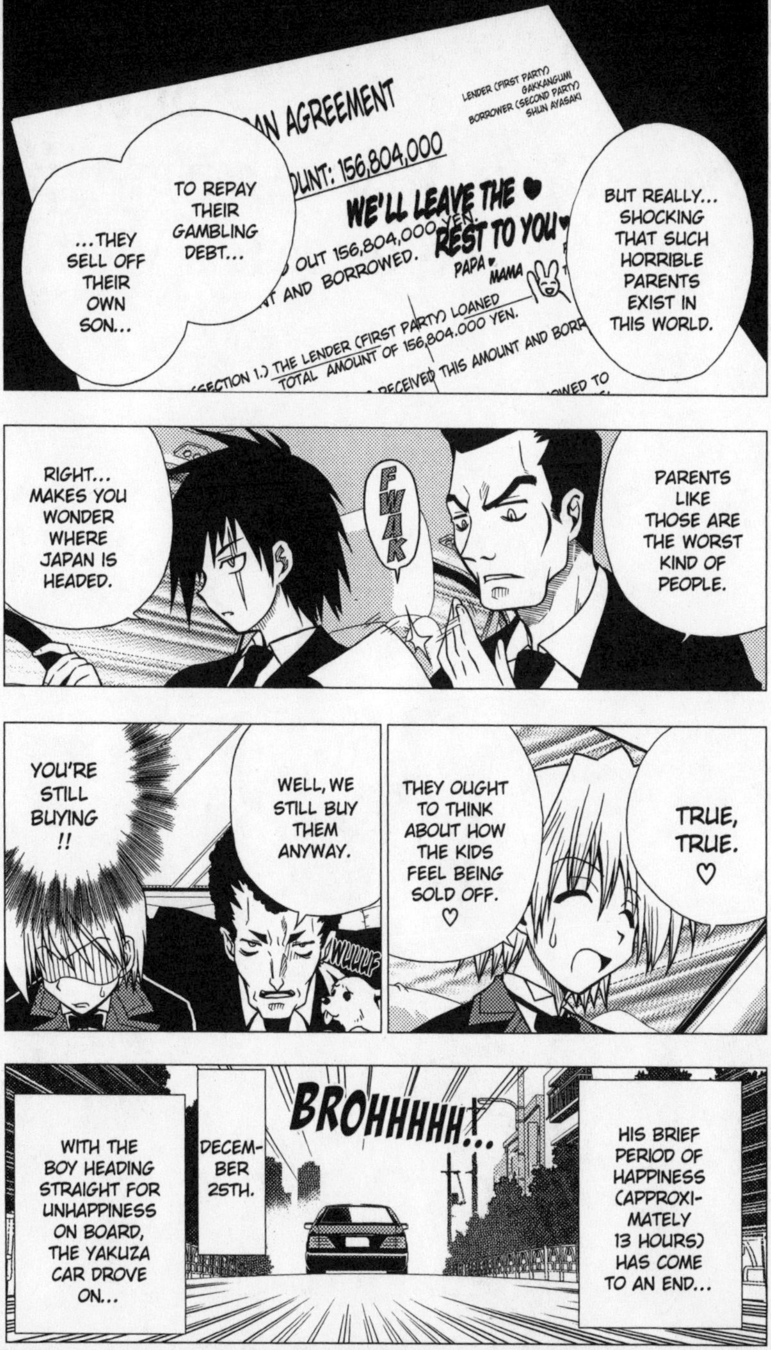

LENDER (FIRST PARTY) GAKKANGUMI
BORROWER (SECOND PARTY) SHUN AYASAKI
BUT REALLY... SHOCKING THAT SUCH HORRIBLE PARENTS EXIST IN THIS WORLD.
WE'LL LEAVE THE ♥ REST TO YOU ♥
PAPA ♥ MAMA
TO REPAY THEIR GAMBLING DEBT...
...THEY SELL OFF THEIR OWN SON...
PARENTS LIKE THOSE ARE THE WORST KIND OF PEOPLE.
FWAK
RIGHT... MAKES YOU WONDER WHERE JAPAN IS HEADED.
TRUE, TRUE. ♡
THEY OUGHT TO THINK ABOUT HOW THE KIDS FEEL BEING SOLD OFF. ♡
WELL, WE STILL BUY THEM ANYWAY.
YOU'RE STILL BUYING !!
HIS BRIEF PERIOD OF HAPPINESS (APPROXI-MATELY 13 HOURS) HAS COME TO AN END...
BROHHHHH!...
DECEM-BER 25TH.
WITH THE BOY HEADING STRAIGHT FOR UNHAPPINESS ON BOARD, THE YAKUZA CAR DROVE ON...

Episode 5: "Even If You Become a Newtype, Silence is a Virtue"

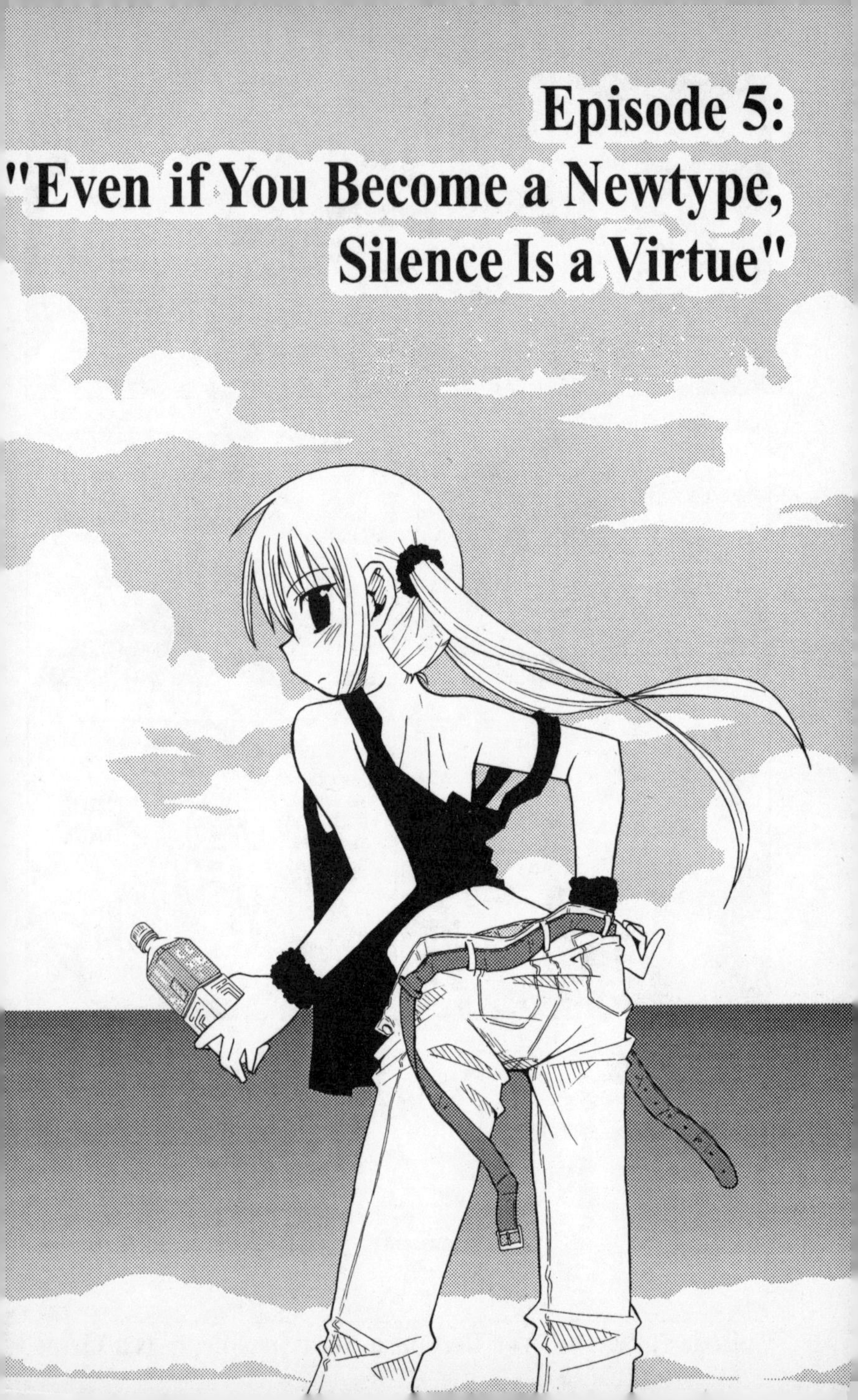
Episode 5:
"Even if You Become a Newtype,
Silence Is a Virtue"

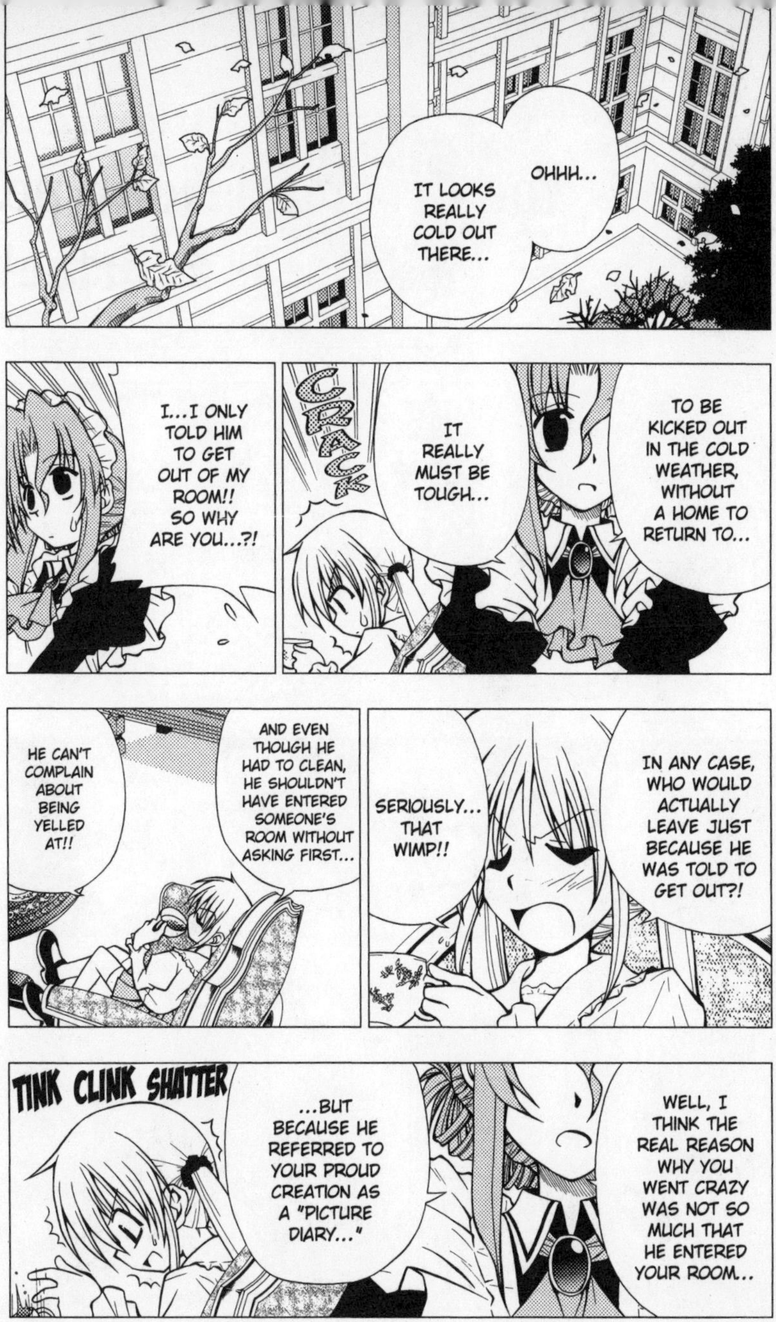
OHHH...
IT LOOKS REALLY COLD OUT THERE...
TO BE KICKED OUT IN THE COLD WEATHER, WITHOUT A HOME TO RETURN TO...
IT REALLY MUST BE TOUGH...
CRACK
I...I ONLY TOLD HIM TO GET OUT OF MY ROOM!! SO WHY ARE YOU...?!
IN ANY CASE, WHO WOULD ACTUALLY LEAVE JUST BECAUSE HE WAS TOLD TO GET OUT?!
SERIOUSLY... THAT WIMP!!
AND EVEN THOUGH HE HAD TO CLEAN, HE SHOULDN'T HAVE ENTERED SOMEONE'S ROOM WITHOUT ASKING FIRST...
HE CAN'T COMPLAIN ABOUT BEING YELLED AT!!
WELL, I THINK THE REAL REASON WHY YOU WENT CRAZY WAS NOT SO MUCH THAT HE ENTERED YOUR ROOM...
...BUT BECAUSE HE REFERRED TO YOUR PROUD CREATION AS A "PICTURE DIARY..."
TINK CLINK SHATTER

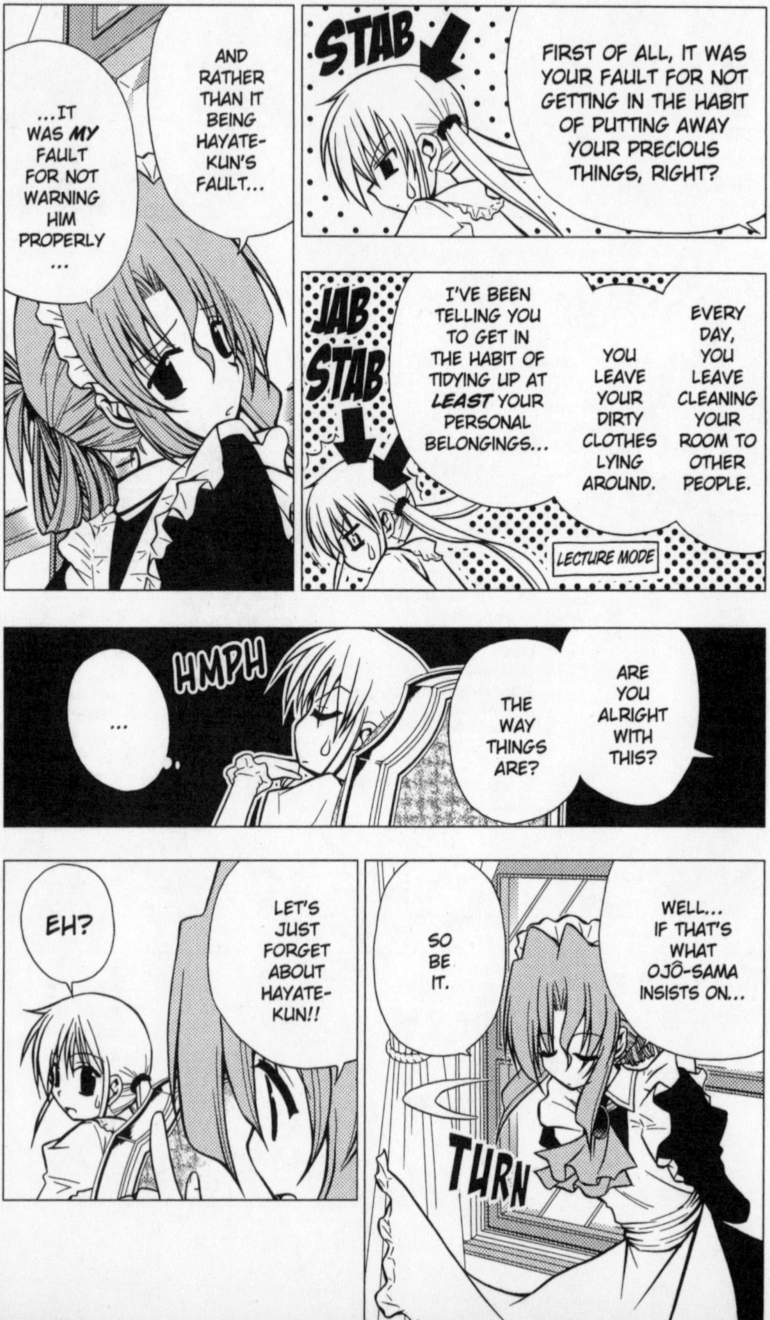
STAB
FIRST OF ALL, IT WAS YOUR FAULT FOR NOT GETTING IN THE HABIT OF PUTTING AWAY YOUR PRECIOUS THINGS, RIGHT?
JAB STAB
EVERY DAY, YOU LEAVE CLEANING YOUR ROOM TO OTHER PEOPLE.
YOU LEAVE YOUR DIRTY CLOTHES LYING AROUND.
I'VE BEEN TELLING YOU TO GET IN THE HABIT OF TIDYING UP AT *LEAST* YOUR PERSONAL BELONGINGS...
LECTURE MODE
AND RATHER THAN IT BEING HAYATE-KUN'S FAULT...
...IT WAS *MY* FAULT FOR NOT WARNING HIM PROPERLY...
ARE YOU ALRIGHT WITH THIS?
THE WAY THINGS ARE?
HMPH
...
WELL... IF THAT'S WHAT OJÔ-SAMA INSISTS ON...
SO BE IT.
TURN
LET'S JUST FORGET ABOUT HAYATE-KUN!!
EH?

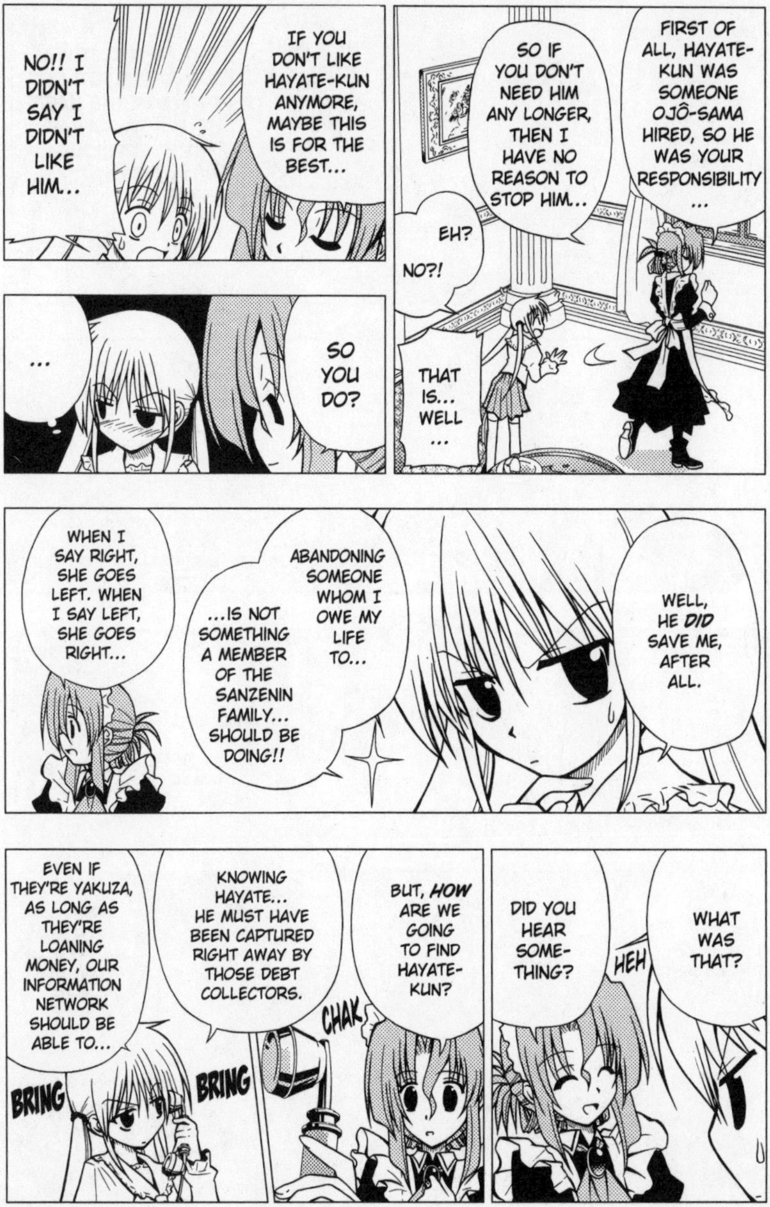
FIRST OF ALL, HAYATE-KUN WAS SOMEONE OJÔ-SAMA HIRED, SO HE WAS YOUR RESPONSIBILITY...
SO IF YOU DON'T NEED HIM ANY LONGER, THEN I HAVE NO REASON TO STOP HIM...
EH?
NO?!
THAT IS... WELL...
IF YOU DON'T LIKE HAYATE-KUN ANYMORE, MAYBE THIS IS FOR THE BEST...
NO!! I DIDN'T SAY I DIDN'T LIKE HIM...
SO YOU DO?
...
WELL, HE *DID* SAVE ME, AFTER ALL.
ABANDONING SOMEONE WHOM I OWE MY LIFE TO...
...IS NOT SOMETHING A MEMBER OF THE SANZENIN FAMILY... SHOULD BE DOING!!
WHEN I SAY RIGHT, SHE GOES LEFT. WHEN I SAY LEFT, SHE GOES RIGHT...
WHAT WAS THAT?
HEH
DID YOU HEAR SOME-THING?
BUT, *HOW* ARE WE GOING TO FIND HAYATE-KUN?
CHAK
KNOWING HAYATE... HE MUST HAVE BEEN CAPTURED RIGHT AWAY BY THOSE DEBT COLLECTORS.
EVEN IF THEY'RE YAKUZA, AS LONG AS THEY'RE LOANING MONEY, OUR INFORMATION NETWORK SHOULD BE ABLE TO...
BRING
BRING

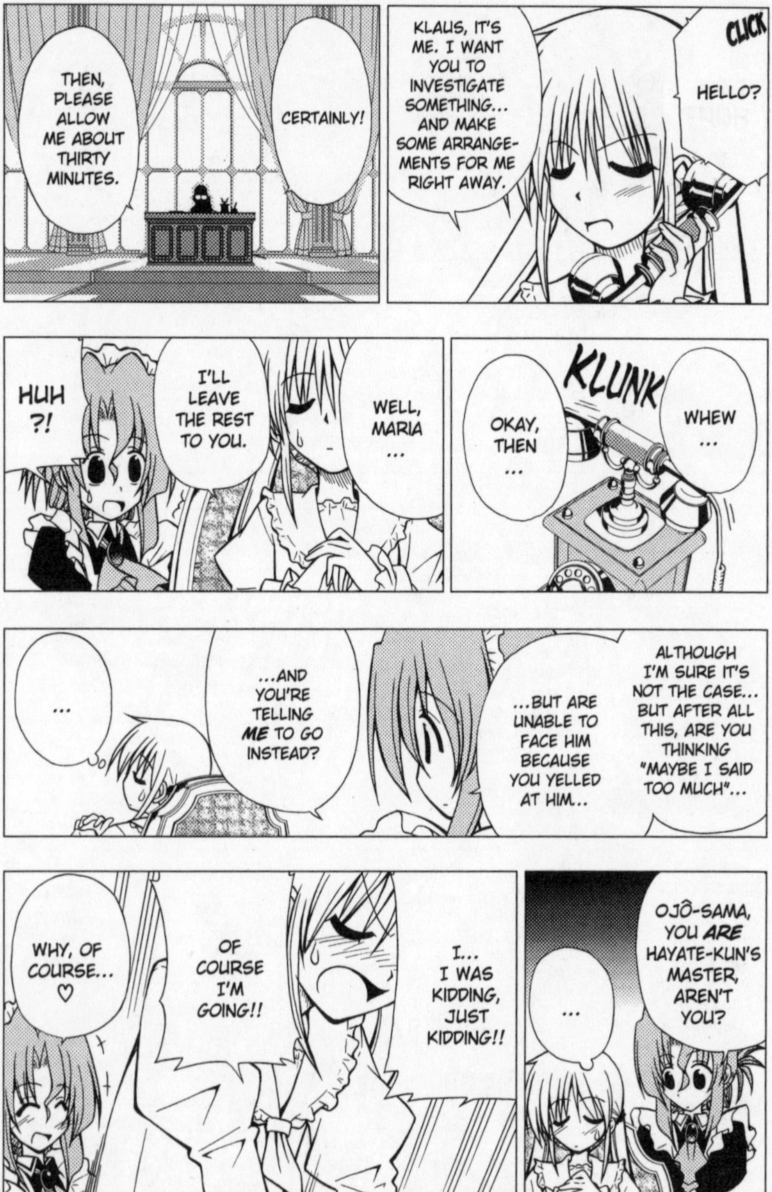
CLICK
HELLO?
KLAUS, IT'S ME. I WANT YOU TO INVESTIGATE SOMETHING... AND MAKE SOME ARRANGEMENTS FOR ME RIGHT AWAY.
CERTAINLY!
THEN, PLEASE ALLOW ME ABOUT THIRTY MINUTES.
KLUNK
WHEW ...
OKAY, THEN ...
WELL, MARIA ...
I'LL LEAVE THE REST TO YOU.
HUH ?!
ALTHOUGH I'M SURE IT'S NOT THE CASE... BUT AFTER ALL THIS, ARE YOU THINKING "MAYBE I SAID TOO MUCH"...
...BUT ARE UNABLE TO FACE HIM BECAUSE YOU YELLED AT HIM...
...AND YOU'RE TELLING *ME* TO GO INSTEAD?
...
OJÔ-SAMA, YOU *ARE* HAYATE-KUN'S MASTER, AREN'T YOU?
...
I... I WAS KIDDING, JUST KIDDING!!
OF COURSE I'M GOING!!
WHY, OF COURSE... ♡

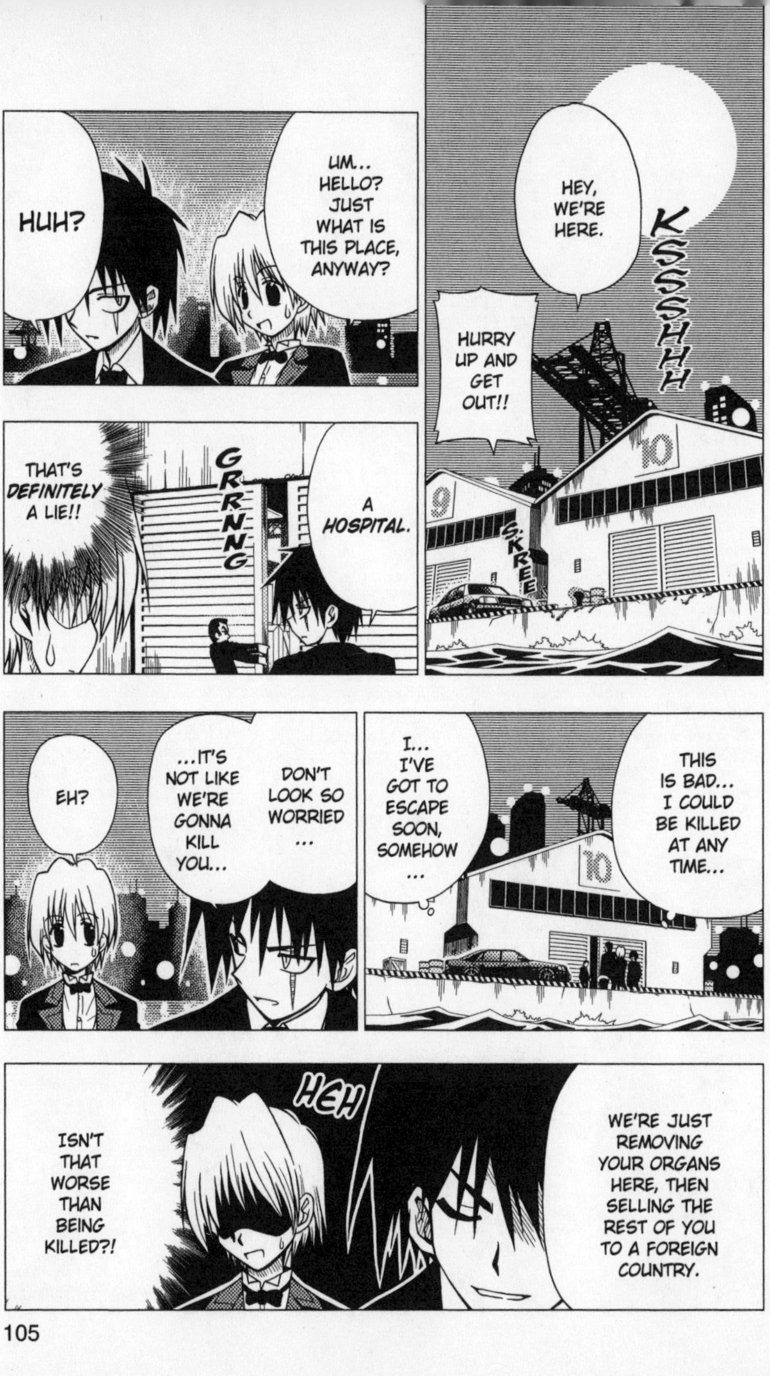
HEY, WE'RE HERE.
KSSSHHH
HURRY UP AND GET OUT!!
SKREE
UM... HELLO? JUST WHAT IS THIS PLACE, ANYWAY?
HUH?
A HOSPITAL.
GRRNNG
THAT'S DEFINITELY A LIE!!
THIS IS BAD... I COULD BE KILLED AT ANY TIME...
I... I'VE GOT TO ESCAPE SOON, SOMEHOW...
DON'T LOOK SO WORRIED...
...IT'S NOT LIKE WE'RE GONNA KILL YOU...
EH?
WE'RE JUST REMOVING YOUR ORGANS HERE, THEN SELLING THE REST OF YOU TO A FOREIGN COUNTRY.
HEH
ISN'T THAT WORSE THAN BEING KILLED?!

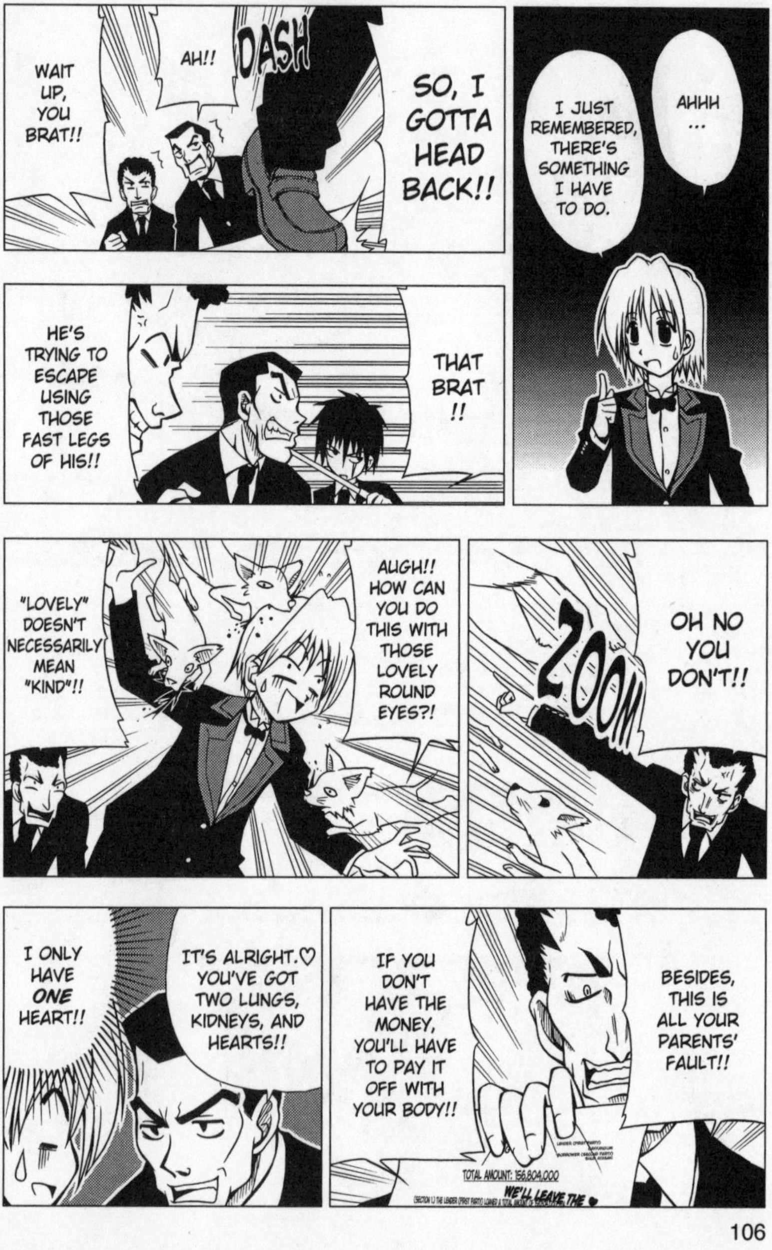
AHHH ...
I JUST REMEMBERED, THERE'S SOMETHING I HAVE TO DO.
SO, I GOTTA HEAD BACK!!
DASH
AH!!
WAIT UP, YOU BRAT!!
THAT BRAT !!
HE'S TRYING TO ESCAPE USING THOSE FAST LEGS OF HIS!!
OH NO YOU DON'T!!
ZOOM
AUGH!! HOW CAN YOU DO THIS WITH THOSE LOVELY ROUND EYES?!
"LOVELY" DOESN'T NECESSARILY MEAN "KIND"!!
BESIDES, THIS IS ALL YOUR PARENTS' FAULT!!
IF YOU DON'T HAVE THE MONEY, YOU'LL HAVE TO PAY IT OFF WITH YOUR BODY!!
TOTAL AMOUNT: 156,804,000
WE'LL LEAVE THE ♥
IT'S ALRIGHT.♡ YOU'VE GOT TWO LUNGS, KIDNEYS, AND HEARTS!!
I ONLY HAVE ONE HEART!!

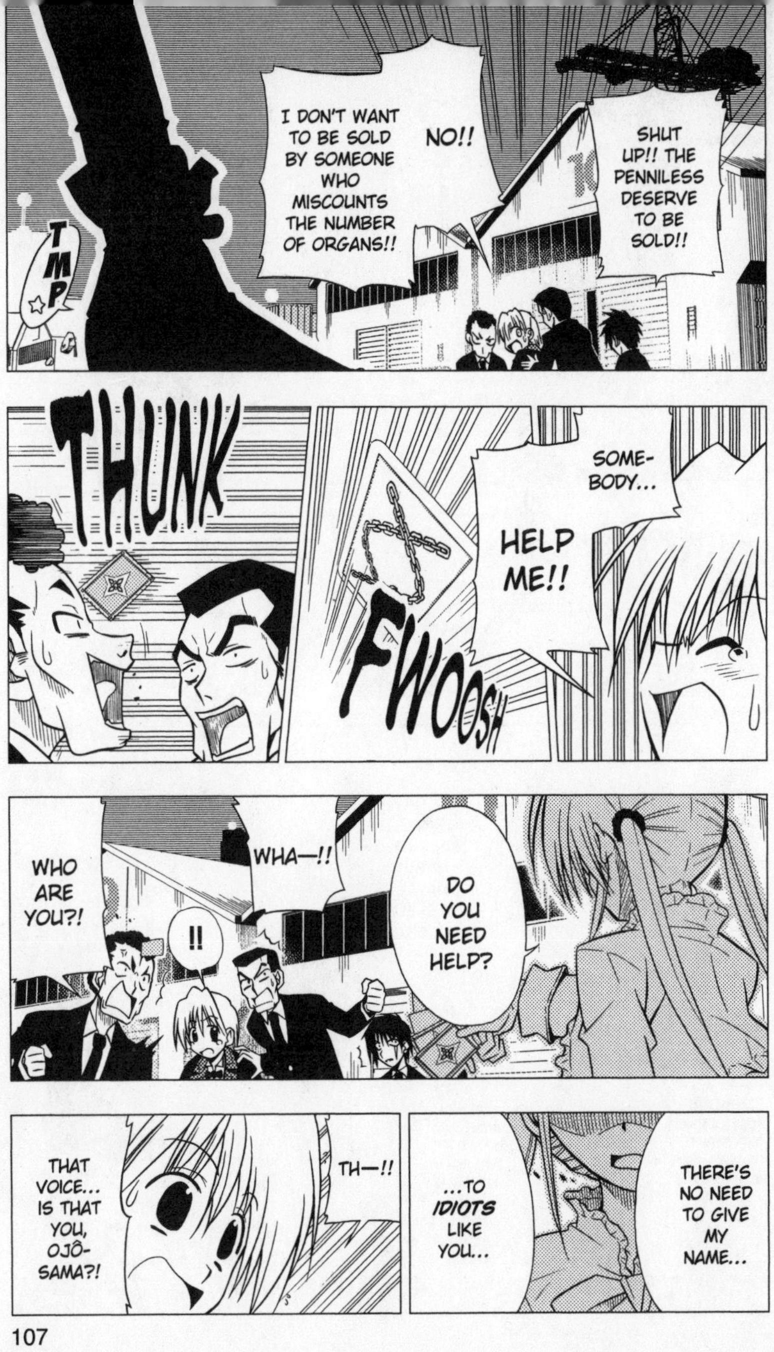
SHUT UP!! THE PENNILESS DESERVE TO BE SOLD!!
NO!!
I DON'T WANT TO BE SOLD BY SOMEONE WHO MISCOUNTS THE NUMBER OF ORGANS!!
TMP
SOME-BODY...
HELP ME!!
FWOOSH
THUNK
DO YOU NEED HELP?
WHA—!!
!!
WHO ARE YOU?!
THERE'S NO NEED TO GIVE MY NAME...
...TO *IDIOTS* LIKE YOU...
TH—!!
THAT VOICE... IS THAT YOU, OJÔ-SAMA?!

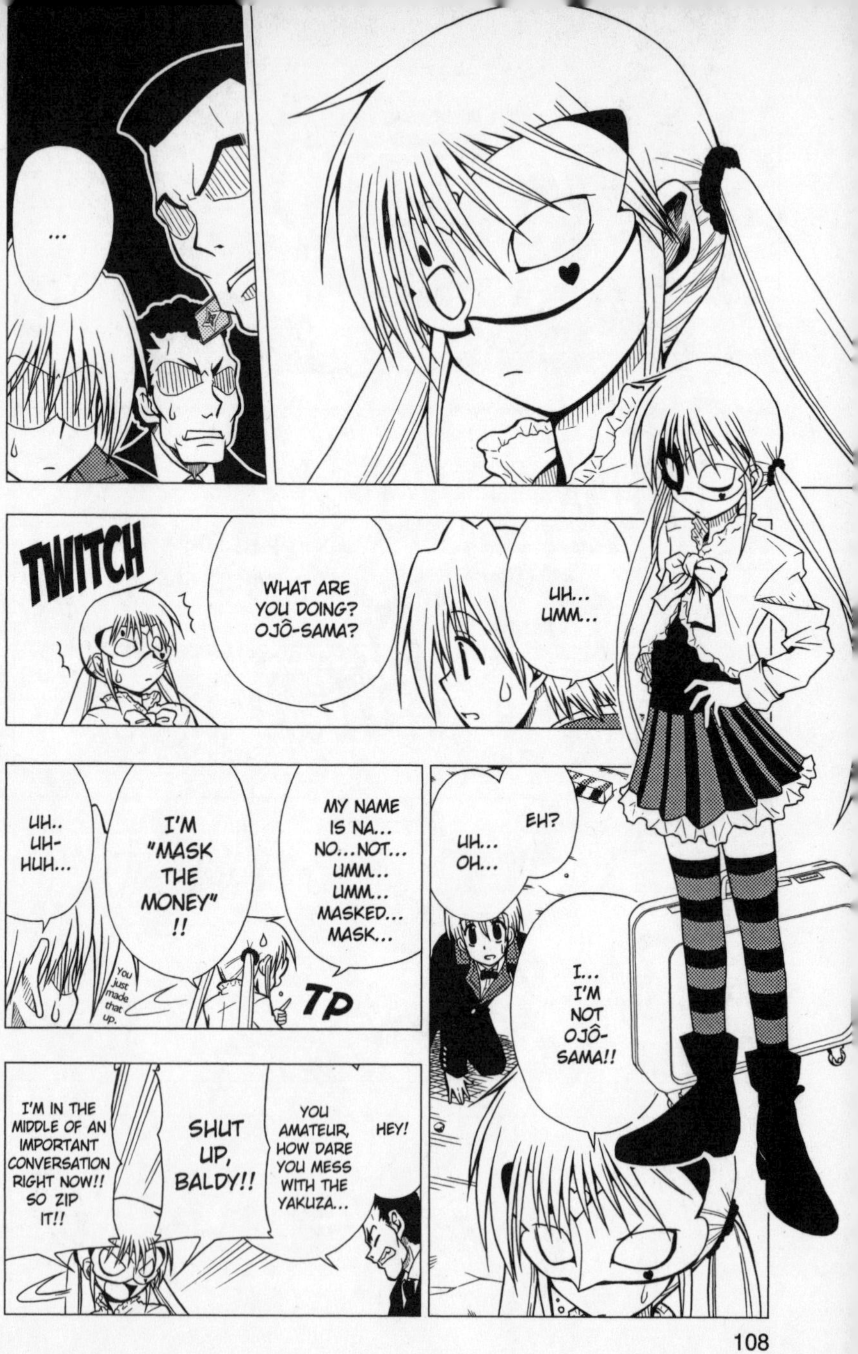
...
UH... UMM...
WHAT ARE YOU DOING? OJÔ-SAMA?
TWITCH
EH?
UH... OH...
I... I'M NOT OJÔ-SAMA!!
MY NAME IS NA... NO...NOT... UMM... UMM... MASKED... MASK...
TP
I'M "MASK THE MONEY" !!
UH.. UH-HUH...
You just made that up.
HEY!
YOU AMATEUR, HOW DARE YOU MESS WITH THE YAKUZA...
SHUT UP, BALDY!!
I'M IN THE MIDDLE OF AN IMPORTANT CONVERSATION RIGHT NOW!! SO ZIP IT!!

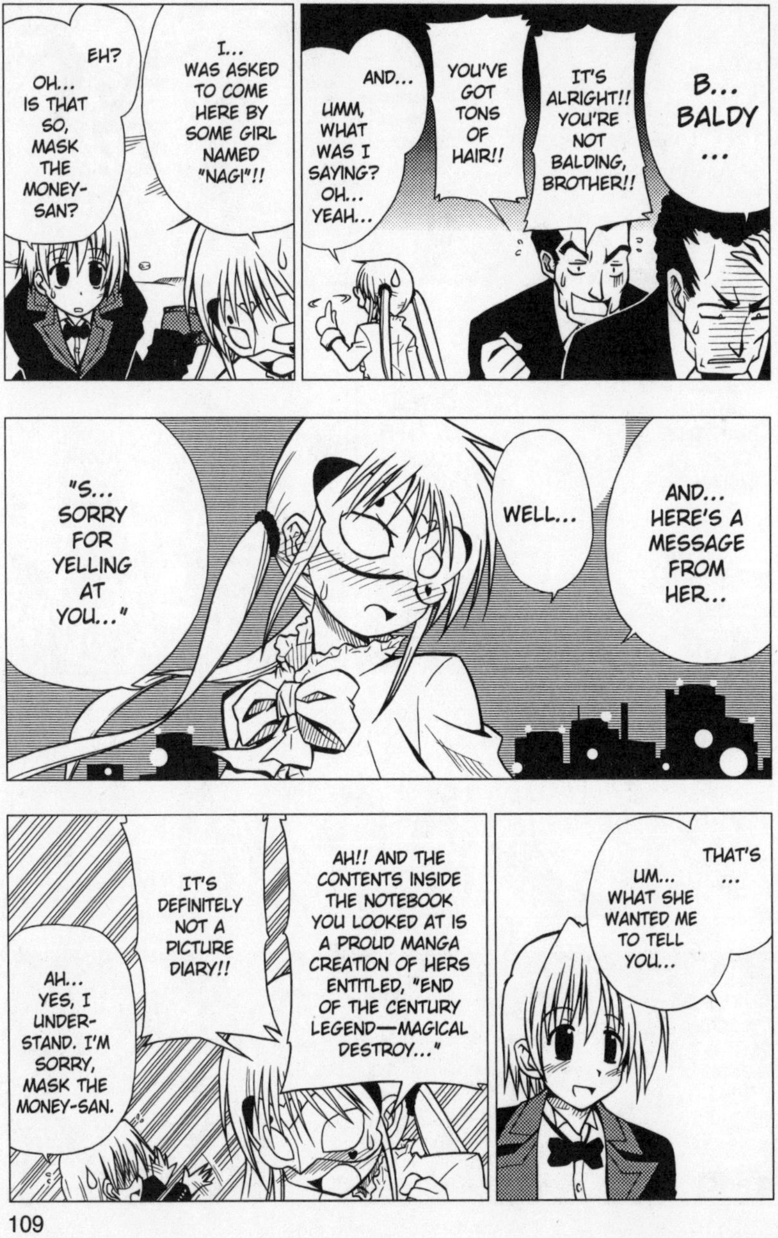
B... BALDY ...
IT'S ALRIGHT!! YOU'RE NOT BALDING, BROTHER!!
YOU'VE GOT TONS OF HAIR!!
AND...
UMM, WHAT WAS I SAYING? OH... YEAH...
I... WAS ASKED TO COME HERE BY SOME GIRL NAMED "NAGI"!!
EH?
OH... IS THAT SO, MASK THE MONEY-SAN?
AND... HERE'S A MESSAGE FROM HER..
WELL...
"S... SORRY FOR YELLING AT YOU..."
THAT'S ...
UM... WHAT SHE WANTED ME TO TELL YOU...
AH!! AND THE CONTENTS INSIDE THE NOTEBOOK YOU LOOKED AT IS A PROUD MANGA CREATION OF HERS ENTITLED, "END OF THE CENTURY LEGEND—MAGICAL DESTROY..."
IT'S DEFINITELY NOT A PICTURE DIARY!!
AH... YES, I UNDERSTAND. I'M SORRY, MASK THE MONEY-SAN.

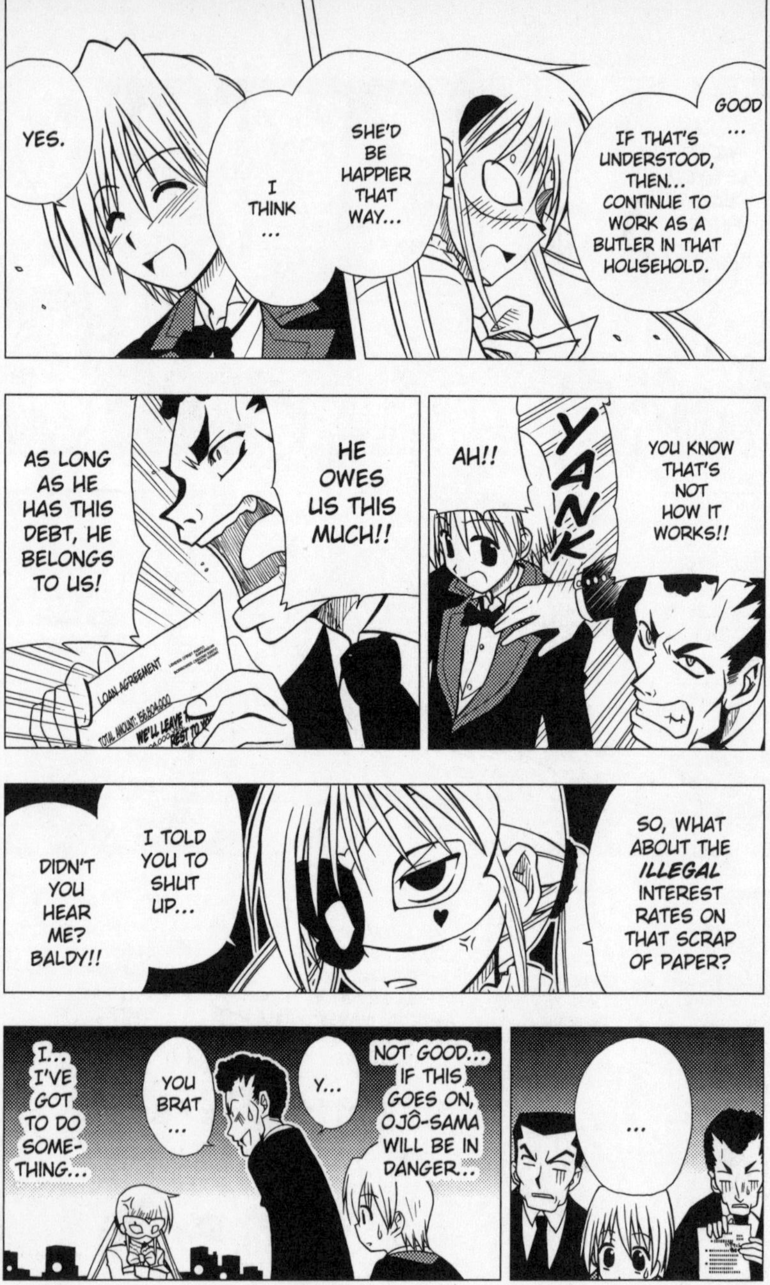
GOOD ...
IF THAT'S UNDERSTOOD, THEN... CONTINUE TO WORK AS A BUTLER IN THAT HOUSEHOLD.
I THINK ... SHE'D BE HAPPIER THAT WAY...
YES.
YOU KNOW THAT'S NOT HOW IT WORKS!!
YANK
AH!!
HE OWES US THIS MUCH!!
AS LONG AS HE HAS THIS DEBT, HE BELONGS TO US!
LOAN AGREEMENT
SO, WHAT ABOUT THE ILLEGAL INTEREST RATES ON THAT SCRAP OF PAPER?
I TOLD YOU TO SHUT UP...
DIDN'T YOU HEAR ME? BALDY!!
...
NOT GOOD... IF THIS GOES ON, OJÔ-SAMA WILL BE IN DANGER...
Y...
YOU BRAT ...
I... I'VE GOT TO DO SOMETHING...

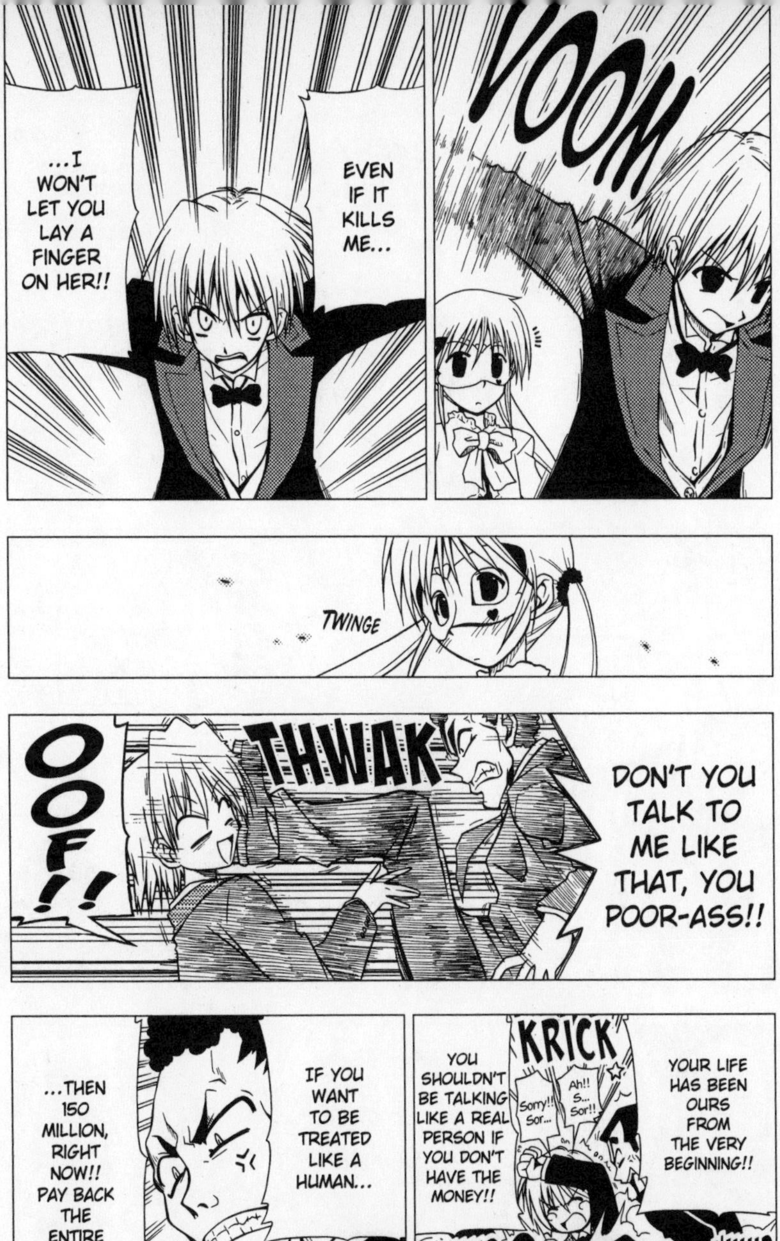
VOOM
EVEN IF IT KILLS ME...
...I WON'T LET YOU LAY A FINGER ON HER!!
TWINGE
DON'T YOU TALK TO ME LIKE THAT, YOU POOR-ASS!!
THWAK
OOF!!
YOUR LIFE HAS BEEN OURS FROM THE VERY BEGINNING!!
KRICK
Ah!! S... Sor!!
Sorry!! Sor...
YOU SHOULDN'T BE TALKING LIKE A REAL PERSON IF YOU DON'T HAVE THE MONEY!!
WHUD
WHUD
IF YOU WANT TO BE TREATED LIKE A HUMAN...
...THEN 150 MILLION, RIGHT NOW!! PAY BACK THE ENTIRE AMOUNT!!

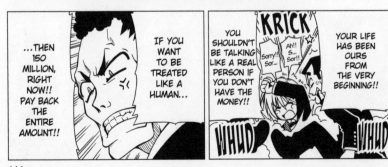

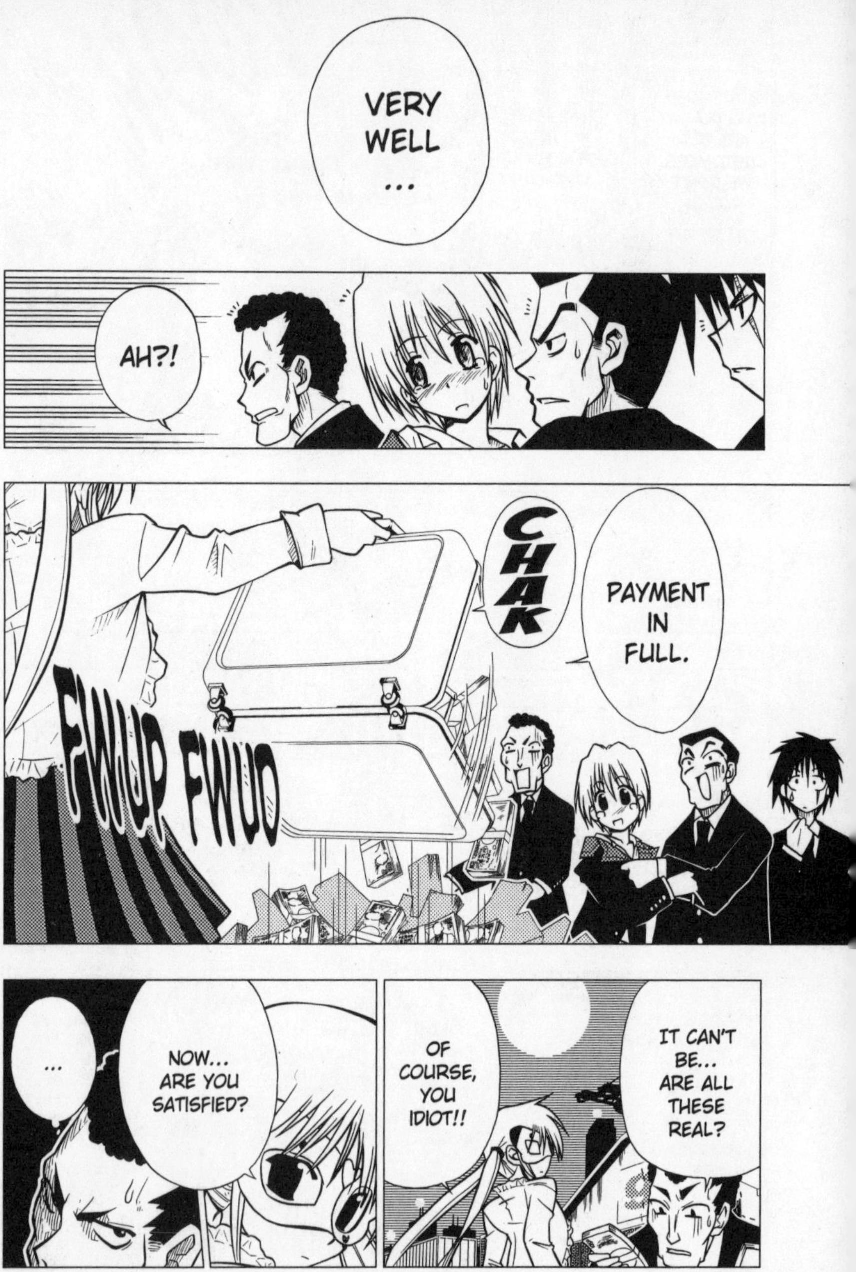
VERY WELL ...
AH?!
PAYMENT IN FULL.
CHAK
FWUUP FWUO
IT CAN'T BE... ARE ALL THESE REAL?
OF COURSE, YOU IDIOT!!
NOW... ARE YOU SATISFIED?
...

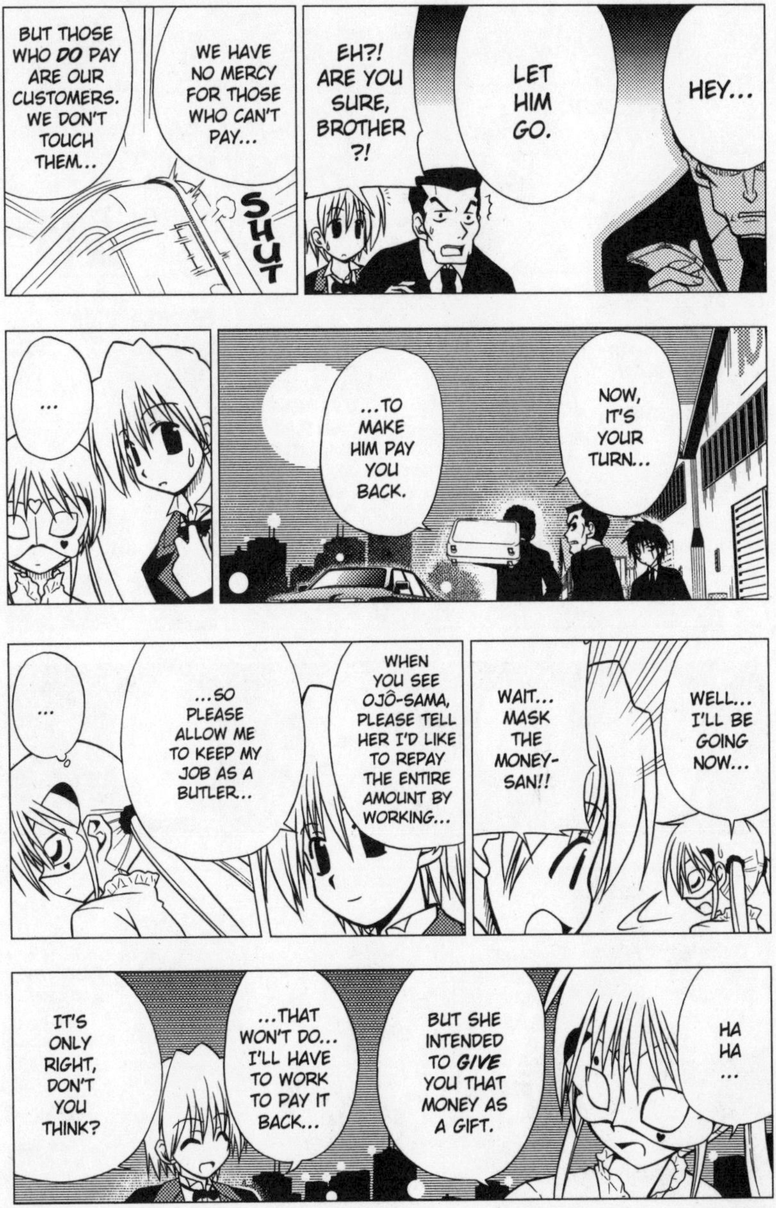
HEY...
LET HIM GO.
EH?! ARE YOU SURE, BROTHER?!
WE HAVE NO MERCY FOR THOSE WHO CAN'T PAY...
BUT THOSE WHO *DO* PAY ARE OUR CUSTOMERS. WE DON'T TOUCH THEM...
SHUT
NOW, IT'S YOUR TURN...
...TO MAKE HIM PAY YOU BACK.
...
WELL... I'LL BE GOING NOW...
WAIT... MASK THE MONEY-SAN!!
WHEN YOU SEE OJÔ-SAMA, PLEASE TELL HER I'D LIKE TO REPAY THE ENTIRE AMOUNT BY WORKING...
...SO PLEASE ALLOW ME TO KEEP MY JOB AS A BUTLER...
...
HA HA ...
BUT SHE INTENDED TO *GIVE* YOU THAT MONEY AS A GIFT.
...THAT WON'T DO... I'LL HAVE TO WORK TO PAY IT BACK...
IT'S ONLY RIGHT, DON'T YOU THINK?

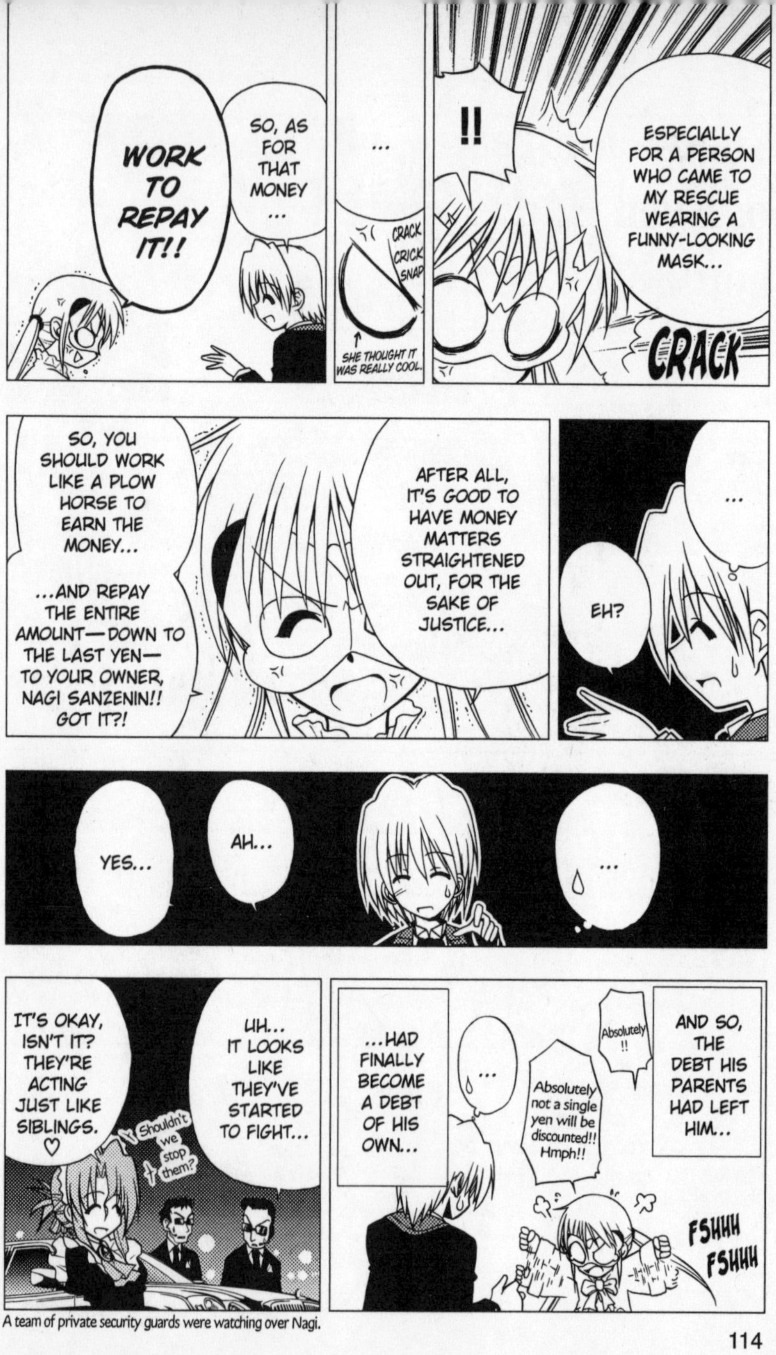
ESPECIALLY FOR A PERSON WHO CAME TO MY RESCUE WEARING A FUNNY-LOOKING MASK...
CRACK
!!
...
CRACK
CRICK
SNAP
SHE THOUGHT IT WAS REALLY COOL.
SO, AS FOR THAT MONEY...
WORK TO REPAY IT!!
...
EH?
AFTER ALL, IT'S GOOD TO HAVE MONEY MATTERS STRAIGHTENED OUT, FOR THE SAKE OF JUSTICE...
SO, YOU SHOULD WORK LIKE A PLOW HORSE TO EARN THE MONEY...
...AND REPAY THE ENTIRE AMOUNT—DOWN TO THE LAST YEN—TO YOUR OWNER, NAGI SANZENIN!! GOT IT?!
...
AH...
YES...
AND SO, THE DEBT HIS PARENTS HAD LEFT HIM...
Absolutely!!
Absolutely not a single yen will be discounted!! Hmph!!
...
...HAD FINALLY BECOME A DEBT OF HIS OWN...
FSHHH
FSHHH
UH... IT LOOKS LIKE THEY'VE STARTED TO FIGHT...
Shouldn't we stop them?
IT'S OKAY, ISN'T IT? THEY'RE ACTING JUST LIKE SIBLINGS. ♡

A team of private security guards were watching over Nagi.

Episode 6:
"Good Children Shouldn't Copy This!! No, Even Bad Children and Adults Shouldn't Copy This Either, Not Ever!"

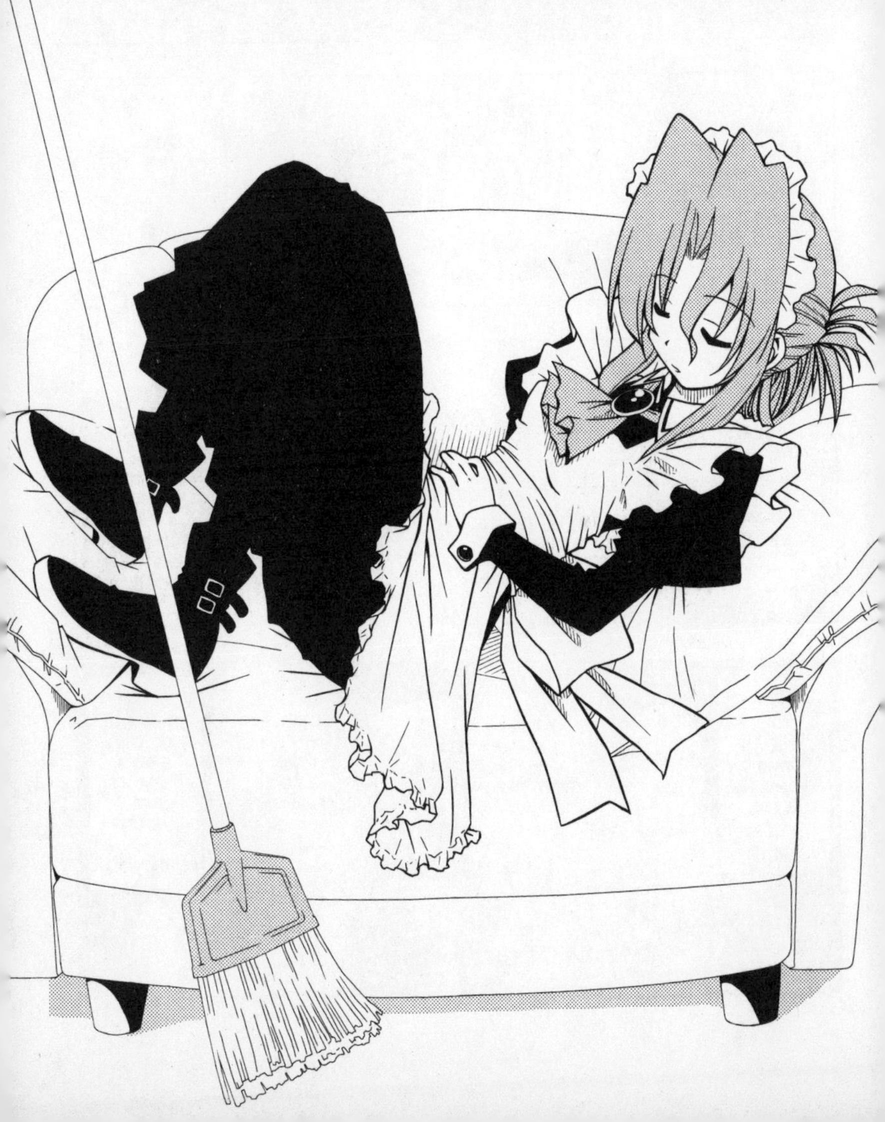

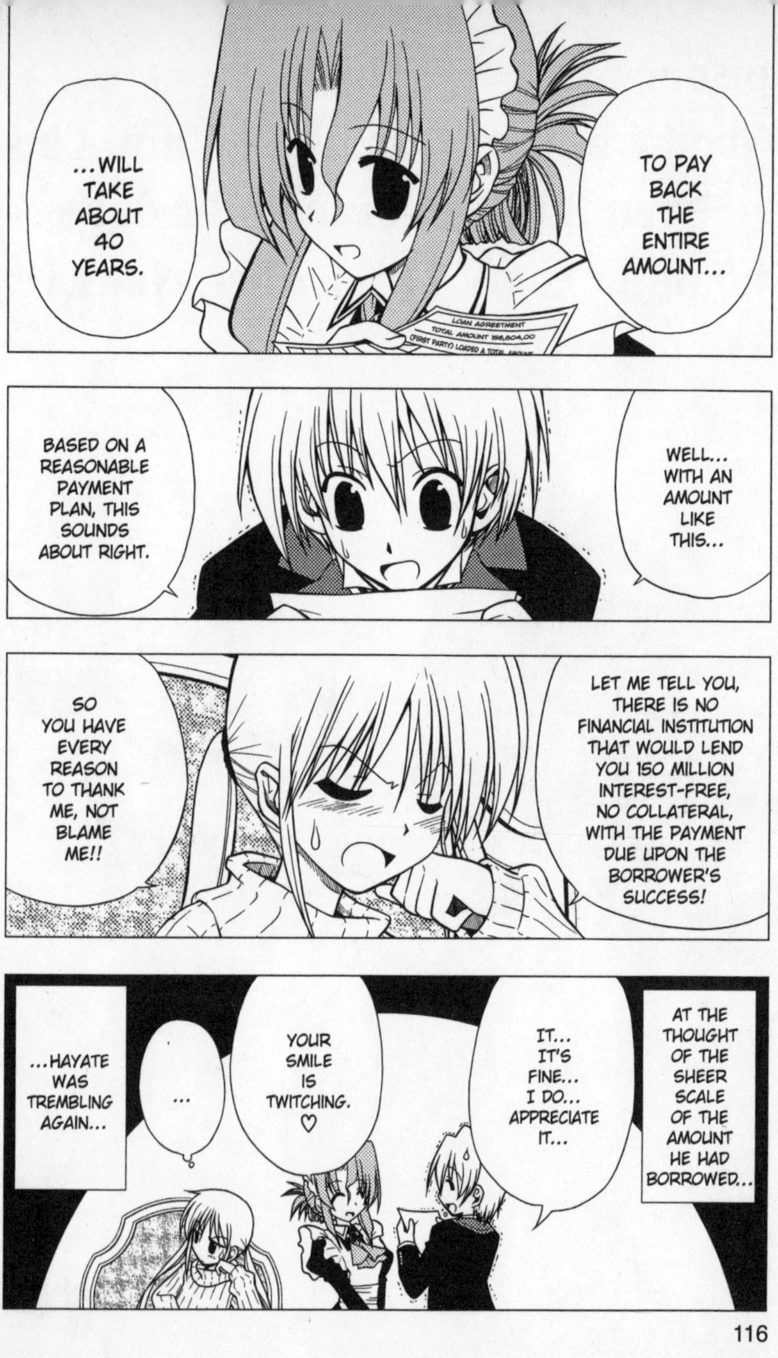
TO PAY BACK THE ENTIRE AMOUNT...
...WILL TAKE ABOUT 40 YEARS.
LOAN AGREEMENT
WELL... WITH AN AMOUNT LIKE THIS...
BASED ON A REASONABLE PAYMENT PLAN, THIS SOUNDS ABOUT RIGHT.
LET ME TELL YOU, THERE IS NO FINANCIAL INSTITUTION THAT WOULD LEND YOU 150 MILLION INTEREST-FREE, NO COLLATERAL, WITH THE PAYMENT DUE UPON THE BORROWER'S SUCCESS!
SO YOU HAVE EVERY REASON TO THANK ME, NOT BLAME ME!!
AT THE THOUGHT OF THE SHEER SCALE OF THE AMOUNT HE HAD BORROWED...
IT... IT'S FINE... I DO... APPRECIATE IT...
YOUR SMILE IS TWITCHING. ♡
...
...HAYATE WAS TREMBLING AGAIN...

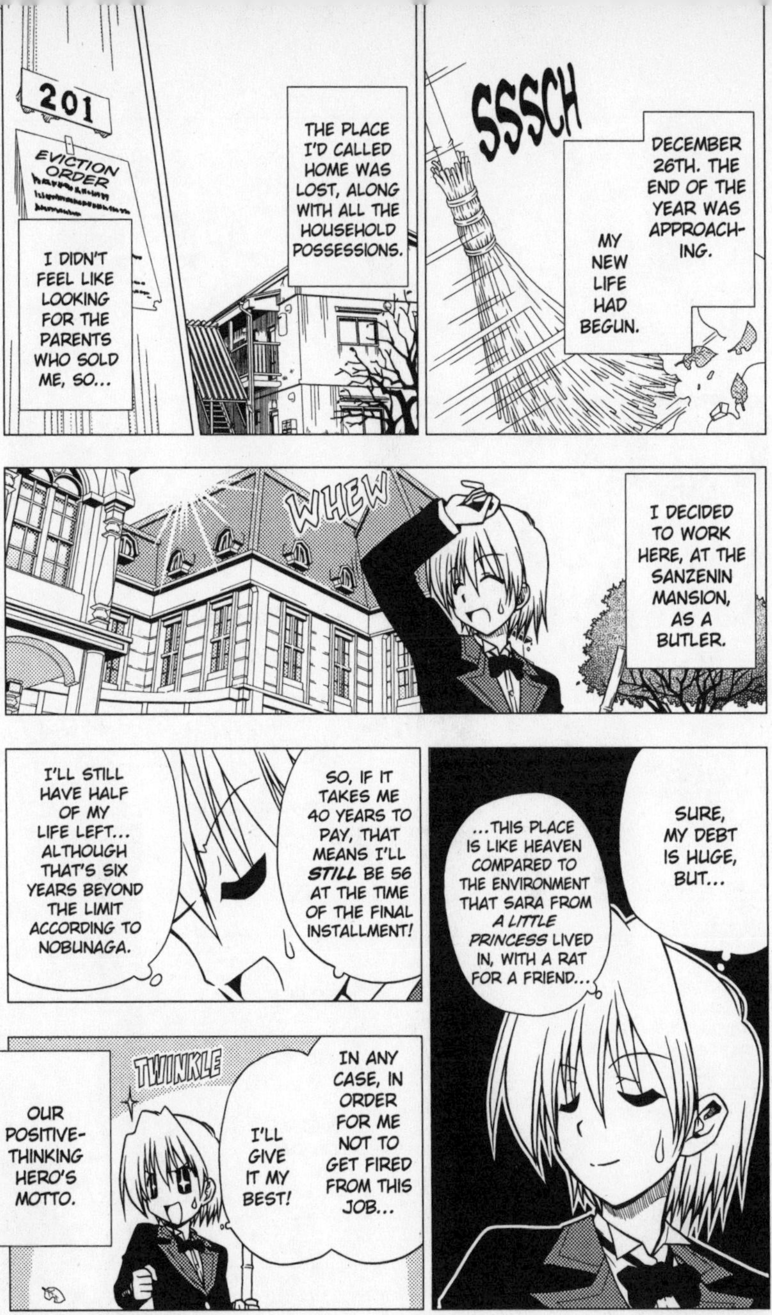
SSSCH
DECEMBER 26TH. THE END OF THE YEAR WAS APPROACHING.
MY NEW LIFE HAD BEGUN.
201
EVICTION ORDER
THE PLACE I'D CALLED HOME WAS LOST, ALONG WITH ALL THE HOUSEHOLD POSSESSIONS.
I DIDN'T FEEL LIKE LOOKING FOR THE PARENTS WHO SOLD ME, SO...
I DECIDED TO WORK HERE, AT THE SANZENIN MANSION, AS A BUTLER.
WHEW
SURE, MY DEBT IS HUGE, BUT...
...THIS PLACE IS LIKE HEAVEN COMPARED TO THE ENVIRONMENT THAT SARA FROM *A LITTLE PRINCESS* LIVED IN, WITH A RAT FOR A FRIEND...
SO, IF IT TAKES ME 40 YEARS TO PAY, THAT MEANS I'LL ***STILL*** BE 56 AT THE TIME OF THE FINAL INSTALLMENT!
I'LL STILL HAVE HALF OF MY LIFE LEFT... ALTHOUGH THAT'S SIX YEARS BEYOND THE LIMIT ACCORDING TO NOBUNAGA.
IN ANY CASE, IN ORDER FOR ME NOT TO GET FIRED FROM THIS JOB...
I'LL GIVE IT MY BEST!
TWINKLE
OUR POSITIVE-THINKING HERO'S MOTTO.

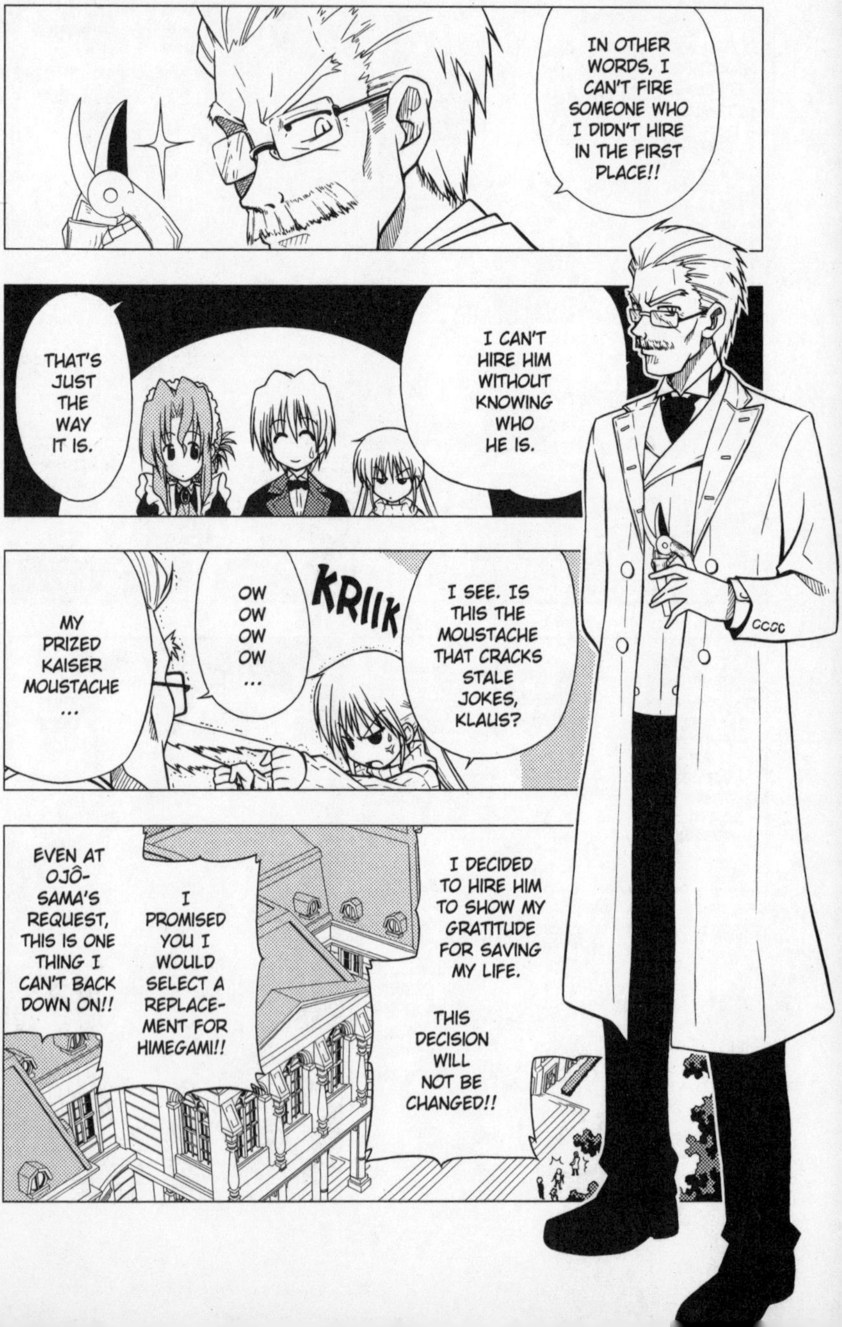
IN OTHER WORDS, I CAN'T FIRE SOMEONE WHO I DIDN'T HIRE IN THE FIRST PLACE!!
I CAN'T HIRE HIM WITHOUT KNOWING WHO HE IS.
THAT'S JUST THE WAY IT IS.
I SEE. IS THIS THE MOUSTACHE THAT CRACKS STALE JOKES, KLAUS?
KRIIK
OW OW OW OW ...
MY PRIZED KAISER MOUSTACHE ...
I DECIDED TO HIRE HIM TO SHOW MY GRATITUDE FOR SAVING MY LIFE.
THIS DECISION WILL NOT BE CHANGED!!
I PROMISED YOU I WOULD SELECT A REPLACE-MENT FOR HIMEGAMI!!
EVEN AT OJÔ-SAMA'S REQUEST, THIS IS ONE THING I CAN'T BACK DOWN ON!!

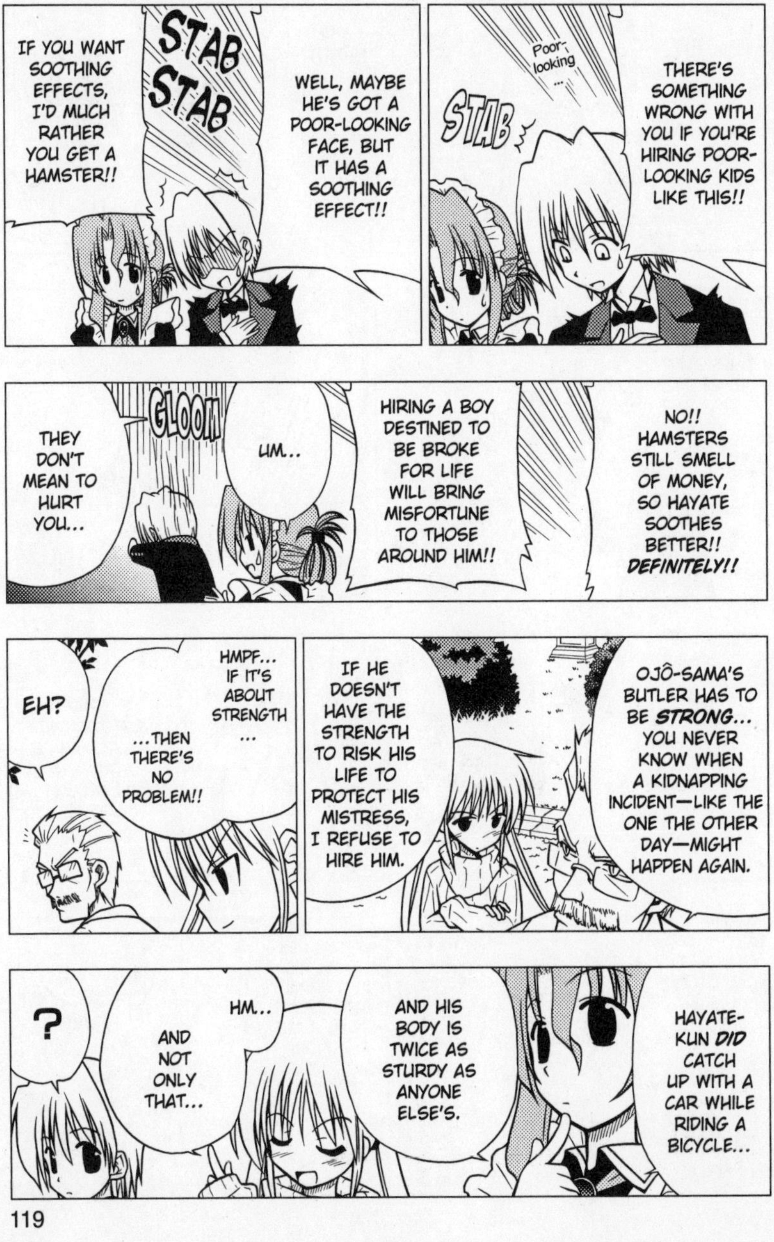
THERE'S SOMETHING WRONG WITH YOU IF YOU'RE HIRING POOR-LOOKING KIDS LIKE THIS!!
Poor-looking ...
STAB
WELL, MAYBE HE'S GOT A POOR-LOOKING FACE, BUT IT HAS A SOOTHING EFFECT!!
STAB STAB
IF YOU WANT SOOTHING EFFECTS, I'D MUCH RATHER YOU GET A HAMSTER!!
NO!! HAMSTERS STILL SMELL OF MONEY, SO HAYATE SOOTHES BETTER!! *DEFINITELY!!*
HIRING A BOY DESTINED TO BE BROKE FOR LIFE WILL BRING MISFORTUNE TO THOSE AROUND HIM!!
UM...
GLOOM
THEY DON'T MEAN TO HURT YOU...
OJÔ-SAMA'S BUTLER HAS TO BE *STRONG*... YOU NEVER KNOW WHEN A KIDNAPPING INCIDENT—LIKE THE ONE THE OTHER DAY—MIGHT HAPPEN AGAIN.
IF HE DOESN'T HAVE THE STRENGTH TO RISK HIS LIFE TO PROTECT HIS MISTRESS, I REFUSE TO HIRE HIM.
HMPF... IF IT'S ABOUT STRENGTH ...
...THEN THERE'S NO PROBLEM!!
EH?
HAYATE-KUN *DID* CATCH UP WITH A CAR WHILE RIDING A BICYCLE...
AND HIS BODY IS TWICE AS STURDY AS ANYONE ELSE'S.
HM...
AND NOT ONLY THAT...
?

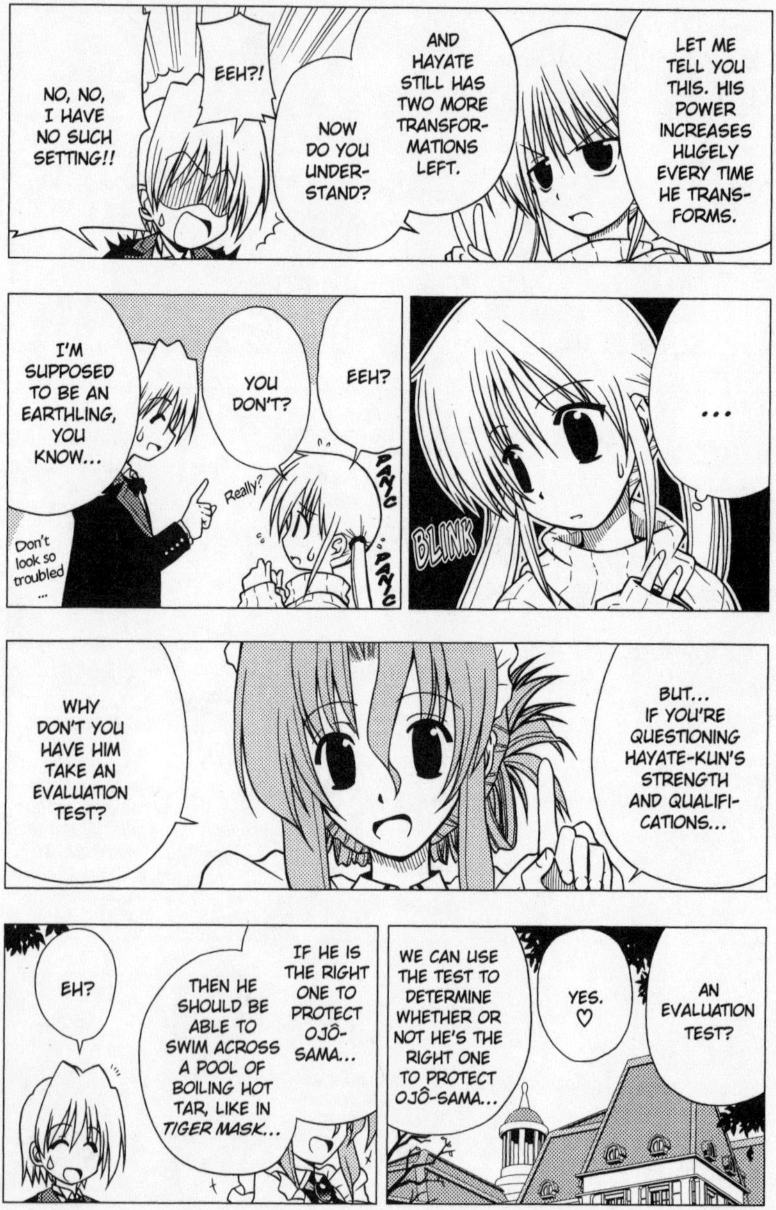

LET ME TELL YOU THIS. HIS POWER INCREASES HUGELY EVERY TIME HE TRANSFORMS.
AND HAYATE STILL HAS TWO MORE TRANSFORMATIONS LEFT.
NOW DO YOU UNDERSTAND?
EEH?!
NO, NO, I HAVE NO SUCH SETTING!!
...
BLINK
EEH?
YOU DON'T?
Really?
I'M SUPPOSED TO BE AN EARTHLING, YOU KNOW...
Don't look so troubled ...
BUT... IF YOU'RE QUESTIONING HAYATE-KUN'S STRENGTH AND QUALIFICATIONS...
WHY DON'T YOU HAVE HIM TAKE AN EVALUATION TEST?
AN EVALUATION TEST?
YES. ♡
WE CAN USE THE TEST TO DETERMINE WHETHER OR NOT HE'S THE RIGHT ONE TO PROTECT OJÔ-SAMA...
IF HE IS THE RIGHT ONE TO PROTECT OJÔ-SAMA...
THEN HE SHOULD BE ABLE TO SWIM ACROSS A POOL OF BOILING HOT TAR, LIKE IN *TIGER MASK*...
EH?

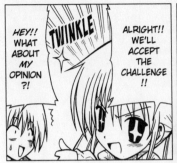

INDEED... HE SHOULD BE ALRIGHT EVEN IF HE WERE TO FALL 2,000 METERS FROM THE SKY, LIKE THE MONSTER GOMORA...
UHH...
AND HE SHOULD BE ABLE TO FIGHT A RAVENOUS BROWN BEAR WITH HIS BARE HANDS, LIKE OYAMA MASUTATSU!!
UM... HELLO ...
ALRIGHT!! WE'LL ACCEPT THE CHALLENGE !!
TWINKLE
HEY!! WHAT ABOUT MY OPINION ?!
WELL THEN, PLEASE WAIT A MOMENT !!
KA-CHUNK
I WILL PREPARE THE TEST RIGHT AWAY!!
OKAY !!
BRING IT ON— EVERYTHING YOU'VE GOT!!
AAH ...
I MEAN, I DON'T KNOW WHAT KIND OF TEST THIS IS...
IS... IS THIS GOING TO BE ALRIGHT?! IN *EVERY* WAY?!
HUH?
IT'LL BE FINE.
HAYATE, I KNOW ...
...YOU'LL MANAGE IT. ♡
...

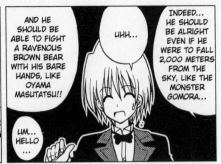

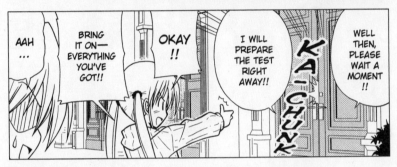

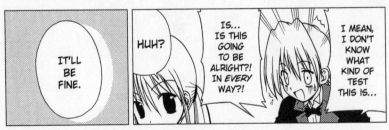

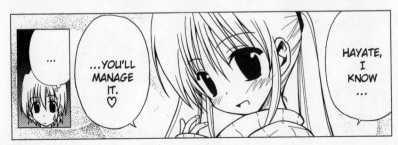

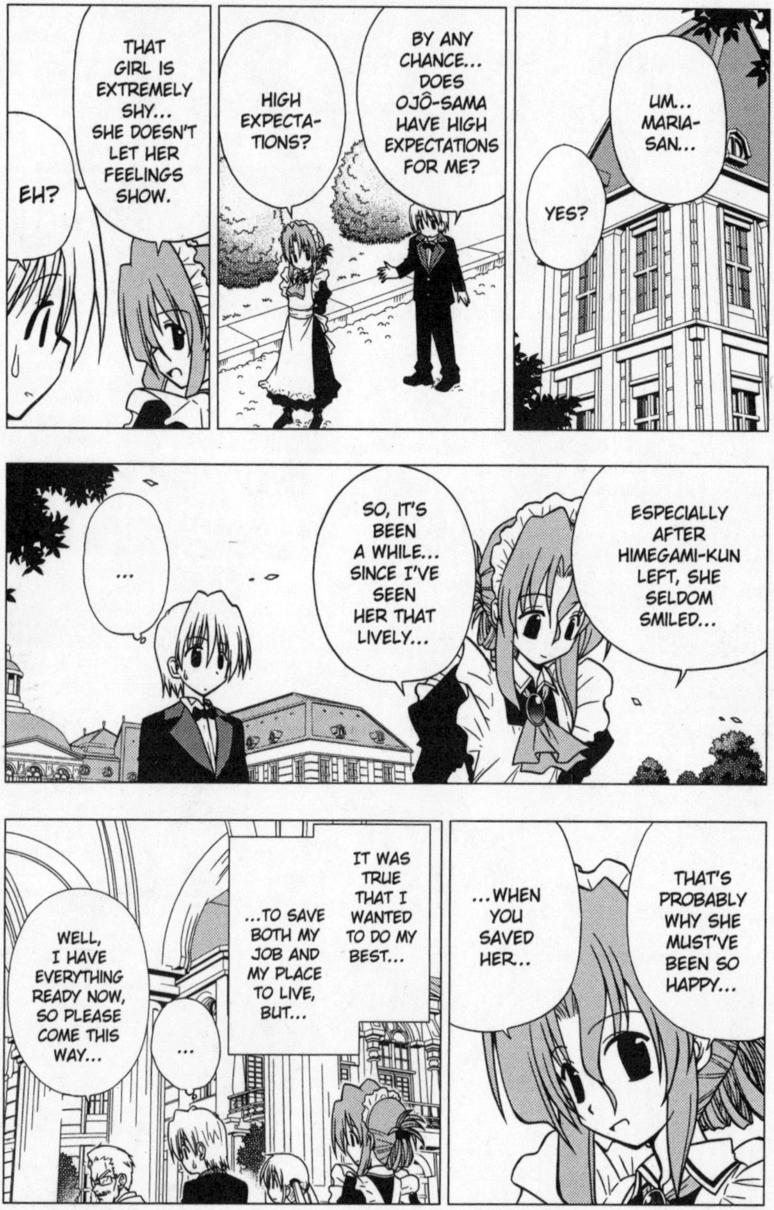
UM... MARIA-SAN...
YES?
BY ANY CHANCE... DOES OJÔ-SAMA HAVE HIGH EXPECTATIONS FOR ME?
HIGH EXPECTA-TIONS?
THAT GIRL IS EXTREMELY SHY... SHE DOESN'T LET HER FEELINGS SHOW.
EH?
ESPECIALLY AFTER HIMEGAMI-KUN LEFT, SHE SELDOM SMILED...
SO, IT'S BEEN A WHILE... SINCE I'VE SEEN HER THAT LIVELY...
...
THAT'S PROBABLY WHY SHE MUST'VE BEEN SO HAPPY...
...WHEN YOU SAVED HER...
IT WAS TRUE THAT I WANTED TO DO MY BEST...
...TO SAVE BOTH MY JOB AND MY PLACE TO LIVE, BUT...
...
WELL, I HAVE EVERYTHING READY NOW, SO PLEASE COME THIS WAY...

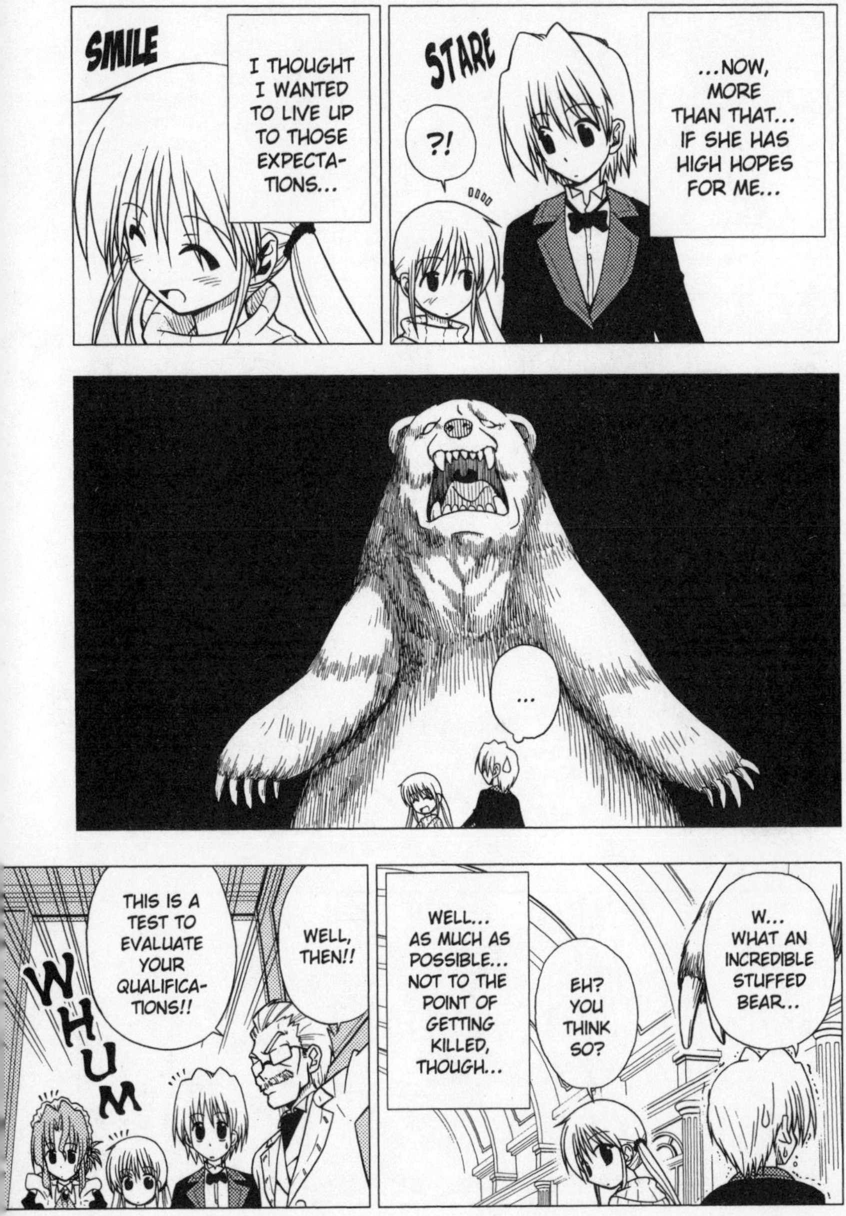
...NOW, MORE THAN THAT... IF SHE HAS HIGH HOPES FOR ME...
STARE
?!
I THOUGHT I WANTED TO LIVE UP TO THOSE EXPECTA-TIONS...
SMILE
...
W... WHAT AN INCREDIBLE STUFFED BEAR...
EH? YOU THINK SO?
WELL... AS MUCH AS POSSIBLE... NOT TO THE POINT OF GETTING KILLED, THOUGH...
WELL, THEN!!
THIS IS A TEST TO EVALUATE YOUR QUALIFICA-TIONS!!
WHUM

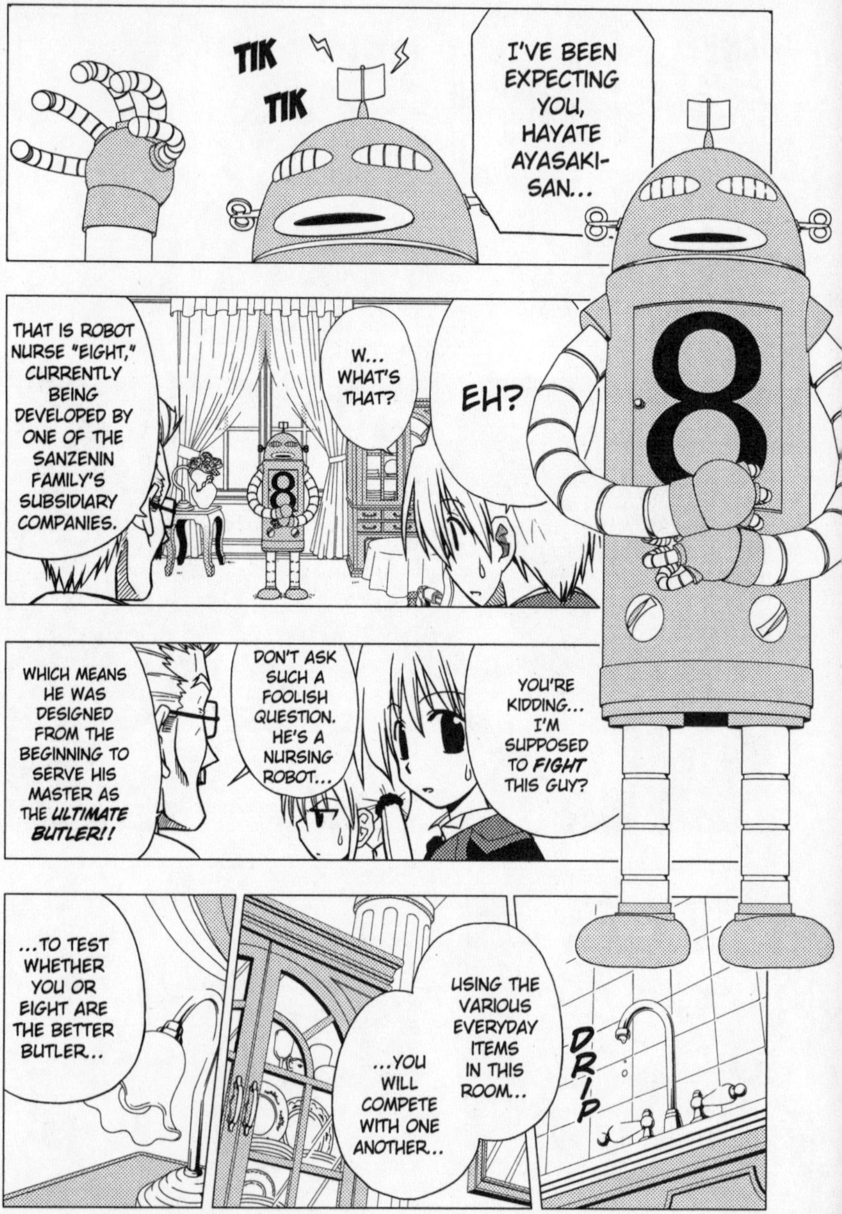
I'VE BEEN EXPECTING YOU, HAYATE AYASAKI-SAN...
TIK
TIK
EH?
W... WHAT'S THAT?
THAT IS ROBOT NURSE "EIGHT," CURRENTLY BEING DEVELOPED BY ONE OF THE SANZENIN FAMILY'S SUBSIDIARY COMPANIES.
YOU'RE KIDDING... I'M SUPPOSED TO *FIGHT* THIS GUY?
DON'T ASK SUCH A FOOLISH QUESTION. HE'S A NURSING ROBOT...
WHICH MEANS HE WAS DESIGNED FROM THE BEGINNING TO SERVE HIS MASTER AS THE *ULTIMATE BUTLER!!*
DRIP
USING THE VARIOUS EVERYDAY ITEMS IN THIS ROOM...
...YOU WILL COMPETE WITH ONE ANOTHER...
...TO TEST WHETHER YOU OR EIGHT ARE THE BETTER BUTLER...

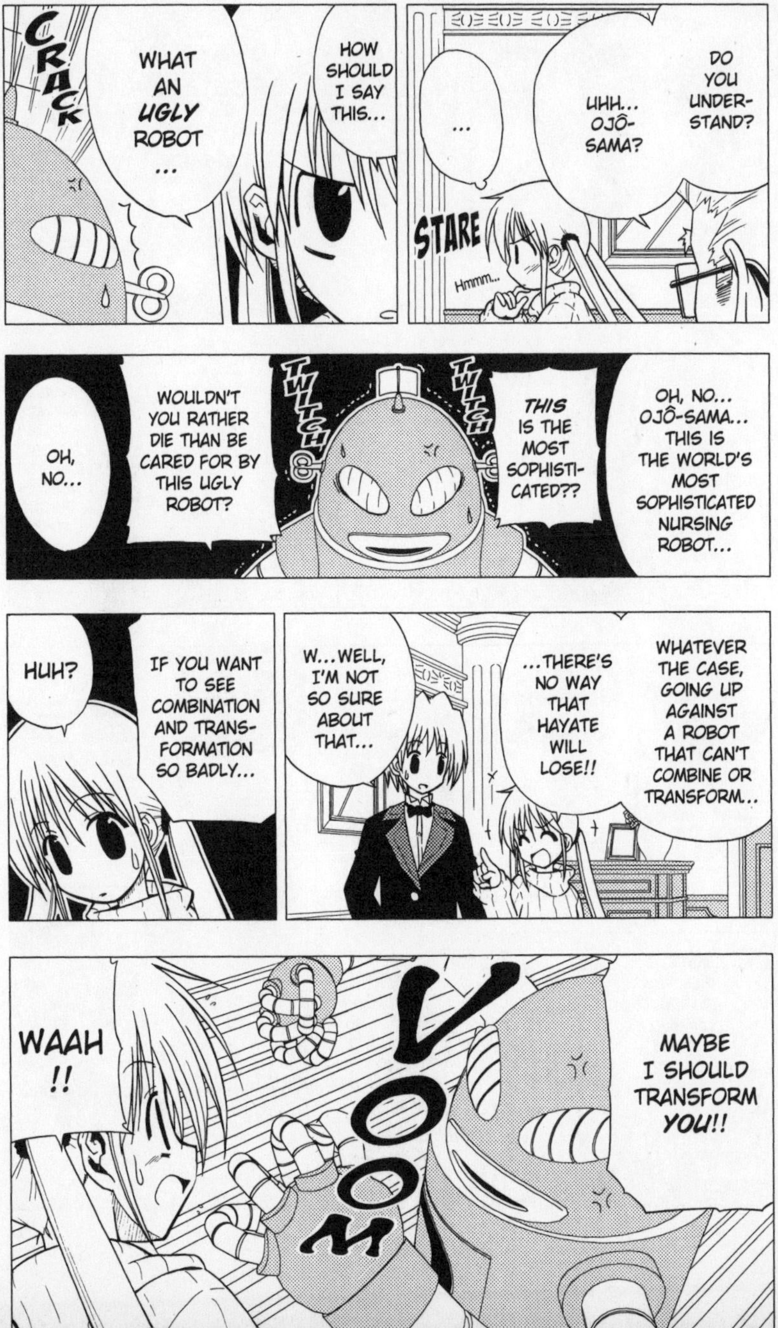
DO YOU UNDERSTAND?
UHH... OJÔ-SAMA?
...
STARE
Hmmm...
HOW SHOULD I SAY THIS...
WHAT AN UGLY ROBOT...
CRACK
OH, NO... OJÔ-SAMA... THIS IS THE WORLD'S MOST SOPHISTICATED NURSING ROBOT...
THIS IS THE MOST SOPHISTICATED??
TWITCH
TWITCH
WOULDN'T YOU RATHER DIE THAN BE CARED FOR BY THIS UGLY ROBOT?
OH, NO...
WHATEVER THE CASE, GOING UP AGAINST A ROBOT THAT CAN'T COMBINE OR TRANSFORM...
...THERE'S NO WAY THAT HAYATE WILL LOSE!!
W...WELL, I'M NOT SO SURE ABOUT THAT...
IF YOU WANT TO SEE COMBINATION AND TRANSFORMATION SO BADLY...
HUH?
MAYBE I SHOULD TRANSFORM YOU!!
VOOOM
WAAH!!

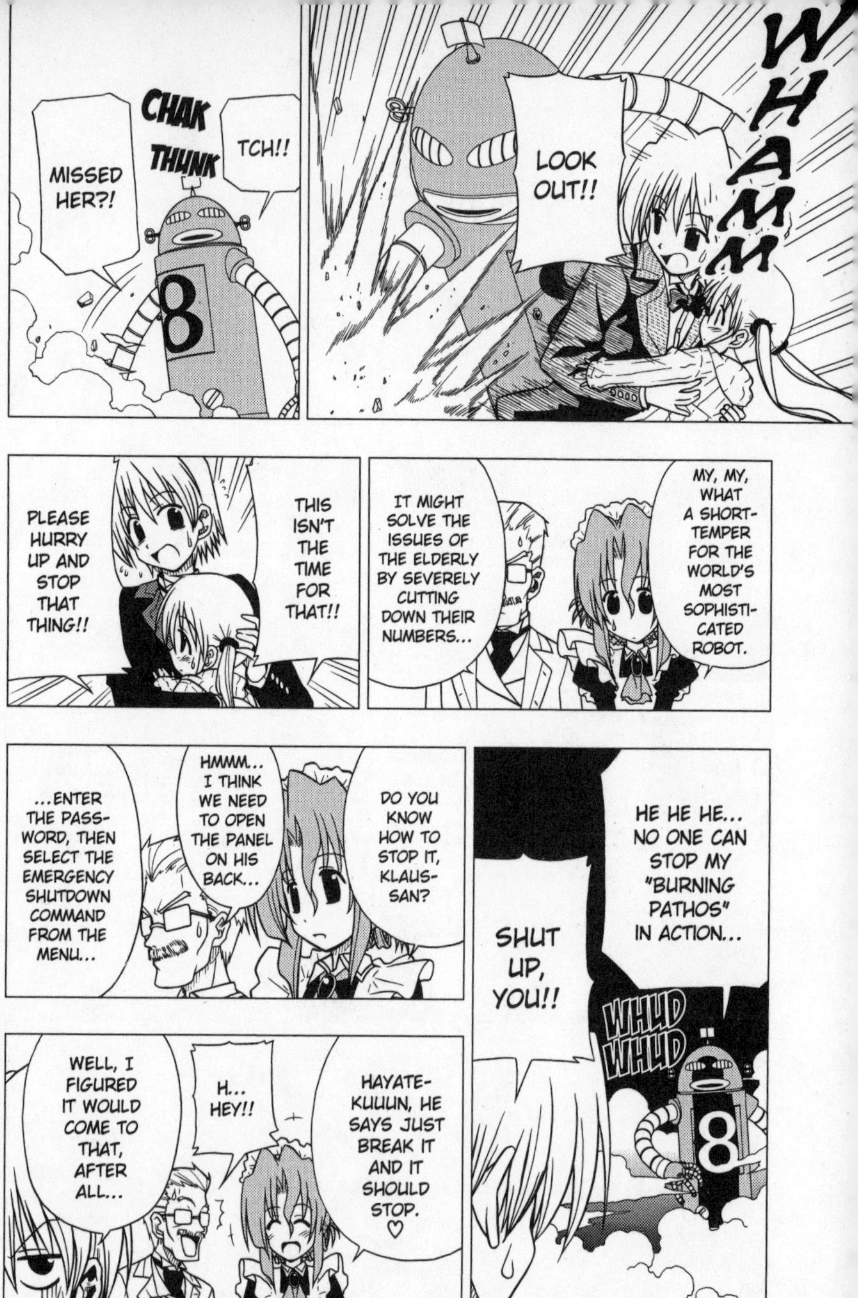
WHAMM
LOOK OUT!!
TCH!!
CHAK THUNK
MISSED HER?!
MY, MY, WHAT A SHORT-TEMPER FOR THE WORLD'S MOST SOPHISTICATED ROBOT.
IT MIGHT SOLVE THE ISSUES OF THE ELDERLY BY SEVERELY CUTTING DOWN THEIR NUMBERS...
THIS ISN'T THE TIME FOR THAT!!
PLEASE HURRY UP AND STOP THAT THING!!
HE HE HE... NO ONE CAN STOP MY "BURNING PATHOS" IN ACTION...
SHUT UP, YOU!!
WHUD WHUD
DO YOU KNOW HOW TO STOP IT, KLAUS-SAN?
HMMM... I THINK WE NEED TO OPEN THE PANEL ON HIS BACK...
...ENTER THE PASS-WORD, THEN SELECT THE EMERGENCY SHUTDOWN COMMAND FROM THE MENU...
HAYATE-KUUUN, HE SAYS JUST BREAK IT AND IT SHOULD STOP. ♡
H... HEY!!
WELL, I FIGURED IT WOULD COME TO THAT, AFTER ALL...

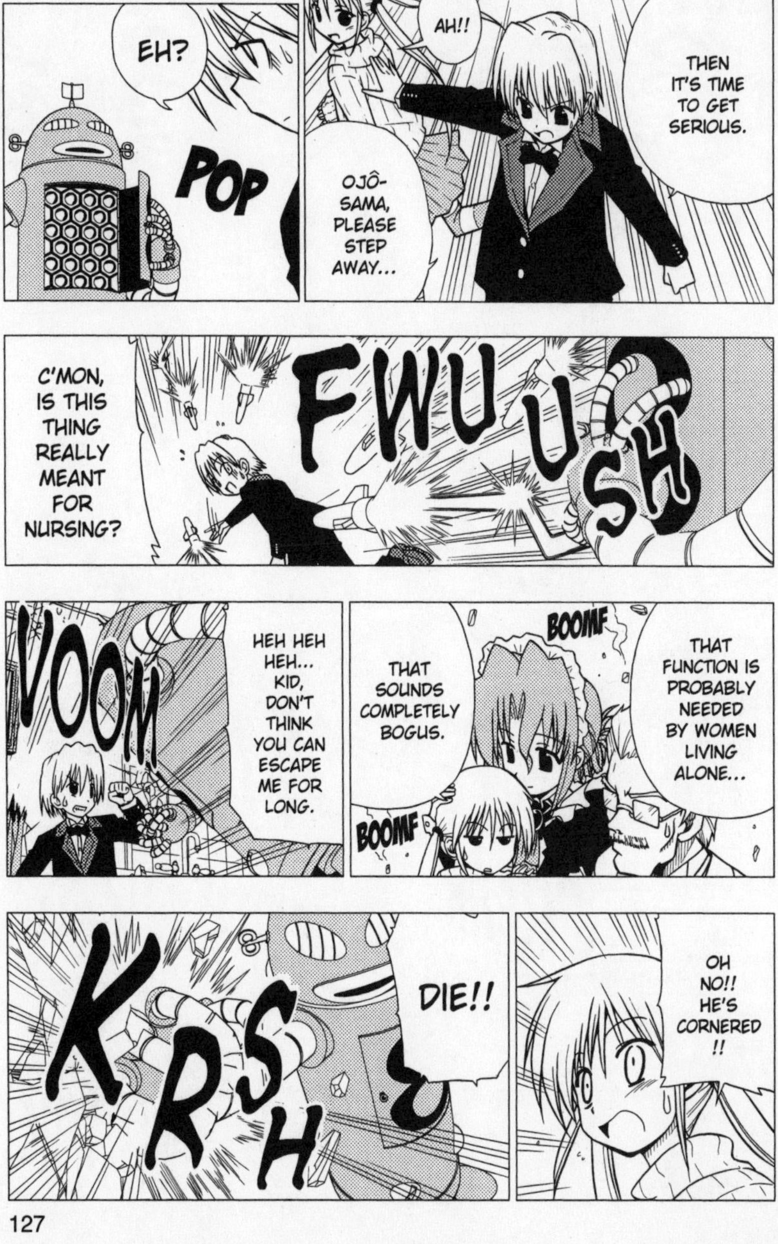
THEN IT'S TIME TO GET SERIOUS.
AH!!
OJÔ-SAMA, PLEASE STEP AWAY...
POP
EH?
FWUUSH
C'MON, IS THIS THING REALLY MEANT FOR NURSING?
THAT FUNCTION IS PROBABLY NEEDED BY WOMEN LIVING ALONE...
BOOMF
THAT SOUNDS COMPLETELY BOGUS.
BOOMF
HEH HEH HEH... KID, DON'T THINK YOU CAN ESCAPE ME FOR LONG.
VOOM
OH NO!! HE'S CORNERED!!
DIE!!
KRSSH

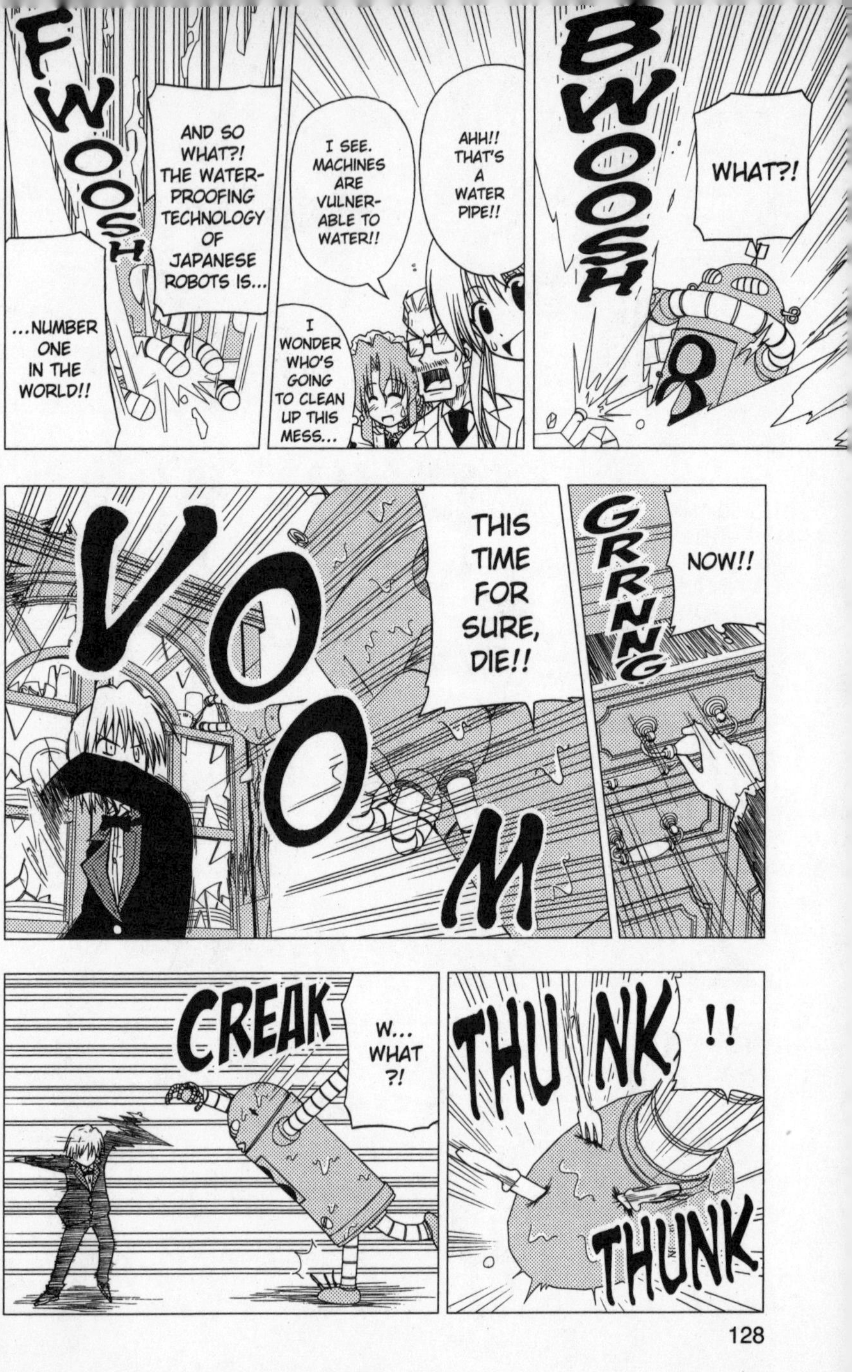
FWOOSH
AND SO WHAT?! THE WATER-PROOFING TECHNOLOGY OF JAPANESE ROBOTS IS...
...NUMBER ONE IN THE WORLD!!
I SEE. MACHINES ARE VULNERABLE TO WATER!!
AHH!! THAT'S A WATER PIPE!!
I WONDER WHO'S GOING TO CLEAN UP THIS MESS...
BWOOSH
WHAT?!
VOOM
THIS TIME FOR SURE, DIE!!
GRRNNG
NOW!!
CREAK
W... WHAT?!
THUNK!!
THUNK

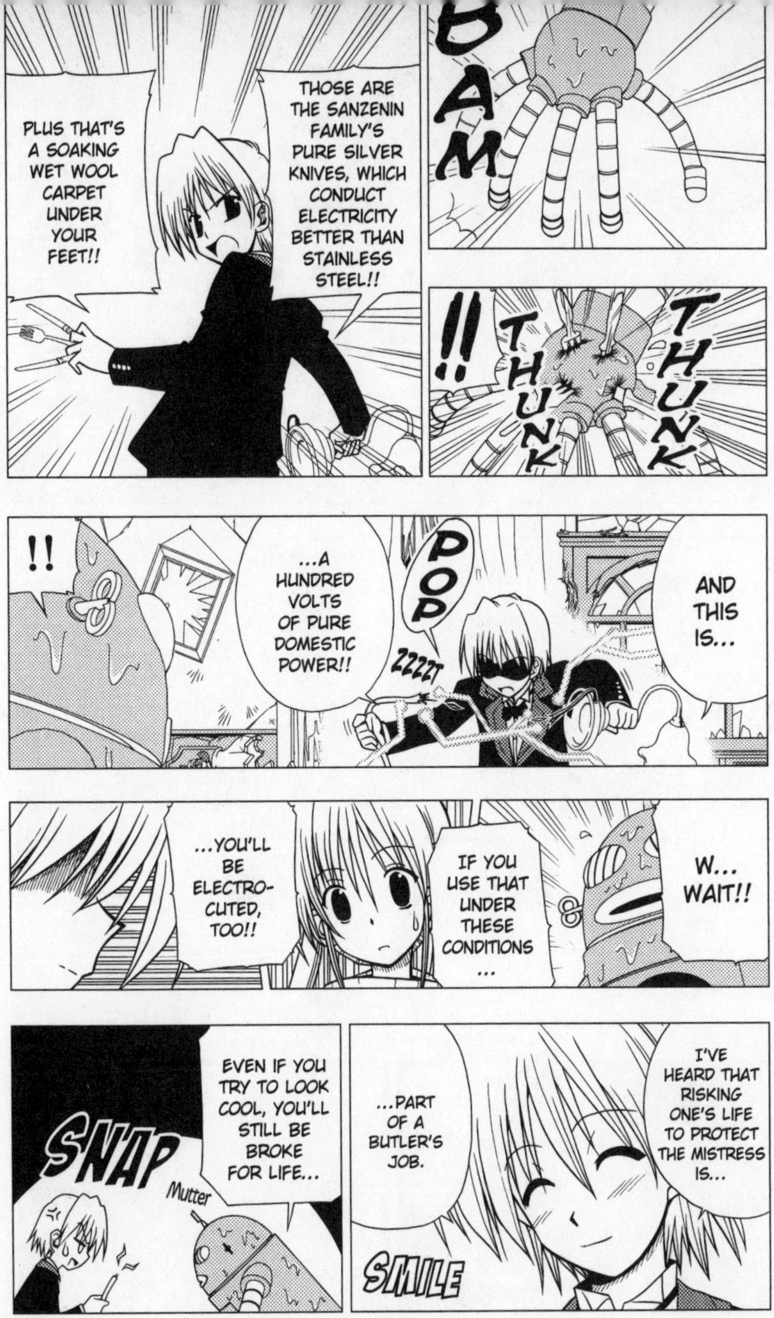
BAM
!!
THUNK
THUNK
THOSE ARE THE SANZENIN FAMILY'S PURE SILVER KNIVES, WHICH CONDUCT ELECTRICITY BETTER THAN STAINLESS STEEL!!
PLUS THAT'S A SOAKING WET WOOL CARPET UNDER YOUR FEET!!
AND THIS IS...
POP
ZZZZT
...A HUNDRED VOLTS OF PURE DOMESTIC POWER!!
!!
W... WAIT!!
IF YOU USE THAT UNDER THESE CONDITIONS...
...YOU'LL BE ELECTROCUTED, TOO!!
I'VE HEARD THAT RISKING ONE'S LIFE TO PROTECT THE MISTRESS IS...
...PART OF A BUTLER'S JOB.
SMILE
EVEN IF YOU TRY TO LOOK COOL, YOU'LL STILL BE BROKE FOR LIFE...
Mutter
SNAP

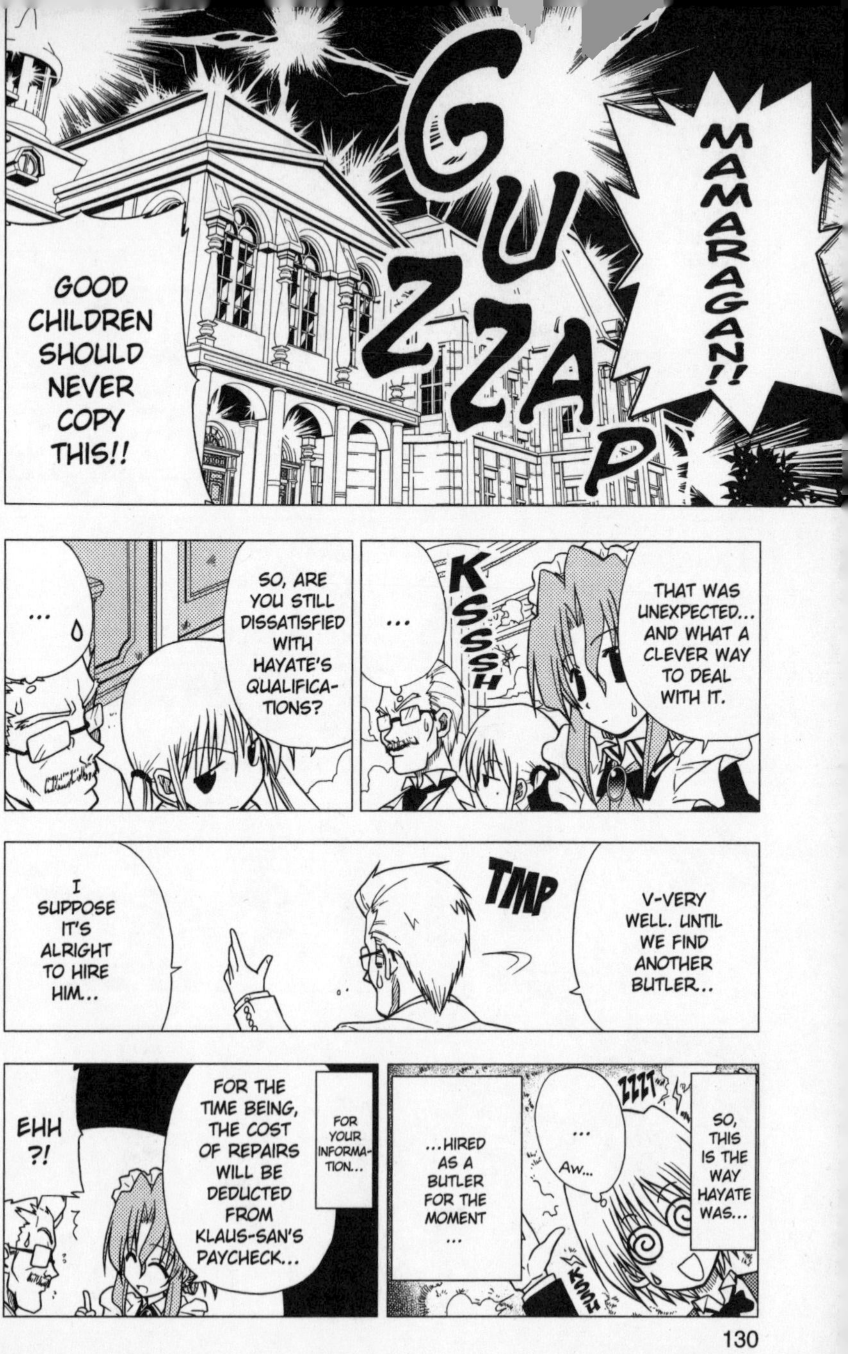
MAMARAGAN!!
GUZZAP
GOOD CHILDREN SHOULD NEVER COPY THIS!!
THAT WAS UNEXPECTED... AND WHAT A CLEVER WAY TO DEAL WITH IT.
KSSSH
...
SO, ARE YOU STILL DISSATISFIED WITH HAYATE'S QUALIFICATIONS?
...
V-VERY WELL. UNTIL WE FIND ANOTHER BUTLER...
TMP
I SUPPOSE IT'S ALRIGHT TO HIRE HIM...
SO, THIS IS THE WAY HAYATE WAS...
ZZZT
...
Aw...
...HIRED AS A BUTLER FOR THE MOMENT...
FOR YOUR INFORMATION...
FOR THE TIME BEING, THE COST OF REPAIRS WILL BE DEDUCTED FROM KLAUS-SAN'S PAYCHECK...
EHH?!

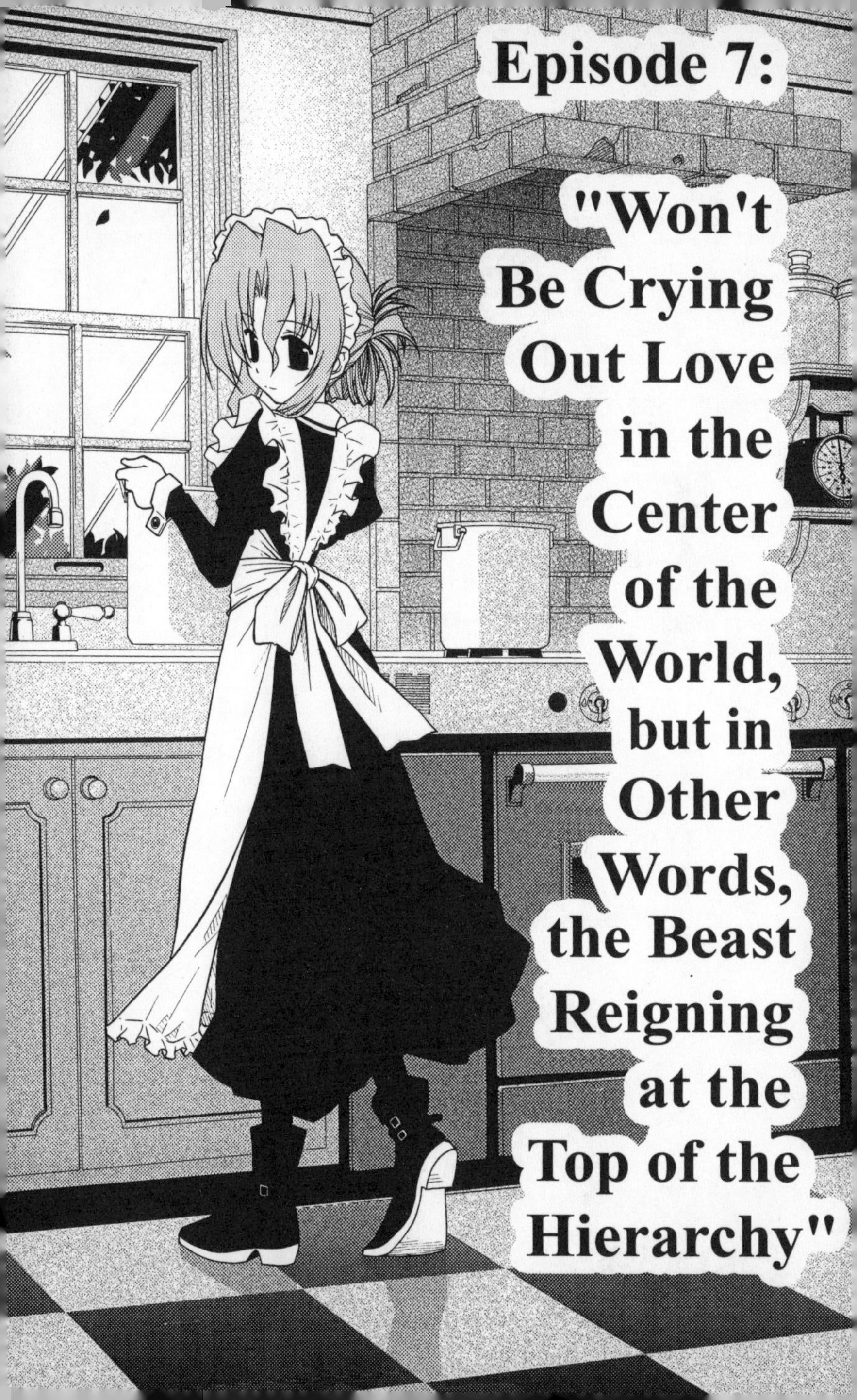
Episode 7:
"Won't Be Crying Out Love in the Center of the World, but in Other Words, the Beast Reigning at the Top of the Hierarchy"

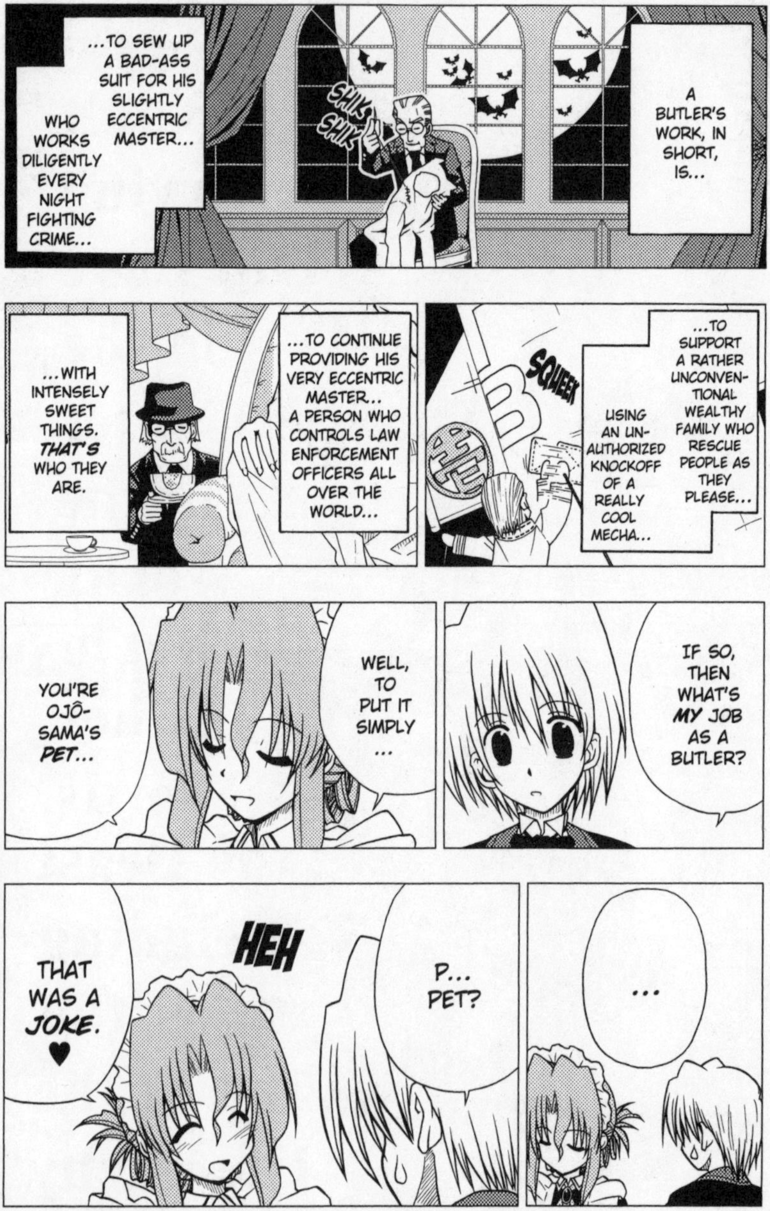
A BUTLER'S WORK, IN SHORT, IS...
SHIK SHIK
...TO SEW UP A BAD-ASS SUIT FOR HIS SLIGHTLY ECCENTRIC MASTER...
WHO WORKS DILIGENTLY EVERY NIGHT FIGHTING CRIME...
...TO SUPPORT A RATHER UNCONVEN-TIONAL WEALTHY FAMILY WHO RESCUE PEOPLE AS THEY PLEASE...
USING AN UN-AUTHORIZED KNOCKOFF OF A REALLY COOL MECHA...
SQUEEK
...TO CONTINUE PROVIDING HIS VERY ECCENTRIC MASTER... A PERSON WHO CONTROLS LAW ENFORCEMENT OFFICERS ALL OVER THE WORLD...
...WITH INTENSELY SWEET THINGS. *THAT'S* WHO THEY ARE.
IF SO, THEN WHAT'S *MY* JOB AS A BUTLER?
WELL, TO PUT IT SIMPLY ...
YOU'RE OJÔ-SAMA'S *PET*...
...
P... PET?
HEH
THAT WAS A *JOKE*. ♥

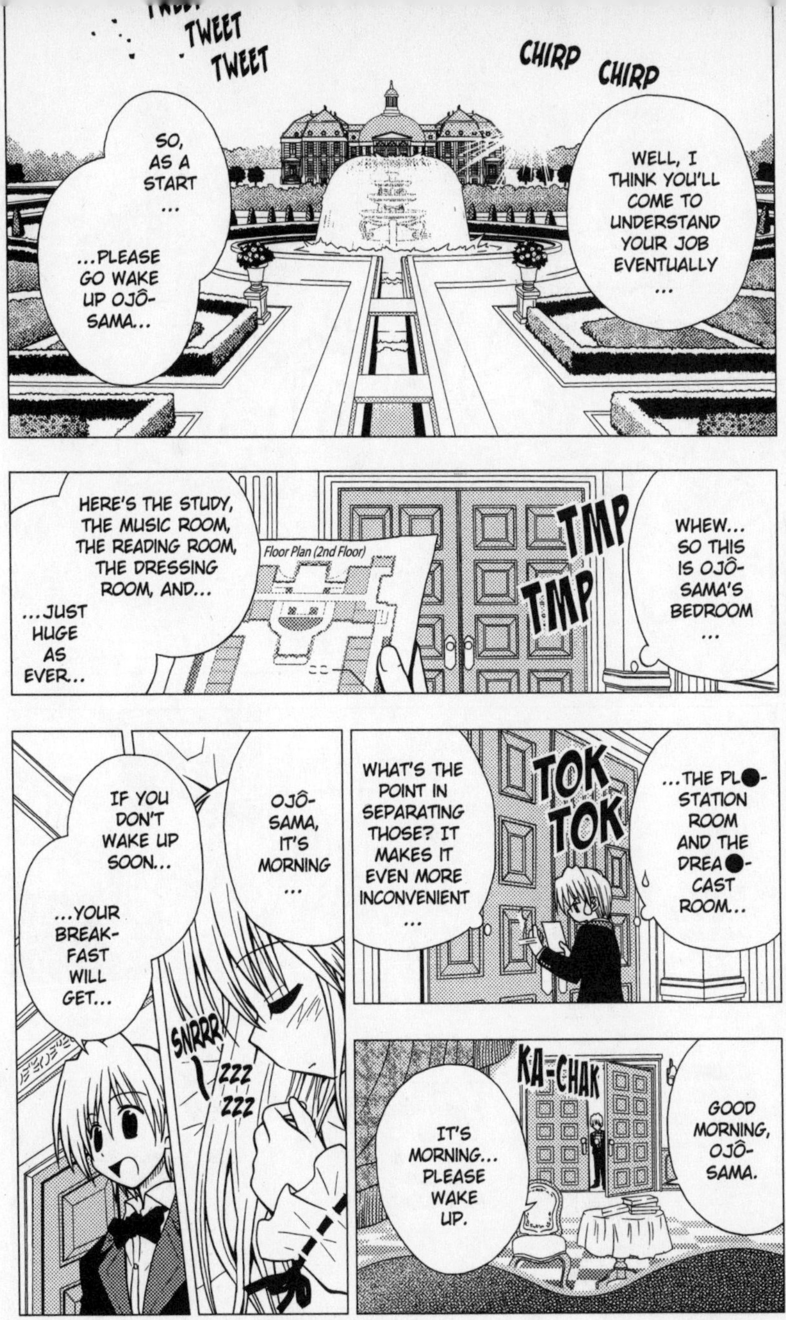
CHIRP
CHIRP
TWEET
TWEET
WELL, I THINK YOU'LL COME TO UNDERSTAND YOUR JOB EVENTUALLY ...
SO, AS A START ...
...PLEASE GO WAKE UP OJÔ-SAMA...
WHEW... SO THIS IS OJÔ-SAMA'S BEDROOM ...
TMP TMP
Floor Plan (2nd Floor)
HERE'S THE STUDY, THE MUSIC ROOM, THE READING ROOM, THE DRESSING ROOM, AND...
...JUST HUGE AS EVER...
...THE PL●-STATION ROOM AND THE DREA●-CAST ROOM...
TOK TOK
WHAT'S THE POINT IN SEPARATING THOSE? IT MAKES IT EVEN MORE INCONVENIENT ...
GOOD MORNING, OJÔ-SAMA.
KA-CHAK
IT'S MORNING... PLEASE WAKE UP.
OJÔ-SAMA, IT'S MORNING ...
IF YOU DON'T WAKE UP SOON...
...YOUR BREAKFAST WILL GET...
SNRRR
ZZZ
ZZZ

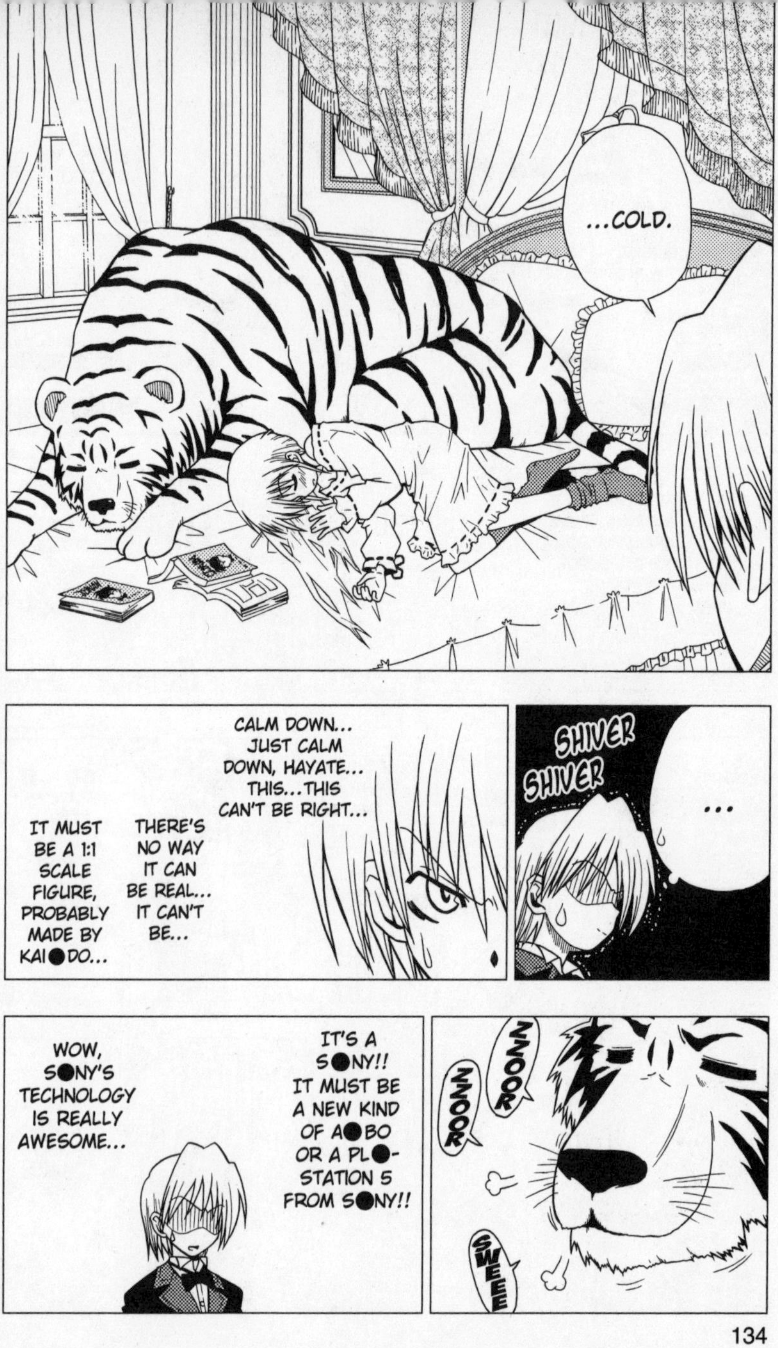
...COLD.
SHIVER SHIVER
...
CALM DOWN... JUST CALM DOWN, HAYATE... THIS...THIS CAN'T BE RIGHT...
THERE'S NO WAY IT CAN BE REAL... IT CAN'T BE...
IT MUST BE A 1:1 SCALE FIGURE, PROBABLY MADE BY KAI●DO...
ZZOOR
ZZOOR
SWEEE
IT'S A S●NY!! IT MUST BE A NEW KIND OF A●BO OR A PL●-STATION 5 FROM S●NY!!
WOW, S●NY'S TECHNOLOGY IS REALLY AWESOME...

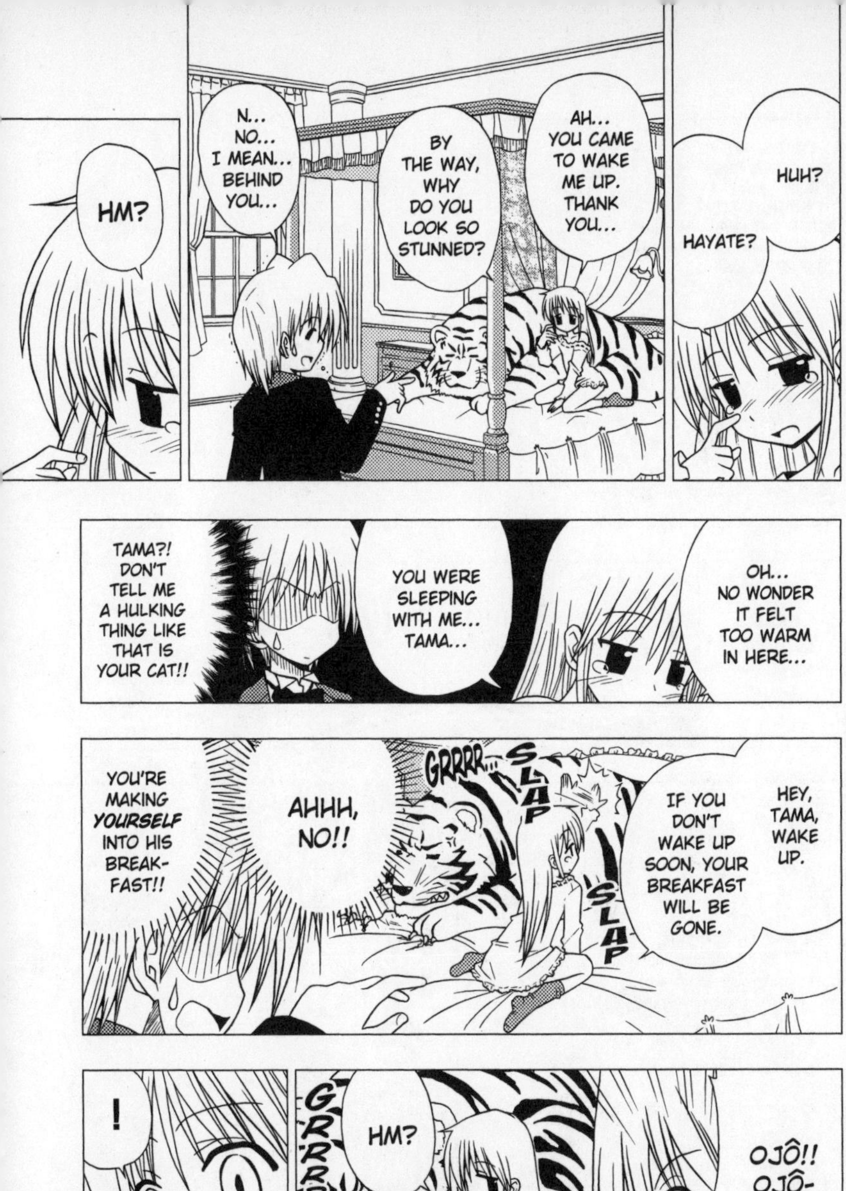
HUH?
HAYATE?
AH... YOU CAME TO WAKE ME UP. THANK YOU...
BY THE WAY, WHY DO YOU LOOK SO STUNNED?
N... NO... I MEAN... BEHIND YOU...
HM?
OH... NO WONDER IT FELT TOO WARM IN HERE...
YOU WERE SLEEPING WITH ME... TAMA...
TAMA?! DON'T TELL ME A HULKING THING LIKE THAT IS YOUR CAT!!
HEY, TAMA, WAKE UP.
IF YOU DON'T WAKE UP SOON, YOUR BREAKFAST WILL BE GONE.
SLAP
SLAP
SLAP
GRRRR...
AHHH, NO!!
YOU'RE MAKING *YOURSELF* INTO HIS BREAK-FAST!!
OJÔ!! OJÔ-SAMA, WAIT!!
HM?
GRRRR
DOINK
DOINK
!
HAH

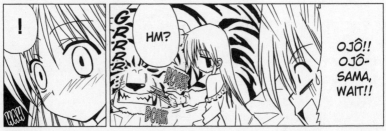

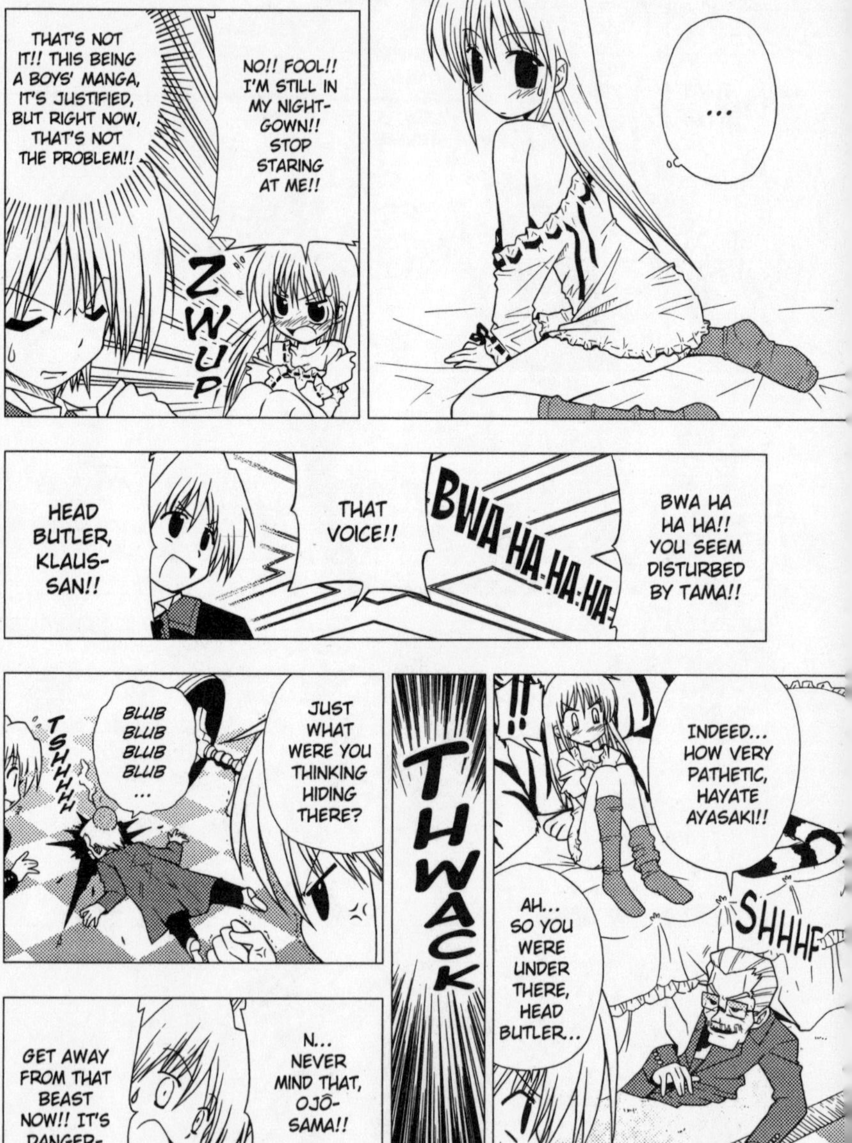
...
NO!! FOOL!! I'M STILL IN MY NIGHTGOWN!! STOP STARING AT ME!!
THAT'S NOT IT!! THIS BEING A BOYS' MANGA, IT'S JUSTIFIED, BUT RIGHT NOW, THAT'S NOT THE PROBLEM!!
ZWUP
BWA HA HA HA!! YOU SEEM DISTURBED BY TAMA!!
BWA-HA-HA-HA
THAT VOICE!!
HEAD BUTLER, KLAUS-SAN!!
!!
INDEED... HOW VERY PATHETIC, HAYATE AYASAKI!!
SHHHF
AH... SO YOU WERE UNDER THERE, HEAD BUTLER...
THWACK
JUST WHAT WERE YOU THINKING HIDING THERE?
BLUB BLUB BLUB BLUB ...
TSHHHHH
N... NEVER MIND THAT, OJÔ-SAMA!!
GET AWAY FROM THAT BEAST NOW!! IT'S DANGER-OUS!!

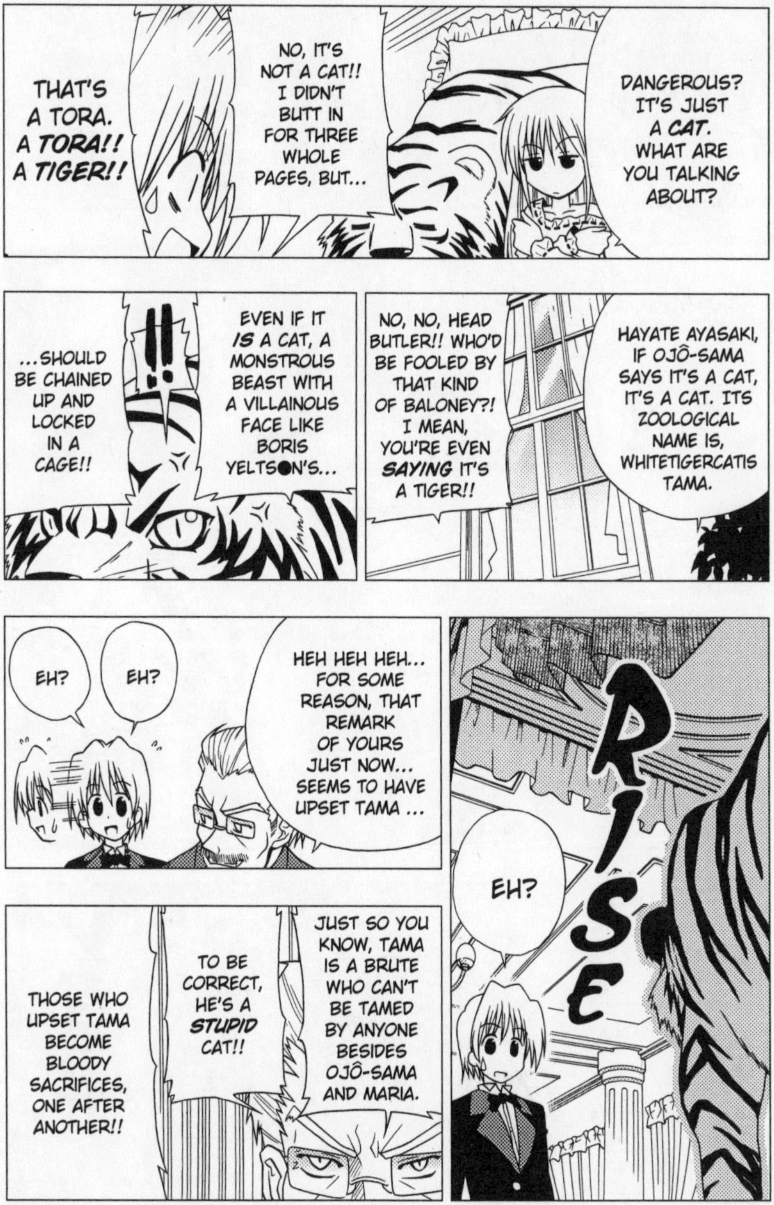

DANGEROUS? IT'S JUST A CAT. WHAT ARE YOU TALKING ABOUT?
NO, IT'S NOT A CAT!! I DIDN'T BUTT IN FOR THREE WHOLE PAGES, BUT...
THAT'S A TORA. A TORA!! A TIGER!!
HAYATE AYASAKI, IF OJÔ-SAMA SAYS IT'S A CAT, IT'S A CAT. ITS ZOOLOGICAL NAME IS, WHITETIGERCATIS TAMA.
NO, NO, HEAD BUTLER!! WHO'D BE FOOLED BY THAT KIND OF BALONEY?! I MEAN, YOU'RE EVEN SAYING IT'S A TIGER!!
EVEN IF IT IS A CAT, A MONSTROUS BEAST WITH A VILLAINOUS FACE LIKE BORIS YELTS●N'S...
...SHOULD BE CHAINED UP AND LOCKED IN A CAGE!!
RISE
EH?
HEH HEH HEH... FOR SOME REASON, THAT REMARK OF YOURS JUST NOW... SEEMS TO HAVE UPSET TAMA ...
EH?
EH?
JUST SO YOU KNOW, TAMA IS A BRUTE WHO CAN'T BE TAMED BY ANYONE BESIDES OJÔ-SAMA AND MARIA.
TO BE CORRECT, HE'S A STUPID CAT!!
THOSE WHO UPSET TAMA BECOME BLOODY SACRIFICES, ONE AFTER ANOTHER!!

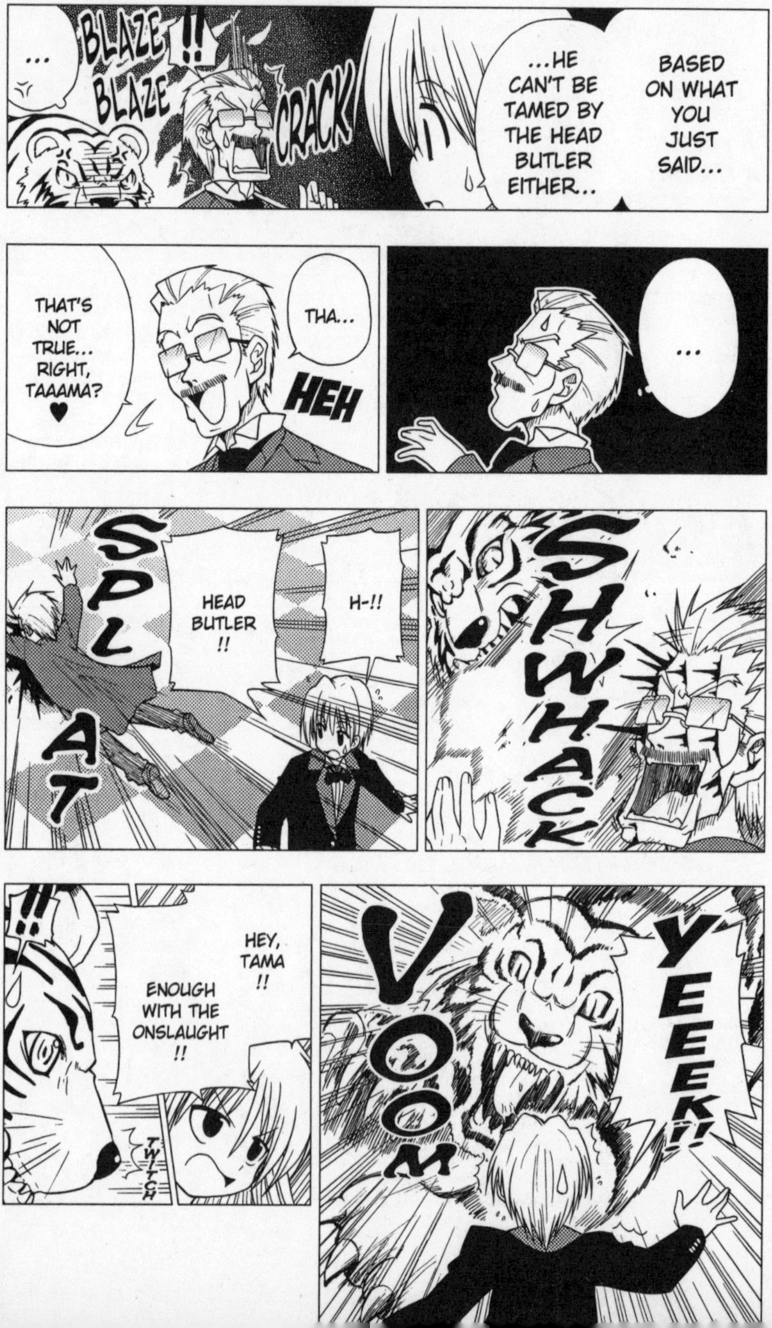
BASED ON WHAT YOU JUST SAID...
...HE CAN'T BE TAMED BY THE HEAD BUTLER EITHER...
CRACK
BLAZE BLAZE
!!
...
...
THA...
HEH
THAT'S NOT TRUE... RIGHT, TAAAMA? ♥
SHWHACK
H-!!
HEAD BUTLER !!
SPLAT
YEEEK!!
VOOM
HEY, TAMA !!
ENOUGH WITH THE ONSLAUGHT !!
TWITCH
!!

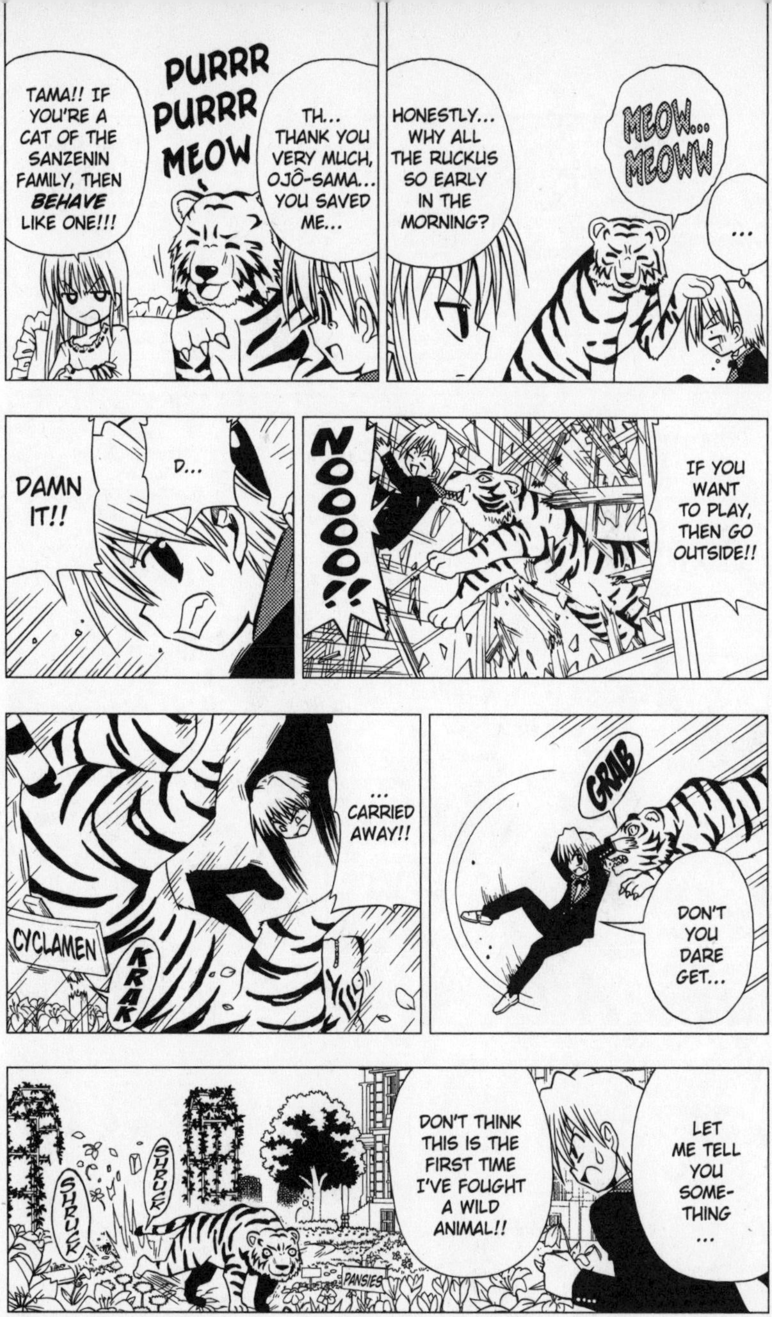
HONESTLY... WHY ALL THE RUCKUS SO EARLY IN THE MORNING?
MEOW... MEOWW
...
TH... THANK YOU VERY MUCH, OJÔ-SAMA... YOU SAVED ME...
PURRR PURRR MEOW
TAMA!! IF YOU'RE A CAT OF THE SANZENIN FAMILY, THEN BEHAVE LIKE ONE!!!
IF YOU WANT TO PLAY, THEN GO OUTSIDE!!
NOOOO!!
D...
DAMN IT!!
GRAB
DON'T YOU DARE GET...
...CARRIED AWAY!!
KRAK
CYCLAMEN
LET ME TELL YOU SOME-THING...
DON'T THINK THIS IS THE FIRST TIME I'VE FOUGHT A WILD ANIMAL!!
SHRUCK
SHRUCK
PANSIES

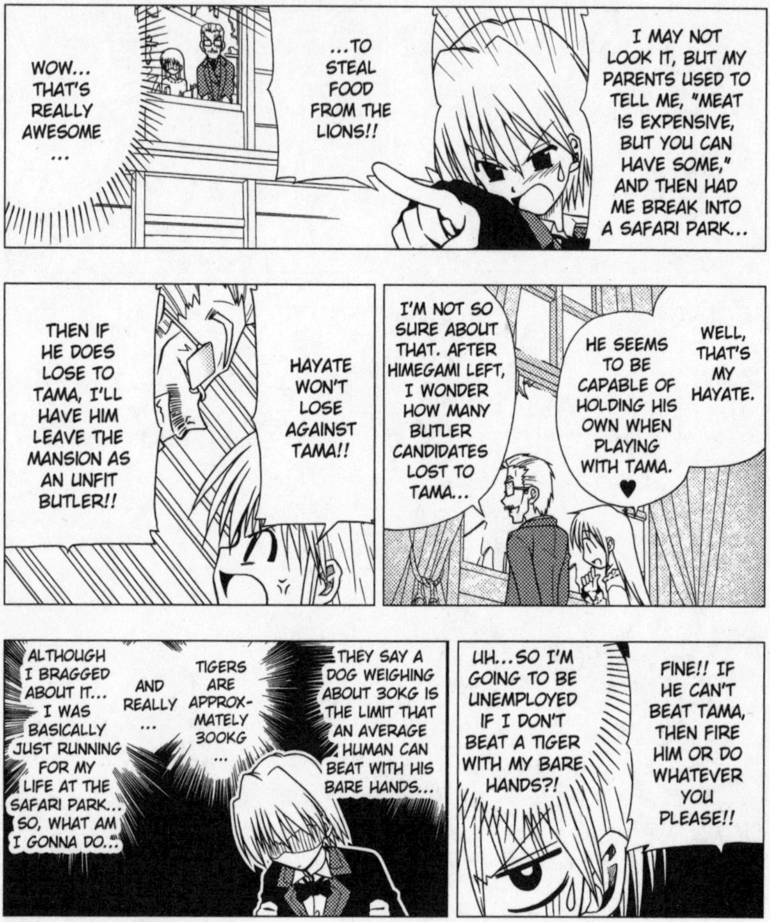
I MAY NOT LOOK IT, BUT MY PARENTS USED TO TELL ME, "MEAT IS EXPENSIVE, BUT YOU CAN HAVE SOME," AND THEN HAD ME BREAK INTO A SAFARI PARK...
...TO STEAL FOOD FROM THE LIONS!!
WOW... THAT'S REALLY AWESOME...
WELL, THAT'S MY HAYATE.
HE SEEMS TO BE CAPABLE OF HOLDING HIS OWN WHEN PLAYING WITH TAMA. ♥
I'M NOT SO SURE ABOUT THAT. AFTER HIMEGAMI LEFT, I WONDER HOW MANY BUTLER CANDIDATES LOST TO TAMA...
HAYATE WON'T LOSE AGAINST TAMA!!
THEN IF HE DOES LOSE TO TAMA, I'LL HAVE HIM LEAVE THE MANSION AS AN UNFIT BUTLER!!
FINE!! IF HE CAN'T BEAT TAMA, THEN FIRE HIM OR DO WHATEVER YOU PLEASE!!
UH...SO I'M GOING TO BE UNEMPLOYED IF I DON'T BEAT A TIGER WITH MY BARE HANDS?!
THEY SAY A DOG WEIGHING ABOUT 30KG IS THE LIMIT THAT AN AVERAGE HUMAN CAN BEAT WITH HIS BARE HANDS...
TIGERS ARE APPROX-MATELY 300KG...
AND REALLY...
ALTHOUGH I BRAGGED ABOUT IT... I WAS BASICALLY JUST RUNNING FOR MY LIFE AT THE SAFARI PARK... SO, WHAT AM I GONNA DO...

*30kg = 66lbs, 300kg = 660lbs

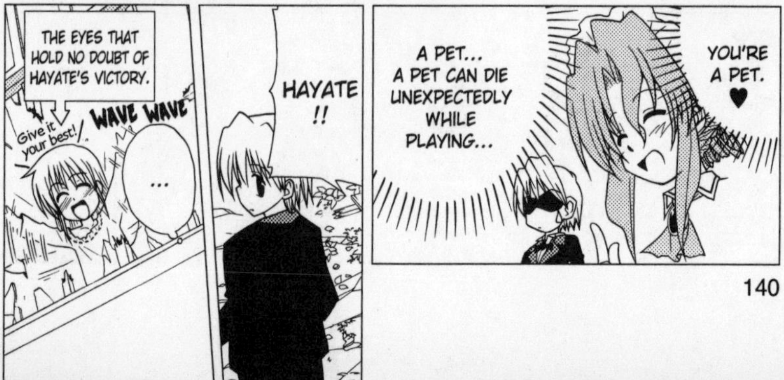
YOU'RE A PET. ♥
A PET... A PET CAN DIE UNEXPECTEDLY WHILE PLAYING...
HAYATE!!
THE EYES THAT HOLD NO DOUBT OF HAYATE'S VICTORY.
WAVE WAVE
Give it your best!
...

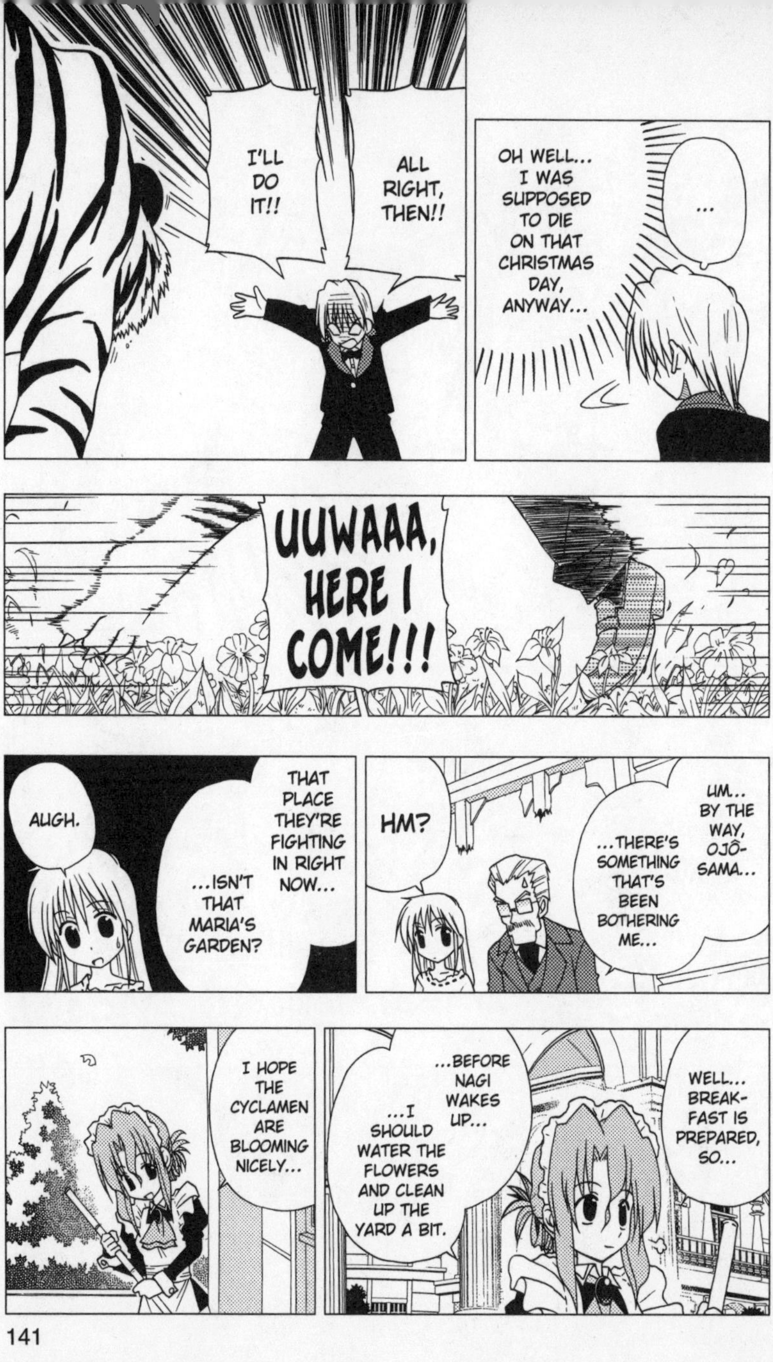
...
OH WELL... I WAS SUPPOSED TO DIE ON THAT CHRISTMAS DAY, ANYWAY...
ALL RIGHT, THEN!!
I'LL DO IT!!
UUWAAA, HERE I COME!!!
UM... BY THE WAY, OJÔ-SAMA...
...THERE'S SOMETHING THAT'S BEEN BOTHERING ME...
HM?
THAT PLACE THEY'RE FIGHTING IN RIGHT NOW...
...ISN'T THAT MARIA'S GARDEN?
AUGH.
WELL... BREAK-FAST IS PREPARED, SO...
...BEFORE NAGI WAKES UP...
...I SHOULD WATER THE FLOWERS AND CLEAN UP THE YARD A BIT.
I HOPE THE CYCLAMEN ARE BLOOMING NICELY...

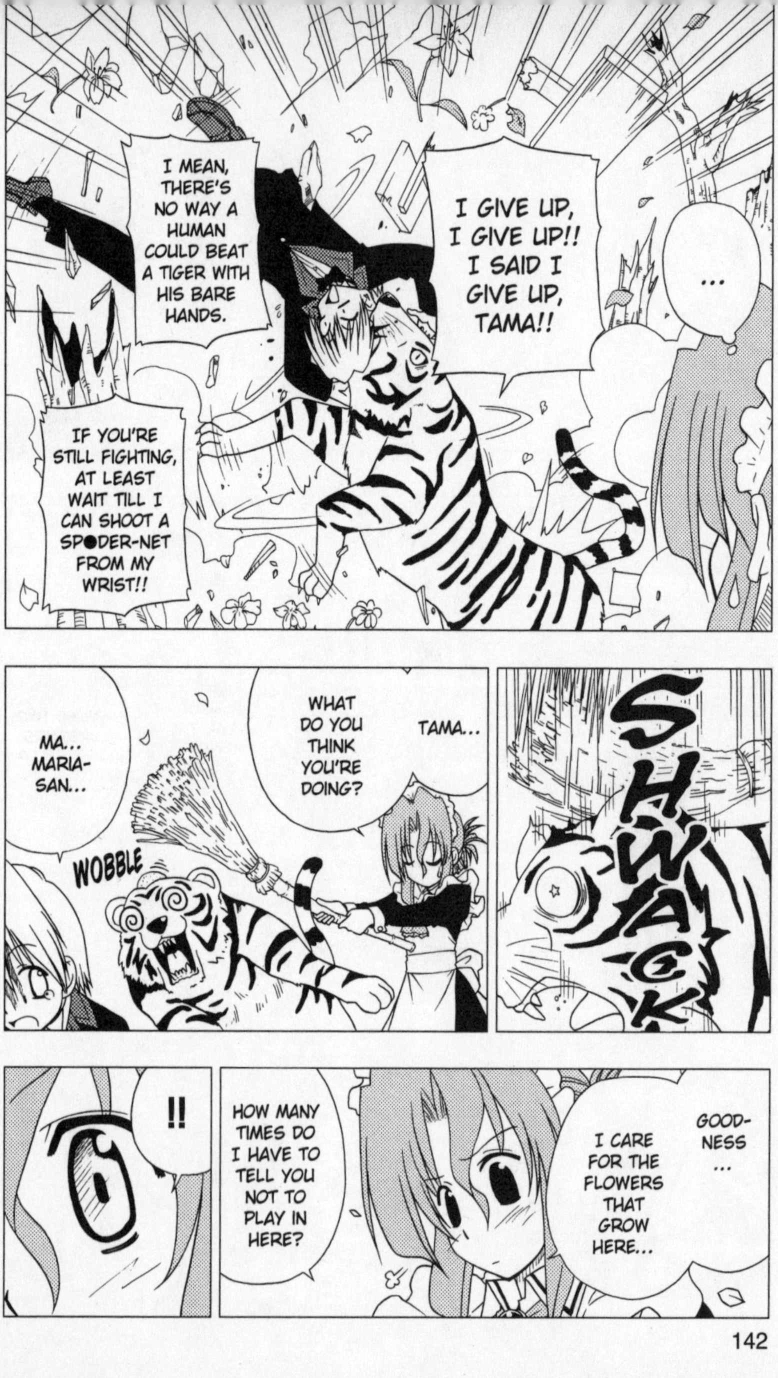
...
I GIVE UP, I GIVE UP!! I SAID I GIVE UP, TAMA!!
I MEAN, THERE'S NO WAY A HUMAN COULD BEAT A TIGER WITH HIS BARE HANDS.
IF YOU'RE STILL FIGHTING, AT LEAST WAIT TILL I CAN SHOOT A SP●DER-NET FROM MY WRIST!!
SHWACK
TAMA...
WHAT DO YOU THINK YOU'RE DOING?
WOBBLE
MA... MARIA-SAN...
GOODNESS...
I CARE FOR THE FLOWERS THAT GROW HERE...
HOW MANY TIMES DO I HAVE TO TELL YOU NOT TO PLAY IN HERE?
!!

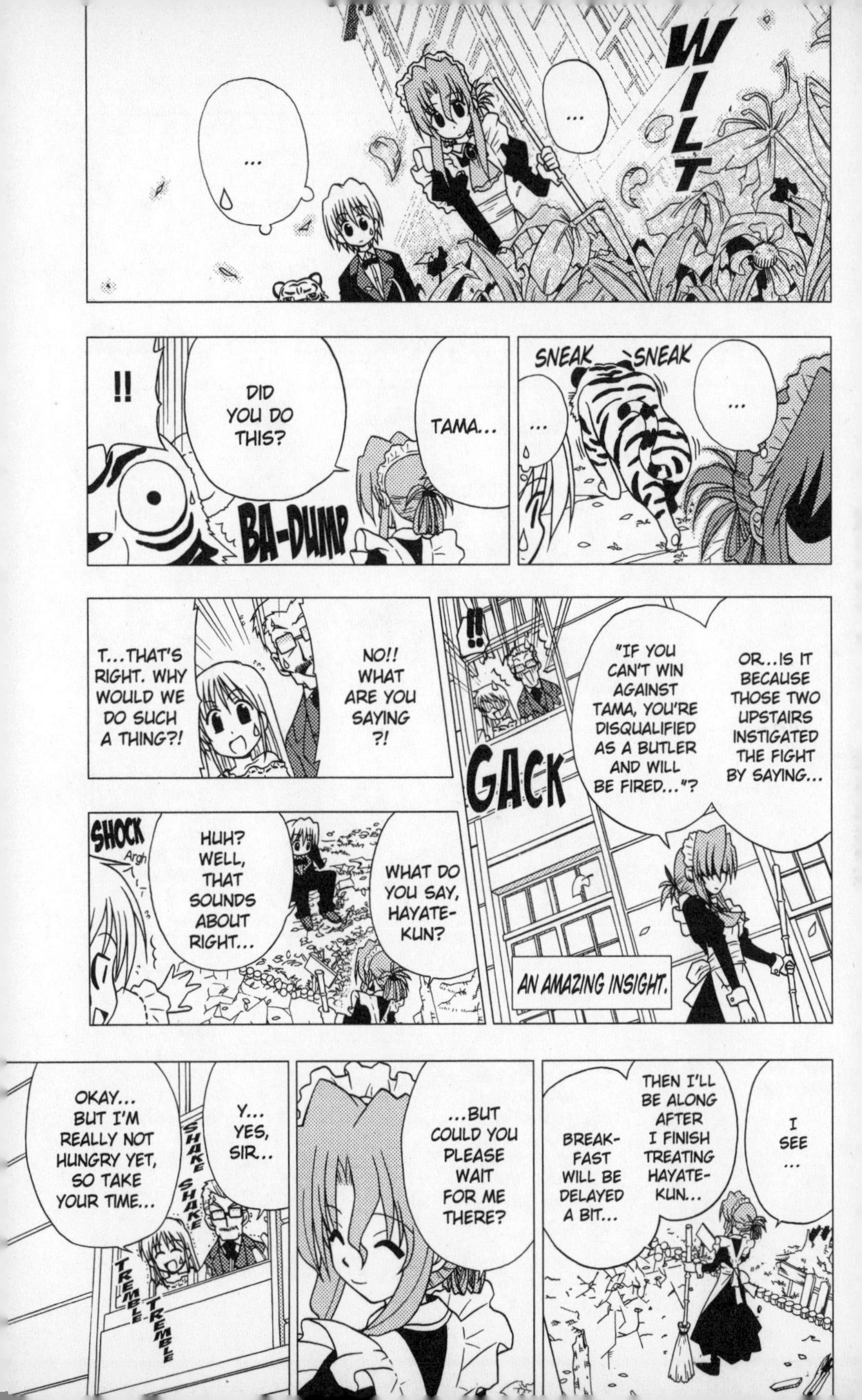
WILT
...
...
SNEAK SNEAK
...
...
TAMA...
DID YOU DO THIS?
!!
BA-DUMP
OR...IS IT BECAUSE THOSE TWO UPSTAIRS INSTIGATED THE FIGHT BY SAYING...
"IF YOU CAN'T WIN AGAINST TAMA, YOU'RE DISQUALIFIED AS A BUTLER AND WILL BE FIRED..."?
!!
GACK
AN AMAZING INSIGHT.
NO!! WHAT ARE YOU SAYING ?!
T...THAT'S RIGHT. WHY WOULD WE DO SUCH A THING?!
WHAT DO YOU SAY, HAYATE-KUN?
HUH? WELL, THAT SOUNDS ABOUT RIGHT...
SHOCK
Argh
I SEE...
THEN I'LL BE ALONG AFTER I FINISH TREATING HAYATE-KUN...
BREAK-FAST WILL BE DELAYED A BIT...
...BUT COULD YOU PLEASE WAIT FOR ME THERE?
Y... YES, SIR...
OKAY... BUT I'M REALLY NOT HUNGRY YET, SO TAKE YOUR TIME...
SHAKE SHAKE
TREMBLE-TREMBLE

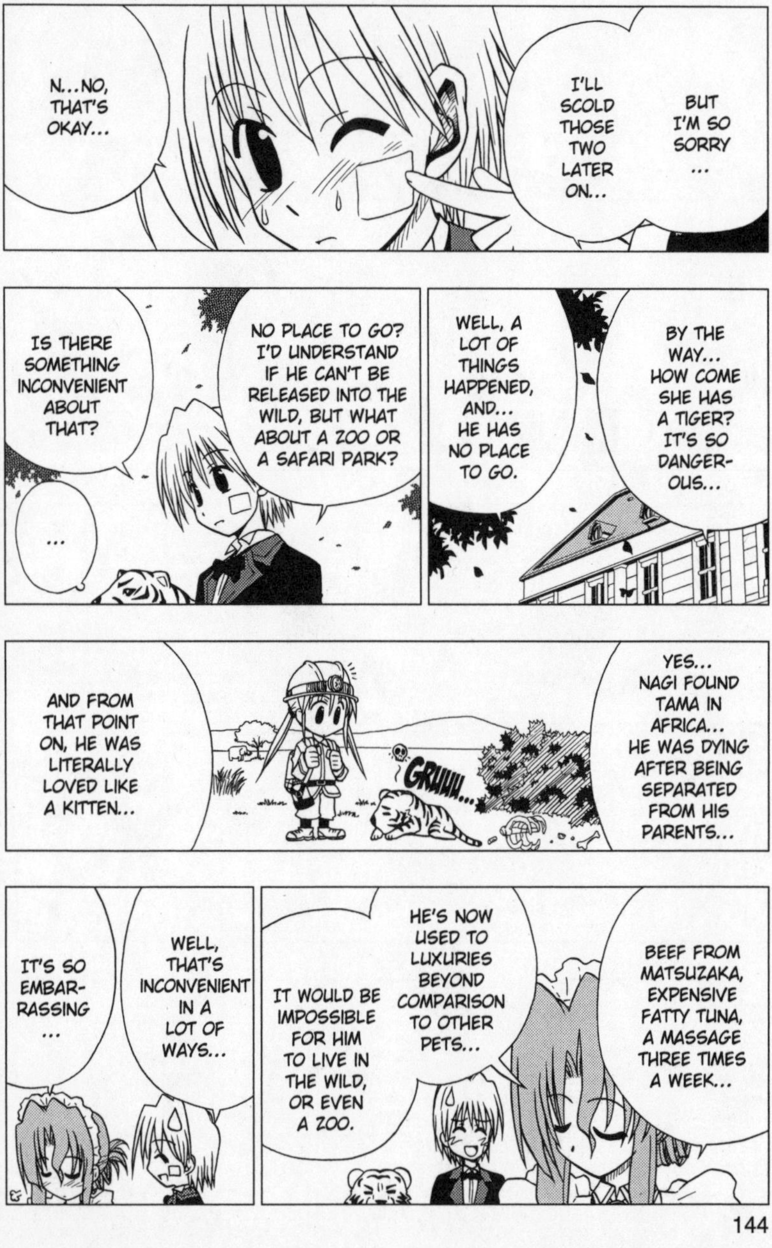
BUT I'M SO SORRY...
I'LL SCOLD THOSE TWO LATER ON...
N...NO, THAT'S OKAY...
BY THE WAY... HOW COME SHE HAS A TIGER? IT'S SO DANGER-OUS...
WELL, A LOT OF THINGS HAPPENED, AND... HE HAS NO PLACE TO GO.
NO PLACE TO GO? I'D UNDERSTAND IF HE CAN'T BE RELEASED INTO THE WILD, BUT WHAT ABOUT A ZOO OR A SAFARI PARK?
IS THERE SOMETHING INCONVENIENT ABOUT THAT?
...
YES... NAGI FOUND TAMA IN AFRICA... HE WAS DYING AFTER BEING SEPARATED FROM HIS PARENTS...
GRUUU...
AND FROM THAT POINT ON, HE WAS LITERALLY LOVED LIKE A KITTEN...
BEEF FROM MATSUZAKA, EXPENSIVE FATTY TUNA, A MASSAGE THREE TIMES A WEEK...
HE'S NOW USED TO LUXURIES BEYOND COMPARISON TO OTHER PETS...
IT WOULD BE IMPOSSIBLE FOR HIM TO LIVE IN THE WILD, OR EVEN A ZOO.
WELL, THAT'S INCONVENIENT IN A LOT OF WAYS...
IT'S SO EMBAR-RASSING...

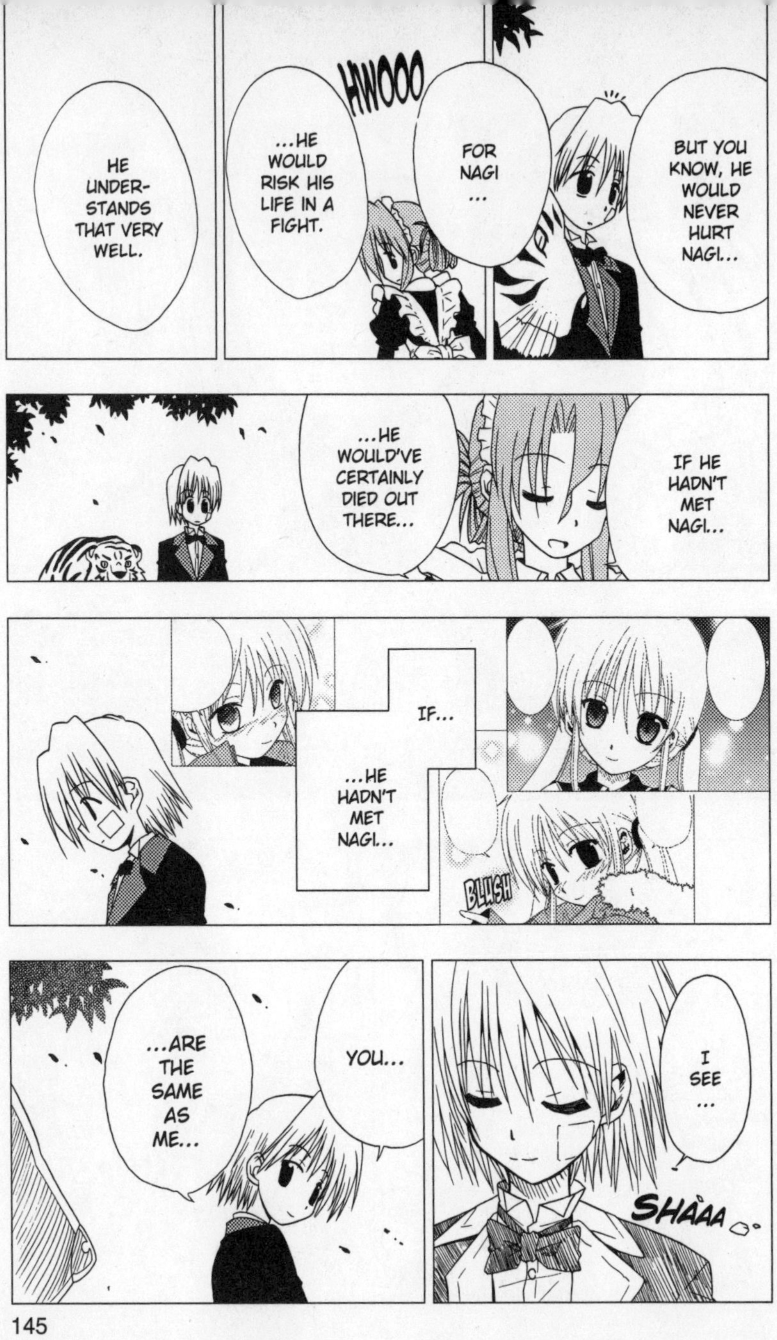
BUT YOU KNOW, HE WOULD NEVER HURT NAGI...
FOR NAGI ...
HWOOO
...HE WOULD RISK HIS LIFE IN A FIGHT.
HE UNDER-STANDS THAT VERY WELL.
IF HE HADN'T MET NAGI...
...HE WOULD'VE CERTAINLY DIED OUT THERE...
IF...
...HE HADN'T MET NAGI...
BLUSH
I SEE ...
SHAAA
YOU...
...ARE THE SAME AS ME...

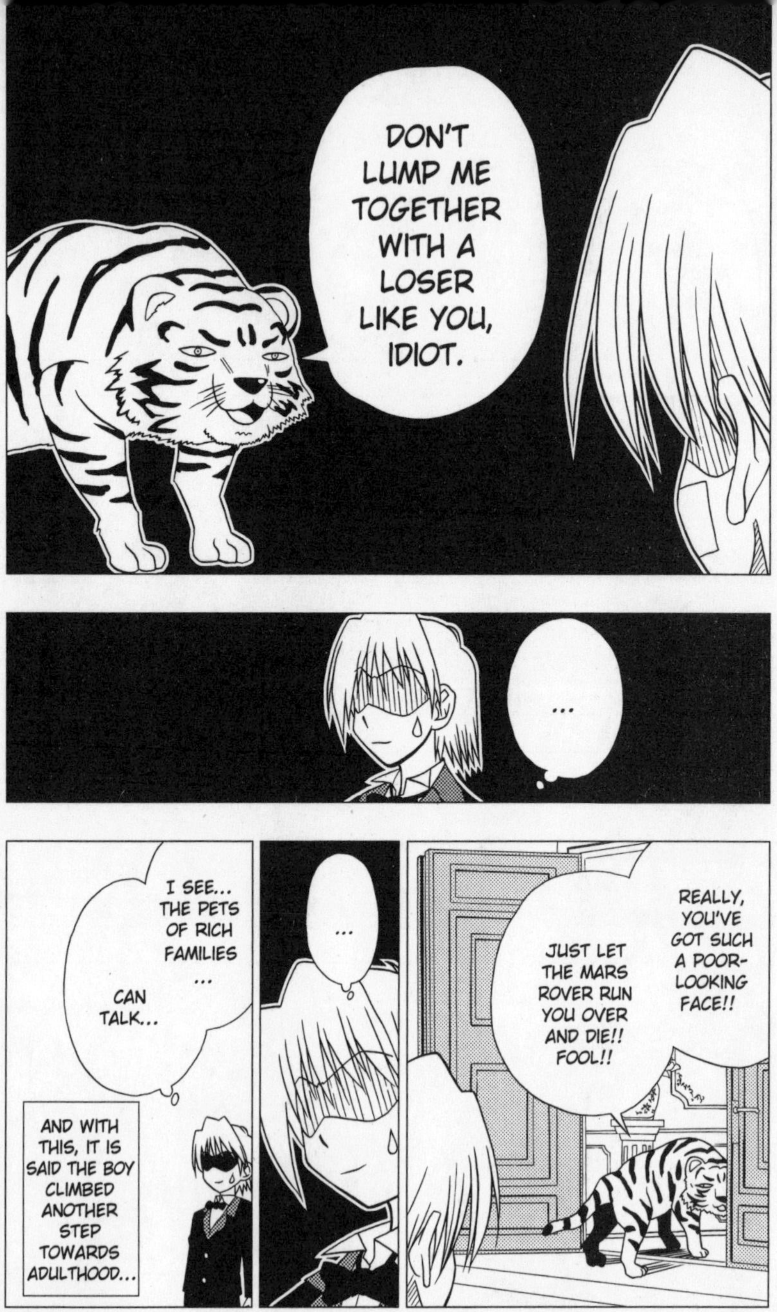
DON'T LUMP ME TOGETHER WITH A LOSER LIKE YOU, IDIOT.
...
REALLY, YOU'VE GOT SUCH A POOR-LOOKING FACE!!
JUST LET THE MARS ROVER RUN YOU OVER AND DIE!! FOOL!!
...
I SEE... THE PETS OF RICH FAMILIES ...
CAN TALK...
AND WITH THIS, IT IS SAID THE BOY CLIMBED ANOTHER STEP TOWARDS ADULTHOOD...

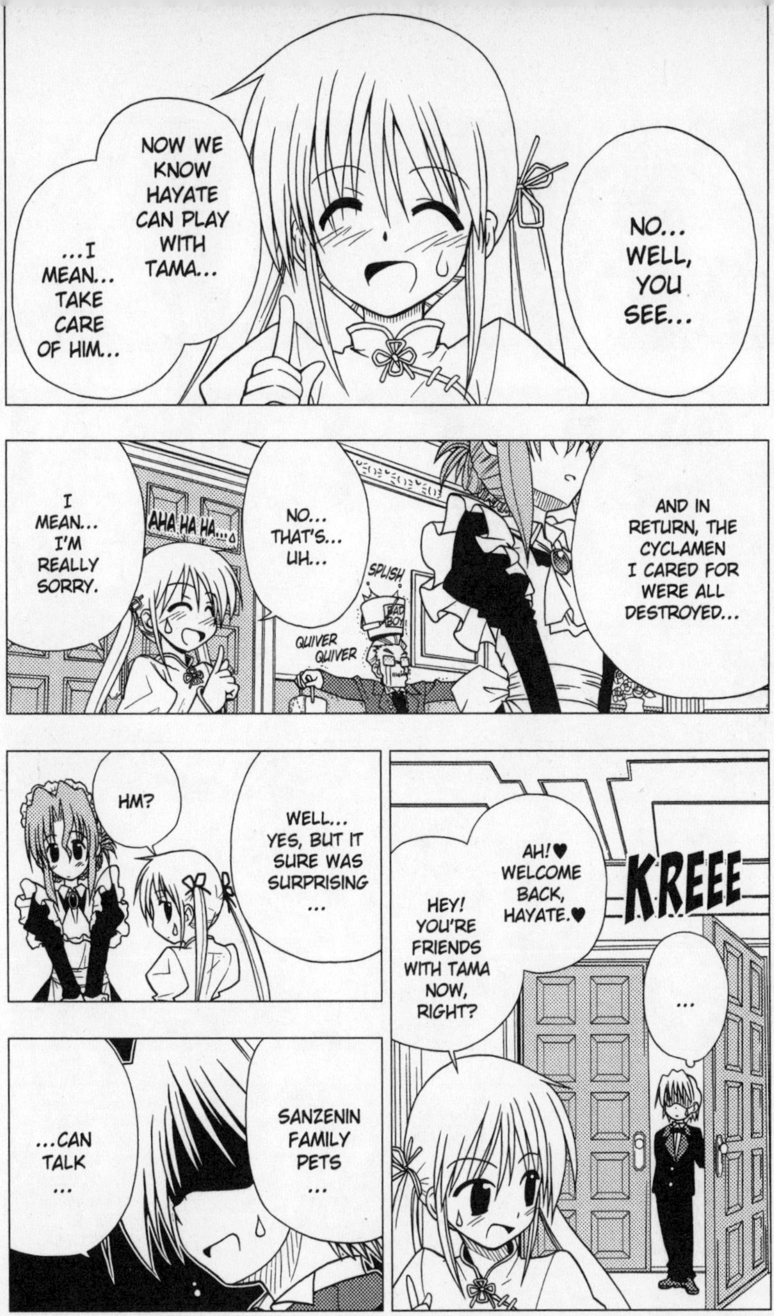
NO... WELL, YOU SEE...
NOW WE KNOW HAYATE CAN PLAY WITH TAMA...
...I MEAN... TAKE CARE OF HIM...
AND IN RETURN, THE CYCLAMEN I CARED FOR WERE ALL DESTROYED...
SPLISH
BAD BOY!
QUIVER QUIVER
NO... THAT'S... UH...
AHA HA HA...
I MEAN... I'M REALLY SORRY.
KREEE
...
AH!♥ WELCOME BACK, HAYATE.♥
HEY! YOU'RE FRIENDS WITH TAMA NOW, RIGHT?
WELL... YES, BUT IT SURE WAS SURPRISING ...
HM?
SANZENIN FAMILY PETS ...
...CAN TALK ...

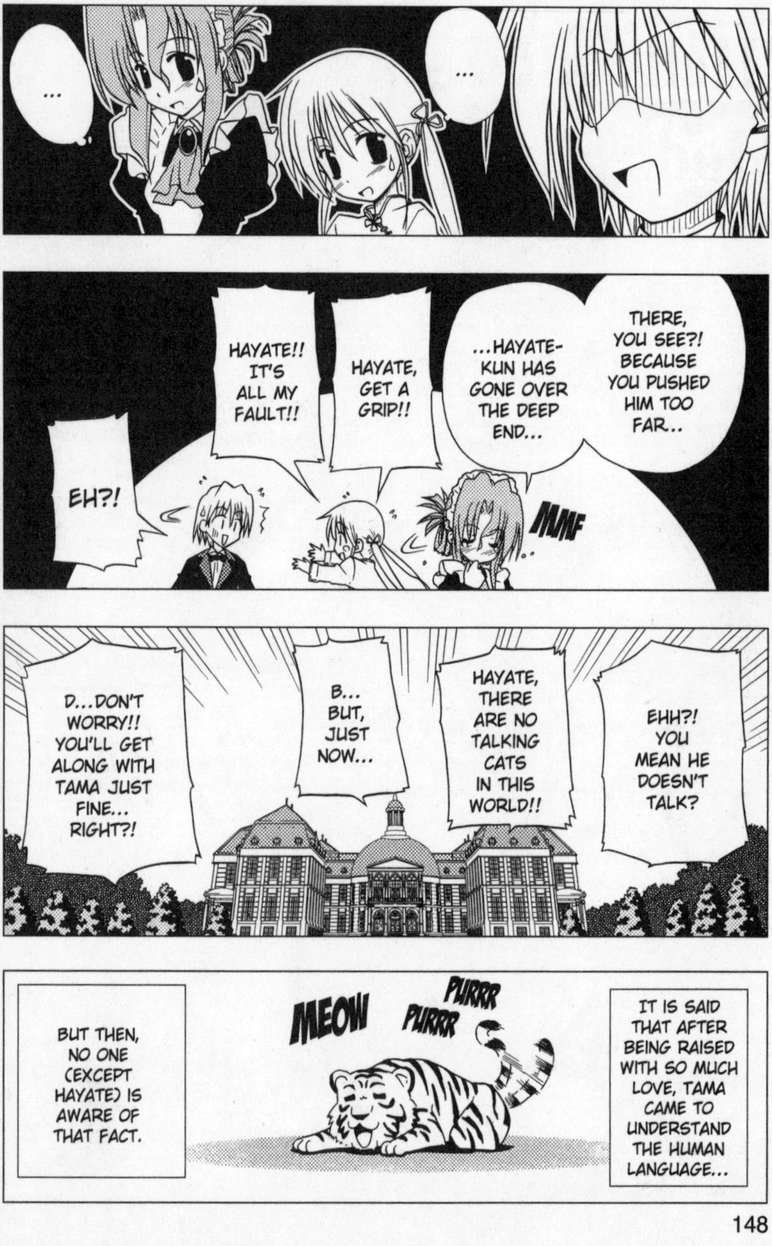
...
...
THERE, YOU SEE?! BECAUSE YOU PUSHED HIM TOO FAR..
...HAYATE-KUN HAS GONE OVER THE DEEP END...
MUNF
HAYATE, GET A GRIP!!
HAYATE!! IT'S ALL MY FAULT!!
EH?!
EHH?! YOU MEAN HE DOESN'T TALK?
HAYATE, THERE ARE NO TALKING CATS IN THIS WORLD!!
B... BUT, JUST NOW...
D...DON'T WORRY!! YOU'LL GET ALONG WITH TAMA JUST FINE... RIGHT?!
IT IS SAID THAT AFTER BEING RAISED WITH SO MUCH LOVE, TAMA CAME TO UNDERSTAND THE HUMAN LANGUAGE...
PURRR
PURRR
MEOW
BUT THEN, NO ONE (EXCEPT HAYATE) IS AWARE OF THAT FACT.

Episode 8: "Hellbound with Neko-mimi Mode"

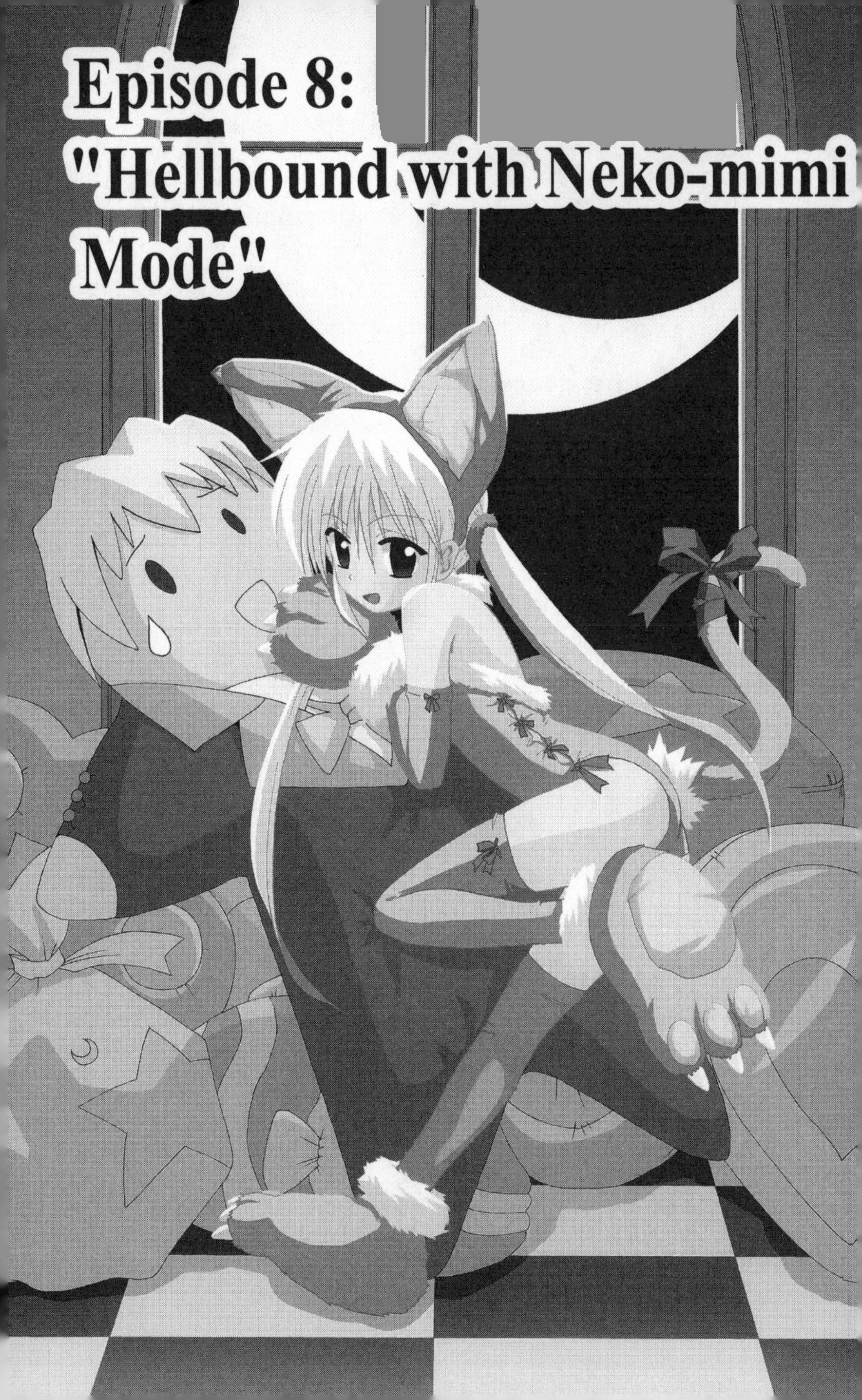

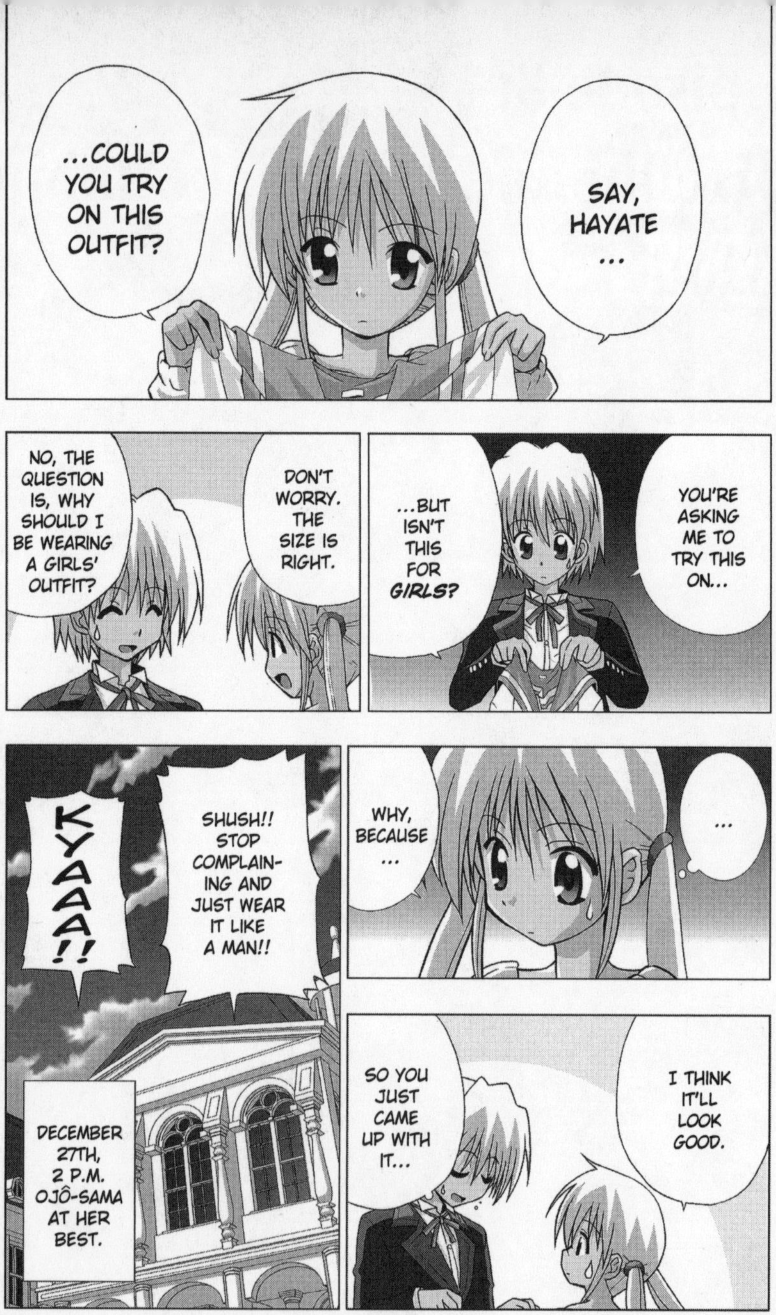
SAY, HAYATE ...
...COULD YOU TRY ON THIS OUTFIT?
YOU'RE ASKING ME TO TRY THIS ON...
...BUT ISN'T THIS FOR GIRLS?
DON'T WORRY. THE SIZE IS RIGHT.
NO, THE QUESTION IS, WHY SHOULD I BE WEARING A GIRLS' OUTFIT?
...
WHY, BECAUSE ...
I THINK IT'LL LOOK GOOD.
SO YOU JUST CAME UP WITH IT...
SHUSH!! STOP COMPLAIN-ING AND JUST WEAR IT LIKE A MAN!!
KYAAA!!
DECEMBER 27TH, 2 P.M. OJÔ-SAMA AT HER BEST.

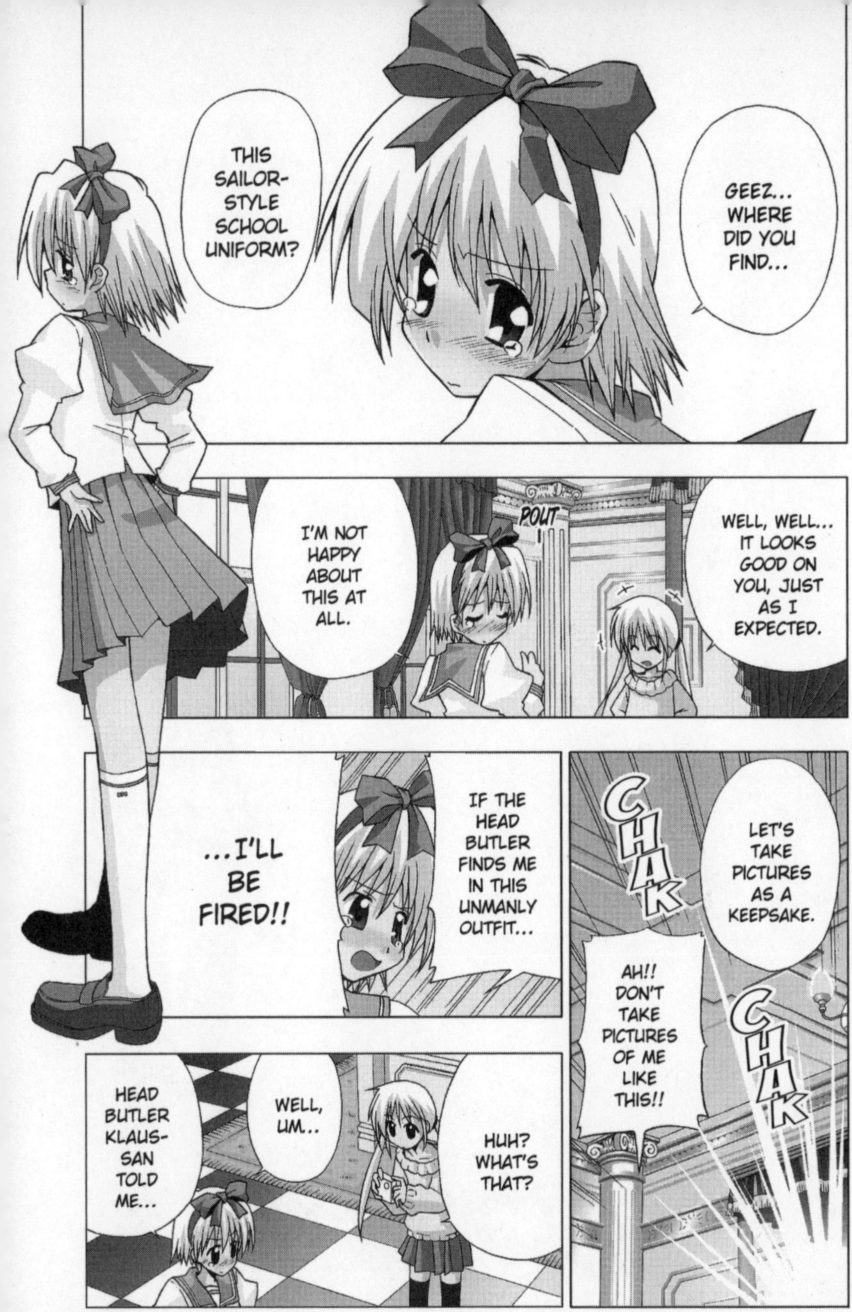
GEEZ... WHERE DID YOU FIND...
THIS SAILOR-STYLE SCHOOL UNIFORM?
WELL, WELL... IT LOOKS GOOD ON YOU, JUST AS I EXPECTED.
POUT
I'M NOT HAPPY ABOUT THIS AT ALL.
LET'S TAKE PICTURES AS A KEEPSAKE.
CHAK
AH!! DON'T TAKE PICTURES OF ME LIKE THIS!!
CHAK
IF THE HEAD BUTLER FINDS ME IN THIS UNMANLY OUTFIT...
...I'LL BE FIRED!!
HUH? WHAT'S THAT?
WELL, UM...
HEAD BUTLER KLAUS-SAN TOLD ME...

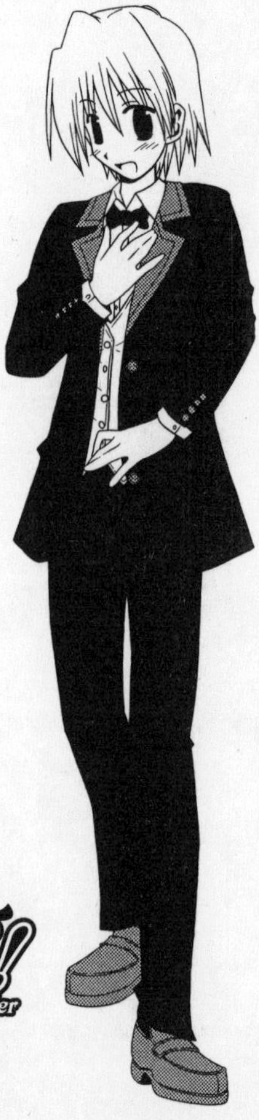

ハヤテのごとく!
Hayate the combat butler

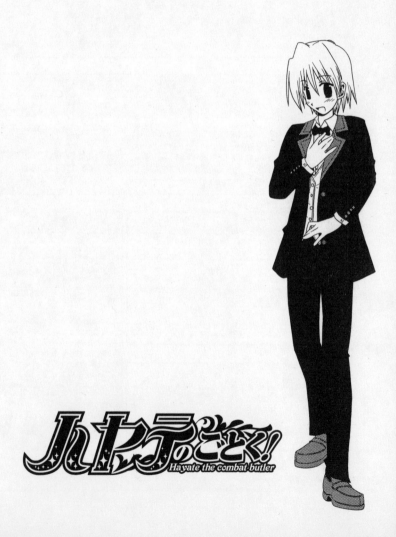

A BUTLER SHOULD BE MANLY!!

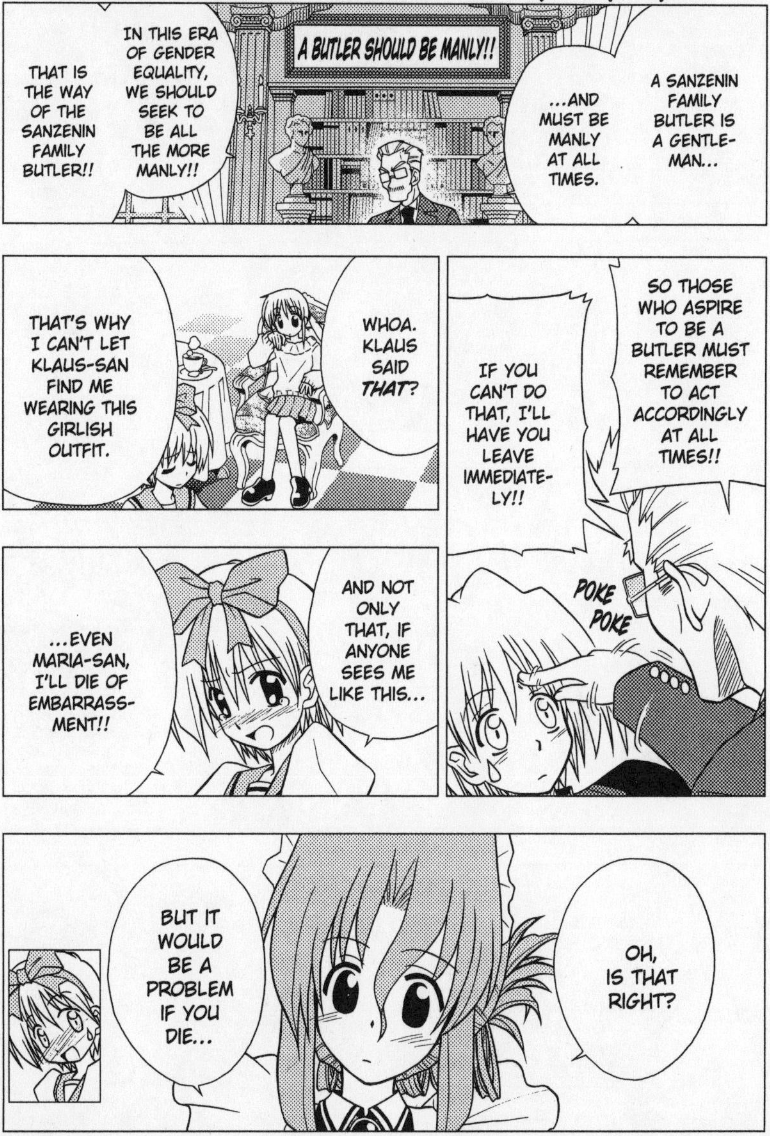
A BUTLER SHOULD BE MANLY!!
A SANZENIN FAMILY BUTLER IS A GENTLEMAN...
...AND MUST BE MANLY AT ALL TIMES.
IN THIS ERA OF GENDER EQUALITY, WE SHOULD SEEK TO BE ALL THE MORE MANLY!!
THAT IS THE WAY OF THE SANZENIN FAMILY BUTLER!!
SO THOSE WHO ASPIRE TO BE A BUTLER MUST REMEMBER TO ACT ACCORDINGLY AT ALL TIMES!!
IF YOU CAN'T DO THAT, I'LL HAVE YOU LEAVE IMMEDIATELY!!
POKE POKE
WHOA. KLAUS SAID *THAT*?
THAT'S WHY I CAN'T LET KLAUS-SAN FIND ME WEARING THIS GIRLISH OUTFIT.
AND NOT ONLY THAT, IF ANYONE SEES ME LIKE THIS...
...EVEN MARIA-SAN, I'LL DIE OF EMBARRASSMENT!!
OH, IS THAT RIGHT?
BUT IT WOULD BE A PROBLEM IF YOU DIE...

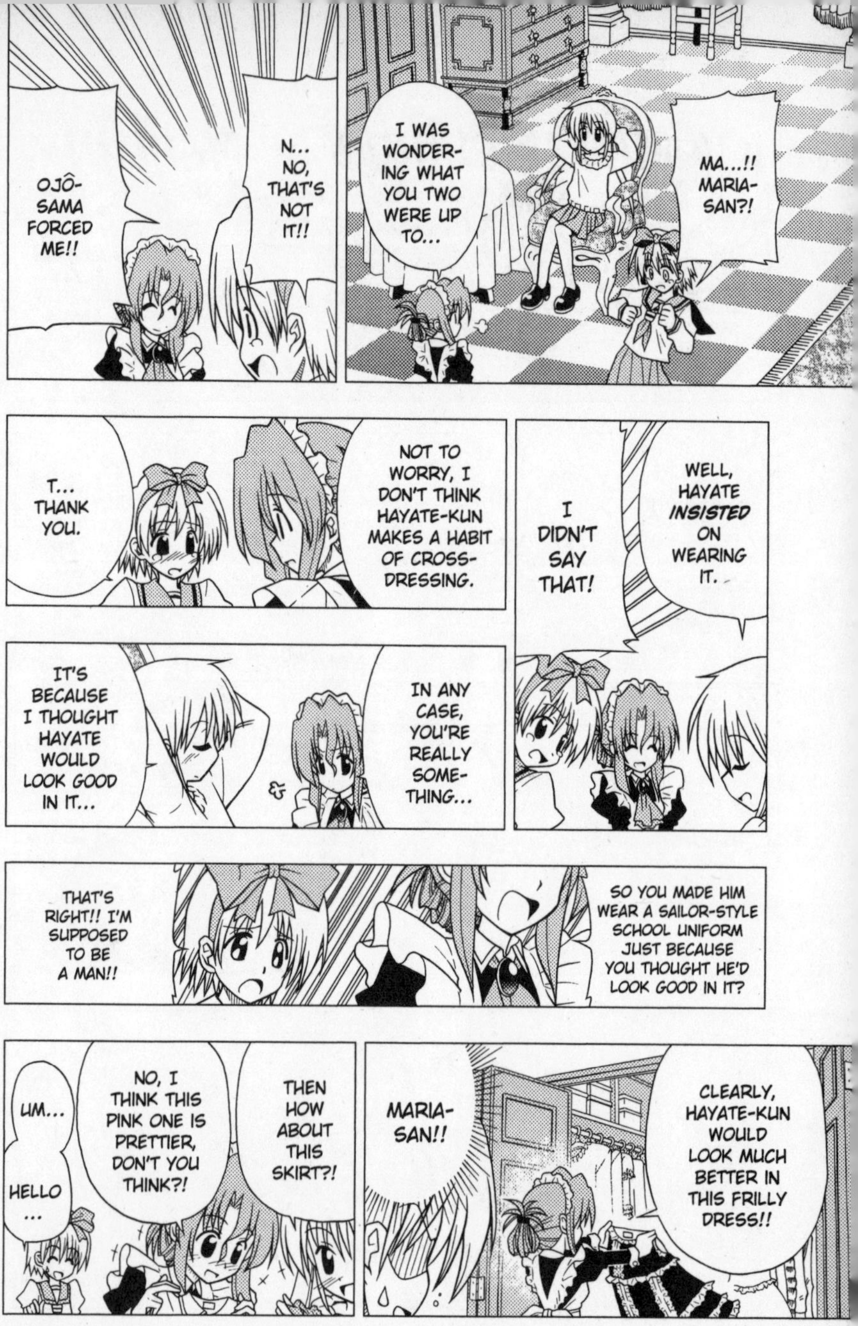
MA...!! MARIA-SAN?!
I WAS WONDERING WHAT YOU TWO WERE UP TO...
N... NO, THAT'S NOT IT!!
OJÔ-SAMA FORCED ME!!
WELL, HAYATE INSISTED ON WEARING IT.
I DIDN'T SAY THAT!
NOT TO WORRY, I DON'T THINK HAYATE-KUN MAKES A HABIT OF CROSS-DRESSING.
T... THANK YOU.
IN ANY CASE, YOU'RE REALLY SOMETHING...
IT'S BECAUSE I THOUGHT HAYATE WOULD LOOK GOOD IN IT...
SO YOU MADE HIM WEAR A SAILOR-STYLE SCHOOL UNIFORM JUST BECAUSE YOU THOUGHT HE'D LOOK GOOD IN IT?
THAT'S RIGHT!! I'M SUPPOSED TO BE A MAN!!
CLEARLY, HAYATE-KUN WOULD LOOK MUCH BETTER IN THIS FRILLY DRESS!!
MARIA-SAN!!
THEN HOW ABOUT THIS SKIRT?!
NO, I THINK THIS PINK ONE IS PRETTIER, DON'T YOU THINK?!
UM...
HELLO...

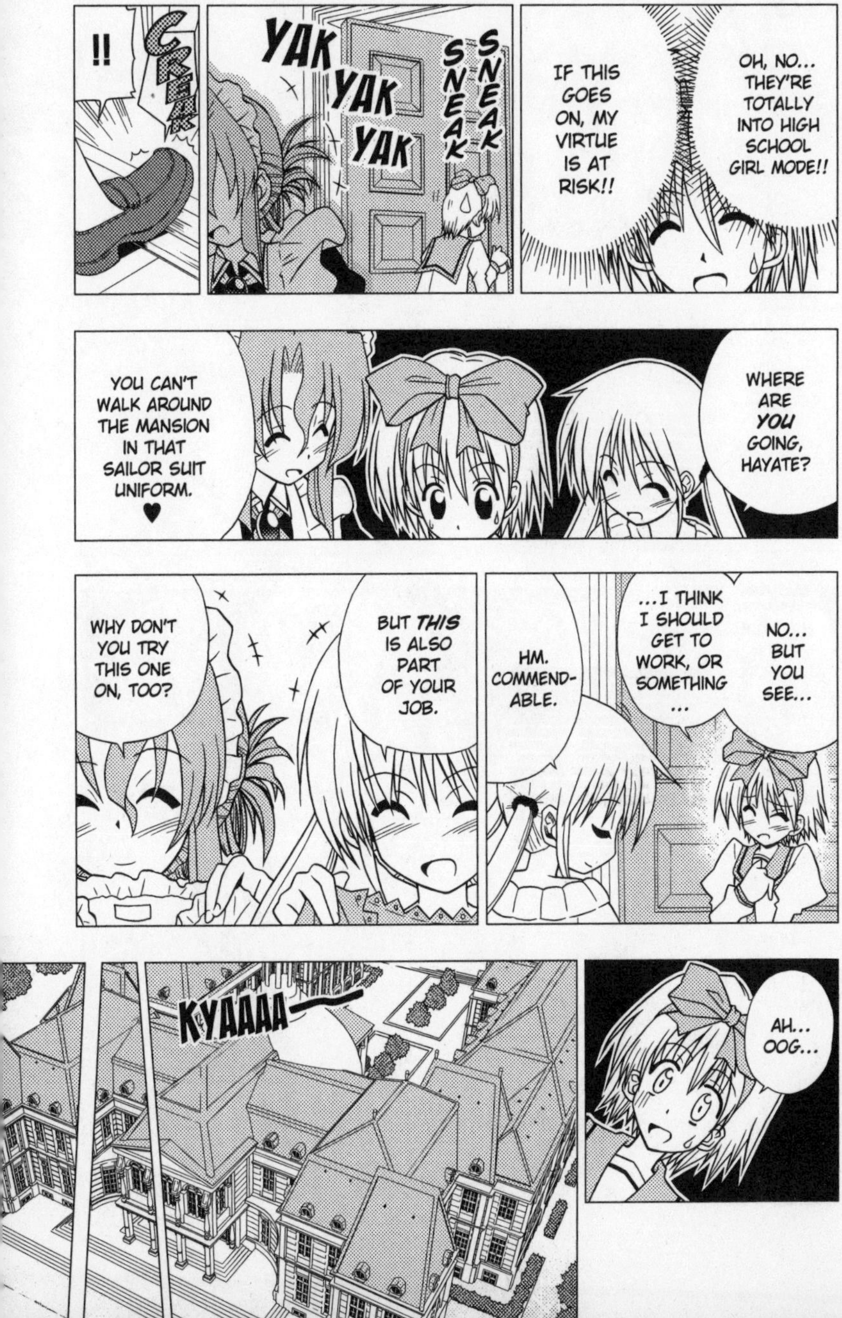
OH, NO... THEY'RE TOTALLY INTO HIGH SCHOOL GIRL MODE!!
IF THIS GOES ON, MY VIRTUE IS AT RISK!!
SNEAK SNEAK
YAK YAK YAK
CREAK
!!
WHERE ARE *YOU* GOING, HAYATE?
YOU CAN'T WALK AROUND THE MANSION IN THAT SAILOR SUIT UNIFORM. ♥
NO... BUT YOU SEE...
...I THINK I SHOULD GET TO WORK, OR SOMETHING...
HM. COMMEND-ABLE.
BUT *THIS* IS ALSO PART OF YOUR JOB.
WHY DON'T YOU TRY THIS ONE ON, TOO?
AH... OOG...
KYAAAA—

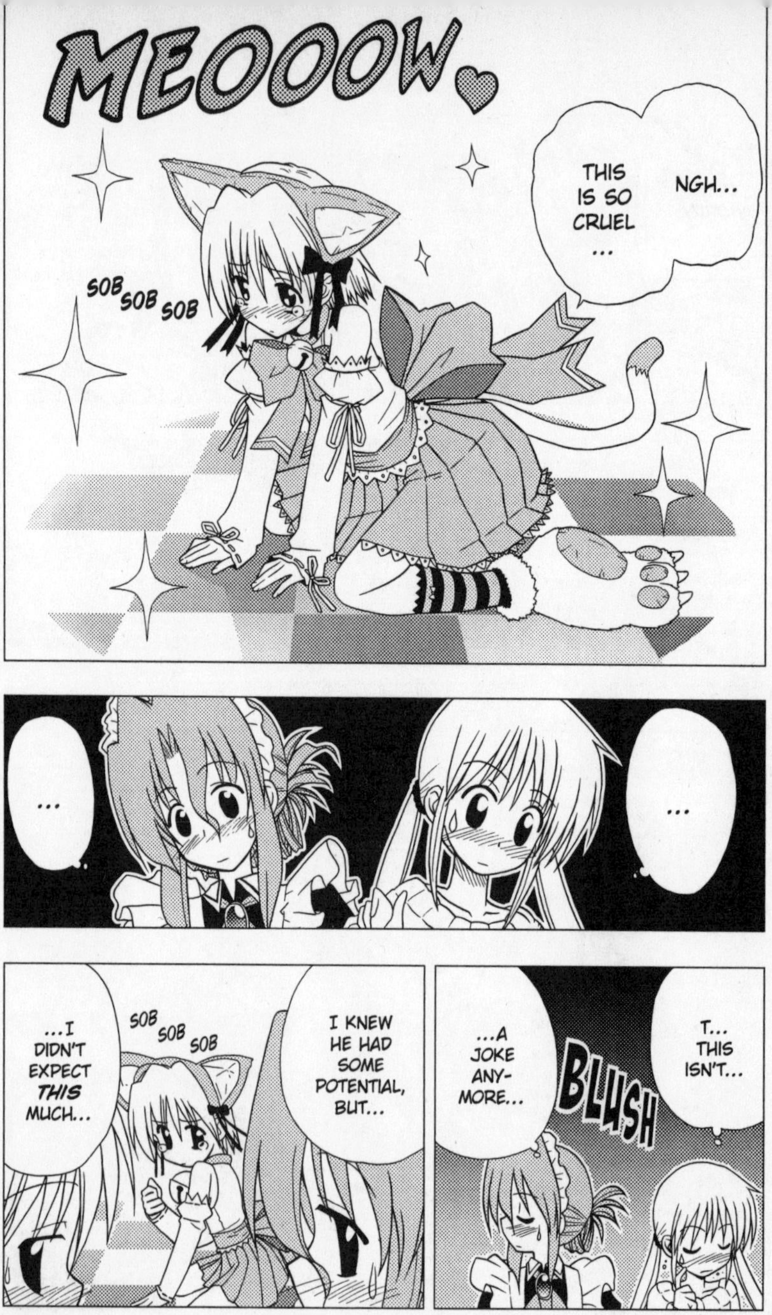
MEOOOW♥
NGH...
THIS IS SO CRUEL ...
SOB SOB SOB
...
...
T... THIS ISN'T...
BLUSH
...A JOKE ANY-MORE...
I KNEW HE HAD SOME POTENTIAL, BUT...
SOB SOB SOB
...I DIDN'T EXPECT *THIS* MUCH...

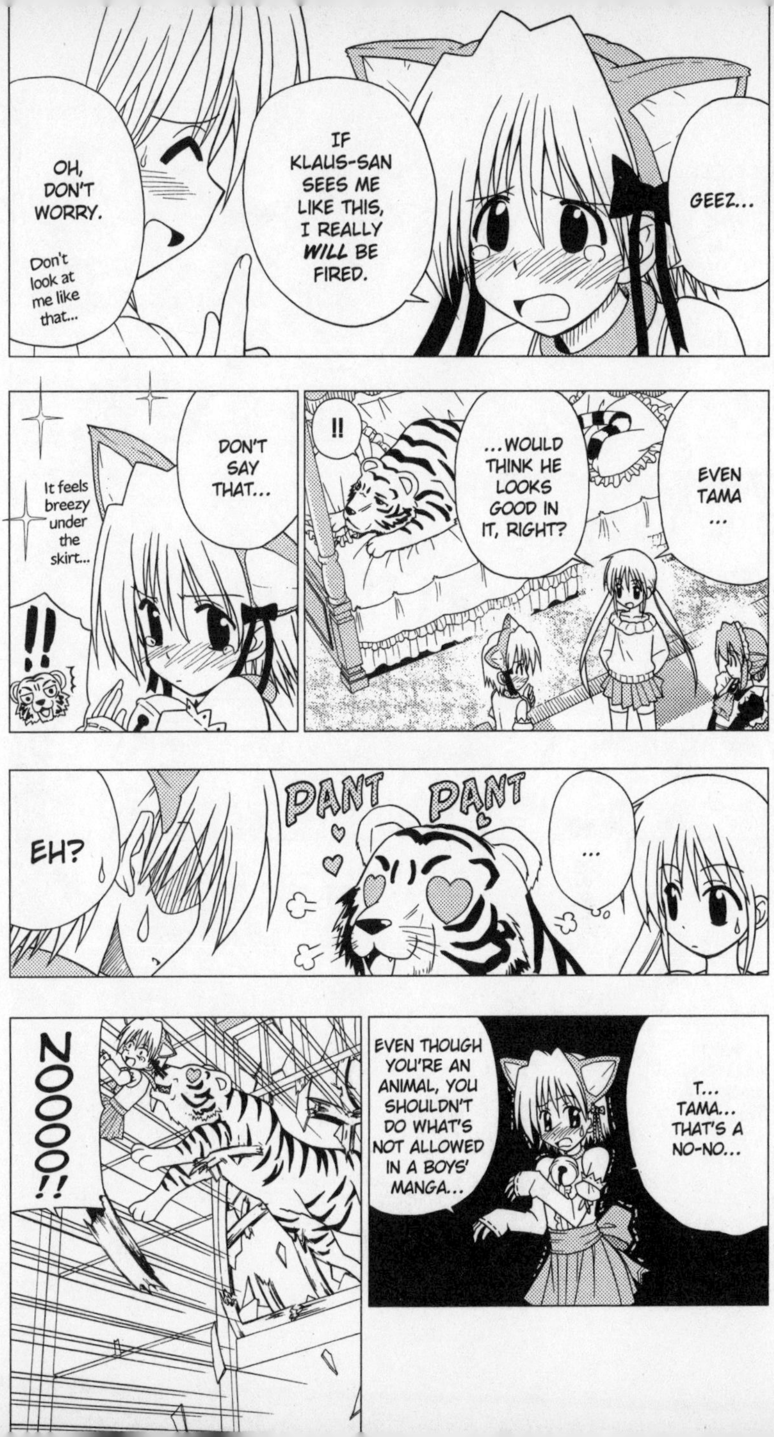
GEEZ...
IF KLAUS-SAN SEES ME LIKE THIS, I REALLY WILL BE FIRED.
OH, DON'T WORRY.
Don't look at me like that...
EVEN TAMA...
...WOULD THINK HE LOOKS GOOD IN IT, RIGHT?
!!
DON'T SAY THAT...
It feels breezy under the skirt...
!!
...
PANT PANT
EH?
T... TAMA... THAT'S A NO-NO...
EVEN THOUGH YOU'RE AN ANIMAL, YOU SHOULDN'T DO WHAT'S NOT ALLOWED IN A BOYS' MANGA...
NOOOOO!!

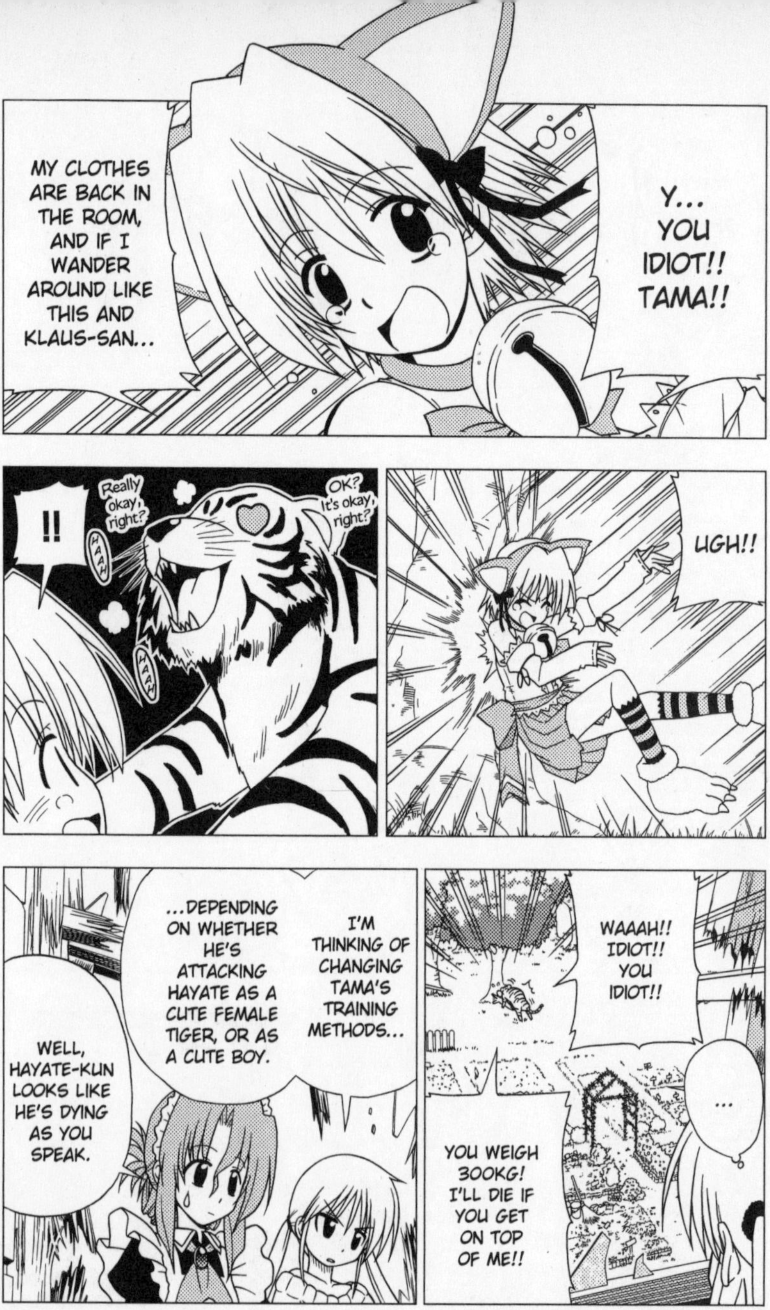
Y... YOU IDIOT!! TAMA!!
MY CLOTHES ARE BACK IN THE ROOM, AND IF I WANDER AROUND LIKE THIS AND KLAUS-SAN...
UGH!!
OK? It's okay, right?
Really okay, right?
HAAH
HAAH
!!
WAAAH!! IDIOT!! YOU IDIOT!!
YOU WEIGH 300KG! I'LL DIE IF YOU GET ON TOP OF ME!!
...
I'M THINKING OF CHANGING TAMA'S TRAINING METHODS...
...DEPENDING ON WHETHER HE'S ATTACKING HAYATE AS A CUTE FEMALE TIGER, OR AS A CUTE BOY.
WELL, HAYATE-KUN LOOKS LIKE HE'S DYING AS YOU SPEAK.

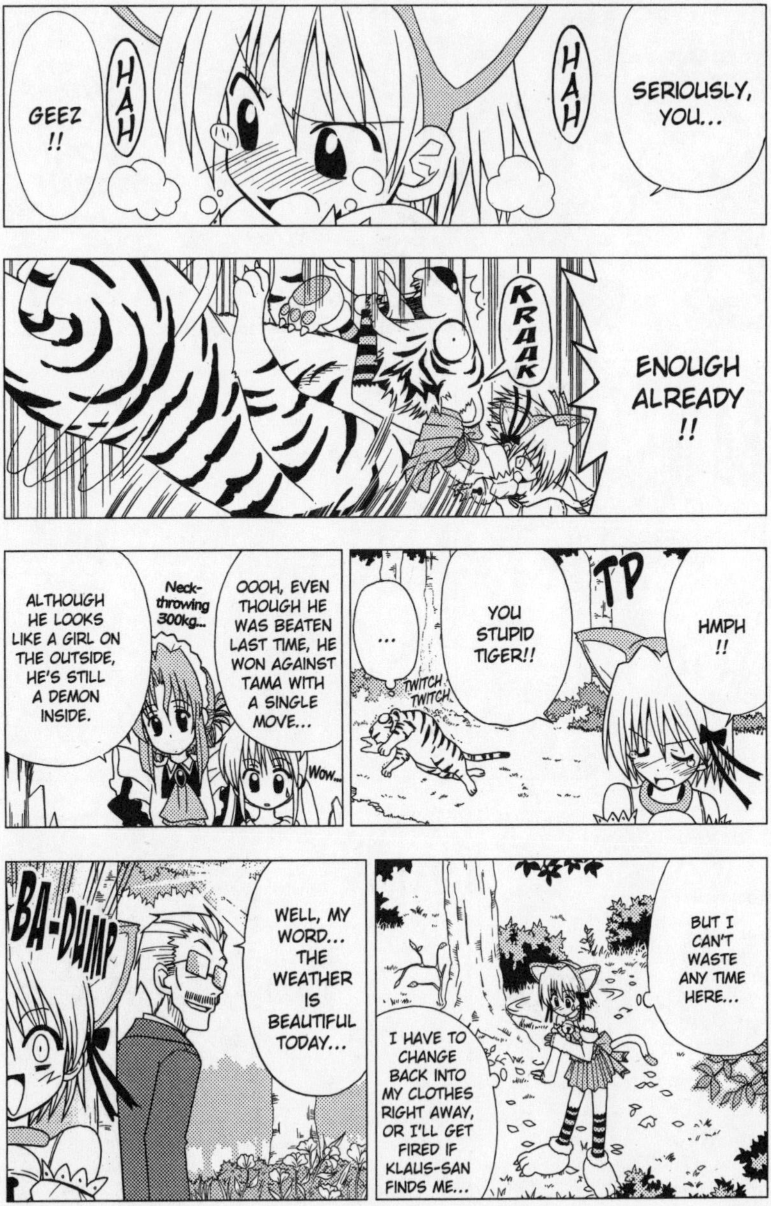
SERIOUSLY, YOU...
HAH
HAH
GEEZ !!
ENOUGH ALREADY !!
KRAAK
HMPH !!
TP
YOU STUPID TIGER!!
...
TWITCH TWITCH
OOOH, EVEN THOUGH HE WAS BEATEN LAST TIME, HE WON AGAINST TAMA WITH A SINGLE MOVE...
Neck-throwing 300kg...
ALTHOUGH HE LOOKS LIKE A GIRL ON THE OUTSIDE, HE'S STILL A DEMON INSIDE.
Wow...
BUT I CAN'T WASTE ANY TIME HERE...
I HAVE TO CHANGE BACK INTO MY CLOTHES RIGHT AWAY, OR I'LL GET FIRED IF KLAUS-SAN FINDS ME...
WELL, MY WORD... THE WEATHER IS BEAUTIFUL TODAY...
BA-DUMP

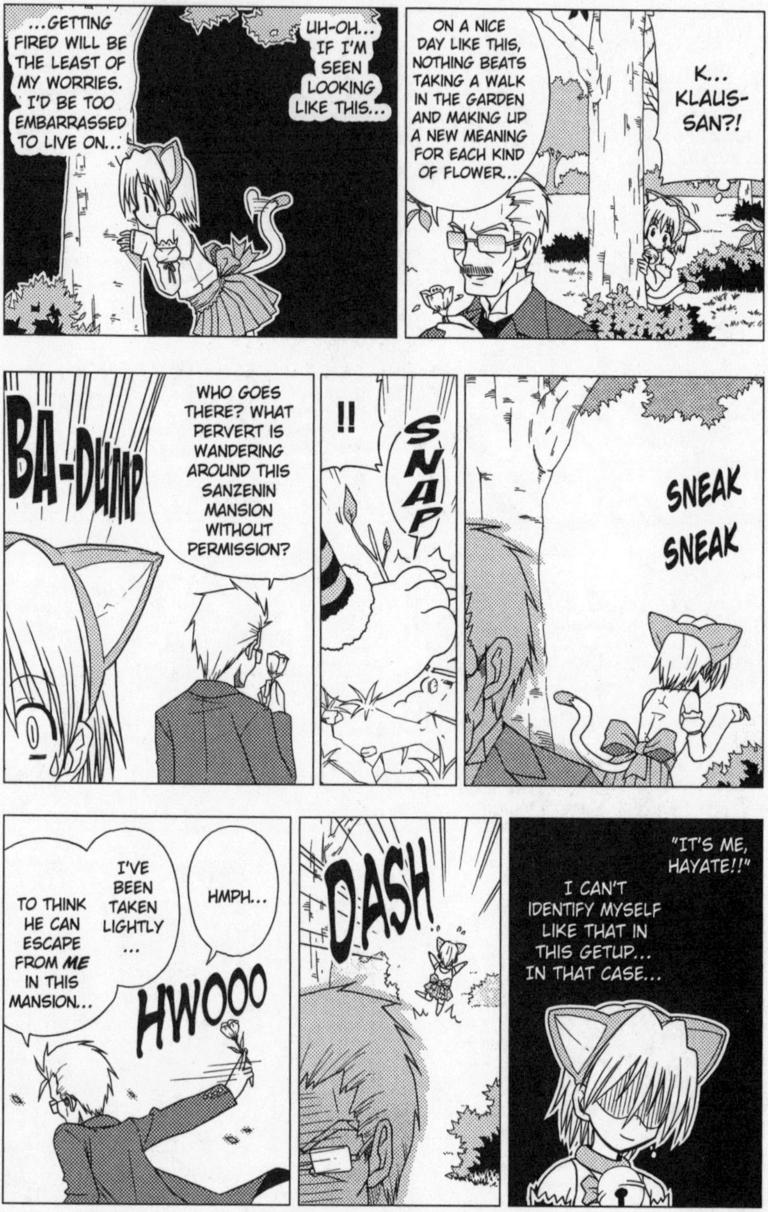
ON A NICE DAY LIKE THIS, NOTHING BEATS TAKING A WALK IN THE GARDEN AND MAKING UP A NEW MEANING FOR EACH KIND OF FLOWER...
K... KLAUS-SAN?!
UH-OH... IF I'M SEEN LOOKING LIKE THIS...
...GETTING FIRED WILL BE THE LEAST OF MY WORRIES. I'D BE TOO EMBARRASSED TO LIVE ON...
SNEAK
SNEAK
!!
SNAP
WHO GOES THERE? WHAT PERVERT IS WANDERING AROUND THIS SANZENIN MANSION WITHOUT PERMISSION?
BA-DUMP
"IT'S ME, HAYATE!!"
I CAN'T IDENTIFY MYSELF LIKE THAT IN THIS GETUP... IN THAT CASE...
DASH
HMPH...
I'VE BEEN TAKEN LIGHTLY...
TO THINK HE CAN ESCAPE FROM *ME* IN THIS MANSION...
HWOOO

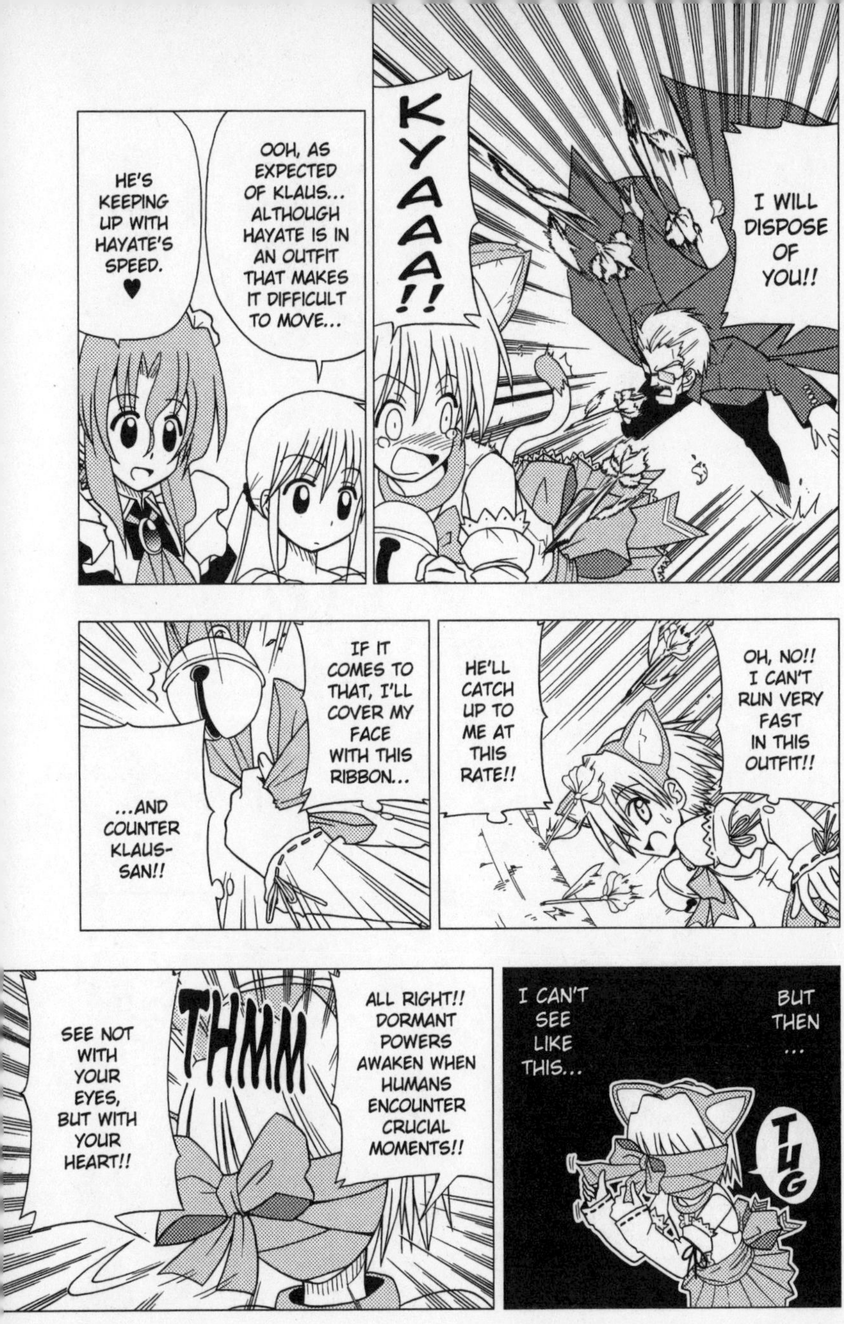
I WILL DISPOSE OF YOU!!
KYAAAA!!
OOH, AS EXPECTED OF KLAUS... ALTHOUGH HAYATE IS IN AN OUTFIT THAT MAKES IT DIFFICULT TO MOVE...
HE'S KEEPING UP WITH HAYATE'S SPEED. ♥
OH, NO!! I CAN'T RUN VERY FAST IN THIS OUTFIT!!
HE'LL CATCH UP TO ME AT THIS RATE!!
IF IT COMES TO THAT, I'LL COVER MY FACE WITH THIS RIBBON...
...AND COUNTER KLAUS-SAN!!
BUT THEN...
I CAN'T SEE LIKE THIS...
TUG
ALL RIGHT!! DORMANT POWERS AWAKEN WHEN HUMANS ENCOUNTER CRUCIAL MOMENTS!!
THMM
SEE NOT WITH YOUR EYES, BUT WITH YOUR HEART!!

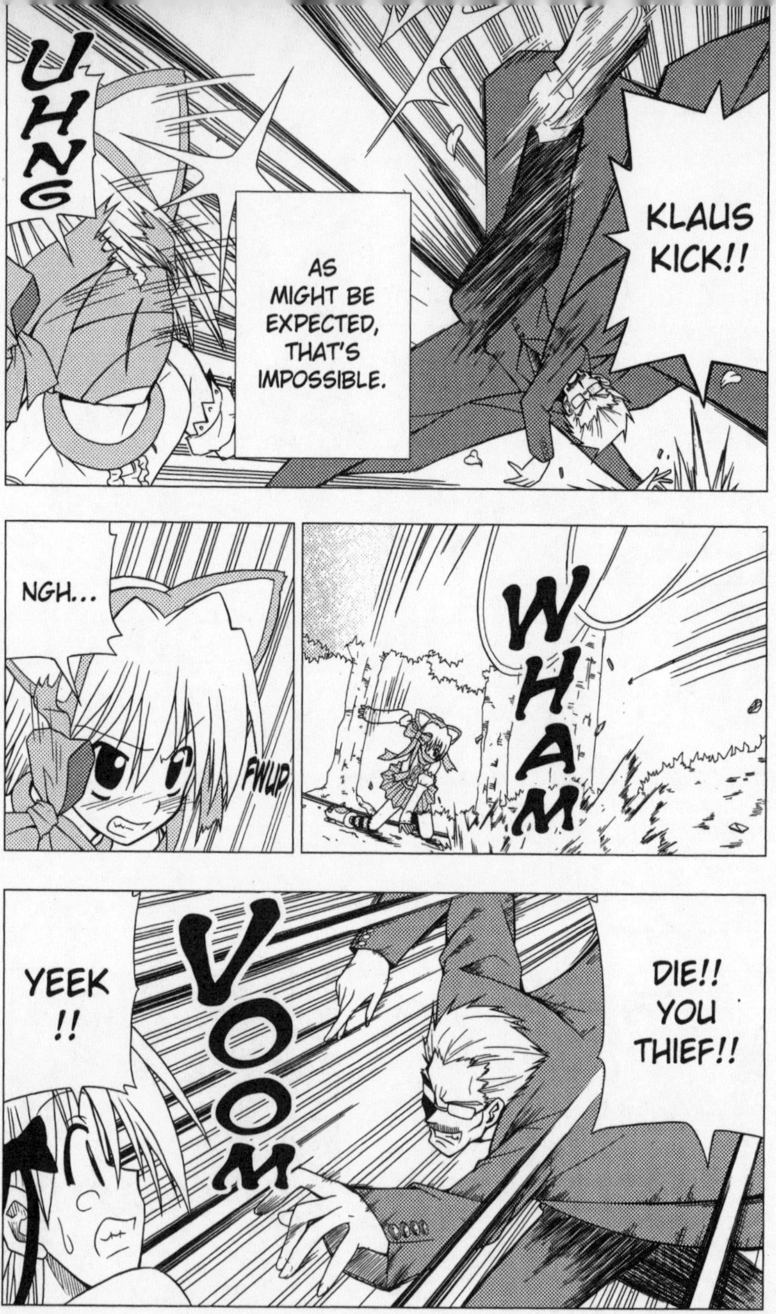

KLAUS KICK!!
AS MIGHT BE EXPECTED, THAT'S IMPOSSIBLE.
UHNG
WHAM
NGH...
FWUP
DIE!! YOU THIEF!!
VOOM
YEEK !!

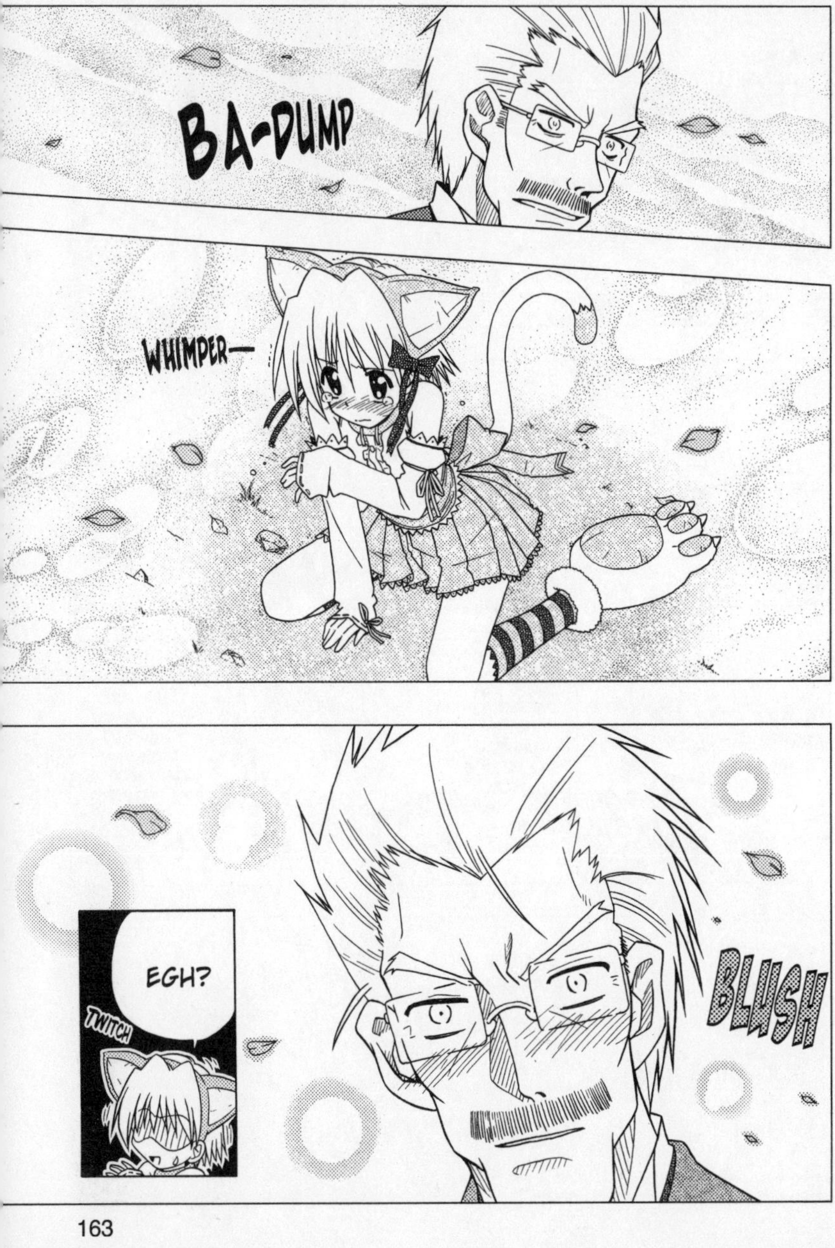
BA-DUMP
WHIMPER—
BLUSH
EGH?
TWITCH

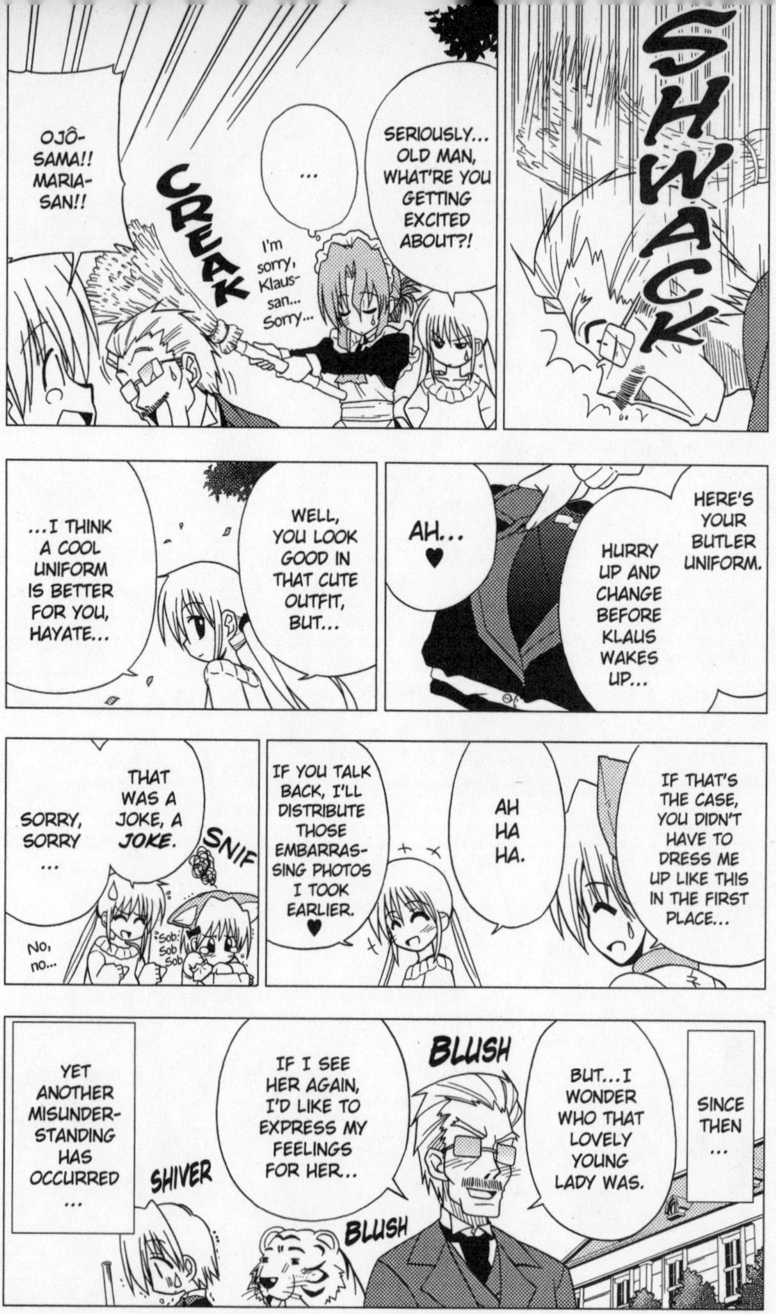
SHWACK
SERIOUSLY... OLD MAN, WHAT'RE YOU GETTING EXCITED ABOUT?!
...
I'm sorry, Klaus-san... Sorry...
CREAK
OJÔ-SAMA!! MARIA-SAN!!
HERE'S YOUR BUTLER UNIFORM.
HURRY UP AND CHANGE BEFORE KLAUS WAKES UP...
AH... ♥
WELL, YOU LOOK GOOD IN THAT CUTE OUTFIT, BUT...
...I THINK A COOL UNIFORM IS BETTER FOR YOU, HAYATE...
IF THAT'S THE CASE, YOU DIDN'T HAVE TO DRESS ME UP LIKE THIS IN THE FIRST PLACE...
AH HA HA.
IF YOU TALK BACK, I'LL DISTRIBUTE THOSE EMBARRASSING PHOTOS I TOOK EARLIER. ♥
THAT WAS A JOKE, A *JOKE*.
SNIF
SORRY, SORRY ...
Sob Sob Sob
No, no...
SINCE THEN ...
BUT...I WONDER WHO THAT LOVELY YOUNG LADY WAS.
BLUSH
IF I SEE HER AGAIN, I'D LIKE TO EXPRESS MY FEELINGS FOR HER..
BLUSH
SHIVER
YET ANOTHER MISUNDERSTANDING HAS OCCURRED ...

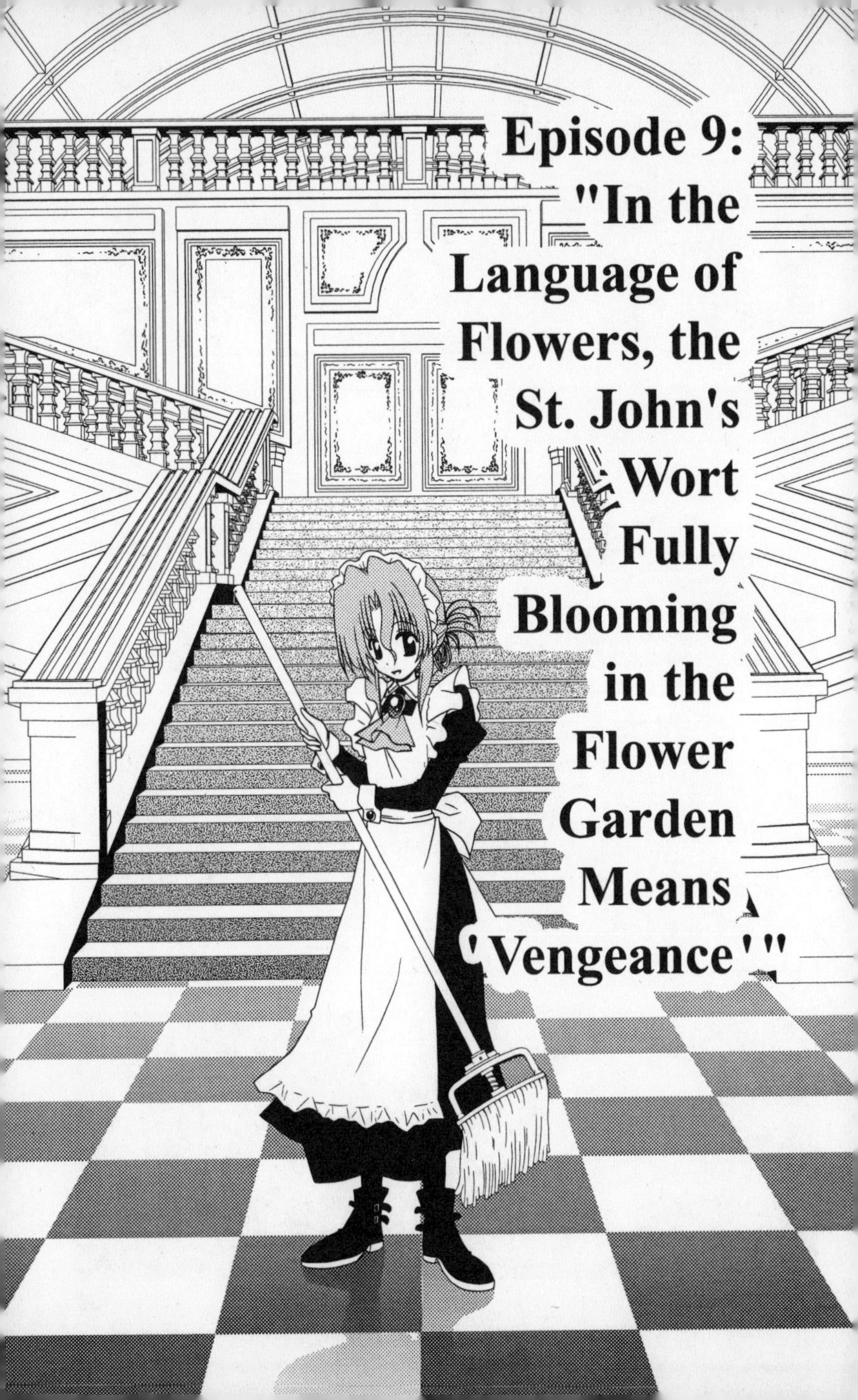
Episode 9: "In the Language of Flowers, the St. John's Wort Fully Blooming in the Flower Garden Means 'Vengeance'"

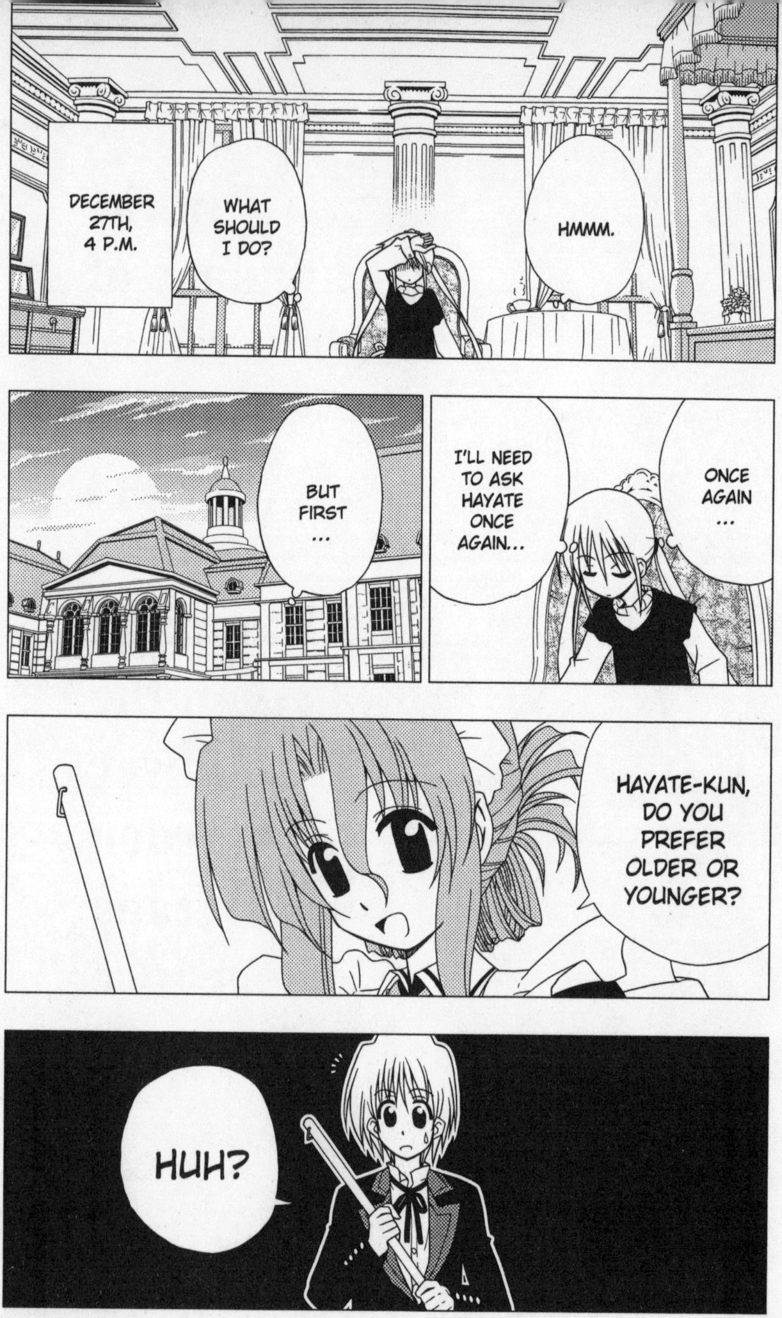
HMMM.
WHAT SHOULD I DO?
DECEMBER 27TH, 4 P.M.
ONCE AGAIN...
I'LL NEED TO ASK HAYATE ONCE AGAIN...
BUT FIRST...
HAYATE-KUN, DO YOU PREFER OLDER OR YOUNGER?
HUH?

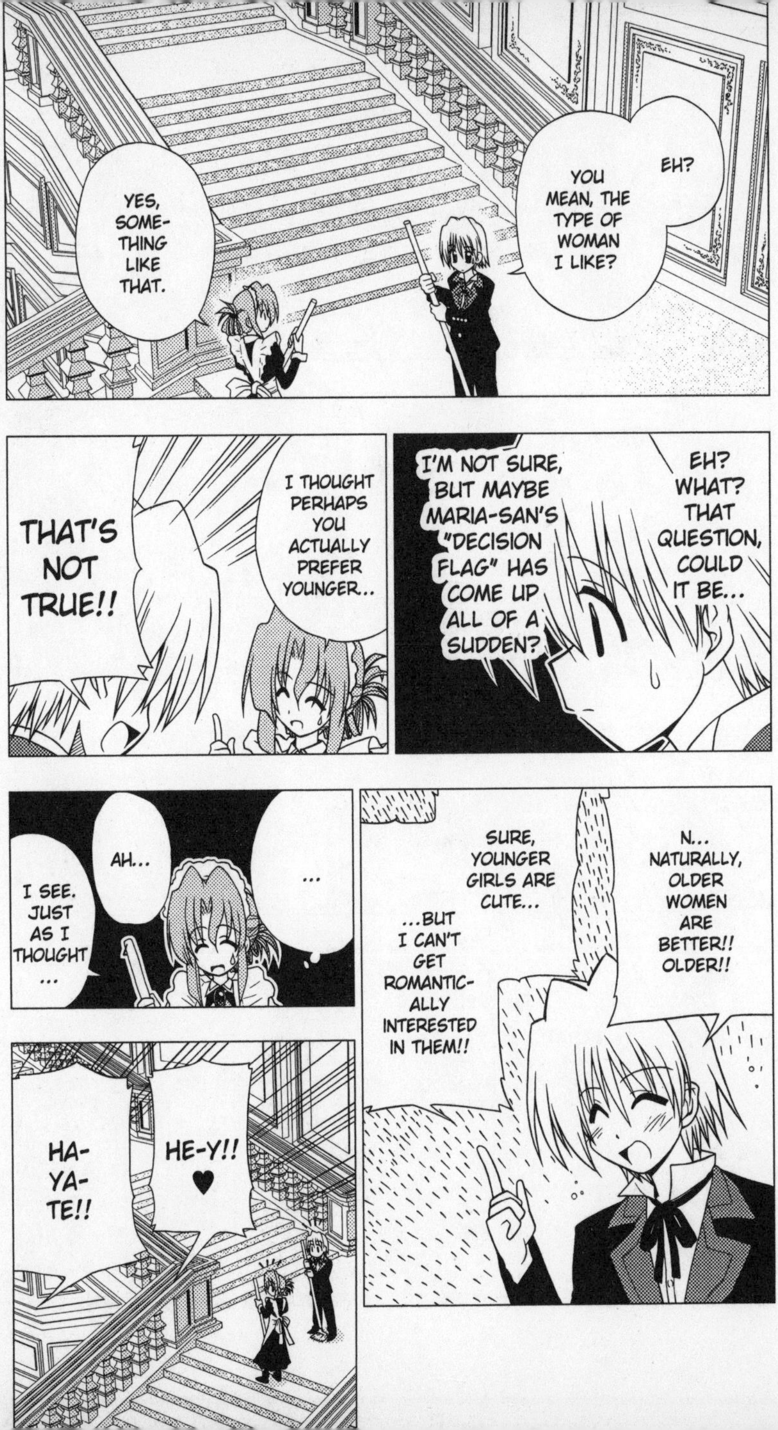
EH?
YOU MEAN, THE TYPE OF WOMAN I LIKE?
YES, SOMETHING LIKE THAT.
EH? WHAT? THAT QUESTION, COULD IT BE...
I'M NOT SURE, BUT MAYBE MARIA-SAN'S "DECISION FLAG" HAS COME UP ALL OF A SUDDEN?
I THOUGHT PERHAPS YOU ACTUALLY PREFER YOUNGER...
THAT'S NOT TRUE!!
N... NATURALLY, OLDER WOMEN ARE BETTER!! OLDER!!
SURE, YOUNGER GIRLS ARE CUTE...
...BUT I CAN'T GET ROMANTICALLY INTERESTED IN THEM!!
...
AH...
I SEE. JUST AS I THOUGHT...
HE-Y!! ♥
HA-YA-TE!!

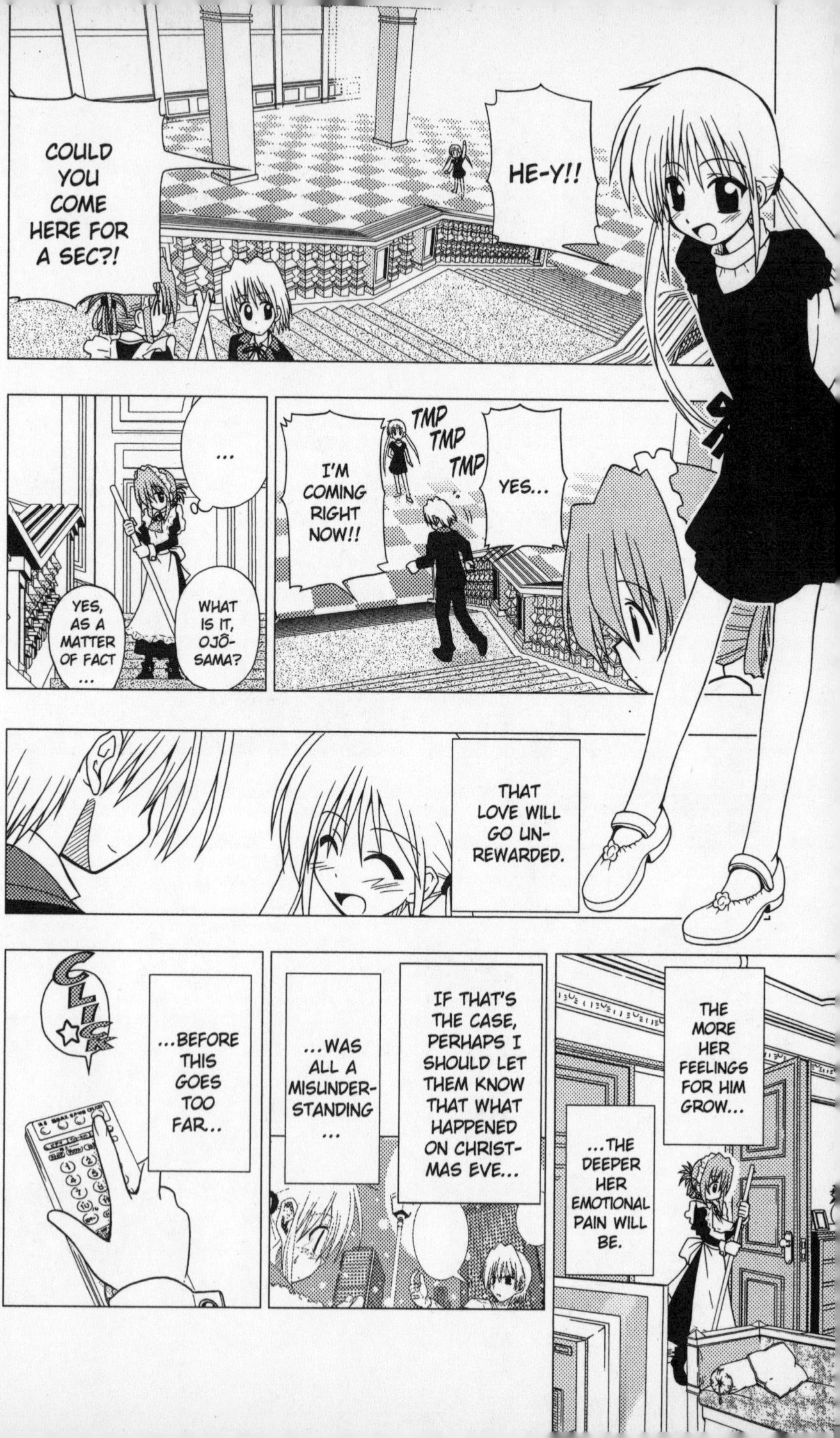
HE-Y!!
COULD YOU COME HERE FOR A SEC?!
YES...
TMP TMP TMP
I'M COMING RIGHT NOW!!
...
WHAT IS IT, OJÔ-SAMA?
YES, AS A MATTER OF FACT...
THAT LOVE WILL GO UN-REWARDED.
THE MORE HER FEELINGS FOR HIM GROW...
...THE DEEPER HER EMOTIONAL PAIN WILL BE.
IF THAT'S THE CASE, PERHAPS I SHOULD LET THEM KNOW THAT WHAT HAPPENED ON CHRIST-MAS EVE...
...WAS ALL A MISUNDER-STANDING...
...BEFORE THIS GOES TOO FAR...
CLICK

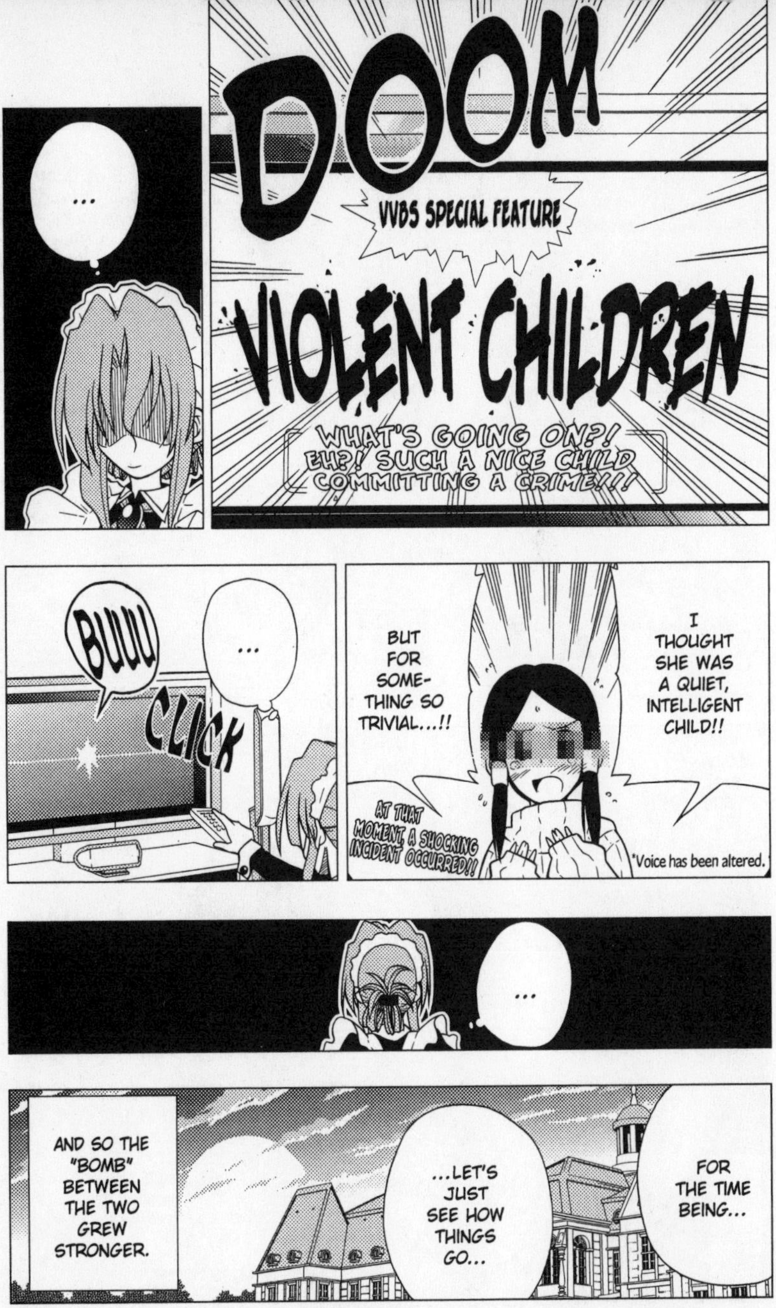
DOOM
VVBS SPECIAL FEATURE
VIOLENT CHILDREN
WHAT'S GOING ON?! EH?! SUCH A NICE CHILD COMMITTING A CRIME!!!
...
I THOUGHT SHE WAS A QUIET, INTELLIGENT CHILD!!
BUT FOR SOME-THING SO TRIVIAL...!!
AT THAT MOMENT, A SHOCKING INCIDENT OCCURRED!!
*Voice has been altered.
...
BUUU
CLICK
...
FOR THE TIME BEING...
...LET'S JUST SEE HOW THINGS GO...
AND SO THE "BOMB" BETWEEN THE TWO GREW STRONGER.

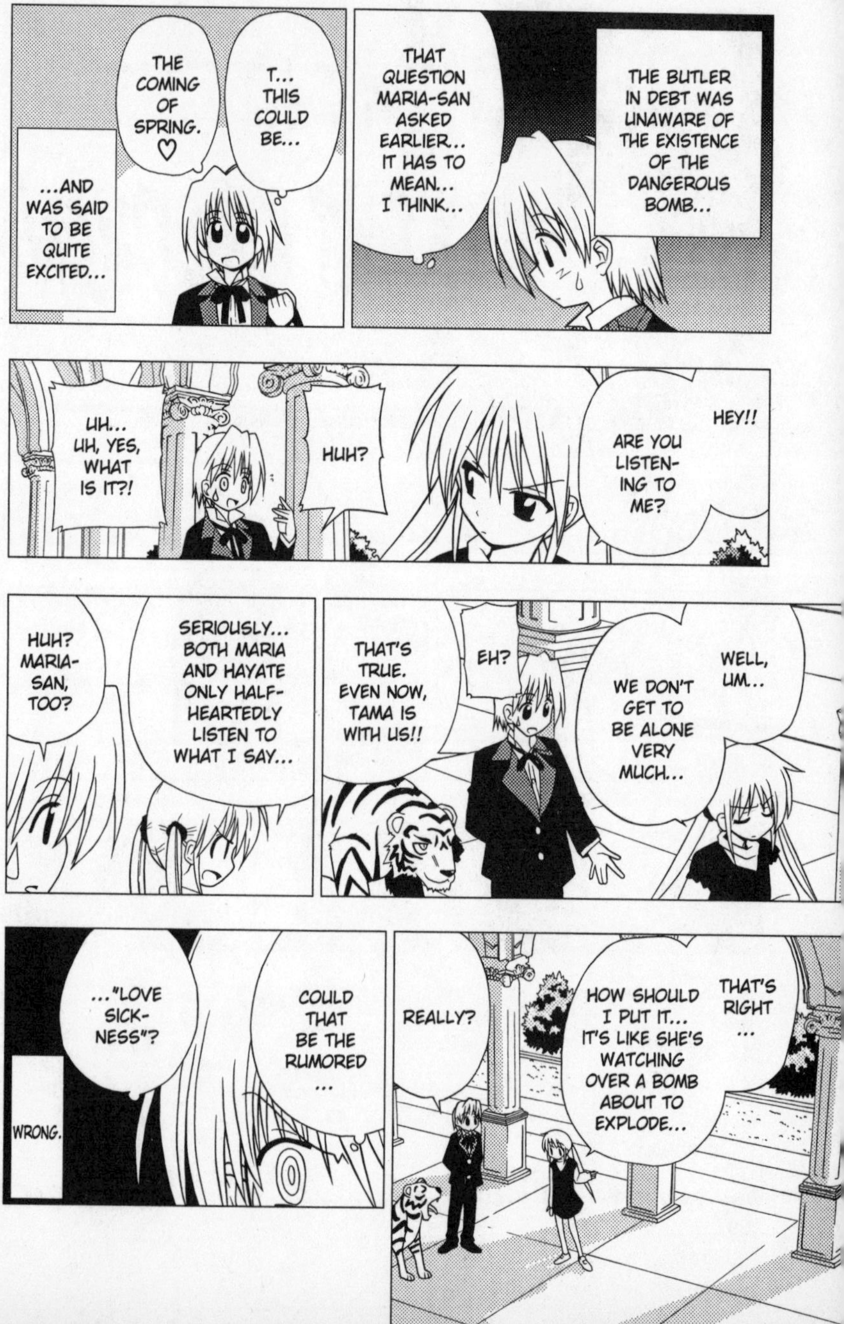
THE BUTLER IN DEBT WAS UNAWARE OF THE EXISTENCE OF THE DANGEROUS BOMB...
THAT QUESTION MARIA-SAN ASKED EARLIER... IT HAS TO MEAN... I THINK...
T... THIS COULD BE...
THE COMING OF SPRING. ♡
...AND WAS SAID TO BE QUITE EXCITED...
HEY!!
ARE YOU LISTENING TO ME?
HUH?
UH... UH, YES, WHAT IS IT?!
WELL, UM...
WE DON'T GET TO BE ALONE VERY MUCH...
EH?
THAT'S TRUE. EVEN NOW, TAMA IS WITH US!!
SERIOUSLY... BOTH MARIA AND HAYATE ONLY HALF-HEARTEDLY LISTEN TO WHAT I SAY...
HUH? MARIA-SAN, TOO?
THAT'S RIGHT...
HOW SHOULD I PUT IT... IT'S LIKE SHE'S WATCHING OVER A BOMB ABOUT TO EXPLODE...
REALLY?
COULD THAT BE THE RUMORED...
..."LOVE SICKNESS"?
WRONG.

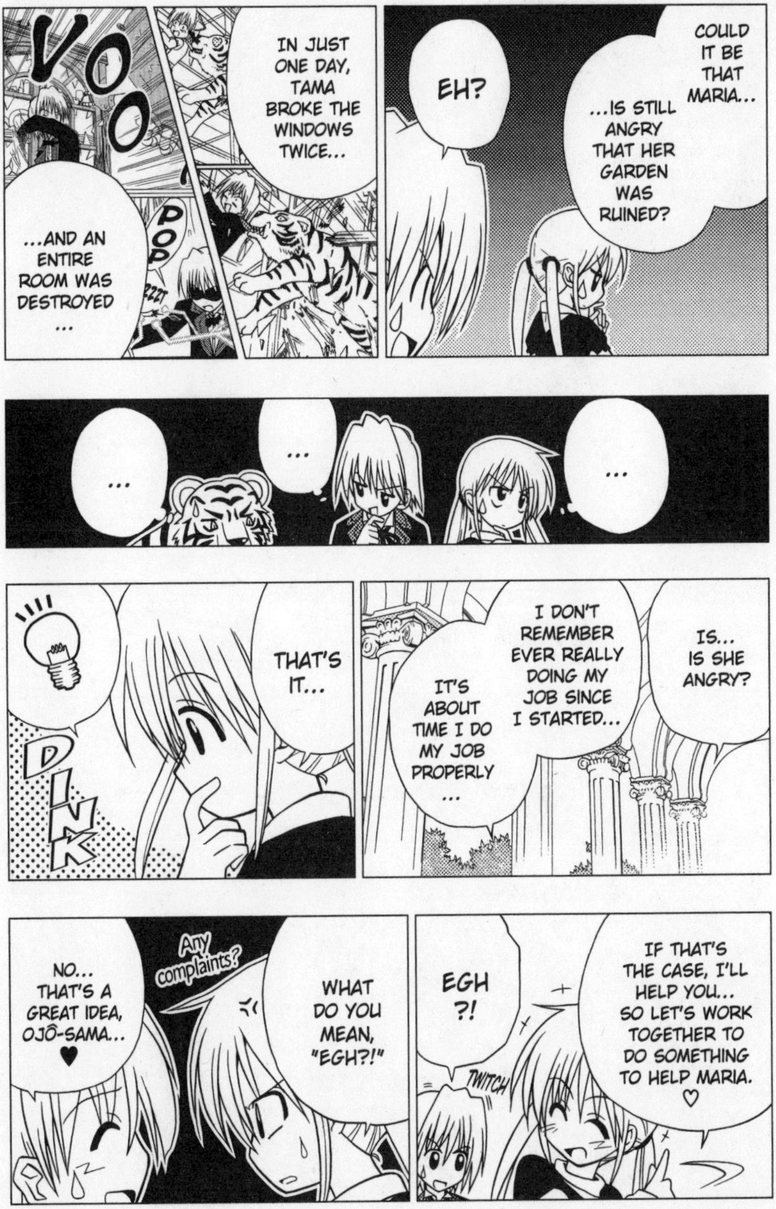
COULD IT BE THAT MARIA...
...IS STILL ANGRY THAT HER GARDEN WAS RUINED?
EH?
IN JUST ONE DAY, TAMA BROKE THE WINDOWS TWICE...
VOOO
POP
ZZZT
...AND AN ENTIRE ROOM WAS DESTROYED...
...
...
...
IS... IS SHE ANGRY?
I DON'T REMEMBER EVER REALLY DOING MY JOB SINCE I STARTED...
IT'S ABOUT TIME I DO MY JOB PROPERLY...
THAT'S IT...
DINK
IF THAT'S THE CASE, I'LL HELP YOU... SO LET'S WORK TOGETHER TO DO SOMETHING TO HELP MARIA. ♡
EGH ?!
TWITCH
WHAT DO YOU MEAN, "EGH?!"
Any complaints?
NO... THAT'S A GREAT IDEA, OJÔ-SAMA... ♥

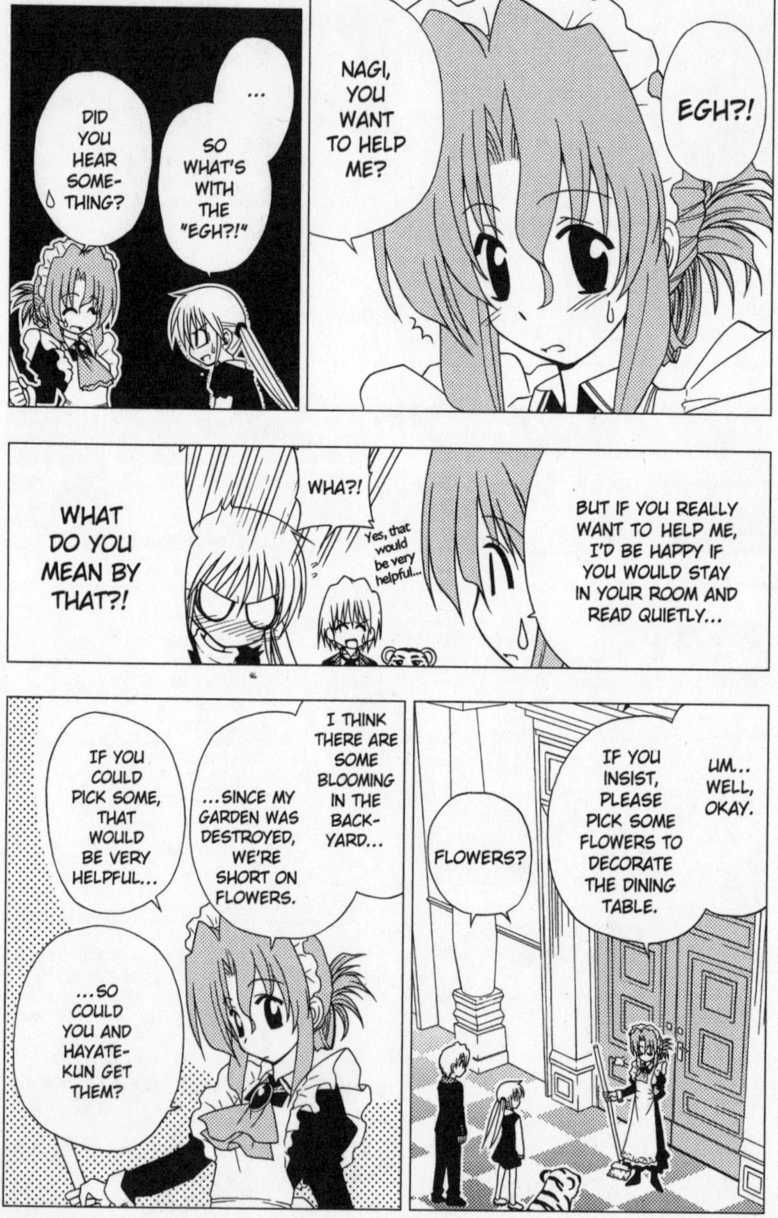
EGH?!
NAGI, YOU WANT TO HELP ME?
...
SO WHAT'S WITH THE "EGH?!"
DID YOU HEAR SOME-THING?
BUT IF YOU REALLY WANT TO HELP ME, I'D BE HAPPY IF YOU WOULD STAY IN YOUR ROOM AND READ QUIETLY...
Yes, that would be very helpful...
WHA?!
WHAT DO YOU MEAN BY THAT?!
UM.. WELL, OKAY.
IF YOU INSIST, PLEASE PICK SOME FLOWERS TO DECORATE THE DINING TABLE.
FLOWERS?
I THINK THERE ARE SOME BLOOMING IN THE BACK-YARD...
...SINCE MY GARDEN WAS DESTROYED, WE'RE SHORT ON FLOWERS.
IF YOU COULD PICK SOME, THAT WOULD BE VERY HELPFUL...
...SO COULD YOU AND HAYATE-KUN GET THEM?

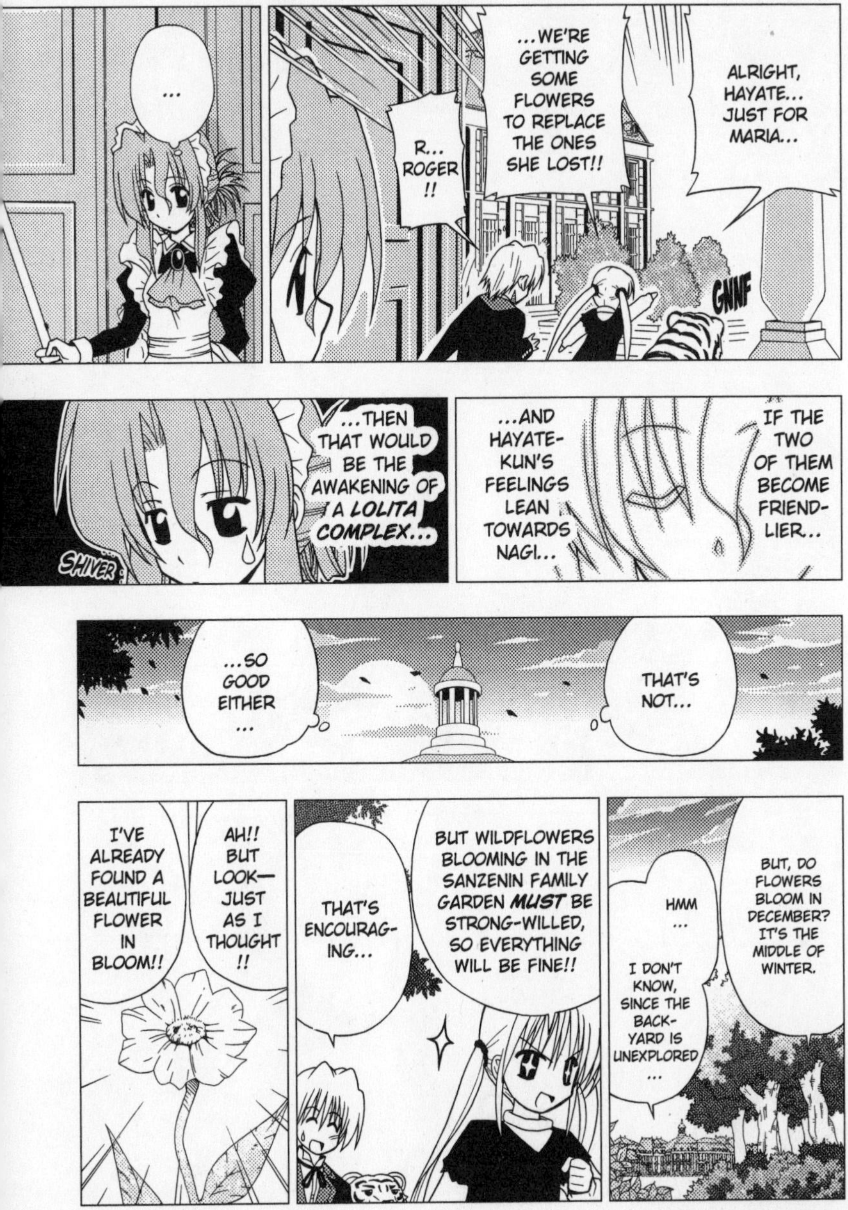
ALRIGHT, HAYATE... JUST FOR MARIA...
...WE'RE GETTING SOME FLOWERS TO REPLACE THE ONES SHE LOST!!
GNNF
R... ROGER!!
...
IF THE TWO OF THEM BECOME FRIENDLIER...
...AND HAYATE-KUN'S FEELINGS LEAN TOWARDS NAGI...
...THEN THAT WOULD BE THE AWAKENING OF A LOLITA COMPLEX...
SHIVER
THAT'S NOT...
...SO GOOD EITHER...
BUT, DO FLOWERS BLOOM IN DECEMBER? IT'S THE MIDDLE OF WINTER.
HMM...
I DON'T KNOW, SINCE THE BACKYARD IS UNEXPLORED...
BUT WILDFLOWERS BLOOMING IN THE SANZENIN FAMILY GARDEN MUST BE STRONG-WILLED, SO EVERYTHING WILL BE FINE!!
THAT'S ENCOURAGING...
AH!! BUT LOOK—JUST AS I THOUGHT!!
I'VE ALREADY FOUND A BEAUTIFUL FLOWER IN BLOOM!!

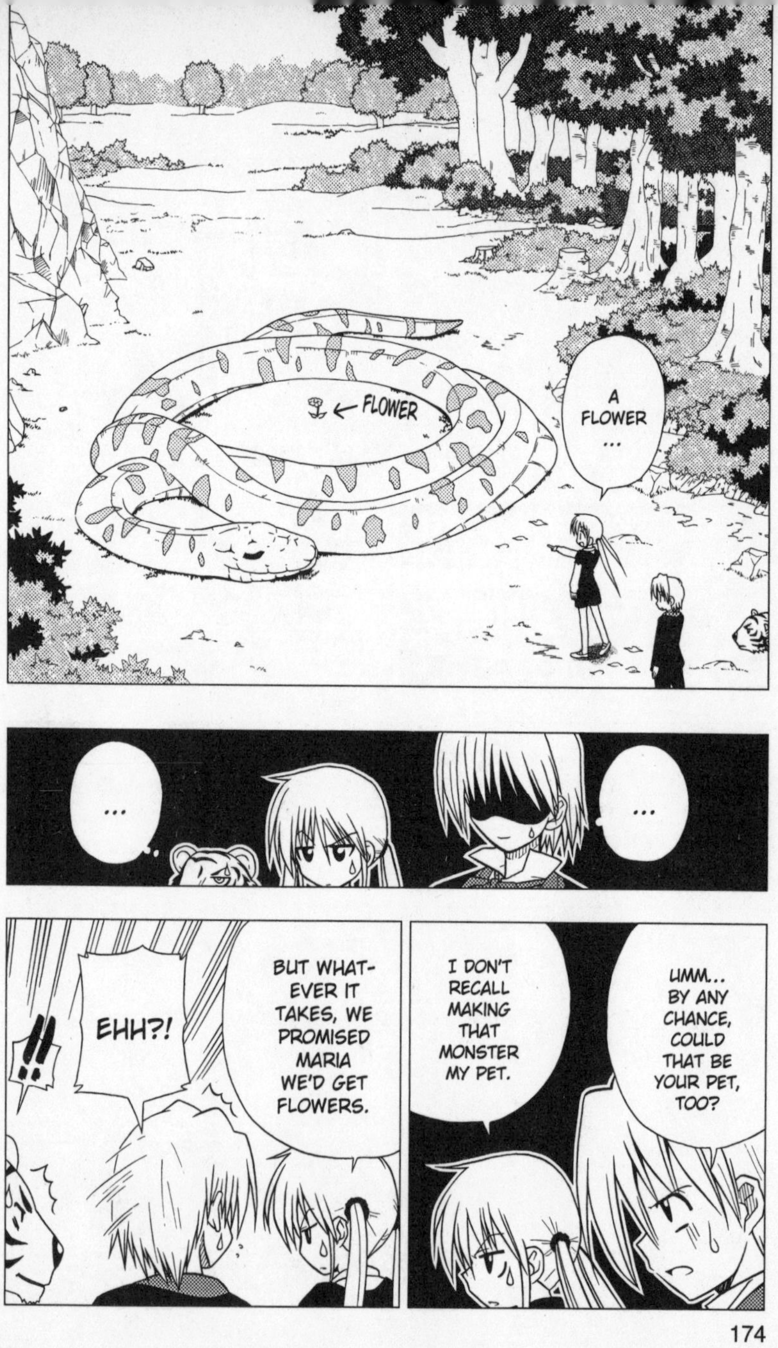
FLOWER
A FLOWER ...
...
...
UMM... BY ANY CHANCE, COULD THAT BE YOUR PET, TOO?
I DON'T RECALL MAKING THAT MONSTER MY PET.
BUT WHAT-EVER IT TAKES, WE PROMISED MARIA WE'D GET FLOWERS.
EHH?!
!!

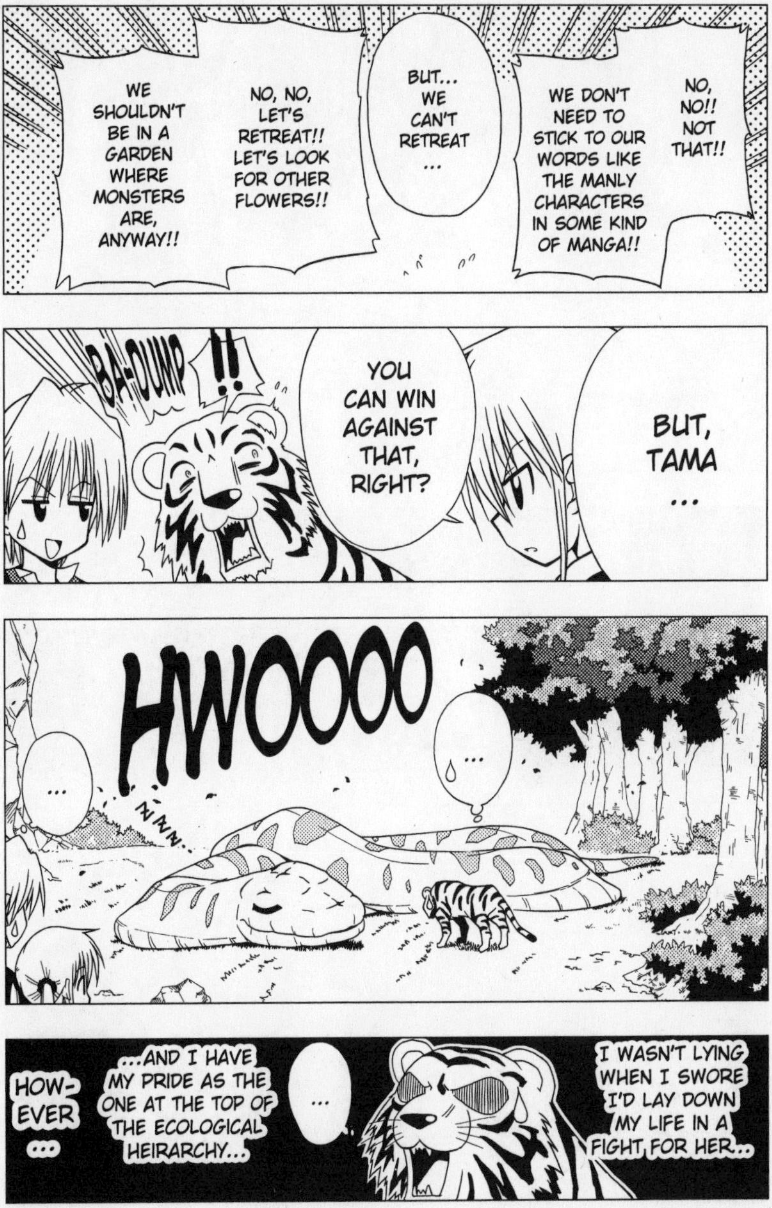
NO, NO!! NOT THAT!!
WE DON'T NEED TO STICK TO OUR WORDS LIKE THE MANLY CHARACTERS IN SOME KIND OF MANGA!!
BUT... WE CAN'T RETREAT ...
NO, NO, LET'S RETREAT!! LET'S LOOK FOR OTHER FLOWERS!!
WE SHOULDN'T BE IN A GARDEN WHERE MONSTERS ARE, ANYWAY!!
BUT, TAMA ...
YOU CAN WIN AGAINST THAT, RIGHT?
!!
BA-DUMP
...
HWOOOO
...
I WASN'T LYING WHEN I SWORE I'D LAY DOWN MY LIFE IN A FIGHT FOR HER...
...
...AND I HAVE MY PRIDE AS THE ONE AT THE TOP OF THE ECOLOGICAL HEIRARCHY...
HOW-EVER ...

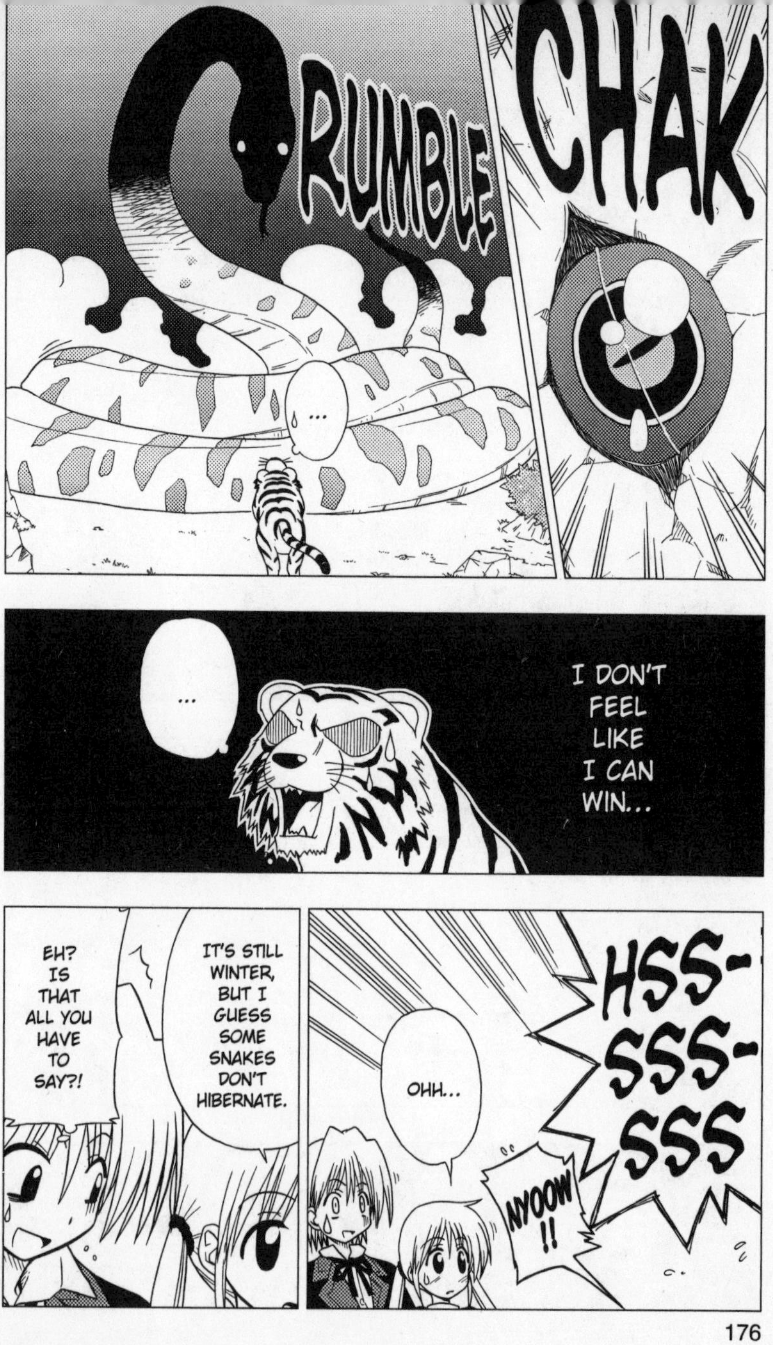

CHAK
RUMBLE
...
I DON'T FEEL LIKE I CAN WIN...
...
HSS-SSS-SSS
NYOOW!!
OHH...
IT'S STILL WINTER, BUT I GUESS SOME SNAKES DON'T HIBERNATE.
EH? IS THAT ALL YOU HAVE TO SAY?!

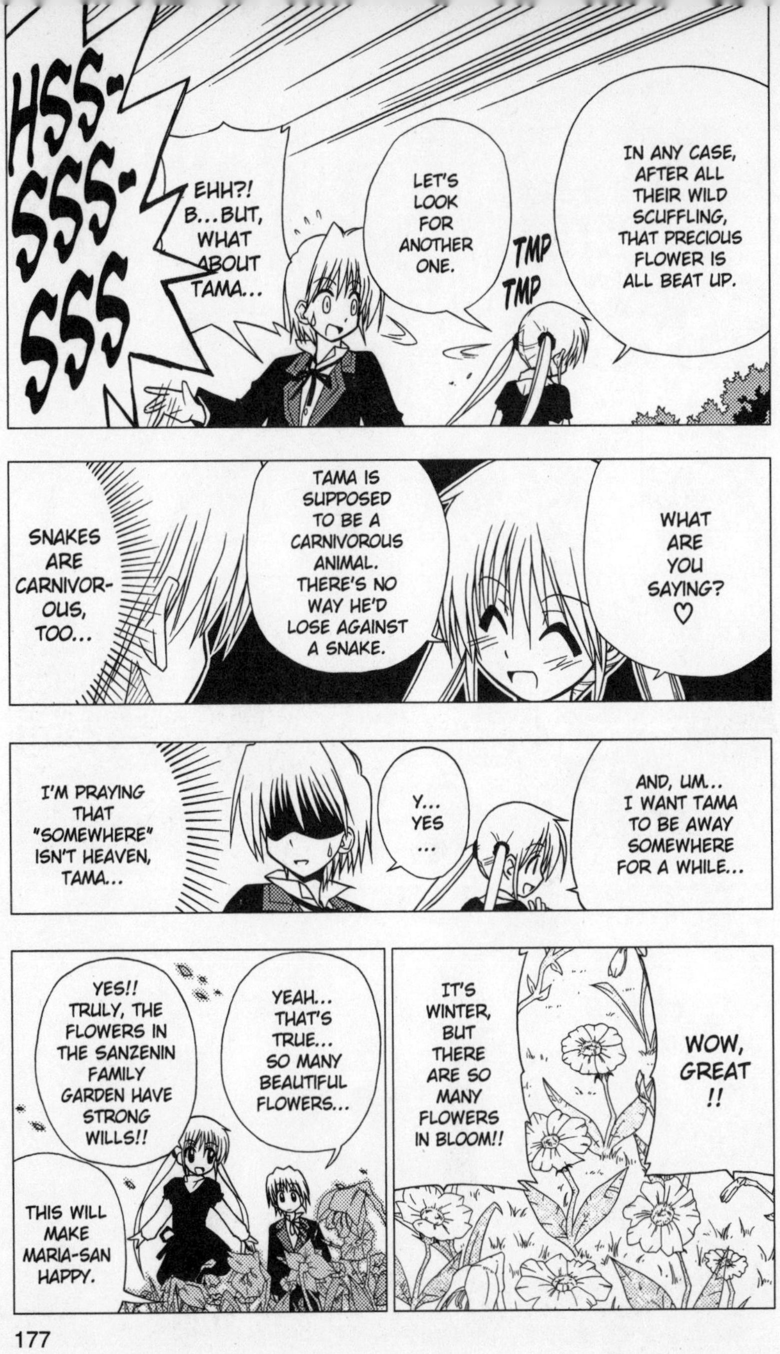
IN ANY CASE, AFTER ALL THEIR WILD SCUFFLING, THAT PRECIOUS FLOWER IS ALL BEAT UP.
TMP TMP
LET'S LOOK FOR ANOTHER ONE.
EHH?! B...BUT, WHAT ABOUT TAMA...
HSS-SSS-SSS
WHAT ARE YOU SAYING? ♡
TAMA IS SUPPOSED TO BE A CARNIVOROUS ANIMAL. THERE'S NO WAY HE'D LOSE AGAINST A SNAKE.
SNAKES ARE CARNIVOR-OUS, TOO...
AND, UM... I WANT TAMA TO BE AWAY SOMEWHERE FOR A WHILE...
Y... YES ...
I'M PRAYING THAT "SOMEWHERE" ISN'T HEAVEN, TAMA...
WOW, GREAT !!
IT'S WINTER, BUT THERE ARE SO MANY FLOWERS IN BLOOM!!
YEAH... THAT'S TRUE... SO MANY BEAUTIFUL FLOWERS...
YES!! TRULY, THE FLOWERS IN THE SANZENIN FAMILY GARDEN HAVE STRONG WILLS!!
THIS WILL MAKE MARIA-SAN HAPPY.

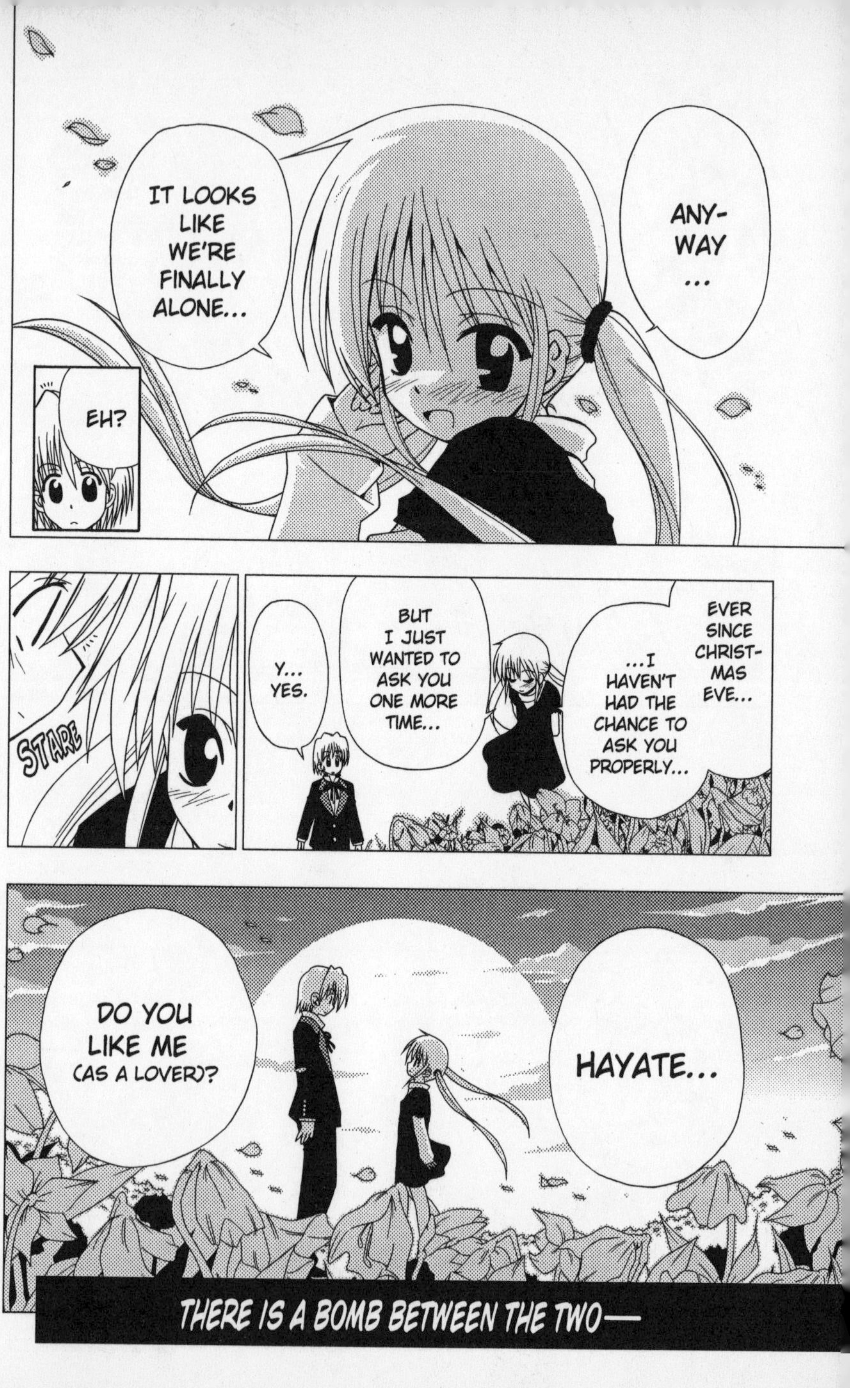
ANY-WAY...
IT LOOKS LIKE WE'RE FINALLY ALONE...
EH?
EVER SINCE CHRISTMAS EVE...
...I HAVEN'T HAD THE CHANCE TO ASK YOU PROPERLY...
BUT I JUST WANTED TO ASK YOU ONE MORE TIME...
Y... YES.
STARE
HAYATE...
DO YOU LIKE ME (AS A LOVER)?
THERE IS A BOMB BETWEEN THE TWO—

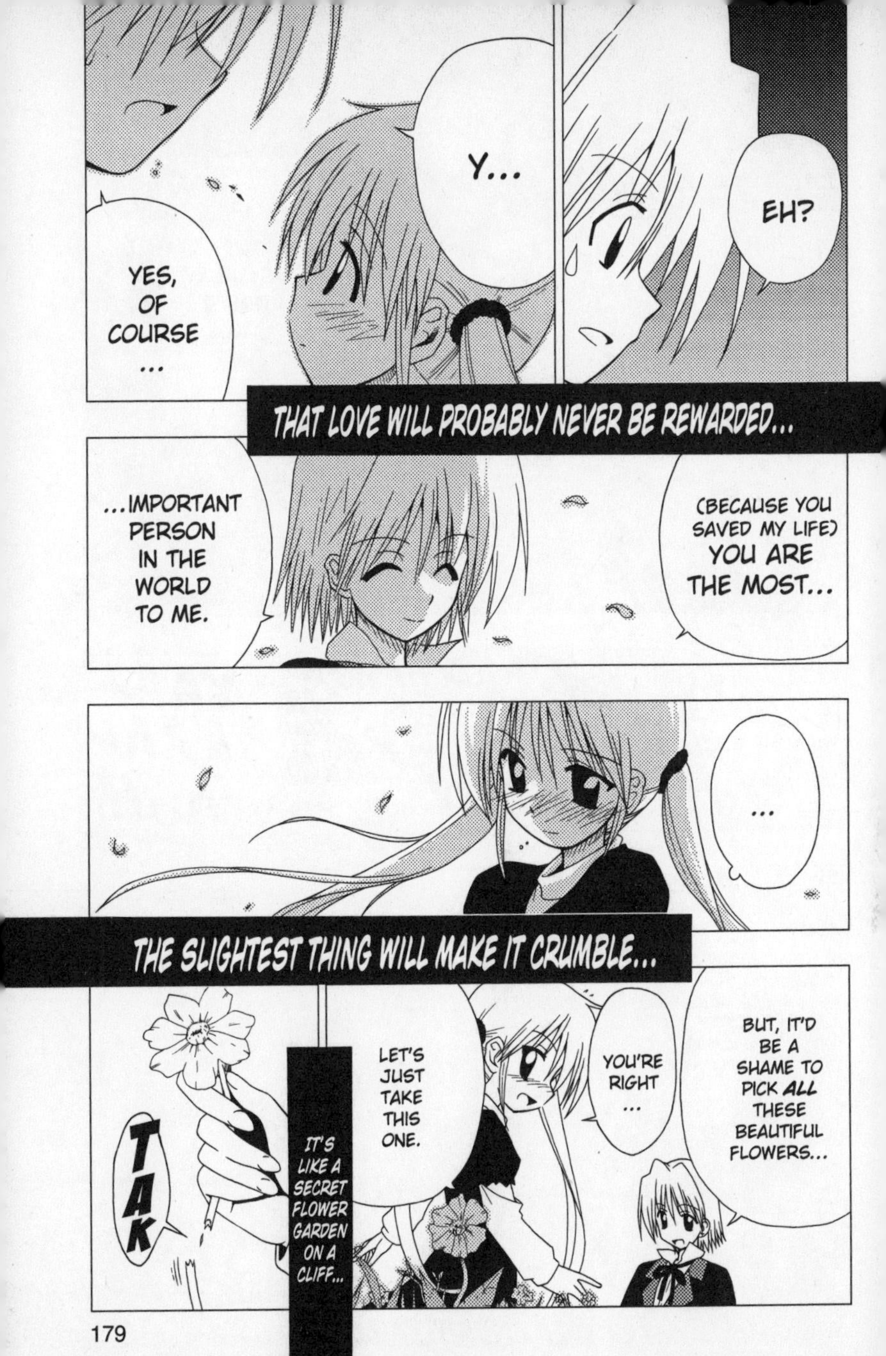
EH?
Y...
YES, OF COURSE ...
THAT LOVE WILL PROBABLY NEVER BE REWARDED...
(BECAUSE YOU SAVED MY LIFE) YOU ARE THE MOST...
...IMPORTANT PERSON IN THE WORLD TO ME.
...
THE SLIGHTEST THING WILL MAKE IT CRUMBLE...
BUT, IT'D BE A SHAME TO PICK ALL THESE BEAUTIFUL FLOWERS...
YOU'RE RIGHT ...
LET'S JUST TAKE THIS ONE.
IT'S LIKE A SECRET FLOWER GARDEN ON A CLIFF...
TAK

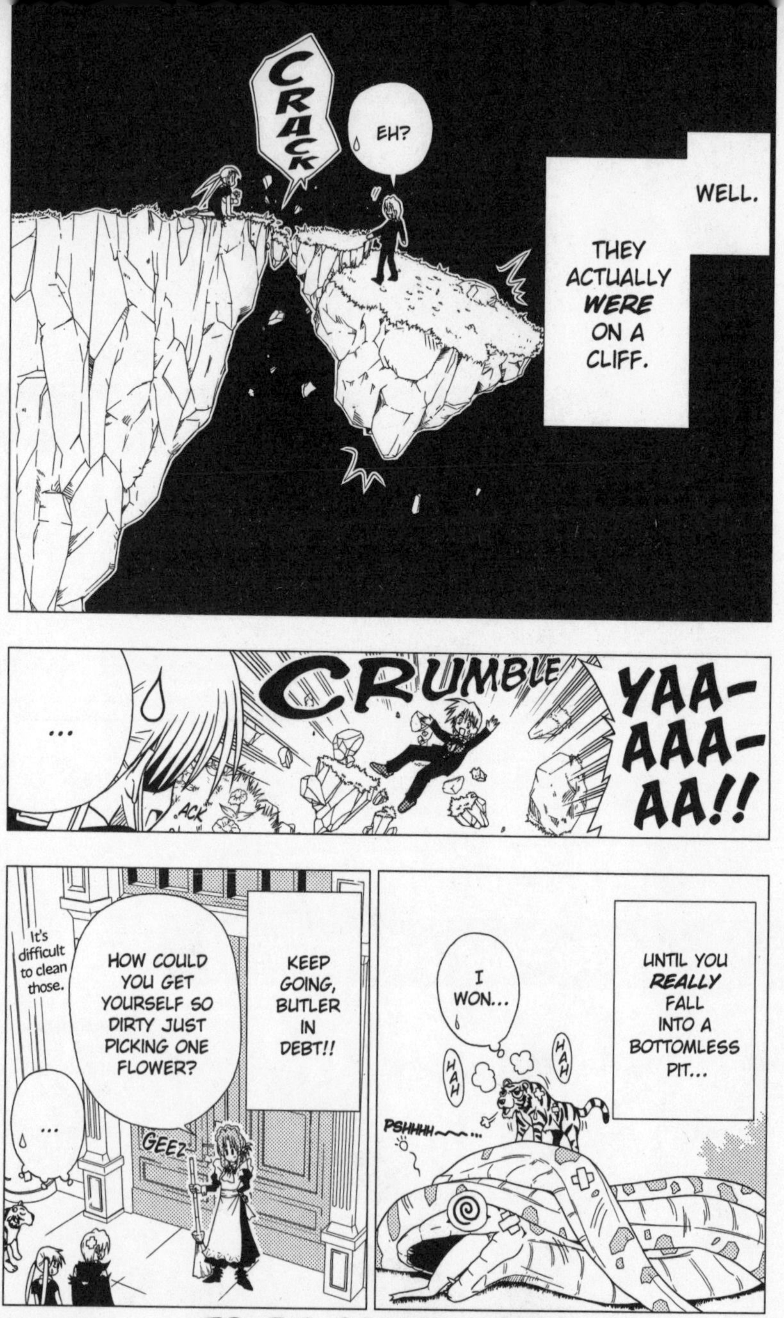
CRACK
EH?
WELL.
THEY ACTUALLY WERE ON A CLIFF.
YAA-AAA-AA!!
CRUMBLE
ACK
...
UNTIL YOU REALLY FALL INTO A BOTTOMLESS PIT...
I WON...
HAH
HAH
PSHHHH~~~...
KEEP GOING, BUTLER IN DEBT!!
HOW COULD YOU GET YOURSELF SO DIRTY JUST PICKING ONE FLOWER?
It's difficult to clean those.
GEEZ
...

TO BE CONTINUED!

HAYATE THE COMBAT BUTLER

BONUS PAGE

TITLE TEXT: RITSUKO HATA (MOTHER)

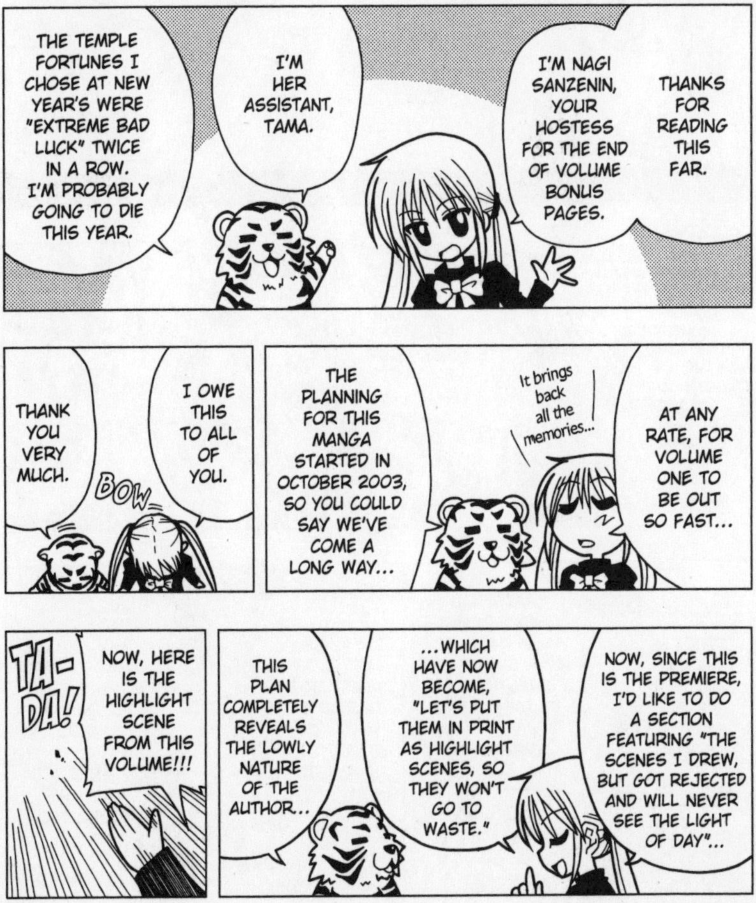

THANKS FOR READING THIS FAR.
I'M NAGI SANZENIN, YOUR HOSTESS FOR THE END OF VOLUME BONUS PAGES.
I'M HER ASSISTANT, TAMA.
THE TEMPLE FORTUNES I CHOSE AT NEW YEAR'S WERE "EXTREME BAD LUCK" TWICE IN A ROW. I'M PROBABLY GOING TO DIE THIS YEAR.
AT ANY RATE, FOR VOLUME ONE TO BE OUT SO FAST...
It brings back all the memories...
THE PLANNING FOR THIS MANGA STARTED IN OCTOBER 2003, SO YOU COULD SAY WE'VE COME A LONG WAY...
I OWE THIS TO ALL OF YOU.
BOW
THANK YOU VERY MUCH.
NOW, SINCE THIS IS THE PREMIERE, I'D LIKE TO DO A SECTION FEATURING "THE SCENES I DREW, BUT GOT REJECTED AND WILL NEVER SEE THE LIGHT OF DAY"...
...WHICH HAVE NOW BECOME, "LET'S PUT THEM IN PRINT AS HIGHLIGHT SCENES, SO THEY WON'T GO TO WASTE."
THIS PLAN COMPLETELY REVEALS THE LOWLY NATURE OF THE AUTHOR...
TA-DA!
NOW, HERE IS THE HIGHLIGHT SCENE FROM THIS VOLUME!!!

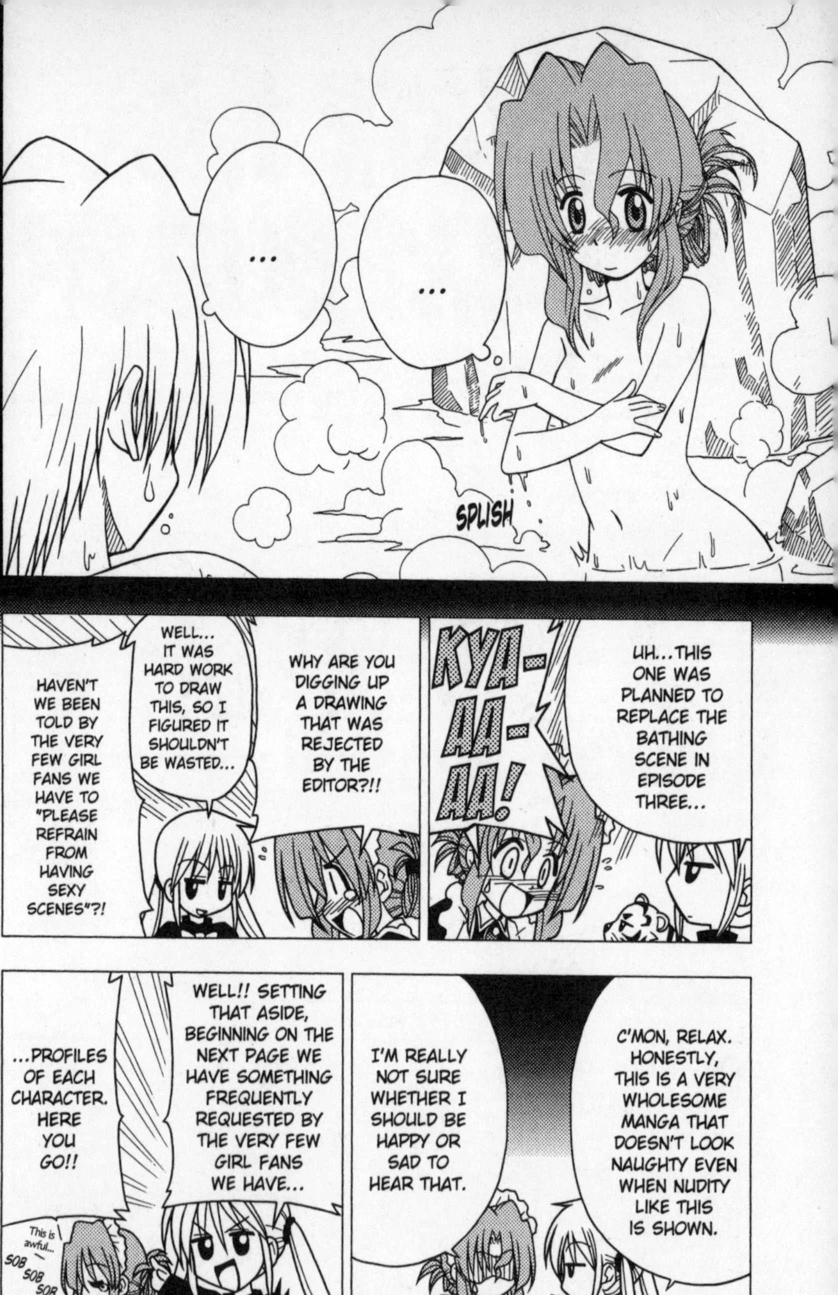
...
...
SPLISH
UH...THIS ONE WAS PLANNED TO REPLACE THE BATHING SCENE IN EPISODE THREE...
KYA-AA-AA-AA!
WHY ARE YOU DIGGING UP A DRAWING THAT WAS REJECTED BY THE EDITOR?!!
WELL... IT WAS HARD WORK TO DRAW THIS, SO I FIGURED IT SHOULDN'T BE WASTED...
HAVEN'T WE BEEN TOLD BY THE VERY FEW GIRL FANS WE HAVE TO "PLEASE REFRAIN FROM HAVING SEXY SCENES"?!
C'MON, RELAX. HONESTLY, THIS IS A VERY WHOLESOME MANGA THAT DOESN'T LOOK NAUGHTY EVEN WHEN NUDITY LIKE THIS IS SHOWN.
I'M REALLY NOT SURE WHETHER I SHOULD BE HAPPY OR SAD TO HEAR THAT.
WELL!! SETTING THAT ASIDE, BEGINNING ON THE NEXT PAGE WE HAVE SOMETHING FREQUENTLY REQUESTED BY THE VERY FEW GIRL FANS WE HAVE...
...PROFILES OF EACH CHARACTER. HERE YOU GO!!
This is awful...
SOB SOB SOB

PROFILE

[Age] 16

[Birthday] November 11th

[Blood Type] A

[Family Structure]
Father (Missing)
Mother (Missing)
Elder Brother (Missing)

[Height] 168 cm

[Weight]
57 kg
(Body fat percentage
in the single digits)

[Strengths/Likes]
Violin, survival
(he can survive anywhere)

[Weaknesses/Dislikes] Girls

Hayate Ayasaki

His name in Kanji is "綾崎颯."
But since it can't be read accurately, Katakana is used in the manga.
He is this story's hero. A heroine at times.
Even though he doesn't defeat the Andro Army like Casshan,
he is a man with an invincible body.
But before he knew it, Hayate had become a terribly unfortunate boy,
probably due to the fact that the author loved the often-tragic
World Masterpiece Theater anime series so much that he wanted to
become an animator. Naturally, there are no plans for him to be
happy in the future. (Not for a while, anyway...)
By the way, even though this manga is an episodic comedy,
a sense of continuity is maintained because the author likes
"the feel" of *World Masterpiece Theater*.
It is said that Hayate acquired the reflexes and body of a
superhuman through rigorous hard labor since childhood,
but there may or may not be other reasons...

By the way, the butler portrayed in this manga is, in short, like
"Doraemon resolving various difficult and unusual problems by
force, and without secret tools." Even today, he is striving to resolve
the unreasonable demands of his mistress...

PROFILE

[Age] 13

[Birthday] December 3rd

[Blood Type] AB

[Family Structure]
Grandfather

[Height] 138 cm

[Weight] 29 kg

[Strengths/Likes]
Manga (Reading and Drawing)
Finance
Learning

[Weaknesses/Dislikes]
Hot and spicy food
Dark rooms

Nagi Sanzenin

Her name in Kanji is "三千院凪."
Having received a custom-tailored education for gifted children ever since she was small, she is in fact an intelligent, talented young lady.
Her parents passed away in an accident a few years ago.
Her mind is possessed with her own thoughts, she hates to lose and is a strong-willed girl, but she also has many weaknesses, such as not being able to sleep alone, not being athletic, and not being able to eat spicy foods.
The original plot was to have the misunderstanding of Hayate's kidnapping of Nagi being a confession of love resolved (more like exposed) around episode eight,
and continue on to a new development, but…
There's no indication that she's noticed this at all.
I mean, it's already gone beyond the initial stage where it could be laughed off, so it's starting to become a headache and a heartache in different ways. Well, naturally I'm still thinking about it…
At any rate, this naturally spontaneous girl that's somewhat socially withdrawn is supporting this manga, so I want her to do her best.
By the way, if this series continues for more than 100 episodes, I've been told it would be all right for me to use the weekly page allotment to show Nagi's own manga, so I greatly appreciate support on this. I mean, really…

PROFILE

[Age] 17

[Birthday] December 24th
(It's not her actual birthday, but she herself doesn't know when the real one is.)

[Blood Type] O

[Family Structure] None
(She herself doesn't know)

[Height] 158 cm

[Weight] 42 kg

[Strengths/Likes]
Domestic duties
Games (From video games to chess to billiards—all kinds of games)

[Weaknesses/Dislikes]
Dark life forms in the kitchen and such

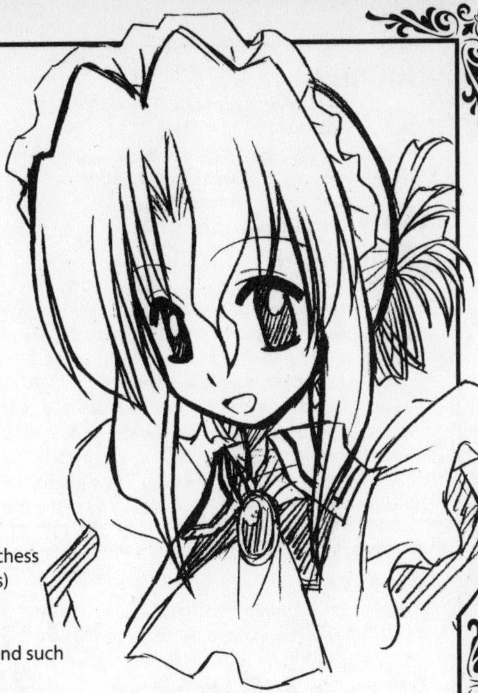

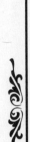

Maria

On Christmas Eve...
She was found in a church in front of a statue of the Virgin Mary and was named after her. Despite the fact she's only 17 years old, she manages many things with skill and grace, and that's because she had lived through many troubles, although in different ways than Hayate. As an otaku-level fan of *World Masterpiece Theater*, I'd love to work on her life story, starting from her birth until now in a *World Masterpiece Theater*-like story and direction, but plotlines with few comedy elements tend to get rejected for this manga, so the odds of it ever being shown to public are very slim. She looks tall because Nagi is always standing next to her, but stands just 158 cm.
Her nature is quiet and gentle, but because she's surrounded by idiots, she's been given the role of "straight man" to expedite the story progression, so her character is that of a pitiable girl in a rather disadvantageous position.
To Nagi, she is maid, mother, and big sister—and at this point, she is the most precious person to Nagi.
By the way, Maria calls Nagi "ojô-sama" only when others are around and there's a need for her to put up a good front, and when she makes little sarcastic remarks. It was decided at a very early stage that Maria would not address Nagi as ojô-sama, but when the time came to start the series, there was concern that it may be difficult for the readers to understand why she does that. So, after giving it a lot of thought, I devised a plan to make full use of various expressions, so that readers wouldn't find it odd when Maria addresses her as "Nagi" without an honorific.

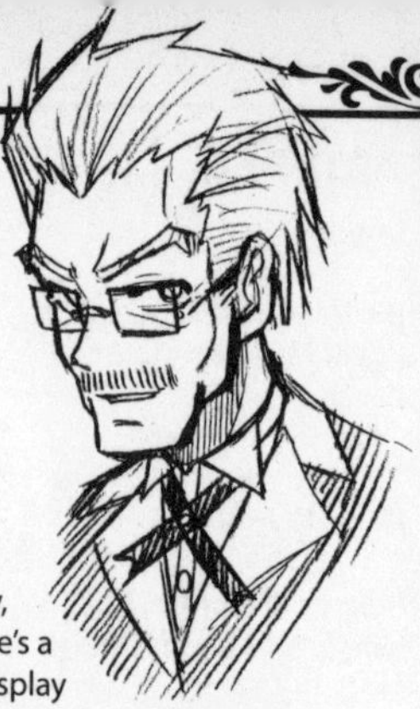

PROFILE

[Age] 58 **[Birthday]** April 18th **[Blood Type]** A
[Family Structure] Single **[Height]** 181 cm
[Weight] 80 kg (He is well-muscled)
[Strengths/Likes] Cars, Motorcycles, Drifting (the motorsport kind)
[Weaknesses/Dislikes] Alcohol, Cigarettes, Women

Klaus

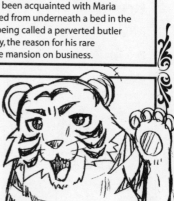

His real name is Kurausu Seishiro. He's pure-blooded Japanese. Being the Head Butler of the Sanzenin family, he's actually a man in an extremely high position, but he's a modest and pleasant middle-aged man who doesn't display that kind of attitude in the slightest. He's actually been acquainted with Maria longer than he's known Nagi. Because he appeared from underneath a bed in the episode where Tama first appears, he ended up being called a perverted butler by the readers… That's not the case… By the way, the reason for his rare appearances is because he is often away from the mansion on business.

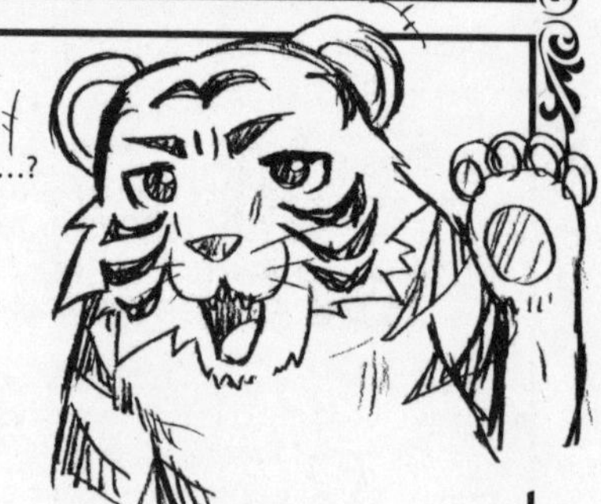

PROFILE

[Age] Uh...um… **[Birthday]** Well…
[Blood Type] Do tigers have blood types, too…?
[Family Structure]
(He thinks:) Maria>a wall you can't go around>Nagi>himself>Hayate>Klaus
[Height] Pretty big
[Weight] Super heavy
[Strengths/Likes] Nagi, Maria
[Weaknesses/Dislikes] Himegami-kun

Tama

Tama is a talking tiger who's popular among female readers for some reason. He's the most puzzling creature in this manga. When I wrote in the story that "he was saved in Africa by Nagi," I received comments from many readers that, "There are no tigers in Africa." So I reflected on that mistake after I realized it had been a blind belief on my part for over 20 years. "I see… I thought Africa would have all sorts of carnivorous animals…" So, when the time came to publish all of volume one, I thought about revising that part, but I realized that "saved in Africa" would make it easier to create a plot later on, so it was left untouched. The story of a how a tiger was saved in Africa will be featured as a side story some other time…
In this manga, I wrote, "It is said that after being raised with so much love, Tama came to understand the human language," but there's supposed to be a particular reason why he learned to talk. But who cares if I explain that now, so we'll just let it go… None of the readers pointed out that "talking tigers are strange" either… By the way, there's a reason Nagi thinks Tama is a cat, and it was supposed to be in episode seven, but it got left out at some point while I was revising the dialogue, and I entirely missed the opportunity to explain it. Well, again, none of the readers have asked, "Why does Nagi insist that Tama is a cat?" so I suppose an opportunity to show the reason will never arrive…

WELL, HOW DID YOU LIKE THE VOLUME ONE
OF HAYATE THE COMBAT BUTLER?

I REALLY HAD PLANNED TO INCLUDE MORE BONUS PAGES,
BUT I WAS DRAWING A PROMOTIONAL MANGA FOR THE EVENT
DISTRIBUTION, A COLOR POSTER FOR BOOKSTORE WINDOWS,
CREATING GIFT BOOKMARKS FOR 1,000 READERS,
AND SO MANY OTHER THINGS, THAT I USED UP ALL OF MY
NEW YEAR'S HOLIDAY, AND BY THE TIME I REALIZED IT,
THE BONUS SECTION TURNED OUT LIKE THIS...

I'M SORRY. I'LL TRY TO DO BETTER FOR THE
NEXT VOLUME. SO PLEASE SUPPORT ME.

TO BE MORE SPECIFIC, PLEASE BUY MORE THAN TWO COPIES,
SEND ME FAN LETTERS, AND WHILE YOU'RE AT IT, PLEASE
MARK HAYATE ON SHŌNEN SUNDAY'S QUESTIONNAIRE
AS THE FUNNIEST STORY—AND DISCREETLY MAIL IT OUT.

I'M SURE THAT SOMETHING GOOD WILL
HAPPEN TO SOMEONE—YOU NEVER KNOW.

NO, I CAN'T GUARANTEE THAT IT'LL HAPPEN TO YOU.

BUT JUST THINK OF IT AS TRAINING AND PLEASE PUT
IT INTO PRACTICE. I'M SURE YOU'LL GET TO SEE A
GODLIKE PERSON SOMEDAY. UM, WELL...
ACTUALLY, HE'S PROBABLY LIKE A GOD,
BUT NOT REALLY A GOD,
SO THERE WON'T BE ANY DIVINE GRACE.

WELL, WITH THAT SAID, I HOPE YOU'LL ENJOY
THE SECOND VOLUME AND BEYOND.

AND, I'M UPDATING MY COLUMN IN WEB SHŌNEN SUNDAY*
EVERY WEEK, SO WHEN YOU GET A CHANCE, PLEASE VISIT!
WELL, I'LL SEE YOU AGAIN IN THE NEXT VOLUME...☆

*ONLY AVAILABLE IN JAPANESE —ED

The Preface Manga

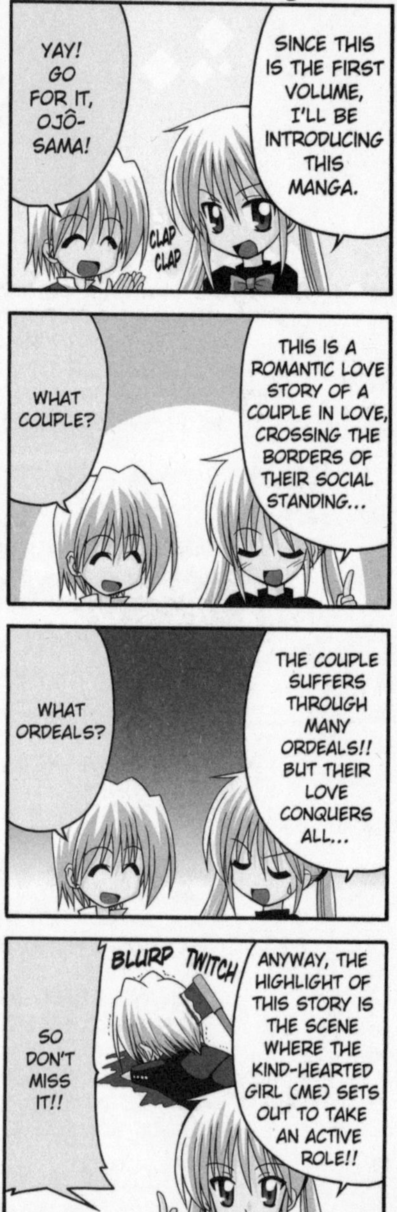
SINCE THIS IS THE FIRST VOLUME, I'LL BE INTRODUCING THIS MANGA.
YAY! GO FOR IT, OJÔ-SAMA!
CLAP CLAP
THIS IS A ROMANTIC LOVE STORY OF A COUPLE IN LOVE, CROSSING THE BORDERS OF THEIR SOCIAL STANDING...
WHAT COUPLE?
THE COUPLE SUFFERS THROUGH MANY ORDEALS!! BUT THEIR LOVE CONQUERS ALL...
WHAT ORDEALS?
ANYWAY, THE HIGHLIGHT OF THIS STORY IS THE SCENE WHERE THE KIND-HEARTED GIRL (ME) SETS OUT TO TAKE AN ACTIVE ROLE!!
TWITCH
BLURP
SO DON'T MISS IT!!

The Postface Manga

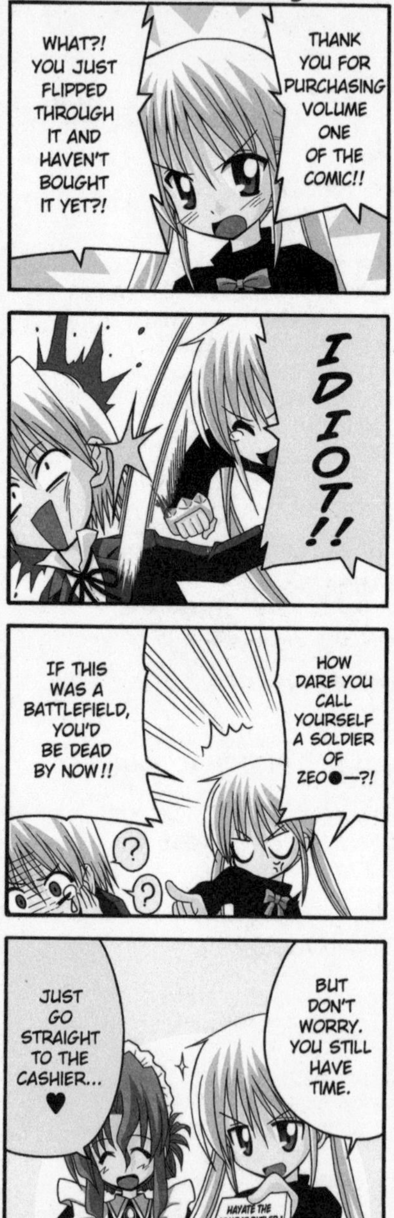
THANK YOU FOR PURCHASING VOLUME ONE OF THE COMIC!!
WHAT?! YOU JUST FLIPPED THROUGH IT AND HAVEN'T BOUGHT IT YET?!
IDIOT!!
HOW DARE YOU CALL YOURSELF A SOLDIER OF ZEO●—?!
IF THIS WAS A BATTLEFIELD, YOU'D BE DEAD BY NOW!!
?
?
BUT DON'T WORRY. YOU STILL HAVE TIME.
JUST GO STRAIGHT TO THE CASHIER... ♥
HAYATE THE COMBAT BUTLER 1

- HAYATE THE COMBAT BUTLER -
[BAD ENDING (I)]

IN REALITY, NO BEAUTIFUL
GIRL APPEARED TO
ASSUME HIS DEBTS...
"THAT ONLY HAPPENS
IN DREAMS"
WAS THE PUNCH LINE. ♥

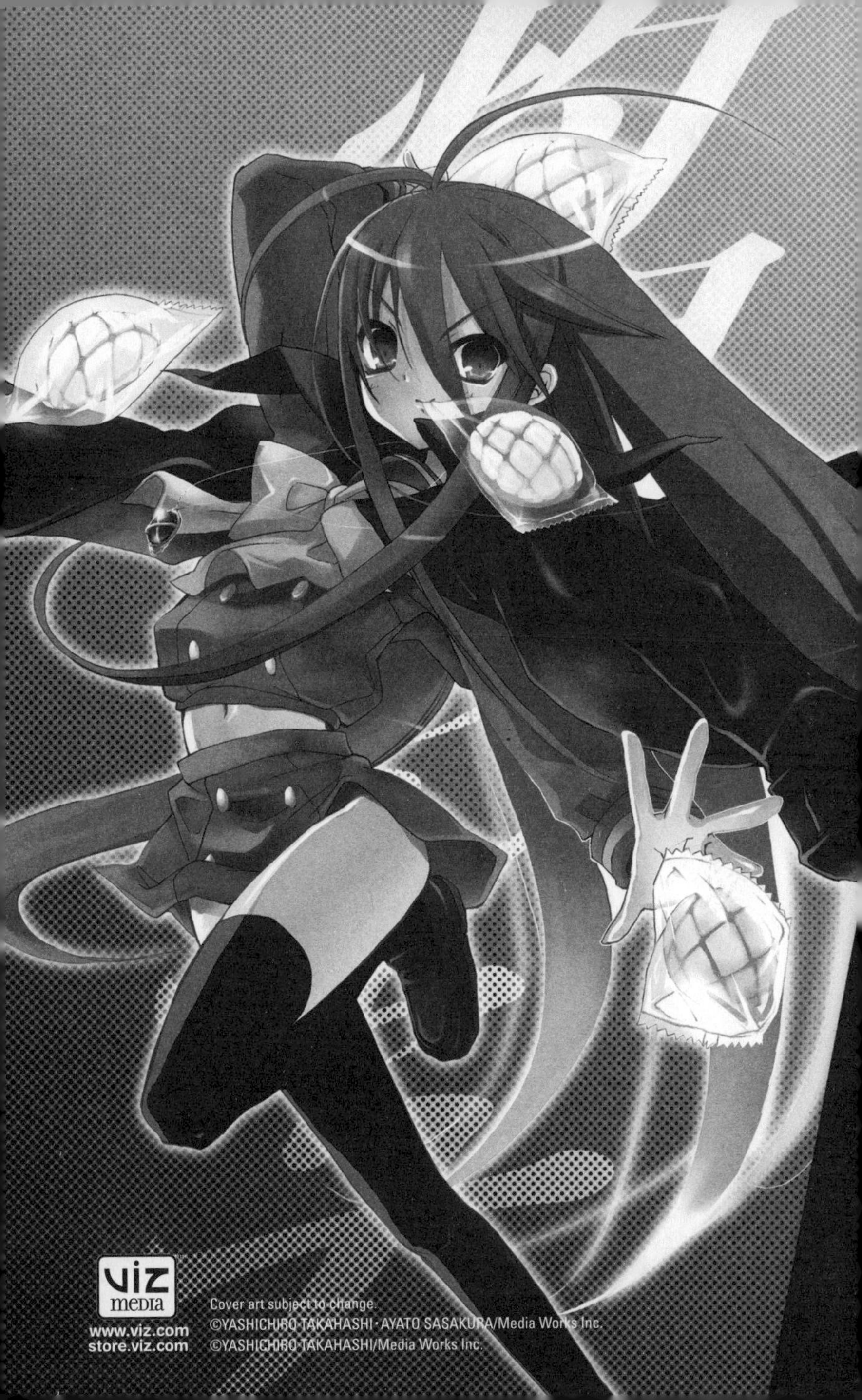